Spanish cinema 1973–2010

MANCHEStER
1824

Manchester University Press

Spanish cinema 1973–2010

Auteurism, politics, landscape and memory

Edited by
MARIA M. DELGADO
and
ROBIN FIDDIAN

Manchester University Press
Manchester and New York

distributed in the United States exclusively
by PALGRAVE MACMILLAN

Published by Manchester University Press
Oxford Road, Manchester M13 9NR, UK
and Room 400, 175 Fifth Avenue, New York, NY 10010, USA
www.manchesteruniversitypress.co.uk

Distributed in the United States exclusively by
Palgrave Macmillan, 175 Fifth Avenue, New York,
NY 10010, USA

Distributed in Canada exclusively by
UBC Press, University of British Columbia, 2029 West Mall,
Vancouver, BC, Canada V6T 1Z2

British Library Cataloguing-in-Publication Data
A catalogue record for this book is available from the British Library

Library of Congress Cataloging-in-Publication Data applied for

ISBN 978 07190 8711 0 hardback

First published 2013

Typeset in 10.5/12.5 Adobe Garamond
by Servis Filmsetting Ltd, Stockport, Cheshire
Printed in Great Britain
by The MPG Books Group, Bodmin

To Peter W. Evans
mentor, friend and colleague

Contents

List of illustrations

Notes on contributors

CELESTINO DELEYTO is Professor of Film and English Literature at the University of Zaragoza, Spain. He is the author of *The Secret Life of Romantic Comedy* (MUP, 2009) and co-author, with María del Mar Azcona, of *Alejandro González Iñárritu* (University of Illinois Press, 2010). At the moment he heads a research project on transnational cinema and the representation of borders in contemporary film.

MARIA M. DELGADO is Professor of Theatre and Screen Arts at Queen Mary, University of London. She has published widely in the areas of twentieth-century Spanish theatre and film, with a particular interest in the work of performers and directors and the intersections between stage and screen cultures. Her books include *Federico García Lorca* (Routledge, 2008) and *'Other' Spanish Theatres* (MUP, 2003), as well as seven co-edited volumes. She has been a programme advisor to the BFI London Film Festival since 1997 and contributes regularly to *Sight & Sound* and BBC Radio's *The Strand*, *Night Waves* and *Saturday Review*.

MARÍA DONAPETRY is Lecturer in Spanish at Balliol College, Oxford, where she teaches modern literature, film and women's studies. She has published widely on European and Hispanic film and is the author of titles including *La otra mirada* (University Press of the South, 1998), *Toda ojos* (KRK, 2001) and *Imaginación: la feminización de la nación en el cine español y latinoamericano* (Fundamentos, 2006). She is a founder member of the programme of Women's Studies at the University of Oviedo, where she is a regular collaborator in projects and teaching.

MARVIN D'LUGO is Professor of Spanish and Comparative Literature at Clark University, Worcester, MA, where he teaches courses on Spanish and Latin American cinema. He is author of *The Films of Carlos Saura: The Practice of Seeing* (Princeton University Press, 1991), *Guide to the Cinema of Spain* (Greenwood Press, 1997) and *Pedro Almodóvar* (University of Illinois Press, 2006). Since 2008 he has served as principal editor of *Studies in Hispanic Cinemas*.

JO EVANS is Senior Lecturer at University College, London, where she teaches undergraduate and postgraduate courses on Spanish film. She is the author of a book on the Francoist poet, Ángela Figuera Aymerich, and of *Julio Medem* (Grant & Cutler, 2007). Her research interests include psychoanalytic and feminist film theory, and her articles on Spanish film and narrative have appeared in *Screen, New Cinemas, Studies in Hispanic Cinemas*, the *Hispanic Research Journal* and the *Bulletin of Hispanic Studies*. Forthcoming publications include book chapters on Iciar Bollaín, Spanish women filmmakers and the Argentine poet, journalist and playwright, Alfonsina Storni.

ROBIN FIDDIAN is Professor of Hispanic Studies at the University of Oxford and Fellow of Wadham College. He has published widely on Spanish and Spanish American literature and is the author of monographs on Ignacio Aldecoa, Gabriel García Márquez and Fernando del Paso. His work on Spanish cinema includes essays on Almodóvar, Borau and Colomo, amongst others. With Peter William Evans, he co-authored *Challenges to Authority: Fiction and Film in Contemporary Spain* (Tamesis, 1987). With Ian Michael, he co-edited *Sound on Vision: Studies on Spanish Cinema* (University of Glasgow, 1999).

SUE HARRIS is Reader in Film Studies at Queen Mary, University of London. She is the author of *Bertrand Blier* (MUP, 2001), co-author (with Tim Bergfelder and Sarah Street) of *Film Architecture and the Transnational Imagination: Set Design in 1930s European Cinema* (Amsterdam University Press, 2007), and co-editor of two volumes of essays: *France in Focus: Film and National Identity* (Berg, 2000), with Elizabeth Ezra, and *From Perversion to Purity: The Stardom of Catherine Deneuve* (MUP, 2007), with Lisa Downing. She is currently completing *An American in Paris* for the BFI Film Classics series.

MARÍA JOSÉ MARTÍNEZ JURICO is an artist based in Nottingham. She has a background in fine art, critical theory and counselling and has also worked as a teacher and a translator. As an artist, she has exhibited video-installation and mixed-media works. Her main medium at present is painting.

MARK MILLINGTON is Professor of Latin American Studies at the University of Nottingham. He has published on numerous Latin American novelists and the theory of cross-cultural reading. His last book was *Hombres in/visibles: la representación de la masculinidad en la ficción latinoamericana 1920–1980* (Fondo de Cultura Económica de España, 2010). His current research is on intellectual life in early twentieth-century Mexico and in particular the autobiography of José Vasconcelos.

ALBERTO MIRA is Reader in Film Studies at Oxford Brookes University, where he teaches courses on Spanish cinema, and classical Hollywood narration and stars. He co-devised the Film Studies undergraduate program at Brookes in 2004, and also contributes to the postgraduate MA in Popular Cinema. Between 1997 and 1999 he was Queen Sofía Research Fellow at Exeter College, Oxford. He has published extensively on Francoist cinema, gender in Spanish cinema, Iván Zulueta and Pedro Almodóvar for various Spanish, British and US journals. Alberto is the author of *De Sodoma a Chueca* (Egales, 2004), as well as a monograph on gay and lesbian cinema: *Miradas insumisas: gays y lesbianas en el cine* (Egales, 2008). Other publications include the *Historical Dictionary of Spanish Cinema* (Scarecrow, 2010) and critical editions and Spanish translations of plays by Oscar Wilde and Edward Albee.

CHRIS PERRIAM is Professor of Hispanic Studies at the University of Manchester and is lead researcher on the AHRC-funded project 'Queer Cinema from Spain and France'. He is joint author, with Phil Powrie, Bruce Babington and Ann Davies, of *Carmen on Film: A Cultural History* (Indiana University Press, 2006/07) and joint editor, with Peter William Evans and Isabel Santaolalla, of *The Transnational in Iberian and Latin American Cinemas* (special issue of the *Hispanic Research Journal*, 2007), as well as of *Theorizing World Cinema*, with Lúcia Nagib and Rajinder Dudrah (I.B. Tauris, 2011).

STEPHEN ROBERTS is Associate Professor and Reader in Modern Spanish Literature and Intellectual History at the University of Nottingham. He has published on the work of early twentieth-century Spanish and Spanish American thinkers and poets, including Unamuno, Rodó, Juan Ramón Jiménez, Neruda and Lorca, and on Spanish and US cinema (Juan Antonio Bardem, John Huston, Hollywood biopics). His current research focuses on the phenomenon of exile.

AGUSTÍN SÁNCHEZ VIDAL is Professor of Art History specialising in cinema and media studies at the University of Zaragoza, where he has also taught Spanish literature for more than 20 years. He has held posts as visiting professor in a number of universities including Princeton and the University of Nanterre, France. The author of more than 50 books on art, literature and film studies, he has published monographs on Borau and Carlos Saura, amongst others.

PAUL JULIAN SMITH is Distinguished Professor in the Ph.D. Program in Hispanic and Luso-Brazilian Languages and Literatures at the Graduate Center, City University of New York (CUNY). He was for 20 years Professor of Spanish in the University of Cambridge, UK. He is the author of 15 books, including *Desire Unlimited: The Cinema of Pedro Almodóvar* (Verso 1994; translated into Chinese and Turkish), *Amores Perros: Modern Classic* (BFI and University of California Press, 2003; translated into Spanish), *Laws of Desire: Questions of Homosexuality in Spanish Writing and Film* (Oxford University Press, 1992; also translated into Spanish) and *Spanish Screen Fiction: Between Cinema and Television* (Liverpool University Press and Chicago University Press, 2009).

ROB STONE is Professor of European Film at the University of Birmingham. He is the author of *Spanish Cinema* (Longman, 2001), *Flamenco in the Works of Federico García Lorca and Carlos Saura* (Edwin Mellen, 2004), *Julio Medem* (MUP, 2007) and *Walk, Don't Run: The Cinema of Richard Linklater* (Columbia University Press and Wallflower, 2012). He is also co-editor of *The Unsilvered Screen: Surrealism on Film* (Wallflower, 2006), *Screening Songs in Hispanic and Lusophone Cinema* (MUP, 2012) and *The Companion to Luis Buñuel* (Wiley-Blackwell, 2013).

KATHLEEN M. VERNON is Associate Professor of Hispanic Languages and Literature at Stony Brook University, New York State. Her areas of research focus primarily on cinema and popular culture, especially popular song, in Spain and Latin America in the twentieth century. With Barbara Morris, she co-edited *Post-Franco, Postmodern: The Films of Pedro Almodóvar* (Greenwood, 1995), and she is co-editor of *Studies in Hispanic Cinemas*.

DUNCAN WHEELER is Lecturer in Spanish at the University of Leeds, where he is also a member of the executive committee of the Centre for World Cinemas. Between 2010 and 2012 he was Leverhulme Research Fellow working on the role of arts and cultural institutions in Spain's transition to democracy, the subject of his second monograph which will be completed in 2013. In addition, he is reviews editor of *New Cinemas* and subject editor (Spanish literature and culture) of *The Literary Encyclopedia* (online).

TOM WHITTAKER is Lecturer in Hispanic Film Studies at the University of Liverpool. He is the author of *The Films of Elías Querejeta: A Producer of Landscapes* (University of Wales Press, 2011). His research has mainly focused on the relationship between film and geography in Spanish cinema, and his publications have appeared in journals such as *Jump Cut*, the *International Journal of Cultural Studies*, the *Journal of British Cinema and Television* and the *Bulletin of Hispanic Studies*. His current research centres on questions of movement and rhythm in Latin American cinema and soundscapes in Spanish cinema.

Acknowledgements

We have accumulated a number of debts in preparing this book. Thanks are due to the scholars who make the volume what it is, our resourceful and imaginative research assistant, Mar Diestro-Dópido, our indexer, Kate Eaton, and the distributors, filmmakers and producers who provided images or assisted us with queries: Pedro Almodóvar and Bárbara Peiró Aso at El Deseo; Robert Beeson of New Wave Films; Neil Bhatt and Edith Chappey at STUDIOCANAL; Víctor Erice; Cesc Gay; Manuel de Juan at Media Art Management; José Luis López-Linares; Lucrecia Martel; Julio Medem, Cecilia Roca and Silvia Gómez at Alicia Produce; Massimo Moretti at Optimum Releasing; Messidor Films; Luis Miñarro at Eddie Saeta S.A.; Ventura Pons at Els Films de la Rambla; Patrizia Raeli at Yume Pictures; and Carlos Saura. We would also like to express our thanks to Rosario Alburquerque Pérez, Rafael Cabrera, José Antonio de Ory and Manuel Llamas at the ICAA, Spanish Ministry of Culture; and Àlex Navarro and Mònica García i Massagué at Catalan Films.

We are also grateful to colleagues in the field who were not able to provide a chapter but whose ideas and scholarship have contributed in many ways to the overall shape and content of the volume: Bruce Babington, Xon de Ros, Richard Dyer, Parvati Nair, Isabel Santaolalla and Nuria Triana-Toribio. Thanks are also due to Matthew Frost and Kim Walker at Manchester University Press (MUP) for their support of this volume; Sandra Hebron; Michael Hayden and the London Film Festival team at the British Film Institute (BFI); Nick James, Kieron Corless and James Bell at *Sight & Sound*; the Office of Cultural and Scientific Affairs, Embassy of Spain in London; and to Joana Granero at the London Spanish Film Festival. We would also like to thank the two anonymous readers who first read the proposal for MUP, and Sarah Wright, who read the final manuscript when it was submitted to the publisher. Their generous feedback was instrumental at formative stages of preparing the volume.

Maria M. Delgado wishes to acknowledge the assistance of Queen Mary, University of London, in preparing the book. Special thanks go to Tom Delgado-Little and Henry Little for their patience and support.

Introduction

Maria M. Delgado

This collection of essays offers a new lens through which to examine Spain's cinematic production following the decades of isolation imposed by the Franco regime. The films analysed in the volume span a period of some 40 years that have been crucial in the development of Spain, Spanish democracy and Spanish cinema. Two 1970s films by Víctor Erice and Luis Buñuel (*El espíritu de la colmena/ The Spirit of the Beehive* [1973], *Cet obscur objet du désir/ That Obscure Object of Desire* [1977]), landmarks in that historical process, remain canonical instances of film-art which retain the power to inspire new critical interpretations, as in the first two chapters of the present volume.[1] A decade later, *El Dorado* (1987) by Carlos Saura feeds off the freedoms enshrined in the democratic Constitution of 1978 and anticipates the landmark year of 1992 – pivotal in global as well as Spanish political and cultural history, and represented here by Julio Medem's *Vacas/Cows* and Erice's *El sol del membrillo/ The Quince Tree Sun* (both 1992). These films provide a context and a threshold for the films of the noughties that form the main body of the volume.

Indeed, at the heart of this project, for which the majority of the films selected come from the opening decade of the twenty-first century, lies an examination of the ways in which established auteurs (Almodóvar, Garci, Saura) and younger generations of filmmakers (Cesc Gay, Alejandro Amenábar, Jorge Sánchez-Cabezudo) have harnessed cinematic language towards a commentary on the nation-state and the politics of historical and cultural memory. In the age of globalisation, it is perhaps not surprising that issues of cultural exchange, transnational collaboration and postcolonial discourse come into play. Thus, Chris Perriam turns his attention to Woody Allen's *Vicky Cristina Barcelona* (2008) – a Spanish/American co-production that performs a particular image of the Catalan capital by drawing on 'authenticating' performances by two of Spain's most prominent cultural exports – Penélope Cruz and Javier Bardem. Maria M. Delgado's treatment of Lucrecia Martel's *La mujer sin cabeza/The Headless Woman* (2008) similarly uses an Argentine–Spanish co-production, realised with the conspicuous support of Pedro Almodóvar's production company, El Deseo, to interrogate issues of historical memory in relation to both Argentina's 'Dirty War' (1976–83) and Spain's Law of Historical Memory (2007). *Vicky Cristina Barcelona* – conducted through the English language – again considers the ways in which language constructs identity in a Europe where economics fracture the ecologies of the nation-state. In *El laberinto del fauno/Pan's Labyrinth* (2006), Mexican auteur Guillermo del Toro provides an outsider's view on the difficult aftermath of the Spanish Civil War, harnessing the horror genre to a subject more often refracted through social-realist prisms.

In terms of the philosophical coherence of the project, association with the canon and a critical reflection on the political status quo are of interest to all the studies gathered here, along with a sharpness of focus on a key aspect or concept pertinent to each of the 17 films covered. The figure of the auteur jostles for attention alongside other features of film, ranging from genre, intertexuality and ethics, to filmic language and aesthetics. The representation of city space is of concern not only to Perriam's assessment of *Vicky Cristina Barcelona* but also a central element in Rob Stone's treatment of José Luis Guerín's *En la ciudad de Sylvia/In the City of Sylvia* (2007) and Sue Harris's study of José Luis Garci's *Ninette* (2005). For his part, Celestino Deleyto examines a new model of spectatorship in Cesc Gay's playful postmodernist *V.O.S.* (2009). The films chosen for study encompass major developments in the artistic and industrial processes of late twentieth- and early twenty-first-century cinema and have secured distribution outside Spain at major international festivals including Cannes, San Sebastián, Venice, Toronto and Berlin. They encompass different genres (horror, thriller, melodrama, documentary), both popular (Almodóvar, Allen, Amenábar) and more select arthouse fare (Guerín, Erice), and are made in different languages: English (as both first and second language), Basque, Castilian, Catalan and French. The focus of the volume is not on homogenisation but rather on locating how the different films treat wider issues of landscape (both rural and urban, abstract and concrete, filmic and theatrical) and memory in relation to the political shifts of Spain's history since the late 1970s.

Auteurism, popular cinema and the box office

Not all cinema can be harnessed to auteurist ends but auteurism remains, nevertheless, a prominent prism through which to analyse Spanish cinema. This is, in part, due to the visibility of a select number of filmmakers who have a global reach through the pervasiveness of the international festival market. Almodóvar is, of course, an international trademark and the visibility of his work through the exhibition sector in Europe, Asia and the Americas has further served to generate interest in Spanish film products. Álex de la Iglesia and Isabel Coixet have had work produced by El Deseo, the Almodóvar brothers' production company, as has the Argentine director Lucrecia Martel, whose 2008 film is discussed in Chapter 14. Beyond the scope of this collection, Pablo Berger's *Torremolinos 73* (2003) and Ayaso and Sabroso's *Los años desnudos/Rated R* (2008) have deployed visual devices popularised by Almodóvar. Certainly the auteur is no longer a figure with mere minority appeal – as may have been the case with Saura, Borau and Erice in the 1970s with films that failed to register with domestic audiences, despite gaining prizes at international festivals. The crossover attraction of popular genres like the thriller, horror and the romantic comedy has propelled particular auteurist works into commercial terrain and muddied the boundaries between 'popular' and 'auteurist': the box-office successes of *[REC]* (Jaume Balagueró and Paco Plaza, 2007), *Abre los ojos/Open Your Eyes* (Alejandro Amenábar, 1997), *El orfanato/The Orphanage* (J.A. Bayona, 2007) and *Los ojos de Julia/Julia's Eyes* (Guillem Morales, 2010) testify to this current, while the distribution possibilities offered by the festival circuit have served not merely to promote the work of more obviously auteurist directors like Julio Medem, Isabel Coixet and Iciar Bollaín, but also to offer markets where popular wares can be peddled to the increasingly powerful Spanish-speaking market in the Americas.

While we have chosen to focus largely on what could be termed auteurist cinema – with contributors stressing the recognisable style and thematics promoted by a filmmaker across a body of work – this is not to negate the significance of work across commercial genres that has enjoyed a degree of box-office success. *Vicky Cristina Barcelona* and *La noche de los girasoles/The Night of the Sunflowers* (Jorge Sánchez-Cabezudo, 2006) use established genres (the romantic comedy, the thriller) towards auteurist ends. *Vicky Cristina Barcelona* has enjoyed considerable commercial success in the process, taking $96,409,300 at the box office.[2] The influence of teen, coming-of-age features is witnessed in the range of films released in Spain at the end of the first decade of the twenty-first century – as with *Héroes* (Pau Freixas, 2010) and *El diario de Carlota/The Diary of Carlota* (Juan Manuel Carrasco, 2010). The concerns of these commercial features have also permeated the arthouse circuit, as with the more experimental *Blog* (Elena Trapé, 2010) and *Verbo* (Eduardo Chapero-Jackson, 2011), using social media as a visual vocabulary in delineating the day-to-day adventures of its 15-year old protagonists. Buddy movies, too, have oscillated between broad comic vehicles like *Primos/Cousins* (Daniel Sánchez Arévalo, 2010), celebrating male solidarity as a reliable force (above the vagaries of romantic attachment), and smaller-budget indie flicks emphasising the importance of social cohesion and community engagement in compromised times, as with *Amigos de Jesús/Friends of Jesús* (Antonio Muñoz de Mesa, 2007), where a group of friends head to New York in search of a good time when one is dumped by his girlfriend.

Slacker movies, too, have functioned as a mode of commentating on the inertia and sense of disillusionment in areas of high unemployment – as with the Seville-set *Déjate caer/Lazy Days* (Jesús Ponce, 2007) – and the dynamics of the tourist economy and Spain's selling of itself abroad – as with *Aislados/Isolated* (David Marqués, 2005). Both straddle the conventions of popular genres with a minimalist aesthetic imported from American independent cinema. With the exception of Luis García Berlanga, perhaps, the relationship between auteurist and popular cinema may have been more clearly drawn when Erice made *The Spirit of the Beehive* in 1973, but as the commercial successes of Almodóvar and Amenábar mapped in this volume evidence, these binarisms have now broken down to a previously unprecedented degree.

Spanish film production has expanded in recent years. In 1998, 65 full-length films were produced; this figure rose to 173 in 2008 and 200 in 2010 (although of these 200 productions only 138 secured distribution). Nevertheless, while investment in production continues to increase – with €80,283,375 handed out by the Instituto de la Cinematografía y las Artes Audiovisuales [ICAA, or Institute for Cinematography and Audiovisual Arts] in 2010 for production and promotion costs – the level of state investment has not been matched by box-office income. Spanish films at the domestic box office secured just 12.12 per cent of the market in 2010 (down by 3.38 per cent from 2009), bringing in 12.92 million spectators (a fall of 4.56 million from the previous year) and generating just €80.3 million (in contrast to the €104.3 million of 2009). It is perhaps not surprising that in a nation-state where, at the time of writing (December 2011), unemployment runs at over 22 per cent, there should be frustration at the level of state support for an industry that is perceived to not pay its own way.[3] During 2010 none of the top ten box-office hits was a home-grown product. Of the 200 films shot in the country only 138 secured cinematic release. Ignasi Guardans, Director General of the ICAA between 27 April 2010 and 22 October 2011, lamented that Spanish cinema had 'la cuota del mercado más baja de Europa' [the lowest market share in Europe] (cited in Seisdedos 2009), introducing a controversial ministerial order that allowed for 50 per cent more subsidy for films directed by women, the maximum amount that film projects could apply for in subsidy cut by a quarter from €2 million to €1.5 million, and concrete plans to fund a smaller percentage of films that he hoped would achieve a wider circulation – perhaps because of their more 'accessible' subject matter or genre.[4] His own positioning of the national Málaga Film Festival (as opposed to the A-list and more conspicuously international San Sebastián Festival) as the central market for Spanish cinema demonstrates the mixed messages that typified his tenure. The headlines that greeted his controversial legislation echo those that characterised Pilar Miró's period as Director General of Cinema (1982–85) in the heady years of Felipe González's first socialist government (1982–86) – with allegations of *amiguismo* [cronyism], a support for 'quality', 'artistic' cinema over more commercial fare, and conspicuous investment in the promotion of Spanish cinema at A-list international festivals.[5] Unlike Miró, Guardans actively promoted a more commercially minded mould of Spanish cinema that he hoped would encourage more profitable screen products with clear international sales potential – like Bayona's *The Impossible* (2012) and Juan Carlos Fresnadillo's *Intruders* (2011), two English-language works both building on the success of Spanish-language horror on the international festival circuit.[6] Spain may have moved away from tax breaks for commercial producers under Miró, but Guardans evidently had different priorities.

It is undeniably the international market and the branding of Spain that remains the key determinant for film in the second decade of the twenty-first century. Film, to co-opt Lefebvre's terminology, produces space and in so doing shapes how we see the world (Lefebvre 1991). Javier Bardem and Penélope Cruz are now global stars whose selling power promotes an image of Spain as alluring, desirable 'other'. The 2010 Venice Festival success of Álex de la Iglesia's *Balada triste de trompeta/ The Last Circus* and the co-production initiatives of Barcelona-based arthouse producer Luis Miñarro – who won the Cannes Palme d'Or in 2010 with Apichatpong Weerasethakul's *Loong Boonmee raleuk chat/ Uncle Boonmee Who Can Recall His Past Lives* – have served to position Spain within circuits that promote particular 'quality' fare. While statistics may show that it is teenagers and young adults under 25 who most frequent the cinema,[7] it is the international art-cinema market that Spanish governmental bodies continue to court with their promotional strategies. In June 2011 at the VI Madrid de Cine-Spanish Film Screenings, the ICAA's director, Carlos Cuadros, continued to stress the importance of selling Spain through its cinema. 'El cine es la mejor herramienta para promocionar la marca de un país y de nuestros productos' [Cinema is the best tool for promoting the brand of a country and of our products] – a position reinforced by Enrique Salazar, Vice-President of the Instituto Español de Comercio Exterior [ICEX or Spanish Institute for Foreign Commerce]: 'España necesita de una imagen exterior y uno de los baluartes para su construcción es el cine, un elemento clave para la economía y la imagen de un país' [Spain needs an international profile and foremost in its creation is cinema, a key element for a country's economy and image].[8] It is possible to argue that in the early 1970s there were 'two' Spanish cinemas: the allegorical ventures of directors like Carlos Saura, Erice and Vicente Aranda that were tolerated by the regime because of their international reverberations and presence at prestigious film markets like Cannes and Berlin, and commercial flicks drawing on the tropes of *costumbrismo* and the *españolada* that could be seen to function within what is commonly (and broadly) understood to be popular cinema.[9] The influence of *costumbrismo* may be evident in Fernando Trueba's Oscar-winning *Belle Epoque* (1992) and Garci's *Ninette* (2005) – analysed by Sue Harris in Chapter 9 – but it is primarily horror and Almodrama – to appropriate the late Cuban writer Guillermo Cabrera Infante's term for the blend of genres that constitute the eclectic screen worlds of the iconic Spanish *auteur*[10] – that have found the international audiences so courted by the Spanish authorities. And it is for this reason that we have included examples of both in this volume.

Politics

The period covered by this volume has seen the political landscape of Spain move from the dictatorial structures that underpinned the state in 1973, when *The Spirit of the Beehive* was made, to a constitutional framework articulating the tenets of a new democracy marked by an acceptance of *autonomías* – the 17 autonomous communities that make up the state of Spain. In the early 1970s Spain was led by a heavily centralised dictatorship that prioritised Castilian as the sole official language. Democracy has brought with it recognition that Spain is a state where linguistic difference is acknowledged (if not always celebrated). Catalan, Galician, Basque and Aranese are all spoken within what is understood to be Spain, with regional governments funding cinematic organisations to assist with the production and dissemination of films in their *autonomía*. The Generalitat de Valencia has funded the Ciudad de la Luz studios in Alicante to the tune of €46 million for a total of over 50 productions (EFE 2011), where films as diverse as *The Last Circus, Todas las canciones hablan de mí/Every Song is About Me* (Jonás Trueba, 2009), *Lo que sé de Lola/Lola* (Javier Rebollo, 2006), *Astérix en los juegos olímpicos/Asterix at the Olympic Games* (Frédéric Forestier and Thomas Langmann, 2008) and *The Diary of Carlota* have been shot.[11] The 19 productions made there between 2005 and 2007, for example, made the sum of €69.5 million, generated contracts with 1,107 local businesses and employed 1,220 resident technicians.[12] Barcelona-based Catalan Films received €1,090,000 in 2011 (down from €1,475,000 in 2005) from the Generalitat de Catalunya and has completed a total of 703 productions since it was founded in 1986. The Kimuak initiative, running since 1998 with the support of the Basque government and the Basque Filmoteca [Film Institute] has offered a standard for the production and distribution of short films (on DVD) in the Basque Country. While the early 1990s saw a crop of young Basque-born directors – Juanma Bajo Ulloa, Daniel Calparsoro and Julio Medem – set films within the Basque Country, all have gradually moved away from the landscape, social realities and myths of this *autonomía* in their twenty-first-century work. Only Medem in *La pelota vasca: la piel contra la piedra/Basque Ball: Skin against Stone* (2003) shot material in the Basque language, and while the film proved contentious in its treatment of ETA [Euskadi ta Askatasuna],[13] other films have more readily been able to articulate a national(ist) sentiment that has resonated internationally through its engagement with gay politics – as with Jon Garaño and José Mari Goenaga's *80 egunean/For 80 Days* (2010), seen at Karlovy Vary, and Roberto

Castón's *Ander* (2009) at Berlin's Panorama. In her Chapter 6 on *Vacas*, Jo Evans does not trace the film's debt to the Basque ethnographic documentary tradition which is such a feature of José María de Orbe's *Aita/Father* (2010), but rather chooses to explore its formal links to Goya's *Saturn* and *Leocadia* and Coppola's *Apocalypse Now* (1979) as a way of deconstructing the mechanics of assimilated fascism that it confronts.[14]

So while this volume does engage with the political implications of cinema made across the different languages of Spain (see Chapters 3, 6, 13 and 17), the political is inflected across a range of different modes. A number of contributors engage with what it means to make a political film or be categorised as a political filmmaker. In *The Spirit of the Beehive,* Erice offers the model of a restrained and understated storyline that can be read as an allegory of post-Civil War Spain (see Evans 1982; Kinder 1983), elaborated on here in Robin Fiddian's assertion of a debt to a politically charged precursor text (see pp. 30–2). The final film discussed in the volume, *También la lluvia/Even the Rain* (Iciar Bollaín, 2010), offers a different type of political filmmaking rooted in a social realism that has proved a dominant trend in post-Franco cinema. The need for metaphorical narratives that might 'escape' the censor's watchful gaze in many ways died with Franco – Saura's *Cría cuervos/Raise Ravens* (1975), produced in the year of Franco's death, is in many ways the pinnacle of this genre: a tale of stunted children in a closed-off female household where the death of their philandering military father signals the possibility of a new order.

Indeed, the post-Franco era has largely seen the enigmatic, metaphorical and elliptical jettisoned in favour of a social realism where politics is clearly worn on the sleeve. The in-yer-face exploitation *flics* of Eloy de la Iglesia, the permissive urban romantic comedies of Fernando Trueba and Fernando Colomo, the topical genre films of Imanol Uribe and the character-driven examinations of marginalised social-strata narratives of Fernando León de Aranoa have promoted what has proved to be a dominant trope in post-Franco Spanish filmmaking. The pop-cum-trash aesthetics of Iván Zulueta and Pedro Almodóvar pursued a bold intertextuality that looked outside Spain to music and the visual arts, comic books and the B-movie, but social realism has looked to Spain – its foibles and fears, corruptions and scandals, newsworthy stories and topical debates – in crafting its cinematic tales. As Duncan Wheeler indicates in Chapter 17, social realism's strong foothold in Spanish cinema has proffered a form of engaging with debates of the day. Iciar Bollaín and Javier Balaguer tackled domestic violence in *Te doy mis ojos/Take my Eyes* (2003) and *Sólo mía/Mine Alone* (2001), respectively, at a time when the Spanish media was obsessively focusing on what was perceived to be a problem of escalating proportions.[15] In the aggressively capitalist years of the UK's Thatcher governments, Ken Loach offered an angry voice of dissent to match the dark television dramas of Alan Bleasdale and Mike Leigh. Benito Zambrano in *Solas/Alone* (1999), Léon de Aranoa in *Los lunes al*

sol/Mondays in the Sun (2001) and Bollaín in *Mataharis* (2007) have all followed
Loach's lead in crafting deft features that have looked at the personal malaise that
comes from an unemployment that can be traced to the demise of certain key
industries in Spain.[16] The integrity of particular ways of making films that have
drawn on Loach's methodologies – extensive research, shooting on location as
opposed to in the studio, everyday settings, careful work with performers (sometimes non-professionals) – is touched on by Duncan Wheeler in his assessment
of Bollaín's *Even the Rain*. The types of female experience that women filmmakers like Bollaín, Isabel Coixet and Chus Gutiérrez have chosen to engage with in
their films – life/work balance, single parenting, the patriarchal ideologies that
underpin the workplace – suggest that the issues of gender parity, female agency
and equality remain a work in progress in post-Franco Spain.[17]

Crucially, the fall of the right-of-centre Partido Popular [PP, or People's
Party] government in 2004 witnessed a shift towards different thematic concerns and experiences – including a marked focus on issues of migration and
immigration and the shifting demographics of the metropolis. In the eight years
during which the Partido Socialista Obrero Español [PSOE, or Spanish Socialist
Workers' Party], held power, between 2004 and 2011, there was a dramatic
increase in immigration to Spain – from 923,879 in 2000 to 3,034,326 in 2004
and 5,730,667 in 2011;[18] and an escalation of unemployment mainly owing to
the global recession that burst the bubble of Spain's construction boom – the
average ministerial budget (in thousands of euros) increased from 727 in 1999
to 2,719 in 2008 (the climax of the boom).[19] Ventura Pons's *Ocaña. Retrat
intermitent/Ocaña. An Intermittent Portrait* (1977), analysed by Alberto Mira
in Chapter 3, explores the cultural legacy of the first wave of immigrants who
flocked to the industrial centres of northern Spain in search of employment and
a better standard of living in the 1960s. The films of Zapatero's Spain offer a
picture of a radically different demographic. *V.O.S.*, examined in Chapter 16, is
set in a Barcelona that similarly brings together inhabitants from other nations
within the Spanish state – this time the educated Basques who are part of the
distinct cultural infrastructure of the city and who switch languages from Basque
to Castilian and Catalan, thereby suggesting a degree of integration that evades
the immigrants that arrive from the developing world in González Iñárritu's
Biutiful (2010). *Ander* and *Rabia/Rage* (Sebastián Cordero, 2009) engage with
the issue of cheap immigrant labour in rural settings, refracting the debate
through the prisms of gay politics and gender exploitation. *La mujer sin piano/
Woman without Piano* (Javier Rebollo, 2009) and *Forasters/Strangers* (Ventura
Pons, 2008) deconstruct the isolation, stigmatism and vulnerability that can
accompany the position of the *forastero*, or outsider.

Spanish cinema's engagement with changes to the national demographic
generated by the economic growth of the 1980s is evident in a range of works
from Montxo Armendáriz's *Las cartas de Alou/Alou's Letters* (1990) to León

de Aranoa's *Amador* (2010). In Chapter 17, Duncan Wheeler discusses the postcolonialist features of both *Flores de otro mundo/Flowers from Another World* (Bollaín, 1999) and *Rage* when assessing the social issues that Bollaín has chosen to engage with in her work. The legacy of Spain's empire in the Americas hovers over the migrants who arrive in Spain in search of employment. The feminisation of migration undertaken in films like León de Aranoa's *Princesas/Princesses* (2005) and *Amador* functions as a pertinent reminder of the masculine discourses of colonialist mobility interrogated by Agustín Sánchez Vidal in his treatment of Saura's *El Dorado* in Chapter 4. In *Even the Rain* Bollaín too is shown to negotiate transnational considerations that engage with narratives of imperialist expansion, investigating the mechanisms through which colonial power was consolidated by Columbus during his time as Governor in the Caribbean (1493–96). A shared language – Castilian commonly referred to as Spanish – has allowed for a circuit of transnational traffic between Spain and the Americas consolidated through such initiatives as Ibermedia – a collaboration between Spain and 13 Spanish-speaking countries established in 1997 (www.programaibermedia.com). The potentially uneven dynamics of such relationships, however, are also explored within the volume in three chapters (13, 15 and 17) that both question the construct of a Spanish 'national' cinema, and engage with wider issues around an international currency which arguably functions through the very culture of global exchange that such films may seek to denounce.

Landscape

Landscape – offering a correlation between physical and emotional space – is also an essential feature of many of the films in the volume. In *The Spirit of the Beehive* the sparse rural terrain of Castile is an embodiment of the psychological states of mind of the mother and father both trapped in emotional voids brought about by the devastation wrought by the Civil War and its aftermath. The landscape captured by Luis Cuadrado's camera is as yellow as dried parchment, with honeyed hues that replicate the palette of the beehive. *Los abrazos rotos/Broken Embraces* (Almodóvar, 2009) picks up on the town/country binary that has proved such a powerful trope in Spanish culture, juxtaposing the danger of Madrid with the rural, magical paradise of Lanzarote. In *El Dorado* the gilded beauty of this Atlantis offers an image of a paradise idyll shattered by the extraneous forces represented by the sixteenth-century explorer Lope de Aguirre and the colonialist culture he represents. In *Even the Rain*, Bollaín shows how the rich natural resources of the Americas have been harnessed towards the commercial gain of a few, leaving a significant proportion of the population without basic provision. In *The Headless Woman*, too, the reservoir in which the boy's body is found functions as a metaphor for the murky depths of the middle-class psyche willing to erase all traces of the possible crime. María Donapetry powerfully explores the resonances of space in her treatment of *Tesis/ Thesis* (Amenábar, 1996) (Chapter 7) through a comparison with the visual landscape of Hieronymus Bosch's *The Garden of Earthly Delights*. Jo Evans, in Chapter 6, reads Medem's *Vacas* through two of Goya's Black Paintings as a means of exploring ways of seeing and the ethics of filmmaking.

From Berlanga and Bardem's *¡Bienvenido Mr Marshall!/ Welcome Mr. Marshall!* (1952), it is possible to view Spanish cinema's engagement with the historical transformations that the country has experienced both under Franco and beyond. The *desarrollismo* [modernisation] of the late 1950s and 1960s was interrogated in three of Saura's most corrosive works (*La caza/ The Hunt* [1965], *El jardín de las delicias/ The Garden of Delights* [1970] and *Stress es tres, tres/ Stress is Three* [1968]). Erice's *The Spirit of the Beehive* continues this vein of social engagement realised through elliptical vocabularies that prioritise the episodic and the observational. The tone is elegiac although not nostalgic, and offers a potent antidote to the more sanitised and narrative-driven filmmaking of the social-realist filmmakers discussed earlier in this introduction. Tom Whittaker, too, maps landscapes of 'loss, trauma and fragmentation' (p. 159) in his treatment of *The Night of the Sunflowers* in Chapter 11. While the picturesque village wants to capitalise on the rural tourism market that the discovery of the cave might bring, the film exposes the Spanish countryside as anything but peaceful and passive. The ravages of time are evident in the tired buildings as well as in the two weathered faces of the village's elderly, cantankerous inhabitants. Whittaker traces a trend in twenty-first-century Spanish filmmaking – evident in works as diverse as Gonzalo López-Gallego's *El rey de la montaña/ King of the Hill* (2007) and Mercedes Álvarez's *El cielo gira/ The Sky Turns* (2004) – in which the rural is both trope and setting. As Almodóvar signals in *Volver* (2006), the pastoral idyll may only have existed in the national imaginary; here Carmen Maura's ghost functions as a potent metaphor for a landscape haunted by the 'other' of urbanisation and the legacy of feuds and disputes that eventually lead the rural world to implode with terrifying consequences in *The Night of the Sunflowers*. Indeed, the anxieties of neoliberalism have frequently been played out in Spanish cinema in the tensions between the urban and the rural.

The urban metropolis also functions as a powerful trope in many of the films presented in this volume. In her discussion of *Ninette* in Chapter 9, Sue Harris shows how Paris functions as an alternative cultural landscape to the provincial world represented by Murcia, signifying 'political freedom, sexual identity and modern cosmopolitanism, as well as cinematic escapism' (p. 137). Madrid and Barcelona have both featured as characters in the films of Pedro Almodóvar and Ventura Pons, respectively. Almodóvar challenged the images of the drab, grey Madrid represented in post-Civil War Spanish fiction and film. Pons provided an alternative to the modernist bourgeois city of popular contemporary mythology or the avant-garde vision of the Barcelona School with a libertarian vision of a city infused with a playful sensuality. In *The Night of the Sunflowers*, the city (Madrid) embodies the danger that intrudes on and disrupts the civic ecology of the town of Angosto. In *Broken Embraces*, too, it is a space of danger and entrapment, surveillance and observation that Penélope Cruz's Lena and Lluís Homar's Mateo Blanco hope to escape when they elope to Lanzarote. (Again, here, 'the city' invades their protected space when Rayo-X tracks them down.) *Vicky Cristina Barcelona* presents an idealised city landscape, more myth than reality – and a veritable 'other' to the 'invisible' Barcelona of a film like González Iñárritu's *Biutiful*, set in the northern populated suburbs of Santa Coloma and Badalona. The multiethnic Barcelona of *Biutiful* is also visible in Ventura Pons's *Strangers*, which similarly explores the patterns of immigration to the city as waves of migrants – *charnegos* – from Andalusia and Extremadura in the 1950s, 1960s and 1970s have been followed by a new generation of political and economic migrants from Africa, China and Central and South America. Neither *Biutiful* nor *Strangers* are covered in this volume, but their representation of the urban metropolis offers a useful reference point for both *Vicky Cristina Barcelona* and *V.O.S.*, where Barcelona's status as a cosmopolitan city is both celebrated – in the former – and interrogated – in the latter.

The city is also a powerful theme in Guerín's *In the City of Sylvia*, analysed by Rob Stone in Chapter 12. Here the material body of the city 'speaks' of the mysterious woman and the unnamed young man – a modern-day *flâneur* – who follows her. Guerín interweaves a physical, emotional and cinematic journey through a cityscape that eschews national markers. As Stone indicates, the film constructs, deconstructs and reconstructs a particularly contemporary European intuition of time and space, making reference to the theories of time and its *durée* posited by Henri Bergson and the psychogeography of the *dérive* as promoted by Guy Debord and the Situationist International (pp. 169–70). *In the City of Sylvia* may have been promoted as Spanish arthouse fare, but its paradigms are decisively shown to be those of a modernist ideal of European time and place.

For Mark Millington, in his treatment of Buñuel's *That Obscure Object of Desire* (1977), landscape is not about the locations that serve as the backdrops of the meetings between Mathieu and Concha – Switzerland, Paris, Seville – but rather about Buñuel's technique: his opting primarily for the two- and three-shots, and his 'occasionally tightly controlled shots containing up to six or seven characters' (pp. 39–40). Millington charts a landscape that is not about montage but rather about arranging characters in an environment, about grouping and regrouping, about repetition and variation.

In their chapter on *The Quince Tree Sun*, too, María José Martínez Jurico and Stephen G.H. Roberts show how patterns of composition (in painting, drawing and filmmaking) are harnessed to deal with the passing of time. Erice's process of capturing artist Antonio López as he paints a quince tree in the period between autumn 1990 and spring 1991 is shown to echo that of the painter at work. In engaging with the space of artistic creation, Erice creates a landscape of observation where the very process of representation is itself exposed as objects are 'transferred' into an artistic space where they become an 'other' entity.

With *The Spirit of the Beehive*, Erice introduces a further dimension, a film within a film, in this case excerpts from James Whale's *Frankenstein* (1931), to construct a metaphor for the protagonist Ana's own alienation. Telling the story solely from Ana's point of view also allows Erice to blur the boundary between reality and fiction, in order to highlight the gap between official rhetoric and the gruesome reality of the country. In this light, the house functions as a potent metaphor for a wider social landscape of entrapment. Erice's own evolution as a filmmaker – as both *The Quince Tree Sun* and his 2006 filmed correspondence with Abbas Kiarostami[20] indicate – points to a desire to continue investigating how cinema can depict or describe a mode of working, tell a story and patiently engage with the textures, sounds, sights, smells and rhythms of the world without ever succumbing to the accelerated narratives of much commercial cinema. His influence is evident both in the work of filmmakers represented in this study (like Guerín and José Luis López-Linares) and further auteurs working in Spanish cinema. Javier Rebollo, for example, deploys an economical performance register where the accelerated rhythm of contemporary consumerist culture is expertly dissected. Albert Serra has produced a cinema of gentle observation and slow demeanour, in which eccentric characters incarnated by non-professional actors bring new dimensions to well-known fictional and religious archetypes. Serra, like Jaime Rosales, Isaki Lacuesta, Erice and Guerín, has worked with the museum sector – the CCCB's Correspondencia series (2006/11) – on commissioned works that both take cinema as a mode of discourse – a way of 'writing' to a contemporary about what they do and how they do it – and a mode of presenting their relationship with the world through their engagement with art practice. Cinema may have moved into the domestic space embodied by the DVD and the streaming/downloading of films, but the endemic problems with pirating – over 77 per cent of the digital content viewed in Spain during the first six months of 2011 was downloaded from non-legal channels – have had an impact on revenues generated for motion pictures' production, distribution and exhibition industries, with estimated losses costing the music, film, publishing and gaming sectors over \$7.2 billion during this period alone (Rolfe 2011). While Álex de la Iglesia protested at the introduction of a new law in February 2011 to close down file-sharing websites that boasted excessive copyrighted material (Anon. 2011a), El Deseo mentioned piracy as the reason for choosing to release *La piel que habito/The Skin I Live in* (2011) theatrically in Spain after Cannes rather than prior to the festival, as had habitually been the case with Almodóvar's films in the noughties (Almodóvar 2011). At a time when DVD sales in Spain have reached an all-time low, with one independent producer referring to the nation as a '1950s' market' where significant funds are only generated from cinema screenings and television broadcast rights (Anon. 2011b), cinema is having to look to new modes of distribution and exhibition.

Initiatives such as the CCCB's Correspondencia series demonstrate the ways in which both filmmakers and exhibitors in Spain are reconfiguring the role of film within museum spaces in a context that recognises how each filmic artefact is an engagement with the ghosts of a cinematic past, and the realities of a digital world where social isolation and fragmentation are a way of life. It is perhaps no coincidence that Guerín, one of Spain's most internationally acclaimed filmmakers, grounds his films in metaphors of rootlessness, displacement and death (see Diestro-Dópido 2011). The cubist puzzle of *In the City of Sylvia* presents the search for an elusive Other that always remains out of the grasp of both the filmmaker and his alter ego. As Rob Stone demonstrates in Chapter 12, in Guerín's earlier *Tren de sombras/ Train of Shadows* (1997) the 'found' home movies of a Parisian lawyer are shown to be a fiction, a mode of constructing the past rather than simply remembering it (pp. 173–4). Kathleen M. Vernon, too, in Chapter 8 demonstrates how López-Linares's *Un instante en la vida ajena/A Glimpse of Other Lives* (2003) engages with the processes of narrating history. Documentary cinema may have been constrained within the propagandist paradigms of the NO-DO (Notario y Documentales) [News and Documentaries] service during the Franco regime but the years covered by this volume, as Vernon shows, have witnessed documentary filmmakers entering into a space of engagement with the role of film in the construction of their nation's past. From Basilio Martín Patino's *Caudillo* (1973) to Jaime Chávarri's *El desencanto/ The Disenchantment* (1976), Medem's *Basque Ball* to *A Glimpse of Other Lives*, the documentary has offered a creative space for an interrogation of memory, landscape and history where the archive collides with memory to disarming effect. The fusion of documentary and fiction in Isaki Lacuesta's choral feature *Los pasos dobles/ The Double Steps* (2011), winner of the grand prize, the Concha de Oro, at San Sebastián's 2011 Festival, questions interpretations of history and myth-creation, but, most importantly, undermines schematic notions of national identity, mirroring the changes that have occurred in Spanish society since Franco's death.

Memory

In a nation haunted by the legacy of a fratricidal conflict that left approximately 750,000[21] dead and sent over 500,000 into exile (of which around 300,000 decided to return to Spain after the war, and over 200,000 remained in France), it is perhaps no surprise that memory should prove such a potent topic in Spanish filmmaking. In *The Spirit of the Beehive,* the trauma of the Civil War hovers over the characters as an unarticulated malcontent. The mass unmarked graves of the nation appear to haunt the landscape of *Pan's Labyrinth* from which the undead that pursue the child protagonist appear. Paul Julian Smith's analysis of the latter film in Chapter 10 positions it within the Spanish branding of horror known as *cine fantástico* and charts its evolution in Spain. The Mexican-born Guillermo del Toro has spoken of the influence Spanish exiles from the Civil War exerted on Mexican culture during his youth (Smith 2007). As director of *El espinazo del diablo/ The Devil's Backbone* (2001) and *Pan's Labyrinth*, and co-producer of Bayona's debut feature *The Orphanage,* he has contributed greatly to the shaping of a genre that has served as a potent transnational currency, albeit with films set in a recognisably Spanish landscape.

Since the beginning of the twenty-first century, a range of directors have used horror as a way of probing issues of the personal and collective subconscious: *The Devil's Backbone* is set during the fratricidal Civil War, *Pan's Labyrinth* is set in the *años de hambre* [years of hunger] that followed, and its child protagonist also evokes the curious Ana of *The Spirit of the Beehive*. *The Orphanage*, while ostensibly set in twenty-first-century Spain, harks back to the dictatorship era with a fey young boy, like Ana in Saura's *Raise Ravens*, who offers a connection to the other-worldly. Geraldine Chaplin, the ghost-mother of *Raise Ravens*, is here an obvious link: the spectral medium brought in by the young boy's mother, Laura (Belén Rueda), to unearth whatever may be hiding in the old orphanage. The leitmotif of the haunted-house – and the house, of course, as Paul Julian Smith (2011) aptly notes, has proved a dominant trope in Spanish filmmaking – allows for the exploration of the inheritance of an unearthed past. It is perhaps no coincidence that at a time when Spain was debating the merits (or otherwise) of introducing a Law of Historical Memory, finally pushed through by Zapatero's socialist government in 2007, Spanish horror films were engaging with revenants and zombies, phantoms and the living dead. The ghosts of those civilians – anything between 30,000 and 150,000, depending on whose statistics you choose to believe – who opposed the right-wing Nationalists during the Civil War and its aftermath, lie in multiple mass graves across the nation. *Pan's Labyrinth* is one of a significant number of features – *Los otros/ The Others* (Amenábar, 2001), *[REC]*, *The Orphanage*, *Julia's Eyes* – that deploy ghosts to explore the inheritance of a past marked by traumatic excesses. *Pan's Labyrinth* revisits the traumatised children of *The Spirit of the Beehive*, haunted by the ravages of dictatorship in both its domestic and institutional forms.

Horror's resonance in a nation still coming to terms with both the Civil War and the 36-year legacy of Franco's dictatorship may, in part, explain its commercial and critical success. Paul Julian Smith charts the box-office success of *Pan's Labyrinth* in Chapter 10 (p. 146). *The Orphanage* proved *the* Spanish box-office hit of 2007, besting Hollywood blockbusters like *Pirates of the Caribbean: At World's End* and *Shrek 3*,[22] while Fresnadillo's *Intruders* and Bayona's *The Impossible* have both followed Amenábar's example in 'exporting' the genre to the global mainstream with an English-language cast (Clive Owen features in the former; Ewan McGregor in the latter).

It is not merely through horror, however, that memory is conceived as a thematic through this volume. In *That Obscure Object of Desire* Concha (played by two actors) remains an enigma, existing as a memory conjured through Mathieu's storytelling.[23] The idea of the unattainable woman idealised by the male imagination dominates both Buñuel's film and Guerín's *In the City of Sylvia*. The tension between personal and collective memory is articulated in the conflict between the Mendiluze and Irigibel families in *Vacas*. Modes of tackling the nation's historical past – as *Vacas* pertinently demonstrates – have moved beyond singular notions of historical 'truth'.

Empire and its discontents, tainted with the brush of Francoism's attempts to bind the nation through *hispanidad,* have subsequently been subject to caustic treatments, evidenced in the readings of *El Dorado* and *Even the Rain* proffered in Chapters 4 and 17, respectively. *El Dorado* signalled a historical paradigm that presented an ambition for wealth and power bound up with reckless ambition and greed – a greed in evidence in the multinationals that hover over the Bolivian social landscape in *Even the Rain*. The early modern world has also proved the backdrop to the swashbuckling adventures of Agustín Díaz Yanes's *Alatriste* (2006), as well as Manuel Iborra's adaptation of Lope de Vega's *La dama boba/The Silly Lady* (2006), which itself built on the success of Pilar Miró's 1995 adaptation of *El perro del hortelano/Dog in a Manger*.[24] *Even the Rain* itself interrogates the discourses of historical filmmaking, probing the ways in which particular ideological positions are promoted by screen represen-tations of the historical. While the rhetorical excesses of historical filmmaking under Franco were parodied in the transition era – as Wheeler indicates in Chapter 17 – there remains a need for film to engage with the complexity of historical paradoxes in models that go beyond the biopic case of *Salvador* (*Puig Antich*) (Manuel Huerga, 2006), the comic treatment offered by *Ninette* or the stolid melodrama of *Las 13 rosas/13 Roses* (Emilio Martínez Lázaro, 2007). Reappraisals of the Spanish Civil War appear to have especially fallen into such generic paradigms, functioning through a burlesque comic register (*¡Ay, Carmela!* [Carlos Saura, 1990]) or sweeping treatments of star-crossed lovers caught across enemy lines (*La voz dormida/The Sleeping Voice* [Benito Zambrano, 2011]).

In this respect both Alberto Morais's debut feature *Las olas/The Waves* (2011) and del Toro's *The Devil's Backbone* revolve around the ghostly legacy of the Civil War. In the former a Spanish refugee returns to the concentration camp at Argelès-sur-Mer where he was held over half a century earlier – the conflict-marked symbolic landscape as redolent as that of Saura's earlier *The Hunt*; in the latter the voice-over that opens the film sets out the spectral legacy of a war whose ghostly presence continues to dominate the ecology of the nation.

Spectres feature as both a thematic motif in a number of the films considered in this collection and as a way of conceiving both the nation's history and its cinematic past. The prevalence of tropes, motifs and characteristics present in Peter William Evans's landmark volume, *Spanish Cinema: The Auteurist Tradition* (1999), testifies both to a degree of self-referentiality and a shared political and cultural context that has informed the stylistic and thematic considerations of the filmmakers whose work is analysed in this collection. From the need to cultivate foreign interests evident in both *Welcome Mr. Marshall!* and *Vicky Cristina Barcelona* to the violent brutality masked by the benign pastoral idyll of rural Castile in *Furtivos/Poachers* (José Luis Borau, 1975) and *The Night of the Sunflowers*, the politics, landscape and memory of the nation's psyche remain prominent concerns. The extended discussion of specific films presented in *Spanish Cinema 1973–2010: Auteurism, Politics, Landscape and Memory* provides both a link to Evans's volume (with *The Spirit of the Beehive* and *Vacas* featuring across both books) and a contribution (and complement) to the scholarship on landscape (Davies 2012; Faulkner 2006; Smith 2000; Whittaker 2011), national identity (Triana-Toribio 2003) and memory (Labanyi 2008) that has emerged in the twenty-first century. It also demonstrates the ways in which film has created new prisms (indeed, one could argue, stereotypes) that have determined how Spain is positioned in the global marketplace.[25]

Notes

1 We cite both Spanish titles and their English translation on first use. After that, for ease and consistency, we opt for the English translation of the title, unless the film is known in English by its Spanish title, as with *Vacas* and *Volver*.

2 See http://boxofficemojo.com/movies/?id=vickycristinabarcelona.htm [accessed 10 January 2012].

3 These figures are published in the Ministry of Culture's 'Boletín Informativo de Cine' for 2010; see www.mcu.es/cine/docs/MC/BIC/2010/Boletin_2010.pdf [accessed 9 January 2010]. Note that these figures are contested by other sources, which argue for takings of just €69.7 million (as opposed to the €80.3 claimed by the Ministry of Culture; see Martínez 2011). The year 2011 proved a more positive one, with a 15.3 per cent quota of the market and €95.7 million generated in takings. See Belinchón 2011.

4 The order met with opposition from a grouping of professionals, 'Cineastas contra la Orden' [Filmmakers against the Order] – which included Javier Rebollo, Luis Miñarro, Ventura Pons and Fernando Trueba – who took their protests to the European Commission. For further details, see Belinchón and García (2009); García (2009).

5 See Aguirre (1984); García (1984, 2009).

6 *The Orphanage*, for example, made $71,477,703 at the foreign box-office (as opposed to $7,161,284 in domestic sales). See http://boxofficemojo.com/movies/?id=orphanage.htm [accessed 11 January 2012].

7 See Time Consultants (2006); Repiso (2009); EGEDA (2010).

8 Quotes taken from 'El cine español como marca de un país' on the website of the Academia de las Artes y las Ciencias Cinematográficas de España, www.academia decine.com/la_academia/noticia.php?id_noticia=370 [accessed 19 October 2011].

9 Here I am adopting one of Raymond Williams's (1976) useful articulations of popular culture as an artefact or form consumed by considerable numbers of individuals, although not produced by them. A useful and compact history of Spanish popular cinema is offered by Antonio Lázaro-Reboll and Andrew Willis (2004).

10 Indeed, we would also argue that the volume makes a contribution to Almodóvar studies in a number of ways. From Alberto Mira's pertinent observations in Chapter 3 on the way that the *movida* was interpreted at the start (by Almodóvar and others) as stemming from the jubilation felt at the death of Franco and the opening up of prohibitions, through Delgado's reflection in Chapter 14 on the way that recent films by Almodóvar concentrate on mourning, both institutional and personal, to Marvin D'Lugo's discussion of the ways that *Broken Embraces* might be seen to revise Almodóvar's earlier feelings about the *movida*: all these reflections offer revisionist positions on arguably Spain's most important film director. (With thanks to Sarah Wright for drawing this to the editors' attention.)

11 For further details see the Ciudad de la Luz's website, www.ciudaddelaluz.com/es/ Filmografia/Paginas/indice.aspx [accessed 12 December 2011].

12 See http://web.ciudaddelaluz.com/ES/conocenos/presentacion [accessed 12 December 2011].

13 The Basque acronym for Basque Land and Liberty, ETA is a nationalist separatist movement founded in 1959 that developed into a paramilitary organisation responsible for the deaths of 829 individuals from 1968. On 20 October 2011 ETA announced a definitive termination of its armed activity. For further details, see Woodworth 2002.

14 For readings of *Vacas* through the prism of Basque identities, see de Ros (1997); Santaolalla (1999).

15 On the issue of domestic violence and its treatment in Spanish cinema, see Wheeler (2008) and (2012b); Zanzana (2010).

16 In an interview with me conducted in October 2011, Benito Zambrano also significantly acknowledged a debt to Mike Leigh's improvisational character development when discussing the mode of crafting *Solas*.

17 As regards male and female unemployment, in 1996 (the year that the PP came to power) the difference peaked at 1,279,180 men/1,496,772 women. When PSOE was re-elected in 2004 the gap had almost doubled, peaking at 872,326 men/1,293,094 women. In 2011, the difference had narrowed, peaking at 2,147,953 men/2,212,973 women unemployed. Information found at the Instituto Nacional de Estadística [National Statistics Institute], www.ine.es [accessed 18 December 2011].

18 Information found at the Instituto Nacional de Estadística [National Statistics Institute], www. ine.es [accessed 18 December 2011].

19 Licitación oficial de las administraciones públicas en la construcción [Official Tender in Building], Ministerio de Fomento [Ministry of Development]. Units: thousands of euros. 1999: 15,958,631/2008: 38,514,124. Ministerio de Fomento [Ministry of

Development]. Information found at the Instituto Nacional de Estadística [National Statistics Institute], www.ine.es [accessed 18 December 2011].

20 An exhibition of Erice and Kiarostami's work, first seen at the Centre de Cultura Contemporània de Barcelona [CCCB, or Barcelona Centre for Contemporary Culture] in 2006, was realised through cinematic correspondence and offered a model which was taken up with a series of further commissions of 'filmed conversations' between pairs of filmmakers in 2011 that I deal with later in the paragraph.

21 With total figures ranging from 500,000 to a million, in 2010 the Ministerio de Cultura [Ministry of Culture] created a website documenting the personal details of approximately 750,000 victims on both sides, called 'Víctimas de la Guerra Civil y Represaliados del Franquismo' [Victims of the Civil War and of Repression under Franco], part of the Ministerio de Cultura (www.mcu.es) website.

22 *The Orphanage* grossed €24,317,951,81, *Pirates of the Caribbean* €22,774,989,10 and *Shrek 3* €22.065.328,57; see www.mcu.es/cine/MC/CDC/Anio2007/CinePeliculasRecaudacion.html [accessed 9 January 2012].

23 Gilles Deleuze sees this differently. He reads the characters as 'factual', existing simultaneously in two worlds, and both equally valid; see Deleuze (2005: 100).

24 For further information on the cinematic adaptations of these works and other Golden Age plays, see Wheeler (2012a: 135–88); for a study of literary adaptations in Spanish cinema, see Faulkner (2004).

25 With thanks to Mar Diestro-Dópido, Robin Fiddian, Rob Stone and Sarah Wright for their comments on earlier drafts of this introduction.

Bibliography

Aguirre, Javier (1984) 'Sobre la "ley Miró"', *El País* (26 December), www.elpais.com/articulo/cultura/MIRO/_PILAR/ley/Miro/elpepicul/19841226elpepicul_1/Tes [accessed 10 January 2012].

Almodóvar, Pedro (2011) Interview with the author, Madrid (13 June).

Anon. (2011a) 'Ending the open season on artists', *The Economist* (17 February), www.economist.com/node/18184458 [accessed 4 January 2012].

Anon. (2011b) 'Spotting the pirates', *The Economist* (20 August), www.economist.com/node/21526299 [accessed 5 January 2012].

Belinchón, Gregorio (2011) 'Cifras de asistencia a las salas', *El País* (28 December), p. 38.

—and R. García (2009) 'Conmoción en el mundo del cine por la decisión de Bruselas de bloquear las ayudas a rodajes', *El País* (25 November), www.elpais.com/articulo/cultura/Conmocion/mundo/cine/decision/Bruselas/bloquear/ayudas/rodajes/elpepucul/20091125elpepucul_1/Tes [accessed 20 December 2011].

Davies, Ann (2012) *Spanish Spaces: Landscape, Space and Place in Contemporary Spanish Culture*, Liverpool: Liverpool University Press.

de Ros, Xon (1997) '*Vacas* and Basque Cinema: The Making of a Tradition', *Journal of the Institute of Romance Studies*, 5, 225–34.

Deleuze, Gilles (2005), *Cinema 2: The Time Image* (London: Continuum Impacts).

Diestro-Dópido, Mar (2011) 'Correspondences: Jonas Mekas, José Luis Guerín, Jafar

Panahi', *Sight & Sound* (21 October), www.bfi.org.uk/sightandsound/newsandviews/ festivals/blog/lff-2011–10–21–correspondence.php [accessed 1 December 2011].

EFE (2011) 'Las películas rodadas en la Ciudad de la Luz acaparan 19 nominaciones', *Informacion.es* (11 January), www.diarioinformacion.com/cultura/2011/01/11/ peliculas-rodadas-ciudad-luz-acaparan-19–nominaciones/1083211.html [accessed 10 January 2012].

EGEDA [Entidad de Gestión de Derechos de los Productores Audiovisuales] (2010) 'La imagen del cine español en la sociedad española', *Boletín Informativo EGEDA*, 53 (June), 14–15.

Evans, Peter William (1982) '*El espíritu de la colmena*: The Monster, the Place of the Father, and Growing Up in the Dictatorship', *Vida Hispánica,* 31:3 (Autumn), 13–16.

—(ed.) (1999) *Spanish Cinema: The Auteurist Tradition,* Oxford: Oxford University Press.

Faulkner, Sally (2004) *Literary Adaptations in Spanish Cinema*, London: Tamesis.

—(2006) *A Cinema of Contradiction: Spanish Film in the 1960s*, Edinburgh: Edinburgh University Press.

García, Ángeles (1984) 'Pilar Miró asegura que no hay corrupción ni amiguismo en las subvenciones al cine', *El País* (28 November), www.elpais.com/articulo/cultura/ MIRO/_PILAR/CABAL/_FERMIN/Pilar/Miro/asegura/hay/corrupcion/amiguismo /subvenciones/cine/elpepicul/19841128elpepicul_4/Tes [accessed 2 February 2012].

García, Rocío (2009) 'Cineastas contra la Orden', *El País* (7 August), www.elpais. com/articulo/revista/agosto/Cineastas/Orden/elpeputec/20090807elpepirdv_8/Tes [accessed 10 November 2011].

Kinder, Marsha (1983) 'The Children of Franco in the New Spanish Cinema', *Quarterly Review of Film Studies*, 8:2 (Spring), 57–76.

Labanyi, Jo (ed.) (2008) *The Politics of Memory in Contemporary Spain*, monographic issue of *Journal of Spanish Cultural Studies,* 9:2.

Lázaro Reboll, Antonio and Andrew Willis (eds) (2004) *Spanish Popular Cinema*, Manchester: Manchester University Press.

Lefebvre, Henri (1991) *The Production of Space*, Oxford: Blackwell.

Martínez, Luis (2011) 'El misterio de los 10 "kilos"', *El Mundo* (17 March), www. elmundo.es/elmundo/2011/03/17/cultura/1300364240.html [accessed 10 January 2012].

Ministerio de Cultura (2011), 'Boletín Informativo de Cine. Año 2010', www.mcu.es/ cine/docs/MC/BIC/2010/Boletin_2010.pdf [accessed 15 January 2012].

Repiso, Isabel (2009) 'Los jóvenes levantan el cine', *Público.es*, 12 July, www.publico.es/ culturas/238178/los-jovenes-levantan-el-cine [accessed 30 January 2012].

Rolfe, Pamela (2011) 'Over 77% of Digital Content Consumed in Spain is Pirated', *Hollywood Reporter* (11 August), www.hollywoodreporter.com/news/77–digital- content-consumed-spain-258726 [accessed 10 January 2012].

Santaolalla, Isabel (1999) 'Julio Medem's *Vacas* (1991): Historicizing the Forest', in Evans (ed.), 310–24.

Seisdedos, Iker (2009) 'Guardans aplica la Ley de Igualdad a las ayudas del cine', *El País* (23 September), www.elpais.com/articulo/cultura/Guardans/aplica/Ley/Igualdad/ayu das/cine/elpepucul/20090923elpepicul_5/Tes [accessed 10 December 2011].

Smith, Paul (2000) *The Moderns: Space and Subjectivity in Contemporary Spanish Culture*, Oxford: Oxford University Press.

—(2007) '*Pan's Labyrinth*', *Film Quarterly*, 60:4 (Summer), www.filmquarterly.org/2007/06/pans-labyrinth/ [accessed 5 January 2012].

—(2011) 'Spanish Spring: Spanish Cinema after Franco', *Sight & Sound*, 21:7 (July), 34–7.

Time Consultants (2006) 'Mileuristas. Guapos y pobres. Informe de resultados "Nuevas audiencias potenciales II", for the Centre de Desenvolupament Audiovisual, Barcelona' (October).

Triana-Toribio, Nuria (2003) *Spanish National Cinemas*, London: Routledge.

Wheeler, Duncan (2008) 'Intimate Partner Abuse in Spain (1975–2006)', *Cuestiones de Género*, 3, 173–204.

—(2012a) *Golden Age Drama in Contemporary Spain: The Comedia on Page, Stage and Screen*, Cardiff: University of Wales Press.

—(2012b) 'The Representation of Domestic Violence in Spanish Cinema', *Modern Language Review*, 10:2 (April), 438–500.

Whittaker, Tom (2011) *The Films of Elías Querejeta: A Producer of Landscapes*, Cardiff: University of Wales Press.

Williams, Raymond (1976) *Keywords: A Vocabulary of Culture and Society*, Glasgow: Fontana.

Woodworth, Paddy (2002) *Dirty War, Clean Hands: ETA, the GAL and Spanish Democracy*, New Haven, CT: Yale University Press.

Zambrano, Benito (2011) Interview with the author, London (21 October).

Zanzana, Habib (2010) 'Domestic Violence and Social Responsibility in Contemporary Spanish Cinema: A Portfolio View of Behavioral Dynamics', *Hispania*, 93:3 (September), 380–98.

1

El espíritu de la colmena/ The Spirit of the Beehive (Víctor Erice, 1973): To Kill a Mockingbird as neglected intertext

Robin Fiddian

Six-year-old Ana lives with her older sister, Isabel, and parents Teresa and Fernando on the outskirts of the small provincial town of Hoyuelos in rural Castile. The year is 1940: the Spanish Civil War (1936–39) has not been long over and General Francisco Franco holds the country in an iron grip. The story begins with Ana (Ana Torrent) and Isabel (Isabel Tellería) hurrying to a makeshift cinema in the town hall, where they will watch James Whale's *Frankenstein* (1931). The impression that the film leaves on Ana is particularly profound, and she will come to interpret the wider world of family, politics and social relations through the prism of a monstrous fiction and excited imagination. We see Ana with her fellow pupils in an anatomy class at school; we also see her befriend a political fugitive, to whom she brings some food including an apple, and some clothes belonging to her father. The film treats of the lives of other characters, including Ana's parents, but the focus is mainly on her inner world and susceptibility. Near the end of the story Ana slips away from the house and, in a night-time fantasy sequence, meets up with Dr Frankenstein's monster next to a stream, in the woods. Eventually located by a search party, she is returned to her parents, weak and mute, but alive. The doctor appears confident that Ana will recover, but her last words, standing at an open window and summoning the monster, cast doubt on that prognosis.

Regarded universally as a classic of Spanish arthouse cinema,[1] *El espíritu de la colmena/ The Spirit of the Beehive* (1973) has attracted a wealth of critical attention which has focused on political, historical, psychological and formal aspects of Víctor Erice's co-authored film-text (he wrote the script together with friend and fellow film critic, Ángel Fernández Santos). A particularly rich vein of scholarship has explored the manifold intertextuality of *The Spirit of the Beehive*, ranging from cinematic genres to literary sources to schools of painting. In one of the very first essays devoted to the film, Fernando Savater (1976) drew on links with Mary Shelley's *Frankenstein* in a discussion of *The Spirit of the Beehive*'s analysis of moral and political distemper in the late years of Franco's Spain. Subsequently, a more cinematic approach was taken by Peter Evans, who in a wide-ranging essay of 1982 illustrated Erice's debts to classic films of German Expressionism as well as to the Val Lewton/Jacques Tourneur brand of horror at RKO studios. In particular, Evans considered intertextual references to James Whale's *Frankenstein*, paying close attention to the figure of the monster, on which Marsha Kinder (1993: 127–9) and Linda M. Willem (1998) would further elaborate. Closer to the present day, essays by Rob Stone (2002: 87–94) and Xon de Ros (2005: 139–47) continue to demonstrate the appeal and relevance of intertextual study to *The Spirit of the Beehive*. Given the existence of such a well-defined critical corpus, it is perhaps surprising that no one has identified the literary and film versions of *To Kill a Mockingbird* as intertexts of Erice's film, which was produced by Elías Querejeta and crafted by a team including Pablo del Amo (editor) and Luis Cuadrado (cinematographer). However, as I will seek to show in this opening chapter, a number of commonalities can be established between *To Kill a Mockingbird* and *The Spirit of the Beehive*, starting at the levels of narrative composition and genre and crystallising in a number of musical and visual motifs of which the most significant by far is the figure of the monster. Recognition of these commonalities prompts a reassessment of Erice's film in terms of influence and adaptation and leads ultimately to a nuanced appreciation of its artistic merits and relationship to the canon of Spanish film.

To Kill a Mockingbird (1960, 1962)

Harper Lee published her landmark novel in 1960 and received the Pulitzer Prize for it the following year. Over half a century later, *To Kill a Mockingbird* remains a classic of world literature, widely celebrated in the year of its fiftieth anniversary, and its author consecrated as a national treasure whose reputation extends beyond the English-speaking world. The film version of *To Kill a Mockingbird* was produced by Alan J. Pakula for Universal Pictures and released in 1962. Working in close collaboration with Lee, Horton Foote wrote the screenplay and Robert Mulligan directed. Gregory Peck was one of the stars of the movie, in which 9-year old Mary Badham played the tomboy Jean Louise ('Scout') Finch and Robert Duvall made his screen debut as the mysterious and pallid Arthur ('Boo') Radley. In the year of its release, *To Kill a Mockingbird* was nominated for no fewer than eight Academy Awards and received Oscars for Best Actor, Best Adapted Screenplay and Art Direction.

In both the film and the book, themes of morality and social justice, innocence and racial prejudice, are as compelling half a century on as they were in early-1960s America; many sequences from the film stand out in the memory, especially those involving Gregory Peck in the role of Atticus Finch, the small-town Southern lawyer who agrees to defend Tom Robinson (Brock Peters), falsely accused of raping a young white woman, Mayella Ewell (Collin Wilcox); Atticus's ultimate failure to secure Tom Robinson's acquittal in the charged atmosphere of the local courthouse does not diminish his aura as a man of principle who is ready to take a stand; Tom Robinson's death, shot while trying to escape custody, and a nasty, revenge-driven attack on Atticus's children provide a dramatic conclusion to a narrative set in times of economic hardship and social crisis in the American deep South following the Wall Street Crash of 1929.

In terms of film form, the most conspicuous feature of *To Kill a Mockingbird* is a first-person female voice-over which serves to introduce the story: 'Maycomb [Alabama] was a tired old town even in 1932 when I first knew it.' This differs only minimally from the Harper Lee original: 'Maycomb was an old town, but it was a tired old town when I first knew it' (2002: 5). In both versions, Scout, now a mature woman, looks back over a quarter of a century to a three-year period beginning in 1932, when she was 6 and her brother Jem almost 11. Immediately, we notice a difference between the film narrative of *To Kill a Mockingbird* and *The Spirit of the Beehive*, where events are presented directly and not retrospectively. In fact, there seems to be a closer fit with Erice's later film, *El Sur/The South* (1983), where Iciar Bollaín's Estrella recounts in voice-over a chain of biographical events beginning in northern Spain in the 1940s and culminating in her departure for the south after her father's suicide in the autumn of 1957. However, as Erice told a team of interviewers in October 1973, his original conception of *The Spirit of the Beehive* had accommodated a retrospective voice-over which was to frame the narrative; with only weeks to go before shooting, he changed his mind and replaced the voice-over with a more elliptical and poetic style of narration in which primacy would be granted to the point of view of the child, Ana (Erice and Fernández Santos 1976: 145).

Opening shots

Horton Foote and Robert Mulligan's *To Kill a Mockingbird* opens with the sound of a piano playing the film's theme tune; a child's voice is heard intermittently, humming along to the music and sometimes chuckling. The camera shows a pair of small hands lifting the lid of a wooden box and revealing an assortment of objects that evoke child's play: amongst other things there is a safety pin, a whistle, two carved figurines – one male in appearance, the other female – some coins, some marbles, a harmonica, a ticking watch and some crayons. The intertitle 'To Kill a Mockingbird' now appears on the screen, superimposed over the

1. Child's drawing of a watch in the opening frames of *The Spirit of the Beehive*.

contents of the box. The child, who is out of frame, picks up a crayon and draws a straight vertical line; a second drawing is on the horizontal plane and depicts troughs or waves on the sea; finally, we see the sketch, in two stages of development, of a bird – a mockingbird, perhaps, or a finch (which would constitute a visual pun on the family's surname). Having finished the sketch, the child tears the picture of the bird in two. As the title sequence comes to a close, the voice-over begins the story of Scout, Jem, Atticus and their neighbours in Maycomb, Alabama. On the musical soundtrack, the harmonies of Elmer Bernstein's theme tune are disturbed by a wind instrument playing a discordant note.

For those familiar with Erice's film, the similarities with the opening sequence of *The Spirit of the Beehive* are both numerous and remarkable. There, too, we are presented with a collage of drawings by children (in reality the work of the two child actresses, Ana and Isabel). The drawings, 12 in number, prefigure events, characters and objects that will appear later in Erice's film; perhaps most interestingly, they include a pocket watch similar to the one that is seen and heard at the beginning of *To Kill a Mockingbird*. The atmosphere at this point in *The Spirit of the Beehive* is rich and saturated in make-believe: an effect produced by a haunting musical score, by the inter-title 'Érase una vez' [Once upon a time] and the lyrics of a well-known nursery song, 'Vamos a contar mentiras, tra la la' [Let's tell fibs]. The overall effect is to entice the spectator into a realm of fantasy. There, he or she will experience the world through the eyes and sensibility of Ana, who is the main focaliser of *The Spirit of the Beehive*.

Narrative genres

Proceeding into the main body of their film narrative, Horton Foote and Robert Mulligan follow Harper Lee in the creation of a hybrid text, which is part female

Bildungsroman and part Southern gothic novel.[2] *To Kill a Mockingbird* traces the psychological development, and privileges the perspective, of a 6-year old girl as she learns lessons in life and social relations. Pushed around by an older brother, Scout finds her liberty curtailed by him as much in the playground as at home. Instinctively a tomboy, she resents having to wear a dress for school and is uncomfortable with her society's code of femininity. In the absence of her mother, who has been dead some four years, the principal source of love in the home is her father, who is certainly benevolent and caring. In the summer, when he must continue working, Scout is very much dependent for entertainment on her brother and a friend named Dill. Dill is a small boy, aged 'four-and-a-half going on seven' (7), who first appears (literally) in the cabbage patch in the summer of 1932 and returns to Maycomb annually thereafter to visit his Aunt Rachel and renew his friendships.

Apart from his size, a number of things are significant about Dill. First is the announcement that he makes, that he has no father. This is actually untrue, but it underscores the importance of themes of family and parenting in both Harper Lee's novel and its adaptation for the screen. In Dill, Scout acquires a second, surrogate brother, one who does not push her around but treats her as an equal. A second point about Dill is the fact that he shares Scout's love of reading, and indeed introduces himself as someone who can read, in spite of circumstances. He has also been to the movies 20 times thanks to his mother, who entered him in a Beautiful Child contest and won a $5 prize which she then gave to him. Dill thus brings extra dimensions of imagination to the children's world.

Dill is especially important in linking the narrative of *To Kill a Mockingbird* with the genre of Gothic horror. Early on in the novel, we read that

> Dill had seen *Dracula*, a revelation that moved Jem to eye him with the beginning of respect. 'Tell it to us,' he said.

At Jem's invitation, Dill 'reduced *Dracula* to dust, and Jem said the show sounded better than the book' (8). For whatever reason, the screenplay of *To Kill a Mockingbird* elides this narrative episode and makes no mention of Tod Browning's film of 1931; it also waters down Dill's role as instigator of adventures. However, it involves him fully in the action that takes place around the house and the figure of Boo Radley, which are the central Gothic elements in *To Kill a Mockingbird.*

The Radley house, also called 'the Radley Place', is held in awe by virtually all the neighbourhood. Declared off-limits by adults, including Dill's hysterical Aunt Rachel, it is shot, for the first time in the film, from a cautious distance. On the day he arrives in Maycomb, Dill enquires about it and is told what seems like a tall story by Jem, who alludes to a mysterious figure, imprisoned by his heartless father, who 'only comes out at night'. This is Boo Radley, who, in the mould of the Bogeyman, eats raw squirrels and all the cats he can catch. There's a long, jagged scar that runs all the way across his face. His teeth are yellow and rotten. His eyes are popped. And he drools most of the time.

Although heavily embroidered, Jem's account is backed up in the film by Aunt Rachel, who fills in the details of a back-story of family dysfunction. According to her, Boo had once attacked his father with a pair of scissors as he worked, aged 33, on his scrapbook; subsequently, he had been locked up in the basement of the courthouse 'till he nearly died of the damp'; finally readmitted to the family home, Boo has for years remained a recluse and, like a vampire, only emerges at night.

An early and a late episode in the film convey two very different sides of Boo's relations with Jem, Scout and Dill. In the first episode, the children dare to approach the Radley Place from the street. It is night-time and they are trespassing. As Jem sets a nervous foot on the porch, the boards creak under his weight and he recoils, in classic Gothic mood. Whilst this is happening, Dill and Scout are crouching, motionless, to one side. Suddenly, as Jem tries to prise open a window, he falls under a monstrous shadow coming from right of frame. The children all cower under the figure, which is photographed suggestively from below and could have come straight out of *Nosferatu* (Murnau, 1922) or *Dracula* – whose trademark black, white and greys are reproduced in Mulligan and Pakula's film.[3] We infer that the figure is Boo Radley. For a few seconds, it looks as if the children will all be violated, or worse, but the figure withdraws, slowly, and they run off.

In the other episode, Boo is once more a shadowy presence, coming fully into view only in the final frames. The action takes place at Halloween, which the children celebrate in a pageant at school. Scout attends as a ham, wearing a costume made of chicken wire and old cloth; except for two peepholes, it covers her head and gives protection to most of her body. After the pageant, she and Jem walk home through windswept trees, redolent of the traditional babes in the wood. Sensing that they are being followed, Jem tries to protect both himself and Scout, but they are attacked. For some seconds, we make out three forms, namely the two children and their assailant, all in close-up. Then another form joins in and wrestles with the assailant, whom it apparently subdues. As the episode continues, we (and Scout) see from behind a tall figure carrying Jem, who is unconscious, home in his arms. The figure is Boo Radley, who has intervened as the children's guardian angel. The assailant, we discover, was Bob Ewell, Mayella's abusive father and the personification of nastiness and evil. The dark events of Halloween end with the announcement of the discovery nearby of Bob Ewell's corpse, stabbed between the ribs with a kitchen knife; in a dramatic climax in the Finches' house, Boo Radley emerges into the light from behind the door of the bedroom where Jem lies asleep, nursing a broken arm.

As his nickname indicates, Boo belongs within the 'scary' tradition of Gothic horror. There is a fascinating ambiguity around him because, whilst the narrative comes to vindicate him as the children's saviour and friend, it does nothing to explain or diminish the stigma of violence that darkens his character. His stabbing of Bob Ewell may seem a justified act of retribution, but the much earlier attack on Mr Radley was arbitrary and unprovoked. Even so, Boo's character is redolent of that of the creature in Mary Shelley's canonical novel: a mixture of frightening monstrosity, on the one hand, and playful, childlike innocence and emotional need, on the other.

From a comparative perspective, the combination of elements from the *Bildungsroman* and the Gothic traditions in *To Kill a Mockingbird* resonates very clearly with the story of Ana in *The Spirit of the Beehive*. In both films a little girl embarks on a process of growing up and learns about good and evil – symbolised by the poisonous mushroom in Erice's film and by the figure of Bob Ewell in *To Kill a Mockingbird*. Taking a cue from one or more references to a monster – Dracula; Frankenstein – both narratives evoke scenes and atmospheres which are terrifying, especially to younger children. More specifically, they feature a night-time encounter with a monstrous figure in the woods, resulting in a child's being confined to bed, receiving medical attention from the town doctor. At the close of *The Spirit of the Beehive*, Ana appears locked into a psychotic state from which there may be no release; Scout and Jem are less visibly traumatised, the damage suffered extending no further than a broken arm and a considerable fright.

The figure of the monster

A central area of concern in the works under discussion is their orchestration of contradictory and shifting perspectives on the figure and motif of the monster. In *To Kill a Mockingbird*, Scout and Jem learn over time and through experience no longer to regard Boo as 'a malevolent phantom' (9). Yet, throughout the film, their perspective has been set against others, including Atticus, who tells the children not to interfere with 'those poor people' (a reference to the Radleys), who want nothing more than to be left alone. The fact is that Boo is widely misunderstood and even demonised, both by children 'enacting a strange little drama of their own invention' (320), and by 'people' in general, on all points of the social scale:

> When people's azaleas froze in a cold snap, it was because [Boo] had breathed on them. Any stealthy small crimes committed in Maycomb were his work ... A Negro would not pass the Radley Place at night, he would cut across to the sidewalk opposite and whistle as he walked. (9)

Behind a façade of cosiness and Southern politesse, Maycomb houses elements that are barbarous and inherently monstrous. An illustration is the mob that arrives at the jail late at night baying for the blood of Tom Robinson, who has been taken into protective custody. Then there is Bob Ewell – associated throughout the film with violence, laziness, cowardice and even incest. We get a sense of what to expect of him early on, when a mad dog roams the streets and Heck Tate, the sheriff, gives Atticus the job of shooting it; the subject of the very next sequence is Bob Ewell, clearly identified by the syntax of the film with themes of irrationality, animal behaviour and sickness.[4]

Forms of monstrosity are no less prevalent in the narrative of *The Spirit of the Beehive*. The monster created by Dr Frankenstein is the first to appear in Erice's film, in a series of excerpts from the James Whale classic shown in its entirety to an audience gathered in the town hall of Hoyuelos; Boris Karloff's monster is internalised almost immediately by Ana, who remains obsessed from that point. After Frankenstein, attributes of monstrosity permeate a spectrum of characters including Ana's father, whose heavy footsteps on the floor as he goes to bed early one morning are redolent of the episode where Boo catches Jem trespassing on the Radley porch; General Francisco Franco, who, though never seen or mentioned in Erice's film, is assimilated to the type of Frankenstein by his names; and the political fugitive: cast in the role of Other by a regime bent on hunting down and destroying its political enemies, who are to be dealt with as ruthlessly as the poisonous mushroom which Fernando identifies and crushes underfoot during an educational outing with his daughters into the countryside.

Education and imagination are in fact crucial in the construction of the figure of the monster, and Erice's film again mirrors significant details of Harper Lee's narrative in this regard. Most pertinently, the Halloween pageant at school features 'a House of Horrors' in which the children are invited by 'the temporary ghoul in residence' to touch 'the component parts of a human being':

> 'Here's his eyes,' we were told when we touched two peeled grapes on a saucer. 'Here's his heart,' which felt like raw liver. 'These are his innards,' and our hands were thrust into a plate of cold spaghetti. (295)

Emptied of any real horror by the more knowing perspective of the adult Scout, the episode picks up on an earlier one in which Jem constructs a 'Morphodite' (84) out of a range of materials gathered in the backyard. Using first mud and then snow, Jem produces a shape that comes to resemble a neighbour, Mr Avery:

> Gradually Mr Avery turned white.
> Using bits of wood for eyes, nose, mouth, and buttons, Jem succeeded in making Mr Avery look cross. A stick of stovewood completed the picture. Jem stepped back and viewed his creation.
> 'It's lovely, Jem,' [Scout] said. 'Looks almost like he'd talk to you.' (76)

Unbeknown to the children, but clearly understood by both the author and her readers, Jem and Scout are effectively re-enacting Dr Frankenstein's creation of a

2. Don José's gaze in the classroom sequence of *The Spirit of the Beehive.*

monster near the start of James Whale's film. Equally to the point, even though neither the ghoulish episode from Halloween, nor that of the Morphodite, finds their way into Foote and Mulligan's screenplay, they enter the very bloodstream of *The Spirit of the Beehive*, where body parts and their amalgamation into the figure of a monster are dramatised in a number of sequences. Early in the story, Isabel seeks to persuade her impressionable younger sister that she has seen the monster from James Whale's film: it is a spirit that lives in hiding, she says, outside the town. In reply, Ana insists that the monster she saw on the screen had body parts: 'it has feet, it has hands, it has everything' (Erice and Fernández Santos 1976: 56), and is therefore more than just a spirit. Isabel continues to play on Ana's credulous nature, and it will not be long before Ana believes that she has really found the monster, hiding in a deserted farm-building outside the town. But before that, she takes part in an exercise at school which consists in fixing body parts and organs onto a dummy called Don José. This imaginary character is introduced by the teacher as if he were a real person visiting the school and requiring deferential treatment. The situation would be comic, were the teacher's attitude not wholly condescending and a deliberate mystification of young minds. Foremost amongst these, of course, is Ana, who, according to Erice's script, 'watches closely, in fascination' (Erice and Fernández Santos 1976: 66) as first one and then another child places the heart, the lungs, a kidney and the stomach in the right places on the dummy. Finally, Ana is called on to supply a key item that is missing, which are Don José's eyes: these she positions correctly and returns to her seat.

The anatomy class is a turning point in Ana's life: whilst Isabel and other older children have seen it all before, Ana undergoes a vital initiation into mysteries of the human organism. Being more imaginative than the other children, Ana is more deeply affected by the lesson of Don José and more convinced, we sense, that she has taken part in the creation of (a simulacrum of) a human being. In the very final lines of the sequence, Ana undergoes an effect which the film's notes describe in unusual detail:

> Don José looks at the children 'for real' [*de verdad*]. And Ana, very close to that ambiguous figure, feels more than ever that she is being looked at intensely. (67).

This moment, in which Ana feels the full force of Don José's silent gaze, is critical in the development of her sense of self. In the context of the plot, the moment prepares the viewer for Ana's encounter with the political fugitive, which will be similarly charged with silence and ambiguity. In the windswept buildings which she will visit first with her sister and then alone, Ana will be sure that she has found the embodied spirit of Frankenstein's monster: a being who is both human and therefore mortal – he needs food and is bleeding from a wound to his leg – and mysterious – he bewitches Ana with legerdemain, making her father's watch disappear up his sleeve. She could hardly ask for more conclusive proof that this is the sympathetic monster of her imaginings. And the spectator, too, is encouraged to establish the connection later, near the end of the film, when the corpse of the fugitive, who has been tracked down and shot, lies stretched out in the town hall, in the exact same space where the movie of Frankenstein had been shown at the start of *The Spirit of the Beehive*. Public space and private fantasy thus coincide as much in the film we are viewing as in the movie Ana and Isabel are watching in the opening sequences of Erice's narrative.

Family resemblance, influence and adaptation

The rich detail and the substance of this comparative analysis suggest a strong family resemblance between *The Spirit of the Beehive* and *To Kill a Mockingbird*. At the level of the narrative, whole swathes of Erice's film echo the stuff of its precursor, which had centred on a 6-year old girl coming to terms, as so many do, with real and imagined monsters. The two films, and the texts from which they derive, share in the same generic mix of the *Bildungsroman* and Gothic horror, with figures of monsters looming large in the story-line. In the context of the Gothic tradition, Harper Lee's novel displays an open affiliation with *Dracula*, whilst Erice references *Frankenstein*. The motif of body parts is essential to both *To Kill a Mockingbird* and *The Spirit of the Beehive*, which have other motifs in common too, including the pocket watch inscribed 'To Atticus, my beloved husband' which reappears, minus inscription, in at least three scenes in *The Spirit of the Beehive*. Add to this the presence, in each work, of a dense web of archetypal material – viz. the names of Arthur Radley, Jem, Scout, etc., and the pervasiveness of the natural order, especially the elements of fire and water, in *The Spirit of the Beehive* – and a common backcloth of social hardship, and we have two texts that are virtually mirror images of each other.

Extending the argument, it is surely legitimate to claim for *To Kill a Mockingbird* the status of a creative template for *The Spirit of the Beehive*. If this proposition is accepted, then we must acknowledge *To Kill a Mockingbird* as a major source and influence on Erice's film, made a full decade after the publication of Harper Lee's novel and its successful translation to the screen. Certain circumstances make it highly plausible that Erice would have seen Pakula's production and the Oscar ceremony at which it made such a stir, in 1962. At that time, Erice was halfway through his practical training at the Madrid-based Instituto de Investigaciones y Experiencias Cinematográficas (Spain's official School of Cinematography), where he studied from 1960 to 1963. As a budding young filmmaker, it is more than likely that he would have followed news reports from the greatest annual event in the global entertainment industry, with keen professional, as well as personal, interest.

However, more important than nailing an influence is the judgement that is to be made concerning the artistic accomplishment of Erice's reworking of the narrative template supplied by *To Kill a Mockingbird*. And here, at least two strategies are available for gauging the outcome of his, and Querejeta's, adaptation of Mulligan and Pakula's film. First, we can regard *The Spirit of the Beehive* as a palimpsest comprising both a surface narrative and a 'ghost' story that lies just below that surface, transmitting a set of meanings and images which percolate upwards into the stories of Ana, Isabel and the other characters in Erice's film. According to this model, *The Spirit of the Beehive* carries within it traces of the psychological and socio-political dramas affecting the lives of Scout, Boo, Atticus and others in *To Kill a Mockingbird*. In finer detail, the fate of the Republican fugitive in Erice's film evokes that of Tom Robinson – the black underdog and object of hatred of rednecks and others in a state such as Alabama both in the 1930s, when the Ku Klux Klan was riding high, but also in the early 1960s, when Harper Lee played an active role in the US Civil Rights movement. The 'ghost' story in Erice's film accordingly serves, amongst other things, to reinforce a bifocal view of history, whereby a series of narrative events set in rural Castile in 1940 do 'double duty' in relation also to the early 1970s in Spain, when *The Spirit of the Beehive* captures the ambience of the Franco dictatorship in terminal decline.

A second model of adaptation allows us to account for essential differences between the precursor narrative and its sequel and to formulate a definitive assessment of the artistic achievement of *The Spirit of the Beehive*. Essential tools here are the concepts of translation or transformation, and re-signification (see Genette 1982). As already stated, *To Kill a Mockingbird* plots the growth in a young girl's understanding of the monstrous elements in her world; besides Boo Radley and Bob Ewell, these also include Tom Robinson – the scapegoat of a racist society which cannot tolerate the idea of a black man being kissed by a white woman in 1930s (or late 1950s) Alabama. In Erice and Fernández Santos's hands, Scout's story is refashioned as a study of growing up a decade later in Franco's Spain, where education and authority are prolific sources of monsters in a little girl's imagination already impacted by a classic horror movie and unsettled by experiences in the heart of the family. Goya's dictum about 'the sleep of reason' engendering monsters seems tailor-made for the story of Ana and her schooling in Hoyuelos in 1940.

Family relations are in fact a key area of re-signification in *The Spirit of the Beehive*. Harper Lee had presented us with a home setting where the mother is dead and the older sibling is male. In a significant variation, Erice describes a family where the parents seem estranged and the older sibling, Isabel, exerts a dark and unsettling influence on her impressionable younger sister. Although Ana's mother, Teresa, is physically present in her daughters' lives, the film leaves us in no doubt that she has a strong emotional attachment outside the family.[5] Meanwhile, her husband Fernando shows only occasional interest in his daughters and takes refuge instead in a world of self-absorption and bee-keeping, insulated inside a suit which makes him look and sound like a monster. When, in the wake of Ana's disappearance, Fernando is called on to exercise parental authority, he overreacts, in marked contrast to the more measured masculinity displayed by Atticus in various episodes of *To Kill a Mockingbird*. The result, in *The Spirit of the Beehive*, is an unflattering depiction of male disorientation, and even impotence, in Spanish society under Franco.

Conclusions

The above analysis gives rise to three interrelated conclusions. First, the identity of *The Spirit of the Beehive* is inseparable from that of its sources, whether cinematic, as in the case of *Frankenstein*,[6] or literary, as in the case of *To Kill a Mockingbird*. Secondly, such an assertion does not imply any depreciation of the technical and artistic merits of *The Spirit of the Beehive*: on the contrary, the ghostly subtext of *To Kill a Mockingbird* enriches the content of Erice's film and further enhances its standing as a universally acclaimed cinematic masterpiece. Thirdly, the long-established prestige of *The Spirit of the Beehive* in the canon of Spanish cinema can be seen, at a distance and perhaps paradoxically, to depend largely on the film's reworking of a composite literary and film text that originated in the lived socio-political and personal experience of mid-twentieth-century subjects in the USA. Yet, as Evans and others noted long ago, Víctor Erice has always recognised an affiliation with a network of transnational cultural traditions, and it seems fitting, on this occasion, to acknowledge not only the creative triumph of the work of re-signification carried out in *The Spirit of the Beehive*, but also the new life that a Spanish film of 1973 is, nearly 50 years later, still capable of breathing into the ever-popular literary and filmic story of innocents and monsters that is Harper Lee's own master-creation.

Notes

1 Paul Julian Smith (1999) studies the construction of the film's and its director's reputation, critiquing auteurist positions which neglect considerations of history.
2 The *Encyclopedia Britannica* defines 'Southern gothic' as a fictional mode unique to US American literature and comprising stories 'characterized by grotesque, macabre, or fantastic incidents'. The attribution of *To Kill a Mockingbird* to the mode is common in the secondary literature devoted to Lee's novel, e.g. Claudia Durst Johnson (1994).
3 Erice spoke openly about mimicking 'aspectos del expresionismo alemán, sobre todo de algunas obras de Fritz Lang, y de "Nosferatu" de Murnau' [aspects of German expressionism, above all some of the works of Fritz Lang, and of Murnau's *Nosferatu*] (Erice and Fernández Santos 1976: 141).
4 Carolyn M. Jones offers an alternative reading of this episode, which is essentially not coherent: 'The mad dog that Atticus shoots represents the mad dog of racism that must be dealt with, not violently, but through persuasion in a public structure of deliberation, the trial' (2002: 416–17).
5 On this aspect of the film, see Celestino Deleyto (1999: 50 and *passim*).
6 Carlos Aguilar suggests a source for Erice's film in *Whistle Down the Wind* (Bryan Forbes, 1961). According to him, the story about two young children and a fugitive from justice 'suspiciously prefigures' that of Ana and Isabel. In the present study, I look at a wider range of convergences with another English-language work.

Bibliography

Aguilar, Carlos (2004) *Guía del cine* (3rd edn 2008), Madrid: Cátedra.
De Ros, Xon (2005) '*El espíritu de la colmena/Spirit of the Beehive*', in Alberto Mira (ed.), *The Cinema of Spain and Portugal*, London: Wallflower Press, 139–47.
Deleyto, Celestino (1999) 'Women and Monsters: *El espíritu de la colmena*', in Robin Fiddian and Ian Michael (eds), *Sound on Vision: Studies on Spanish Cinema*, special issue of *Bulletin of Hispanic Studies* (Carfax Publishing), 76:1, 39–51.
Erice, Víctor and Ángel Fernández Santos (1976) *El espíritu de la colmena*, Madrid: Elías Querejeta Ediciones.
Evans, Peter William (1982) '*El espíritu de la colmena*: The Monster, the Place of the Father, and Growing up in the Dictatorship', *Vida Hispánica* 31:3, 13–17.
Genette, Gérard (1982) *Palimpsestes*, Paris: Editions du Seuil.
Johnson, Claudia Durst (1994) *To Kill a Mockingbird: Threatening Boundaries*, New York: Twayne.
Jones, Carolyn M. (2002) 'Harper Lee', in Carolyn Perry and Mary Louise Weaks (eds), *The History of Southern Women's Literature*, Baton Rouge: Louisiana State University Press, 413–18.
Kinder, Marsha (1993) *Blood Cinema: The Reconstruction of National Identity in Spain*, Berkeley and Los Angeles: University of California Press.
Lee, Harper (2002) *To Kill a Mockingbird*, New York: HarperCollins, Perennial Classics.
Savater, Fernando (1976) 'Riesgos de la iniciación al espíritu', in Erice and Fernández Santos, 9–26.

Smith, Paul Julian (1999) 'Between Metaphysics and Scientism: Rehistoricizing Víctor Erice's *El espíritu de la colmena*', in Peter William Evans (ed.) *Spanish Cinema: The Auteurist Tradition*, Oxford: Oxford University Press, 93–114.
Stone, Rob (2002) *Spanish Cinema*, Harlow: Pearson Education.
Willem, Linda M. (1998) 'Text and Intertext: James Whale's *Frankenstein* in Víctor Erice's *El espíritu de la colmena*', *Romance Languages Annual*, 9, 722–25. Willem's article is originally dated 1997 and can be found at http://tell.fll.purdue.edu/RLA-Archive/1997/Spanish-html/Willem,LindaM.htm [accessed 4 October 2010].

2

Cet obscur objet du désir/ That Obscure Object of Desire (Luis Buñuel, 1977): Buñuel's technique

Mark Millington

[a] duality governs his entire work. On the one hand, ferocity and lyricism, a world of dreams and blood ... On the other, a bare, spare style that is not at all Baroque and produces a sort of exaggerated sobriety. The straight line, not the Surrealist arabesque. (Octavio Paz, 2000: 38–9)

> On a train journey from Seville to Madrid, a middle-aged man, Mathieu (played by Fernando Rey), recounts the story of his relationship with a young woman, Concha (played by Carole Bouquet and Ángela Molina). He tells of his obsessive attempts to consummate his desire for her and of her alternation between responsiveness and rejection. Through numerous episodes, Mathieu seems to get close to his goal, only for disappointment repeatedly to crown his efforts. He thinks that the train is carrying him away from her and that he has put his desire behind him, but Concha is, in fact, on the train, and the end of the journey sees their fraught relationship renew itself.

Luis Buñuel is one of the major *auteurs* of cinema. Film theatres and television channels around the world devote seasons to his films, the presses roll with analyses of his work and references to his 'mastery' are routine. And yet, discussion of that mastery has focused almost exclusively on his ambivalent view of the human condition and the playfulness of his surrealist disruption of conventions and expectations. In short, spectators' and critics' attention has been captured, even dazzled, by the idiosyncrasy of his ideas and vision, while his cinematographic language has tended to pass almost unnoticed, except in passing references to its simplicity. And yet it seems obvious that his technical achievement is the bedrock on which his ideas and vision depend for their impact. And it is on a technical analysis of his last film that I wish now to concentrate in order to prove that point.

Buñuel's technique in *Cet obscur objet du désir/ That Obscure Object of Desire* (1977) is functional and systematic, serving the purpose of presenting action and speech in an unfussy and transparent way, though the meaning of action and speech may be elusive. He uses a variety of techniques in his filming but avoids the extreme ends of cinema's technical resources either in lighting, camera angles and camera mobility or in the duration of shots and editing. He is sparing in his efforts to evoke atmosphere or create mood, and little attempt is made to connect us with characters on an emotional level. His aim is to establish a clear pattern of communication with the spectator, and therefore, at a certain level of spectatorship, to provide security. The transparency of his filming style is crucial in creating an effect of realism to anchor the subversive quality of his idiosyncratic narrative.

Shooting and point of view

Buñuel's standard way with establishing shots precisely demonstrates these points. Each scene or sequence is set up clearly and concisely so that the spectator can quickly locate the action in a recognisable reality. His preference is to start a scene with a long shot using a pan or tracking focused on the movement of a character or vehicle. The camera movement creates a basic dynamism and this, combined with the broad perspective of the long shot, gives an impression of life beyond the frame. A clear example can be seen in the shot on the hotel terrace in Switzerland, which introduces the spectator to a new location (shot 53). A long shot, gradually shortening into medium shot, follows a hotel page who brings newspapers across the terrace to the table of Mathieu, the film's protagonist. In passing, the shot reveals an attractive environment and the tables of others having breakfast. The camera lingers briefly on a medium shot of Mathieu reading the newspapers in order to stabilise our perspective before the subsequent encounter with Concha. A similarly careful establishing shot introduces us to a Parisian bar for the first time (shot 87). This medium shot focuses on a waiter whose movement from the bar around the tables delineates the location. His movement (taking in a table with a quarrelling couple – an echo of Mathieu's stormy relationship with Concha) ends at the table of Mathieu and his cousin, Edouard Foucade. The shot settles on the two men, but with a deep background view, confirming the nature of the location and including a first sighting of the bar manager.

Buñuel's other, though less frequent, establishing technique is to cut to a close-up followed by a pan or track backwards in order to show broader context. This technique is often determined by what happens at the end of the preceding shot. So when Mathieu signals that he will start to tell his story on the train (shot

3. Establishing Mathieu's breakfast location in *That Obscure Object of Desire*.

39), the camera zooms in to a close-up as a sign of intensifying concentration on him. Shot 40 cuts to the meeting with Edouard that Mathieu mentioned in shot 39, and underlines continuity by beginning with a close-up of Mathieu before pulling back and panning left to reveal the whole of Edouard's office. Similarly, after Mathieu's servant, Martin, invites Concha's mother to his master's house, the next shot (shot 77) cuts to a close-up of Mathieu's hand opening a drawer in his study and removing a large sum of money in notes. The camera moves back and pans left to reveal the whole room and establish the space for the entry of Concha's mother. The cut from invitation to close-up on the money neatly suggests the reason for the invitation, so that Mathieu's subsequent behaviour can be viewed sceptically. In other words, the real motive beneath the bourgeois façade of polished manners is laid bare and any inclination to identify with the character is disrupted.

The shared feature of these two kinds of establishing shots is concision. But on a few occasions Buñuel provides more extended establishing sequences, since the scenes which follow contain significant narrative developments. A good example occupies shots 56 to 59. Here we shift from the scene on the hotel terrace in Switzerland to Concha's apartment in Courbevoie. In shot 55 Concha gave her address, and the following four shots lasting one minute twenty-one seconds cut to Mathieu's search for it, a search indicating that he does not know this poor area of Paris. Shot 56 starts with a distant view of tall buildings and pans down and right to follow the movement of the car from which Mathieu emerges. That familiar combination of long shot and pan on movement is followed in shot 57 by a pan on Mathieu in long shot as he walks down a street looking at house numbers. An abrupt cut to Mathieu in medium close-up (as at the start of shots 40 and 77 above) leads to a pan left and a widening view as Mathieu approaches a poorly maintained house. Finally, in shot 59 Mathieu climbs the stairs inside the house in medium shot, rings a doorbell and greets Concha and her mother. This careful establishing sequence takes us from the general to the particular in a characteristically mobile and informative way, and ends when the engagement between characters recommences. The care taken here is significant, as the scene in the apartment which follows is reasonably extended by Buñuel's standards, lasting three minutes and twenty-three seconds, and focuses on the development of a new level of intimacy between Mathieu and Concha. Comparable care (nine shots) is taken with the establishment of Seville as the film's new location from shot 139, taking in the cathedral, street scenes, gypsies, a religious procession and local architecture.

Buñuel's precise way with establishing shots shows that he wants the spectator to have the clarity and security needed to focus on characters and their actions. The environments chosen are familiar and even banally realistic because they are of only incidental interest. An important question in analysing *That Obscure Object* is, therefore, what techniques Buñuel uses to show us his characters. The bulk of the film is structured around Mathieu's narration of his story to a group of strangers who share a compartment on a train travelling between Seville and Madrid. Like Josef von Sternberg (*Shanghai Express* [1932]), Alfred Hitchcock (*The Lady Vanishes* [1938], *Strangers on a Train* [1951], *North by Northwest* [1959]) and numerous other directors, Buñuel uses the reliable narrative device of thrusting together strangers in the confines of a train compartment and observing the reactions and revealing stories which consequentially flow. In this case it seems safe to assume that Mathieu determines the nature of the story and its emphases, and so both the viewer and his listeners on screen are guided by his perspective. But the method of narration does not mean that we wholly share his point of view. It is evident that what we as spectators see is not particularly personalised, and that we are not encouraged to identify or empathise with Mathieu's emotions. For much of the time, even when he is supposedly narrating, we are encouraged to watch him rather than to see with him. On a technical level that effect is fostered by the avoidance of eye-line matches, so that we rarely see things precisely from his perspective. But our impersonal perspective is also encouraged by the obsessive nature of his desire for Concha, which tends to distance us from him. Furthermore, one of the fundamental points of the film is that the bourgeoisie is not as much in control as it believes, so we see that, despite Mathieu's financial advantages and illusions about what money can buy, he is guaranteed nothing as far as desire is concerned.

There are several moments when Mathieu is either not present or not aware of something which spectators can see, and these are signs of how Buñuel encourages us to see beyond him.[1] At the very start of the film when he and Martin first enter the villa in Seville, the camera does not follow them but a man crossing the garden with a sack over his shoulder. Exactly the same thing happens within Mathieu's narration when he and Concha leave the bar in Paris and the camera follows another man carrying a sack. On neither occasion does Mathieu see what we see. Occasionally we are aware of a development before Mathieu, even when he is apparently narrating a scene, with the result that we are able to watch his reaction rather than seeing with him. So we are shown Concha dancing naked for the tourists in Seville before Mathieu reaches the room and are therefore positioned as observers of his behaviour. We are also witness to the scene of the police's deportation of Concha and her mother, an event of which Mathieu is ignorant even though it is apparently part of his narration. Perhaps above all, we know from the start of the journey to Madrid (as he and his listeners on screen do not) that, as he narrates his story, Concha is on the train. The point of his narration is to explain why he threw water over Concha, which he sees as part of finally ridding himself of her, but the fact that she is on the train demonstrates that he has not been able to put her behind him and that his narration is self-deluding.

The spectator's broad perspective also limits the degree of sympathy with Mathieu's emotions in response to Concha's behaviour. In the scene in his country house when he discovers that Concha is wearing a chastity belt, he finally breaks down. And yet the combination of the grotesque nature of the chastity belt, a disruptive cut back to the train compartment and Concha's explanation that what he really wants is that she refuse his advances (as if his weeping were not truthful to his desire) makes a mockery of him and so curtails our sympathy. Similarly, the sequence in Seville when Mathieu is locked out of Concha's house and forced to watch her make love with El Morenito is followed immediately by the almost wordless scene of the hold-up of his taxi. The hold-up punctures any feeling that we might have had for the hurt inflicted by Concha, redirecting our attention away from his emotions.

Montage

Buñuel's approach to montage is as unfussy as his setting-up of individual shots. In general he avoids cuts, so that many scenes consist of just one shot and longer scenes may have no more than three or four. When he employs more editing he seeks to heighten tension. So at the station in Seville, he cuts back and forth between Mathieu looking through the train window and Concha advancing along the platform, six shots lasting 55 seconds which convey Mathieu's increasing anxiety about re-encountering her. And in the sequence leading up to the explosion of the car in Seville, Buñuel puts together five shots lasting just 40 seconds whose rapidity builds to the dramatic effect of the explosion. By contrast, Buñuel largely avoids the cutting involved in the standard shot/reverse-shot technique to articulate dialogue and highlight individual speech and reactions. He does employ this technique once or twice but his standard preference is for two- and three-shots, and occasionally tightly controlled shots containing up to six or seven characters. Two-shots allow him to minimise editing, with the result that he has to concentrate on arranging characters, action and objects within the frame. In minimising editing, the frame becomes a little like a proscenium arch within which he choreographs characters' movements, blocks their positions and has them enter and exit the frame as in the theatre. In shot 90 (located by the cloakroom of the Parisian bar) the restrained use of panning and zooming and the precise movement of six characters both within and in and out of frame is a fine example of the result of downplaying editing. Buñuel avoids any potential awkwardness in this technique by being quite flexible with camera movement so as to create fluidity within shots. His handling of the scenes in the train compartment is particularly skilful in this respect because of the very confined space and the presence of five characters. In this space very little movement is possible, but Buñuel compensates not through the use of multiple cuts and close-ups, but by constantly grouping and regrouping the characters in every combination from two- to five-shots and by moving them back and forward in their seats.

Where Buñuel does employ a cut within a scene it is usually to lay particular emphasis on a point, as when on the terrace of the Swiss hotel he cuts from a two-shot of Mathieu and Concha to a close-up of the latter over Mathieu's shoulder as she answers the vital question about why she disappeared from his house in Paris. Similarly, during Mathieu's first visit to Concha's apartment, Buñuel employs a short sequence of four cuts when they and Concha's mother are seated around the table. The cuts highlight their reactions both to her mother's ingenuous words and to the increasing sexual charge of each other's looks. They also highlight her mother's irrelevance, concentrate attention on their knowing reactions to each other and indicate their understanding of the real purpose of his visit.

The final important aspect of montage in *That Obscure Object* is how Buñuel employs cuts to create efficient narrative momentum. He frequently uses the technique of moving straight from the initial mention of an idea to its enactment. So, Concha mentions that she dances in a club and Buñuel cuts to a scene in which Mathieu sees her dancing. When Mathieu gives Concha the keys for her house she tells him that she will see him the following night and a cut immediately presents him walking towards her house at night. When Edouard says that he will look after getting rid of Concha we cut to the arrival of the police to expel her from France. This narrative efficiency is also apparent in Buñuel's handling of Concha's absences. She disappears from Mathieu's life on several occasions but each absence is brief in screen time (some three to four minutes only). Her rapid reappearances indicate a tight control of narrative essentials on Buñuel's part: what he is interested in is not Mathieu's emotions without Concha but his difficulties in being with her.

Narrative and the realist contract

The organising principle of narrative in the film (as so often in Buñuel) is theme and variations. Narrative structure is built on repetition through a series of episodes, each beginning with an encounter between Mathieu and Concha and ending with a rebuff or separation. Overall there is some gain in intensity and intimacy in the relationship, but there is no overarching causal progression. The story is not built on a series of events developing to a climax but on the relentless, repeating mechanism that is desire. Mathieu is a modern-day Sisyphus, endlessly repeating the same task, and, as Linda Williams points out, he ends up precisely where he started (1981: 190). An example of this theme-and-variation technique are the two scenes in the Parisian bar. In the first, Mathieu re-encounters Concha working in the cloakroom and, when she is admonished by the manager for not paying attention to her work, she resigns. She then suggests that they have a drink in the bar but the manager refuses to serve her. In the second scene, she has a rendezvous with Mathieu in the bar and we anticipate that the manager will again treat her frostily, but instead he offers her champagne. This time it is Concha who reacts coldly by refusing it. This is a characteristically witty reversal, highlighting the inexplicability of human motivation (after all, the key point about Mathieu's behaviour), and that idea is conveyed purely through the technique of repetition with variation. Another scene encapsulates the film's underlying rhythm of endlessly repeated encounter, proximity, rupture, separation and re-encounter. In the scene following Mathieu's discovery of Concha dancing naked in Seville, they move seamlessly in three minutes twenty seconds through encounter, fury, mutual recriminations and desperate ultimatum to his offering to buy her a house. This turnabout is remarkably rapid but is handled effortlessly. Such oscillations are played out at every stage of the film, with a tendency for the extremes to become more pronounced and ultimately violent.

Significant cohesion derives from the theme-and-variations format, but there are other conventional narrative techniques employed to underpin it. A strong narrative lure is created at the outset by Mathieu's throwing water over Concha and his claim to the other passengers that she is the worst of women. That lure is quickly complemented by another which generates spectator interest, namely whether he will ever consummate his desire. It is characteristic of Buñuel that he sets up such well-defined enigmas for the narrative to work with, even if, equally characteristically, they are never resolved (Sandro 1987: 151–2). He also creates cohesion via the intermittent cuts back to the scene in the train compartment. That single scene fragmented across almost the whole film provides a point of focus through the multiple locations and events of Mathieu's story. The returns to the train are carefully managed, with a gradual lengthening of the time between them until the definitive return at the end of Mathieu's narration. Discounting one or two brief exterior views of the train which do no more than punctuate Mathieu's story and re-emphasise the sense of the headlong rush of desire (of which the train is the constant metaphor), the returns become less necessary because the structural reality that it is Mathieu's account of events is well established.

So tight is Buñuel's control of narrative and so focused the commitment to move the narrative forward that coincidences and lacunae in the narrative are unimportant. There are three coincidental meetings between Mathieu and Concha (Switzerland, Parisian bar, Seville) which are vital to enable new episodes in their relationship but which Buñuel does not bother to disguise. There are also certain narrative details which are not adequately explained. When Concha refuses to move into Mathieu's house, accusing him of trying to buy her, he goes to her apartment only to discover that she and her mother have moved out without leaving a forwarding address. And yet later, when Edouard arranges for their deportation, the police go to the same apartment and find them there. At the station in Seville, Concha searches for Mathieu but it is not explained how she knows that he is catching precisely that train to Madrid. Mathieu and Concha return to Paris after meeting on the train, and yet it seems highly unlikely that she could enter France again, having previously been deported. Buñuel does not bother to fill these gaps because explanations would slow narrative progression and distract from the leanness of his story-telling. In that sense, his narrative technique is all about pace and focus on essentials. His visual language and narrative structures are unobtrusive and carefully controlled in order to maximise attention to actions and events. His technique is centred on a commitment to creating a sense of the real, though that sense is complemented by metaphorical elements of communication, as we shall see.

The sense of the real is reliant on a *mise en scène* involving objects and settings of an unremarkable banality. The use of real locations – Paris, Seville, Lausanne – matches on a superficial level the verisimilitude of the story of a middle-aged man who hopelessly desires but is unable to attract a young woman of 18. While it does seem somewhat unlikely that a man of Mathieu's social class would embark on a candid account of his sexual humiliation for a group of strangers, there is a certain realism in his anger and frustration with Concha, even if his reactions are not explored. There is no emotional complexity in Mathieu and no psychology to give depth to his responses: his current desire is not 'placed' in relation to his dead wife or his life history. His is a story of desire, pursuit and frustration without personal inflection. And this is because in *That Obscure Object*, as in many of his films, Buñuel is not interested in exploring characters, bourgeois or otherwise. The idea that there might be a psychological explanation for Concha's or Mathieu's behaviour is wide of the mark, since what is at issue is desire as a force which goes beyond the individual. As a result there is an artificiality about what the characters do and how they respond: the improbability of Mathieu's persistence and the inconsistencies and elusiveness of Concha say nothing about them as individuals. It is no accident that the film's title is impersonal, since this is a story of desire and its object, not about an individual called Mathieu and his obsession with a particular woman.[2]

However, for the primordial truth of desire to be represented Buñuel needs a stable realistic context in which to anchor it, otherwise it could not be grasped. That is why Martin is an important character because he is a source of disruption with his refusal to indulge his master's illusions. In his brutal realism, he is indifferent to Concha and expresses misogynist views of women, and that makes him a key element in the careful interplay of perspectives in the film and in the critical orientation of the spectator. In that respect, a significant part of Buñuel's technique is his deployment of the visual resources of cinema to enable a critical perspective outside diegetic action. He quite often uses visual means to signal a complexity or to convey a truth in counterpoint with what is apparently happening within diegetic reality. Here we see the importance of his creation of a foundational reality against which he can project disruptive elements. This area of technique is concerned with implicit communication with the spectator on a level beyond the reality of his characters.

Metaphor

A prime example of such communication and of the interplay of the real and the metaphorical is the use of two actors in the role of Concha. That there are two actors playing one role is true in terms of visual reality, but that duality does not operate at the level of diegesis. That it is Mathieu who tells the story might seem to account for the fact that nobody acknowledges or even appears to realise that there are two women who constitute Concha: the duality seems explicable as a symptom of his blindness to the truth of who Concha is. But, significantly, the two actors are also both seen outside his narration, at the villa in Seville near the start, on the train at the beginning and end (where both actors are seen by the other passengers) and in the closing arcade scene. The point is that nobody in the film can be allowed to see that there are two Conchas. It is the spectator alone who realises, and that is because the use of two actors is a metadiegetic device by which the director communicates with the audience. The presence of two actors is a metaphor of Mathieu's indifference to all but the object of his desire (which is not Concha as we shall see), and for it to remain a metaphor the physical duality cannot be acknowledged within the diegesis. To do so would expose the device and compromise the realist foundations of the film.

The device of the two actors in one role is a measure of the inventive capacity of Buñuel's visual language and the layering of his thinking. And as so often, that language shows itself to be profoundly witty. His cinema is full of devices which tease and arrest the spectator, and of tongue-in-cheek incongruities and enigmas, which give it its richness. There are numerous examples in *That Obscure*

4. El Morenito's unwieldy instrument in *That Obscure Object of Desire.*

Object. With the arrival in the compartment of the dwarf, Buñuel exploits the incongruity of his size and the discomfort felt by the other adults even though he fits in perfectly in every other respect with the bourgeois values in the compartment. Indeed, the dwarf's profession of psychologist would seem to make him a privileged listener to Mathieu's story.[3] On Concha's first evening as a servant in Mathieu's house he has her bring him a bottle of green Chartreuse, which Martin tells him is mildly aphrodisiac. What Mathieu has in mind is to seduce her, and so it comes as an amusing foretaste of her teasing elusiveness that we see her prepare the bed even though she does not respond to his advances. When Mathieu walks towards Concha's new house in Seville, Buñuel has him pass in front of a café called 'Las cadenas' (the chains), which precisely encapsulates his condition in respect of Concha. These examples of visual wit are complemented by an aural one, when in the arcade the news bulletin on the tannoy is followed by a performance of the rapturous duet between Siegmund and Sieglinde from the end of Act I of Wagner's *Die Walküre*. In the opera the lovers, who have fallen for each other at first sight, are about to consummate their love. The ironic wit of the reference could not be clearer: in the romanticism of Wagner there is an almost instant sexual relationship; between Mathieu and Concha there is none.

Buñuel's technique of metadiegetic communication is also in evidence in his choice of metaphorical objects throughout the film. Not all these objects are obscure; indeed some are quite simple. The fly which drowns in Mathieu's drink and the mouse caught in a trap are both obvious symbols of characters who are ensnared. It is no accident that Concha's possible other lover, El Morenito, is a guitarist: his instrument is obviously phallic. So unwieldy is it when he brings it with him one night to sleep in Concha's room that it proves difficult to keep under control in the narrow corridor, with the result that it knocks over a vase, which has a gaping hole where the flowers should be. Underlining the

5. The blossoming of desire in *That Obscure Object of Desire.*

connection, the other end of the guitar is at the level of Concha's vagina. This symbolic combination is hardly subtle but stands as a sign of the young man's clumsy sexual potency and suggests that he is nearer to success with Concha than Mathieu. And there is another vase with similar metaphorical connotations associated with Concha. On her first entrance in the film, she carries a vase with an exuberant display of red roses. She holds the vase at the level of her vagina, seemingly offering herself as fertile object of passion, although the vase and roses with their prickles look like a barrier between them as much as an offering. Symbolically speaking, this is desire at first sight. And this particular sighting wittily plays off the master's clichéd fantasy of the saucy chambermaid in her neat uniform. Later, when she is expected to come to live with Mathieu, he places a vase of white roses on a chest of drawers in her room (next to a vase with a single red rose), heralding the arrival of the supposedly virginal Concha.[4] When there is a call at the door, Mathieu takes the single red rose and, carrying it proudly upright, goes to the door to present her with it. But when it is not Concha who has called but El Morenito with a note explaining that she is not coming, the rose droops towards the floor as a measure of Mathieu's disappointment. And the metaphorical play with flowers continues because Mathieu immediately goes to find Concha at her apartment but discovers her gone and finds only the elderly concierge. Nonetheless, the latter is carrying a colourful bunch of flowers in her arms, cruelly suggesting that she might be a better match for Mathieu than Concha. However, the flowers are not roses and are not held next to her vagina: desire is absent here. But later, red roses reappear in a vase in the background when Mathieu finds Concha working in the cloakroom of the Parisian bar, signalling to us the rekindling of his desire.

The sack is a further visual metaphor and appears at different moments to be a visualisation of the sack of excrement referred to by Martin when quoting

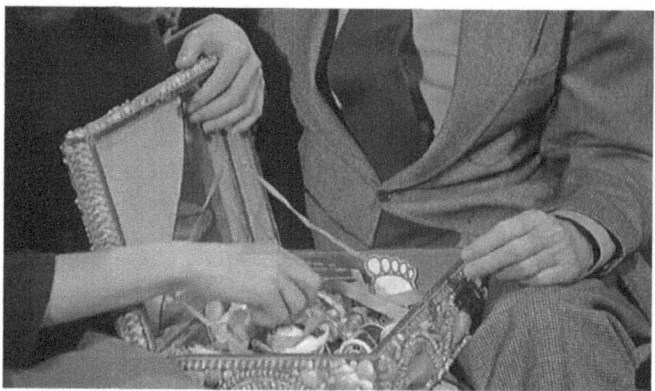

6. A box of oral delights in *That Obscure Object of Desire*.

a friend's view of women. At the end, the same or another sack is opened and a woman takes out a ripped, bloodstained garment and begins to sew it up, as if symbolically repairing the tear in a hymen (a tear which Mathieu has not in reality been able to create in the course of the story).[5] The lace is an object of fascination for Mathieu, just as the obscure object of the film's title has been throughout. But since the lace is associated with the hymen and the loss of virginity it is closely linked with the real object of his desire. That object is not Concha herself and is obscure both because it is mysterious and because it is visible only once in the whole film, when Concha dances naked for the tourists in Seville. The name Concha is a familiar form of the full name: María de la Concepción (appropriately, a reference to the virgin birth). The familiar form, 'Concha', means 'shell', but in slang is a euphemism for *coño* [cunt].[6] This verbal play pinpoints the logic of Mathieu's desire for Concha and the fact that its object is just one part of her body. We may only see that part of her anatomy once but there is also a symbolic displacement of it at one point. At the end of Mathieu's first visit to her apartment she asks him to fetch a box. It is covered in shells and she places it in her lap to leave no doubt of its association with her vagina. When opened, it turns out to contain items for sewing (the hymen has a repair kit ready to hand), a broken mirror (in which a reflection is not wholly what one expects to see), the shape of a foot (a recurrent fetishistic displacement in Buñuel) and some bonbons. Concha proceeds to place one of these bonbons sensually in Mathieu's mouth as Buñuel cuts back to the train, literally and metaphorically plunging into a tunnel. Unfortunately for Mathieu, this is the closest he comes to having sex with Concha. Given that oral sex is rarely alluded to in cinema, let alone represented, this is a daring though amusing piece of implicit communication by Buñuel with the spectator.[7] The object may be obscure, but Buñuel's linguistic and visual metaphors are not difficult to read and lay bare the primordial impulses driving his narrative.

Cinematic mastery

Buñuel's filmmaking has routinely been described as 'masterly' by critics, though few have analysed what is masterly about his technique. Attention has been over-whelmingly centred on what Buñuel is 'saying'. The purpose of this chapter has been to identify at least some of the technical resources that he deploys in *That Obscure Object*. The techniques used in it are all to be found in his films from the 1950s onwards when he established his cinematic language. He knew precisely what parts of the cinematic apparatus he needed to employ and how to make them work for his purposes. Not the least of the fascinating aspects of Buñuel's cinema is how he combines the stylistic sobriety and sparseness to which Octavio Paz alludes with the, at times, daring subversion and wit of his thinking about the contradictions and complexities of human beings.

Notes

1 Since these are instances of visual communication, Mathieu's listeners in the compartment cannot be aware of them either.
2 Williams correctly observes that this is not a realistic depiction of a man and woman in love (1981: 200). Going further and following Deleuze's suggestive analysis of Buñuel as naturalist, one might say that Mathieu allows one to witness the performance of a primary impulse (1992: 123–6).
3 Whether Buñuel intended the dwarf to be 'a visualized pun on shrink', as Marsha Kinder (1993: 336) claims, is debatable, though the pun does work beautifully in English.
4 She has told him that she is *mocita* (a virgin).
5 For a detailed discussion of the lace, see Williams (1981: 205–8). She does not mention that this sewing-up is a symbolic realisation of the act which the jealous Francisco in *Él* (1952) seems intent on performing on his wife. The original publicity poster for *That Obscure Object* picks up this reference with its image of stitches through lips.
6 For a discussion of the object and the name 'Concha', see Evans (1995: 128). It is characteristic of Buñuel's wicked sense of humour that, during one of Mathieu's visits to Concha, she sits on his lap and he runs his hand up her leg towards his ultimate goal as he murmurs its name in its familiar diminutive: 'Conchita, Conchita'.
7 There is another example in Buñuel of metaphorical oral sex in the scene in the garden in *L'Âge d'or* (1930) where Lya Lys sucks the toe of a statue as a substitute for her absent lover.

Bibliography

Deleuze, Gilles (1992 [1983]) *Cinema 1: The Movement-Image*, trans. Hugh Tomlinson and Barbara Habberjam, London: Athlone Press.
Evans, Peter William (1995) *The Films of Luis Buñuel: Subjectivity and Desire*, Oxford: Clarendon Press.

Kinder, Marsha (1993) *Blood Cinema: The Reconstruction of National Identity in Spain*, Berkeley, Los Angeles and London: University of California Press.

Paz, Octavio (2000 [1967]) 'El cine filosófico de Buñuel', in *Luis Buñuel: el doble arco de la belleza y de la rebeldía*, Barcelona: Galaxia Gutenberg and Círculo de Lectores, 36–41.

Sandro, Paul (1987) *Diversions of Pleasure: Luis Buñuel and the Crises of Desire*, Columbus: Ohio State University Press.

Williams, Linda (1981) *Figures of Desire: A Theory and Analysis of Surrealist Film*, Urbana, Chicago and London: University of Illinois Press.

3

Ocaña. Retrat intermitent/Ocaña. An Intermittent Portrait (Ventura Pons, 1977): the Mediterranean *movida* and the passing away of Francoist Barcelona

Alberto Mira

Ocaña is both a documentary and a cinematic essay on the artist José Ocaña, who became a well-known figure in bohemian circles in Barcelona in the 1970s. The backbone of the film is a long interview in which he gives both an account of his life and provides a fascinating discussion on identity and society. Ocaña talks mostly about himself and shows a strong awareness of how his image is an object of cultural consumption, which pre-dates Almodóvar's similar concern with self-presentation. This alternates with scenes which portray Ocaña both in his natural milieu of the Barcelona Ramblas and other more staged performance pieces which cover his theatrical and poetic repertoire.

Responses to the political changes taking place in Spain between the death of Francisco Franco in November 1975 and the electoral victory of the Socialist party in 1982 – with a key turning point being the approval of the 1978 Constitution – were extremely varied and seemed to signal a radical shift in Spanish society. This 'transitional' period produced a wave of self-expression and exploration of difference that is still remarkable; a number of images, narratives and discussions, repeated ad nauseam, fulfilled their function as catalyst even as they disappeared from view as the 1980s progressed and the shock of the new ceased to be marketable. Given their heterogeneity, mapping out cultural manifestations of the period remains a challenge, particularly in terms of sexual mythologies. Some of the texts produced at the time are difficult to make sense of outside the context that made them possible; others still preserve strong values and present us with perspectives which are far from obsolete. *Ocaña. Retrat Intermitent/Ocaña. An Intermittent Portrait*, directed by Catalan filmmaker Ventura Pons in 1977 – that is, at the height of the Barcelona *movida* sometimes referred to as the *llibertari* – is highly representative of the impulse for renewal in Transition cinema and the attempt to document the new social reality: a trend that could also include *El desencanto/ The Disenchantment* (Jaime Chávarri, 1976) and *Queridísimos verdugos/Dearest Executioners* (Basilio Martín Patino, 1977). In an attempt to provide a documentary 'portrait' of an individual who is presented as a symbol of a certain notion of Barcelona, *Ocaña* gestures towards the past to retrieve the kind of stories that had remained unspoken during the dictatorship, and accounts for the speed of change in Spanish society by showing that life thrived beyond the restrictive dictates of Francoism. Pons's film communicated the message that the Spanish transition could only be complete when those narratives became part of the new cultural landscape. Beyond the film's value as a literal representation of a time and place, it remains vitally relevant in presenting debates on identity and sexuality. That said, we must note the absence of epistemological frameworks on gender and sexuality, which made the film unreadable at the time, not least because the gay movement was thinking more or less exclusively in terms of legal change.

On its release, responses to the film focused on its 'Barcelonian-ness' (i.e. rather than 'Catalan-ness', a signifier which would take precedence after 1978) and political freedom, and certainly the film can be seen as the expression of a libertarian agenda. Terenci Moix's review (1978)[1] of the film was very specific in placing Ocaña in the Ramblas and suggesting that Pons's film could be experienced as a tribute to an era which was about to vanish. In the Spanish context, Barcelona was the symbol of an open European city in which different cultural influences could co-exist, whereas in realist fiction of the Franco period, Madrid had been represented as grey and provincial.[2] Another key feature of the film, according to critics, was precisely how vividly Pons represented a particular period in history. So, for José Luis Guarner, writing in *Fotogramas* in May 1978: '*Ocaña* es quizá la primera película parida en nuestro país, donde más claramente se respira un ambiente posfranquista' [*Ocaña* is perhaps the first film spawned in our country where one can breathe most tangibly a post-Francoist atmosphere]. Less precisely articulated at the time were the issues of sexual identity the film raises, and that can only be accounted for theoretically from the standpoint of queer theory. This chapter will provide contexts and frameworks for the understanding of the film both in historical terms and in the way it engages with issues later developed by gender studies.

The libertarian agenda in Catalonian film: cultural coordinates

After the death of Franco, a pressing agenda for change seemed to present itself to artists. Any cultural manifestation, whether journalism, literature or painting, had an implicit subtext: this was the 'new' art, this was the 'new' Spain. 'Change' was a magic word; in fact the Socialists won the general election with the slogan

'Por el cambio' [for change]. Along with other general qualities texts might be expected to possess (i.e. to describe reality, to make people laugh, to shock or thrill), the idea of a clean break with the past was always there, whether as a conscious or subconscious notion. In terms of film, producers felt the encouragement (particularly financial, but also ethical) to make up for decades of censorship: stories that had been repressed – whether they were about the losers of the Civil War, *maudit* artists like the Paneros, or lives that fell outside Francoist morality – could at last be told and there seemed to be a strong demand for them to find their way onto the screen. A number of soft-porn producers, such as José Frade, and some performers – Susana Estrada was typical among the *destape* stars – insisted their films were 'un canto a la libertad' [a song to liberty], a justification parodied in Dunia Ayaso and Félix Sabroso's feature *Los años desnudos/ Rated R* (2008), on the 'S cinema' industry.[3] Each film made in that period is very precisely 'of' the period to a greater extent than it would be at any time after the early 1980s. The membrane between text and history was very thin in the transitional years. In each text, there are elements, whether thematic or just visual motifs, which are pushing the agenda of transition forward. In the perception of Pons's film as expressed in contemporary reviews there is an element of relevance or urgency that would vanish in time.

Films of the early years of democracy have often been read as addressing specifically three areas that had been subjected to the censor's stern eye: first, a certain view of history, which in real terms meant a narrow focus on the Civil War and its consequences – a trend which only intensified after the Socialists came to power; second, a short-lived obsession with political change – visible in films like *Vota a Gundisalvo/ Vote for Gundisalvo* (Pedro Lazaga, 1977), *El día del presidente* [Day of the President] (Pedro Ruiz, 1979), *... Y al tercer año resucitó/ ... And the Third Year, He Resuscitated* (Rafael Gil, 1980) or *El diputado/ Confessions of a Congressman* (Eloy de la Iglesia, 1978); and thirdly, films dealing with morality and specifically sexual issues, as I delineate below. Box-office hits of the period always included some or all of these strands, to the detriment of qualities like challenging aesthetics or well-made plots. Although each of those areas would deserve focused attention, sexual issues were the most prominent obsession in terms of images and pervade all films, whatever else they are about: in those years, nudity was practically a must whether the film was a thriller, a political comedy or horror.

The film industry was also in a state of flux. Between the 1977 abolition of the existing censorship laws – perceived as a sign of government-controlled cinema – and the arrival of another kind of political interference as embodied by the 1983 Pilar Miró legislation which encouraged 'quality' film through government funding, there is a brief, audience-driven period in which filmmakers seemed obsessed with providing the kind of immediate pleasures in competition with the flood of foreign films invading cinemas. Sexual freedom constituted a strategic gateway for maverick filmmakers in need of funding. Vicente Aranda, who, after years in marginal circuits strengthened his career with *Cambio de sexo/Forbidden Love* (1977), is a case in point: some thematic strands in his earlier career – which included genre films like *La novia ensangrentada/The Blood-Spattered Bride* (1972) – remain prominent, but at the same time the film is a consequence of certain conditions of production unique to the immediate post-Franco period. Bigas Luna also used explicit sex to move from the marginality of the avant-garde towards more mainstream projects.

Many other titles of the late 1970s and early 1980s deal obsessively with sexual heterodoxy, as if insisting on making a point about sexual freedom: besides *Ocaña* and Pons's subsequent *El vicari d'Olot/The Vicary of Olot* (1981), Pedro Olea's *Un hombre llamado Flor de Otoño* [A Man Called Autumn Flower] (1978), Almodóvar's *Pepi, Luci, Bom y otras chicas del montón/Pepi, Luci, Bom* (1980), Bigas Luna's *Bilbao* (1978) and *Caniche* (1983), and many others, have sexuality as a central focus in terms of images and plots. It is interesting that, with the possible exception of Almodóvar's film (which actually required the support of Barcelona-based producer Pepón Corominas), all of the films in this list are Catalan productions or are set in Barcelona. If we extend the notion of Catalonia to the south – that is, to include the Valencian Community and the Balearic Islands, the whole of the area of influence of Catalan language known as *Països Catalans* – the films of Carles Mira (*Con el culo al aire/Caution to the Wind* [1980], *La portentosa vida del pare Vicent/The Prodigious Life of Father Vincent* [1978]) are also key contributions to the new view of sexuality in the early Transition years. At the time, certain nineteenth-century mythologies of the Mediterranean as the locus of sensuality were still very much in place and very prominent in Catalan cultures, and they are taken up by Pons and Mira in their filmic works. Such mythologies also, I would argue, made the Catalan perspective distinct from the Madrid-centred version of political change.

These films of the 1978–82 period seem to have taken a cue from Bakhtin's reading of Rabelais with an interpretation of carnival in terms of sexual libera-tion. They dramatise both repression and the upturning of categories in order to take sides at the point of closure and state that there is no turning back: both the endings of *Ocaña* and Pons's second film *The Vicary of Olot*, as well as the Bigas Luna or Carles Mira features mentioned above, signal metonymically the triumph of libertarian ideology. In other words, the films never return audiences to 'nor-mality' – the move towards conservatism which forecloses Bakhtinian carnival at the start of Lent – but propose, progressively, the fiction that the new state of affairs which accepts libidinal variety is desirable and will remain in place. In narrative terms, this results in films which celebrate a variety of sexual identities – and what had until recently been known as 'perversions' – which coexist promiscuously in the plot without ever becoming fixed or easily labelled. The best known examples of this kind of libertarian approach are Almodóvar's *Pepi, Luci,Bom* and *Laberinto de pasiones/Labyrinth of Passion* (1982), two narratives which present a group of urban characters entangled in a series of relationships which are as trivial as they are free and fluid, and which blur the imposed limits between desire, perversion, friendship or simple sex. Although Almodóvar was claiming at the time that the best slap in the face to Francoism was to pretend Franco never existed (Kinder 2004: 55), his films are highly dependent on the mood created by the dictator's death. But in this attitude, Almodóvar was not alone. A parallel Madrid-based exploration of sexual fluidity can be found in Iván Zulueta's *Arrebato/Rapture* (1979). Unlike Almodóvar, Pons or Mira, Zulueta had a career in non-narrative avant-garde film which made his films solipsistically personal.

The Mediterranean films of Pons and Mira constitute even more consistent approaches to this frame of mind before the consolidation of democracy brought with it a standardisation in terms of storytelling (narrative orthodoxy as both an effect of the Ley Miró, which rewarded traditional stories, and a sign of increasing political security where some compromises had been reached and meaning had become more stabilised). Whereas the Madrid *movida* of the early 1980s tended to be linked to New York modernity and the films are evidence of a drug-fuelled lifestyle, Mira used sexuality and anti-clerical feelings as the substance of a Bakhtinian view of carnival, presenting the past as an orgy in *The Prodigious Life of Father Vincent* and *Caution to the Wind*. Ventura Pons sought inspiration in real life with his documentary on *Ocaña*. In later years, he would come to prefer literary frameworks: the premise of his 1981 feature *The Vicary of Olot* is close to the theatrical *sainete* – a short comic farce with popular, stock characters – and a similar perspective would be presented in two network comedies: *Aquesta nit o mai/Tonight or Never* (1991) and *Que t'hi jugues Mari Pili?/What's Your Bet, Mari Pili?* (1991).

A specific aspect the carnivalesque films of the period have in common is a queer approach to sexuality: in *Pepi* the straight/lesbian distinction seems to be dissolved or altogether overcome, whereas in *The Vicary of Olot, Ocaña* and Mira's films sexuality is also presented in manifestations that do not fit easily into traditional classifications. This attitude also affects narrative style: characters proliferate, clash, fight, meet, disappear and/or change, and plot strands are sometimes unfinished and/or open-ended. To some extent, the industrial conditions in which the films were made and their function as a 'quick fix' help to convey this idea of roughness, as if questioning the neatness of classical narrative structures. In thematic terms, police authority and religious bigotry are rendered unthreatening or ridiculed and their power effectively limited; sexuality is praised and identities anything but stable: this was the age in which transvestites and transsexuals seemed to reign in the media, their fascination linked to ambivalence or fluidity, although José Ocaña himself, Pons's protagonist, was wary of such dominance, which he regarded as unauthentic. Indeed, many representations of sexual ambiguity seem to try to have it both ways: homophobically mocking their subjects while at the same time suggesting a certain fascination with the possibilities of sexual ambiguity.

The ending in some of these films is metonymic of new social mythologies: in *Ocaña* through the image of taking one's clothes off and in *The Vicary of Olot*, for instance, this is done with a commitment to change within the Catholic Church. Although markedly different in approach and style, the idea of a new period in history in which old repressions (both political and sexual) are overcome and a new freedom is available that will allow individuals to be 'what they really are' is consistent in both films at the start of Pons's career, and in this they are representative of the explicit message in Transition film. Together, they reflect the cultural moment in Catalonia, if not in terms of reality – always more complex than films could aim to tell – definitely in terms of cultural aspirations.

Socially, the new spirit of the Transition was felt in Barcelona earlier than in Madrid. What has been known as the 'Barcelona *movida*' or *llibertari* movement is clearly a pre-Constitutional phenomenon – it was already fading by the end of 1978 when the Constitution gave credibility to the nationalist project. After Catalan nationalism began to dominate politics, some of the aspects of the iconoclasm discussed here become less momentous and the construction of a new project based on stability, common sense and orthodoxy takes precedence, whereas sex or cultural hybridisation seem less relevant to the new period – Catalan nationalist culture seemed more interested in history, landscape or arts and crafts than in issues of sex or ambivalence. *Ocaña*, on the other hand, was promoted as the 'primer filme catalán hablado en andaluz' [first Catalan film spoken in Andalusian] (Moix 1978), a provocative statement that nevertheless ran against the spirit of the times as the Catalan language acquired primary importance in the nationalist agenda: this slogan would be almost unthinkable in the twenty-first century, when the Catalan language is the central signifier of Catalan cinema. Actually, if libertarianism was articulated in the Catalan capital before Madrid, this was due in part to geographical location – power was felt to emanate from the centre less strongly – but also to a particular symbolic tension between Barcelona and Madrid in which Mediterranean Barcelona was presented as an oasis for artists and intellectuals in search of freedom. By the end of the 1970s the contrast between the specifically Catalan mythologies and this notion of the 'open city' becomes a difficult balancing act, as conservative nationalism is made precariously compatible with cosmopolitanism and progress. Nevertheless, in 1977 this tension was still fruitful, and while care has to be taken to keep nationalism and the Barcelona intelligentsia apart, intellectuals and nationalists had forged strong anti-Franco alliances, and there is a sense that the former fuelled progress and innovation as a way of distinguishing Catalan achievements from those in Madrid in late Francoism. These alliances are the key to the feeling of freedom in films like *Ocaña* and their weakening effectively accounts for the end of the Barcelona *movida*.

The Barcelona depicted in *Ocaña* is therefore the rich pre-constitutional city, a fascinating mix of high and low. Barcelona was always very aware of a Janus-like identity – as described, for instance, in the novels of Juan Marsé such as *Últimas tardes con Teresa* [Last Afternoons with Teresa] (1966) – rooted in historical and geographical reasons: already in late nineteenth-century fiction, extreme conservatism in the *ciudad alta* ('upper' city) seemed to coexist with the world of the port, the prostitutes in the 'lower' city around the port (particularly the *Barrio Chino*), and the dynamics between high and low are entangled historically in ways that follow the Bakhtinian model of interdependence. It was the bourgeois patriarchs (as well as the visiting sailors and sea merchants in the city's teeming port) who made possible the thriving business of prostitution. Already in the early twentieth century, the rougher aspects of the port area were eliciting some concern and fascination from intellectuals, explicit in chronicles of journalists like Ángel Zúñiga, whose 1948 collection of sketches *Barcelona y la noche* [Barcelona and the night] became something of an underground classic during the Transition. At one point in the late 1960s the underworld seems to have taken on a life of its own: suddenly it was not just something that lived in the bourgeois imagination but a subculture starting to 'talk back'. The new protagonists of the 'lower' city cultures were immigrants, working class, often marginal in all senses and, crucially, Castilian-speaking – a substantial section of the bourgeoisie held on to Catalan, even through the Francoist period, and language was a defining sign of social distinction. This permeability is very much the kind of background that makes *Ocaña* and the works of the Barcelona *llibertaris* possible. Lluís Fernández emphasises this in a brief piece, adding that it was Catalan nationalism that reinvented Barcelona culture and forced underground artists to move to Madrid in the late 1970s, giving rise to the Madrid *movida* (Nazario 2004: 186). Whereas for bourgeois intellectuals, nationalist demands were prominent in the early 1970s, I would argue that a nationalist agenda seems to have been absent in the artistic underground. The transition is the brief period where both sides to Barcelona were intensely visible and competing for predominance in representing the city's identity. Some references in responses to Pons's *Ocaña* also seem to show an awareness of the fact that political pressure from the nationalists ended the 'mirage' of what Nazario (2004) refers to as the Barcelona *movida*. Terenci Moix in particular seems to refer to this fact when, in his review of the film, he talks about Barcelona as a city close to Alexandria in its integration of many cultures.

The best account of the Barcelona *llibertari* movement in all of its shocking variety is a book entitled *La Barcelona de los años 70 vista por Nazario y sus amigos* [Barcelona of the 1970s as seen by Nazario and his friends] (2002), a project curated by the artist Nazario. Through a collage of comics, books, record covers, flyers and leaflets, contextualised through brief texts by key participants in the underground culture of the period, the volume shows a fragmented, inconsistent, fascinating view of a period in which underground fantasies emerged slowly into the mainstream. These are complemented with references to sex bars, clubs, prostitution and political demonstrations, throwing into question the vision of Barcelona as bourgeois and 'European'. Writers such as Gil de Biedma, Juan Goytisolo, Terenci Moix, Juan Marsé and Manuel Vázquez Montalbán, among many others, have written extensively about Barcelona's sexual underworld and have built narratives around the links between the upper and lower city. The images in the volume featuring Nazario, Jaume Sisa, Javier Mariscal, Ocaña and the occasional snapshot of Pedro Almodóvar remind us that this had a creative counterpart. Their work of the period remains relatively unexplored by scholars, whereas their later assimilation (in the case of Mariscal, for example) has become canonically representative of Catalan art. Rather than novels or poems, these artists expressed themselves in genres which were themselves marginal – comics, avant-garde performances, sex shows, graffiti, pop music – and are clearer expressions of camp performativity than anything undertaken in Madrid at the end of the decade. A comparison of covers of the Barcelona-edited *Star* or *El Víbora* with the Madrid *La Luna* (a later publication) shows how radical in terms of representation the Barcelona *movida* was. By the time the *movida* wave reached Madrid, the Barcelonian underground was becoming widely known and undergoing gentrification. *Ocaña* is a film poised exactly at this particular moment, immediately before its distinctive character was assimilated into the mainstream. Even today, the extreme, explicit fantasies depicted in Nazario's comics can overwhelm readers with their mix of camp, hard porn and tongue-in-cheek hyperrealism. His targets are those of Ocaña, Pons or Mira: bigots, figures of authority, the Church, the Police; his method usually involves sex. In the figure of Ocaña, Pons chose to gesture towards this underground world as a very specific image of what Barcelona was about.

Portrait of two artists in transition: *Ocaña*

Ventura Pons's extensive body of work is among the most consistent in post-Franco Spanish cinema. He insists on variety and generic diversity, but his films all feature a strong presence of Barcelona, which, as in *Barcelona (un mapa)/ Barcelona (A Map)* (2007) or *Caricies/ Caresses* (1998), becomes a protagonist of sorts. He has often returned to the network narrative in order to provide group portraits: most of his films belong to this category, from *The Vicary of Olot* to *Mil cretins/ A Thousand Fools* (2010). And although he keeps on shifting between original materials and adaptations, his work tends to have a strong theatrical element, in terms of both performers and *mise en scène*: in three decades, his filmmaking has become more stately and more deliberate, and his locations more closed, giving a stronger impression of stage stories. Often shooting in Catalan and close to Catalan literary and cultural traditions and authors, he is also among the most international Spanish filmmakers. In all of these aspects, Pons's films link traditions and locations, and are excellent examples of transcultural film.

Although cinema had always been his vocation, Pons started his professional career as a theatre director. Having spent time in London thanks to a grant from the Anglo-Catalan Society to study the work of Free Cinema documentalists, such as Lindsay Anderson and Karel Reisz, he fell under the spell of 1960s British theatre. At a time when the Catalan intelligentsia was looking towards Paris, Pons chose to focus on Britain – and, later, the USA – for inspiration. He started working professionally at the tail end of the Escuela de Barcelona years. His career in the Catalan independent theatre shows Pons building bridges between Royal Court and West End materials and the Barcelona theatre scene, including productions of Ann Jellicoe's *The Knack* (1969) – Rosa María Sardá's first starring role on stage – Christopher Hampton's *When Did You Last See My Mother?* (1974) and *The Rocky Horror Show* (1975). This is one important sense in which Pons connects the Anglo-American traditions with Barcelona culture. His bold representation of sexual difference is, arguably, further influenced by the radical atmosphere of late 1960s London.

He moved into film in 1977, and although conversant with many intellectuals of the period – he was a personal friend of Terenci Moix and Maria Aurèlia Capmany – he had few contacts among the Barcelona film coteries. He had also no particular interest in the avant-garde (represented, among others, by the cinema of Pere Portabella) or in the experiments of the Escuela de Barcelona that had dominated the late 1960s. In this preference for storytelling, he was not unlike Almodóvar, who was regarded as marginal within the underground for his insistence on making narrative cinema. A documentary turned out to be the ideal choice for Pons: not only had he studied the genre in his British years and was aware of its possibilities, but at a transitional time, it seemed important to chronicle reality as it shifted towards a new era.

Nevertheless, the subject of his first film came to him almost by chance. Ventura Pons was at a dinner to support one of the earliest gay groups in Spain (the FAGC, Front d'Alliberament Gai de Catalunya) [gay liberation front of Catalonia] taking place at a progressive religious school in Barcelona (the Sarrià 'Caputxins', which had a reputation for liberal attitudes not common elsewhere among Spanish clergy). At the dinner – bringing together, in habitual Transition fashion, priests and gay activists (paradoxically and inconsistently) with schoolboys – José Ocaña, a well-known denizen of the lower-city boulevard known as the Ramblas, made a surprise appearance at the end, dressed in full drag, claiming to be 'la Pasionaria de las mariquitas' (Pons 2011: 137). ('La Pasionaria' was the nickname of Dolores Ibárruri, a communist activist during the Civil War, and by invoking her name Ocaña is effectively positioned as 'the defender of the *mariquitas*' [queens].) Pons was immediately fascinated by Ocaña's personality and demeanour, and proposed to interview him on the following day. After this first interview, during which he took copious notes, he decided this would be the perfect subject for his documentary. In his press notes, Pons insisted on two particular aspects of the film: first, that it was very carefully scripted (therefore underlining his own point of view), and secondly that he tried to avoid adorning the character – in particular, he says he avoided turning Ocaña into a stereotype or figure of fun.

In this sense, the film can be seen as a collaboration between Pons, the artist and craftsman, and Ocaña, who provided the raw material. José Ocaña was born in Cantillana, a small Andalusian village near Seville, in 1951, and would die in 1984 as a consequence of an accident suffered when one of his works caught fire. His deep attachment to the place of his childhood is obvious in his recollections. Parallels with Almodóvar's trajectory deserve mention: rural life and characters would remain a source of inspiration, but he found it unbearable to live in the village and chose urban life, with all the possibilities for self-assertion it entailed. Although Almodóvar seems to have changed his view of the past, interviews of the early 1980s show similar conflicted feelings towards rural life. Ocaña in particular was fascinated by religious ritual and imagery, which would achieve centrality in his paintings. His description of life in Cantillana is orgiastic and sexually promiscuous, but at the same time, paradoxically, homophobia seemed to be extraordinarily intense and is mentioned as one of the main causes for his departure: the terms in which he describes his sexual adventures is not dissimilar to yet another instance of rural homosexual childhood, that of Reinaldo Arenas in 1940s Cuba. The first-person anecdotes amount to an acknowledgement of sex and desire as key aspects of the self-assertion narrative. Ocaña becomes 'who he is' by sticking to his desires and acting on them. Authenticity and performance seem to coexist, paradoxically, in his version of the self.

He moved to Madrid to pursue his artistic vocation, but regarded the city as too conservative and ended up settling down in Barcelona, aware of the city's reputation for being more welcoming of difference. It seems it was after a few years in Barcelona that the exhibitionist featured in the film was born. Indeed, the idea of Barcelona as a stage for self-expression is not just part of Ocaña´s story but becomes perfectly realised in Pons's film through a series of scenes in which Ocaña, in drag, parades along the Ramblas. After a series of setbacks he settled in a flat at the Plaza Real (Plaça Reial) and, as he felt the post-Franco winds of change, he embarked on a personal journey of experimentation which led him into building up a popular, instantly recognisable public image. He received a lot of attention from Transition journalists, although in the features written about him he was presented as a freak, something that would make him slightly suspicious of attention at the time of Pons's film. Visual artist Nazario (2004: 218) subsequently acknowledged Ocaña as an inspiration: it was the latter who taught him to push the limits of accepted behaviour. There is something in Ocaña's image which made him audience-friendly, but there is also an orgiastic element which is brought to the fore in Nazario's comics where the Ocaña character appears as mysterious but also promiscuous. The final images of the film, in which Ocaña comes back alone to his flat in the early dawn after a climactic and very public striptease, seem to play on this ambivalence.

Ocaña became part of the city's underground artistic circles which included the painters Javier Mariscal and Miquel Barceló and singer-composer Jaume Sisa. With the Transition and subsequent obsession for *morbo* (a popular word in the period denoting prurient curiosity for what was forbidden) in the press, he was widely interviewed and featured in newspapers and magazine articles. In Pons's film Ocaña shows a keen awareness of his public image, and seeks actively to correct misinterpretations, although he does not come across as an expert in handling his own profile: in his version of those years, attempts to use his notoriety to promote his work as a painter often got out of hand and led to frustration. Furthermore, casual opinions expressed to interviewers landed him in trouble with his family. The idea conveyed is of a struggle to avoid becoming imprisoned by the categories – he views *travesti*, for instance, as a problematic term – journalists want to place him in.

Structurally, Pons's film is divided into two parallel sections. The first is a series of interview sessions with Ocaña in which he speaks very openly and recalls events of his past life. Ocaña discusses political allegiances, the role of religion, sexuality, misogyny, art and inspiration. The *mise en scène* is both austere and theatrical: he appears sitting on his bed, surrounded by blue, sometimes with a black cat on his lap and next to a mirror, which reminds us of the precariousness of any discourse on identity; Ocaña's reflected image is often there to blur any notion we might think we have about the 'real' Ocaña. There is an interesting rapport with the camera in these scenes: he is both self-conscious and seductive, uncomfortable at times as if facing a situation he doesn't quite grasp, but later growing in confidence as he finally finds a way to express what he means. Such hesitations and shifts are part of the film's *modus operandi*: this is not about a stable image which is perfectly controlled or manufactured by the director, along the lines of so many star documentaries, but about a rough character feeling his way into constructing his public image. Ocaña's account of himself in these sections is filled with contradictions, digressions and attempts at definition which are often corrected and contextualised. His engagement with the label 'homosexuality' is complicated with hesitations and denial. Although his somewhat voracious desire for men's bodies is unquestioned and dwelt upon in great detail, he refuses labels and finally settles on being, first and foremost, 'a person', a rhetorical strategy very common at the time to avoid the negative connotations of homosexuality. 'No me gustan las etiquetas' [I don't like labels] had become the motto of many closeted public figures who would neither identify with or deny homosexuality, although this is clearly not the case with Ocaña. He rejects labelling imposed from the outside and proposes some labels of his own (Mira 2004: 458–9).

Something similar happens when he engages with the notion of transvestism: although he uses drag, this is just, he claims, incidental: he just likes it (or, alternatively, because he likes to shock), but he is not 'a transvestite', at least not, he clarifies, in the sense of someone who gets 'pleasure' out of dressing as someone of the opposite sex. In his reluctance to accept labels imposed by cultural orthodoxy, we can distinguish an impulse which is more queer than gay, although this is not a distinction he makes. Interestingly, he claims that he had not heard of 'homosexuality' until he came to Barcelona. One could argue, in Foucaultian fashion, that his experience preceded discursive conceptualisation, and therefore he could not 'be' 'a homosexual'.

Then again, in a manner reminiscent of queer notions of the homosocial, he also claims all men are 'really' homosexuals, although they might not acknowledge it, and the difference between himself and a heterosexual is that he has opted for asserting his own desire in the face of repression, whereas heterosexual men just follow convention. His view on women is even more problematic because of its misogyny and inconsistency. The explicitness of his discourse was unheard of in the cinema at the time: Ocaña discusses promiscuous sex and penises (his own as well as other people's), giving a visibility to the latter which is really exceptional in the cinema.

Pons's working methods are markedly different from those of journalists: in letting him elaborate and digress, and in not editing out inconsistencies or taming Ocaña's discourse in any way, Pons also becomes a proponent of a 'queer' outlook which was already in conflict with the more stable gay identities being proposed at the time. As with so many artists and intellectuals of that era, Pons seems to distrust labels. The hesitations around sexual identity are also prominent in contemporary responses to the film. Fernando Trueba's *El País* review (14 June 1978) also singled out this mistrust of labels as one of the more praiseworthy elements of the film. The libertarian agenda thus steers away from identity. It is also clear that the likes of Ocaña and Nazario had ambivalent feelings towards the gay movement precisely on the grounds that it forced desire to follow certain patterns. On the one hand, they welcome the possibilities of liberation the movement was opening; equality could not be a bad thing after decades of repression. On the other hand, they had no formulated discourse on sexual identity as politics, and believed in approaches to desire that could not be easily locked into categories. Testimonies of the period suggest the mistrust was mutual: gay activists were reluctant to accept drag queens and performers 'taking over' political demonstrations. Ocaña's refusal to accept categories gave his discourse a vitality that has kept it contemporary.

The second strand in the film, which lasts the length of Ocaña's confession (thence the 'Intermittent Portrait' of the title) has to do with a series of performances by Ocaña: he performs highlights of the Quintero brothers'[4] Doña Clarines in full drag, promenades along the Ramblas followed by crowds of onlookers,

7. A Lorca Tribute: Ocaña in one of his performances.

sings the Quintero, León and Quiroga *copla* 'Yo soy esa' [I am that woman] at the Café de L'Òpera, recites from Lorca's work at a cemetery, and at the film's climax removes his clothes at a political-cultural festival at Canet de Mar. This final gesture constitutes a strong closure and has powerful symbolic connotations. From the beginning of the film, Ocaña has been talking about the reason for taking his clothes off and the film seems to be building up his case before it finally shows the action itself. He questions why people wear clothes at all and it seems as if his 'stripteases' – he has problems with the term – are designed to provoke. Ending on this note, Pons is underlining the most controversial aspect of his character and confirming a libertarian point of view for the film.

Such provocation is not without its paradoxical aspects. Pons's portrait effectively shows Ocaña as an *agent provocateur*, as someone who is opposed to everyone else, an individual who seeks self-assertion and identity through provocation. At the same time, however, Ocaña appears very much as what Barcelona was about circa 1977: no one seems shocked or scandalised in the film and his status as some kind of popular celebrity is well established. Although he keeps on mentioning people who may have been offended at his behaviour, the fact remains that this sense of shock or offence has no part in Pons's film or in the Barcelona re-created there.

The film was made with no discernible budget, but after it was completed, Pons managed to secure a degree of funding from established producer Josep M. Forn in order to blow up the 16 mm print to 35 mm and also to inscribe the title in the legal register so the film could 'exist' and be presented at festivals. He had attended the Cannes Film Festival for a few years as a journalist and he submitted the film for a section inaugurated that year: *Un certain regard*. The film proved a critical success and the press conference following the screening featured Ocaña himself singing a *copla* and enjoying the attention of international critics. The film has subsequently been presented at cinemathèques and is now a classic of the gay and lesbian film retrospective circuit. *Ocaña* is a key text of the Spanish Transition, not just for its subject matter, but very specially for the way the subject is presented. Pons's camera understands Ocaña as a contradictory character who represents the vitality of the period and privileges a Catalan perspective that is often overlooked in accounts of films of the period.

Pons's intervention in presenting his subject shows not only an early command of the film image, but also a perspective keenly aware of changes taking place in the period and the mythologies which came to represent the Transition in Catalonia. Thirty-five years after it was first seen, the film feels very much alive, hopeful of change and utopian in its refusal to pin down its main character or to propose a final morality for his life.

Notes

1 A selection of reviews can be found at http://www.venturapons.com/catala.html [accessed 15 May 2011]. See also Campo Vidal (2004: 39-49).

2 The mythology of 'grey Madrid' is prominent in key novels of Francoism such as Camilo José Cela's *La colmena* [*The Beehive*] and Luis Martín Santos's *Tiempo de silencio* [*Time of Silence*]. Almodóvar was very vocal in reacting to this idea of the city in the early 1980s. The idea is developed in his interview with Marsha Kinder (2004).

3 'S Cinema' was the label introduced in 1977 to refer to soft-porn film in the years before legislation for X-rated (or hard-porn) films was introduced in special cinemas.

4 The prolific brothers, Serafín (1871–1938) and Joaquín (1873–1944) Álvarez Quintero wrote over 200 popular plays drawing on the customs, folklore and manners of Andalusia. *Doña Clarines,* first presented in 1909, has as its title protagonist a woman based in a small rural town who obsessively tells the truth and is therefore regarded as half-crazy by the rest of the community. The play unravels her secrets, thus explaining the reasons for her truth-telling.

Bibliography

Campo Vidal, Anabel (2004) *Ventura Pons: La mirada libre*, Madrid: SGAE.

Kinder, Marsha (2004) 'Pleasure and the New Spanish Mentality: A Conversation with Pedro Almodóvar', in Paula Willoquet-Maricondi (ed.), *Pedro Almodóvar: Interviews*, Jackson: University Press of Mississippi, 40–57.

Mira, Alberto (2004) *De Sodoma a Chueca: Una historia cultural de la homosexualidad en España en el siglo XX*, Madrid: Egales.

Moix, Terenci (1978) 'De la diosa Ocaña a Sebastián el martir', www.venturapons.com/catala.html [accessed 23 December 2011].

Nazario (2004) *La Barcelona de los años 70 vista por Nazario y sus amigos*, Barcelona: Ellago Ediciones.

Pons, Ventura (2011) *Els meus (i els altres)*, Barcelona: Proa.

Trueba, Fernando (1978) 'Ocaña. Retrato intermitente', *El País* (14 June).

Various (2002) *Nazario Barcelona 1972–2002*, Barcelona: Ajuntament de Barcelona.

Zúñiga, Ángel (2001) *Barcelona y la noche*, Barcelona: Parsifal.

4

El Dorado (Carlos Saura, 1987): the keys to El Dorado

Agustín Sánchez Vidal
Translated by Mar Diestro-Dópido

In 1560, during the reign of Philip II of Spain, an expedition some three hundred strong sets off up the Amazon, heading for the mythical land of El Dorado. At the head of the expedition is Governor Pedro de Ursúa (Lambert Wilson), together with his lover, the beautiful *mestiza* (mixed-race) Inés de Atienza (Gabriela Roel). He shares command of the expedition with the Basque, Lope de Aguirre (Omero Antonutti), who is accompanied by Elvira (Inés Sastre), his adolescent daughter, also a *mestiza*.

In poor health and only interested in his love affairs, the characterless Ursúa is no match for the cunning veteran, Lope de Aguirre, a man able to secure the expedition's survival. With his officers' agreement, he orders the killing of the governor and appoints in his place the nobleman Fernando de Guzmán (Eusebio Poncela). From this moment on, nothing will be the same. The expedition severs its links with the Crown, setting its sights on a goal more tangible than El Dorado: the taking of power in Peru.

With the breaking of the chain of command, a wave of violence is unleashed. Aguirre eliminates those he suspects of conspiring against him – including Guzmán and Inés de Atienza – and proclaims himself Prince of Freedom, promising a kingdom without either masters or slaves, in an America emancipated from Spain. But he falls ill, and in his feverish delirium he envisions his daughter's slaughter by his own hand. A voice-over summarises the rest of his descent towards death and his posthumous sentencing by the Crown.

Following Franco's death in 1975, Carlos Saura's cinema – characterised by a tendency towards political allegory and an unmistakable resistance to the dictatorship – opened up in new directions. At the beginning of the 1980s his output shows considerable diversification. ¡*Deprisa! !Deprisa!/ Faster! Faster!* (1980) updates Saura's first feature *Los golfos/ The Hooligans* (1959), by virtue of the immediacy of a documentary street style applied to the subject of juvenile delinquency. *Dulces horas/ Sweet Hours* (1981) literally rewrites the circumstances of a Spanish family marked by the past. *Antonieta* (1982) is located in the Mexico of Porfirio Díaz's dictatorship and the Revolution, based on the figure of Antonieta Rivas Mercado, whose biography is reconstructed using a script by Jean-Claude Carrière. *Los zancos/ The Stilts* (1984), devised in collaboration with its male protagonist, Fernando Fernán-Gómez, tackles the relationship between a man who is already old and disillusioned and a young actress. *La noche oscura/ The Dark Night* (1989) centres on the nine months that the Carmelite poet, San Juan de la Cruz, remains imprisoned in Toledo, where he conceives some of his best verse. Meanwhile, ¡*Ay, Carmela!* (1990) scripted by Rafael Azcona, who collaborated on some of Saura's earliest films, develops from José Sanchis Sinisterra's play about two comedians who try to make a living – or just stay alive – during the Spanish Civil War.

These are projects that, on one level, bear little relation to each other. This is especially the case when they are compared with the director's work in the genre of the film musical, realised in collaboration with the dancer Antonio Gades and the producer Emiliano Piedra: *Bodas de sangre/ Blood Wedding* (1981), *Carmen* (1983) and *El amor brujo/ Love, the Magician* (1986).

This is the context that surrounds the shooting of *El Dorado* in 1987, a film which displays characteristics previously absent in Saura's cinema: it could be ascribed to the historical genre, based on real facts, and its format was – at least on the surface – that of an adventure blockbuster. In order to find anything similar in its author's trajectory, we would need to go back to his second feature film, *Llanto por un bandido/ Lament for a Bandit* (1963), about José María Hinojosa, 'El Tempranillo', a famous outlaw back in the time of Francisco de Goya. But this film did not fare well and suffered different kinds of censorship: on the one hand, the government sought to defuse its political charge; on the other, commercial pressures led to its being re-edited in order to look like a Western.

Therefore, it seems appropriate to ponder the reasons behind the 'anomaly' that brought Saura back to historical cinema with *El Dorado*. A project he had been developing for years, it had never managed to find a home with a production company owing to its projected budget, which would end up making it the most expensive film ever envisaged by Spanish cinema: 1,023 million pesetas (about $10 million) when Andrés Vicente Gómez – who had worked with Orson Welles on his final projects, including *The Other Side of the Wind*, begun in the late 1960s – took charge of it in 1986.

Another problem connected with *El Dorado* was finding an actor who could play Lope de Aguirre convincingly, that is, until the appearance of Omero

Antonutti, who had distinguished himself in films such as *Padre padrone/Father and Master* (Paolo and Vittorio Taviani, 1977) and *El sur/The South* (Víctor Erice, 1983). At first, the possibility of Bianca Jagger playing the *mestiza* Inés de Atienza was considered, although in the end it was the Mexican actress Gabriela Roel who took the part.

The team that worked on *El Dorado* ended up comprising actors and technicians from England, Australia, France, Italy, Chile, Argentina, Mexico, Peru, Spain and Costa Rica. The artistic director was Terry Pritchard, who had been responsible for *The French Lieutenant's Woman* (Karel Reisz, 1981) and *The Emerald Forest* (John Boorman, 1985). He was in charge of the design of the drums, costumes and period instruments, as well as a 36-metre-long brig.

Shooting started on 19 January 1987 and finished on 17 May in the canals of the Tortuguero National Park (Costa Rica), on the Atlantic coast. Weather conditions were harsh; almost everyone in the team fell ill with tropical diseases at some point. However, few productions have managed to capture the hostility of this environment on screen. And this was one of the criticisms made of the film during its presentation at the Cannes Film Festival in May 1988. Even though it opened on the Saturday prime slot, the audience received it rather coldly (Collar 1988).

The film did not work commercially either. It seemed to irritate those who were expecting it to extol the conquest of the New World, on the occasion of the fifth centenary of the Discovery of America that was already being prepared for 1992. Some of the media lamented that, with the Discovery celebrations just around the corner, and with so many *exemplary* adventures to retell, the film should have chosen as its subject a conspirator, rebel and murderer such as Lope de Aguirre, thereby offering the world further confirmation of the *leyenda negra* [black legend] (see Santo Job 1988).

Nor were the comments made by Latin American correspondents any kinder; both the figure of Lope de Aguirre and the myth of El Dorado touch some of the most sensitive areas of their imaginary (see Llopis 1988). Going back all the way to 1534, when an Amerindian prisoner informed the Spaniards of the legend of *el Dorado* [the golden Indian], and subsequently narrated by chroniclers such as Gonzalo Fernández de Oviedo, the myth is evoked at the start of Saura's film in the form of Elvira's dream: a *cacique* [local chieftain] anoints his body with resin and is covered with gold dust before immersing himself in a lagoon.

This symbolic and fantastical sensibility was parodied by Voltaire in *Candide or The Optimist* (1759) and would be picked up on again by Howard Hawks in his film *El Dorado* (1966), quoting the homonymous poem by Edgar Allan Poe. And the same could be said of classics such as *The Gold Rush* (Charles Chaplin, 1925) or *The Treasure of Sierra Madre* (John Huston, 1948). But in the case of Lope de Aguirre it is necessary to point out that we are still a long way from such eloquent artistic treatments. For Aguirre and his men, El Dorado could appear

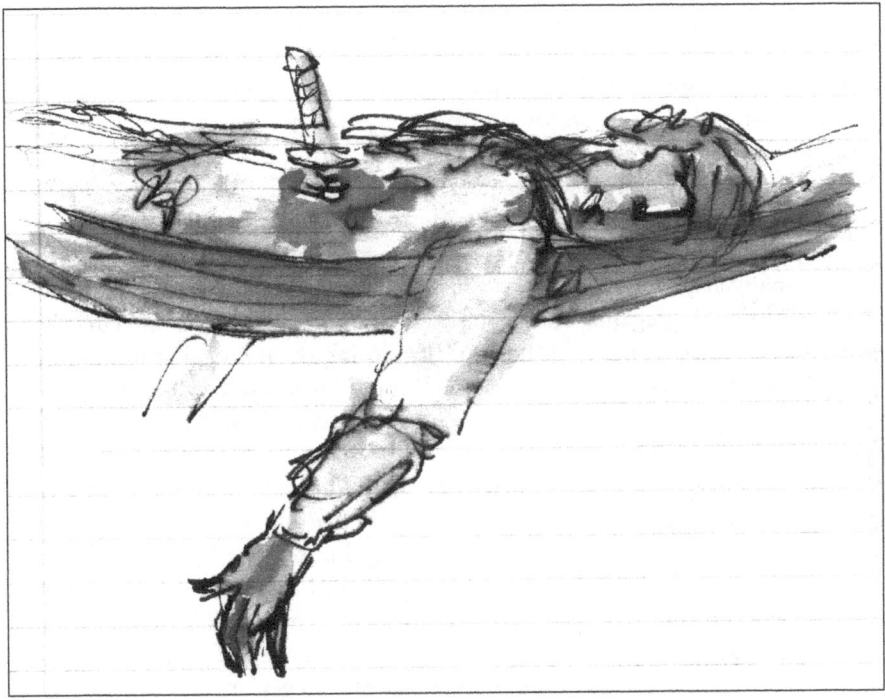

8. Drawing by Carlos Saura of the death of Ursúa.

anywhere, as it did to Hernán Cortés in Mexico or to Francisco Pizarro in Peru. It could turn into real, tangible gold at any moment.

There were other factors shaping the expedition, motivations of a political nature, derived from the bloody civil wars fought by the Spaniards in Peru. The expedition was promoted by the local viceroy, Andrés Hurtado de Mendoza, who was keen to free himself of the hordes of adventurers who were overrunning that territory.

And so on 26 September 1560 Pedro de Ursúa de Topesana set sail with two brigs, nine *chatas* or flat boats, numerous canoes and various rafts. He took with him three hundred Spanish soldiers, three clergymen, seven married women and another five of marriageable age, more than three hundred Amerindian men and women, and about 20 black slaves. It was a considerable mass, made up of the roughest mob elements in Peru, driven by resentment and lacking any experience in the jungle.

Ursúa was from the Baztán Valley in Navarra. Aged 35, he had already acquired a solid prestige by suppressing the uprisings of the Muzos Indians of Colombia and the black *cimarrones* (runaway slaves) of Panama. With him he took Inés de Atienza, a *mestiza* widow of great beauty, and he allegedly devoted more time to her charms than to managing his men, hence provoking their discontent.

For his part, Aguirre is often presented as a failure. Born in Oñate, Guipuzcoa, the second-born son of parents of average means, he thought he could make his fortune in America and emigrated there around 1535. Contemporary chroniclers such as Francisco Vázquez and Pedrarias de Almesto describe him as small-bodied and bad-tempered, with a sharp, lively mind, a forceful man and a workhorse, who hardly slept and who would always go tirelessly on foot, bearing many arms. During the extremely hard civil wars in Peru, he fought on the side of the king against the Spanish rebels and became lame after receiving two shots from a harquebus in his right leg, losing the use of that foot. He was around 50 years old at the time of the El Dorado expedition, and, after a quarter of a century of service to the Crown, he was old and crippled, without either a fortune or any significant rank.

Acknowledging this context, it is easy to understand that for Aguirre, in-fighting between Spaniards came as no surprise. In one of his harangues after taking control of the situation, Lope proclaims himself the Wrath of God, the Prince of Freedom and of the Kingdom of Terra Firma and the provinces of Chile, adopting a curious red-and-black flag that seems almost the precursor of the future anarchist emblem. His demands become more and more extreme: not only is it forbidden to speak even quietly, but also to get up at night (including for the purpose of relieving pressing physiological needs). Aguirre's lieutenant, Portuguese cobbler Antón Llamoso, was given to drinking blood from the open skulls of dead men and eating their brains. In any case, under Aguirre's command, all types of atrocities were committed and his aversion for the clergy became proverbial. It is thought, however, that he did not consent to the rape of women: those who were chaste were treated with respect and prostitutes were locked up in a fortress under Elvira's direction.

In the autumn of 1561 in Nueva Valencia he wrote the famous letter to Philip II, accusing him of being cruel and ungrateful towards the conquistadors. This is an outlandish document, yet one that is not lacking in intelligence and that gives expression to a spirit which, without a doubt, hovered over many expeditionary environments. On 18 September 1821, Simón Bolívar ordered the publication of this letter in Maracaibo's *El Correo Nacional*, because he considered it 'el acta primera de la independencia de América'[the first statement of America's independence]. But Aguirre was much more contradictory. And there have even been those who consider him as the precursor of the despots that have devastated Latin American history, such as Valle-Inclán's novelistic creation *Tirano Banderas* (1927).

This difficulty in pigeonholing Aguirre is illustrated in subsequent publications and controversies. In 1821 the English poet, storyteller and Hispanist Robert Southey, translator of the *Cantar de Mio Cid* [*Chronicle of the Cid*], published his novel *The Expedition of Orsua and the Crimes of Aguirre,* which was recovered in 2010 by Javier Marías for his publishing house Reino de Redonda. It is a short, vigorous account that spares neither blood nor violence and does not disguise the fascination it feels for the character, but without lapsing into the wearisome clichés of the *leyenda negra.*

In the twentieth century, Pío Baroja became interested in Lope de Aguirre in his novel *Las inquietudes de Shanti Andía* [The restlessness of Shanti Andía] (1911) as did Ciro Bayo in *Los Marañones* [The Marañones] (1913). In the 1940s, apart from the biography written by Gonzalo Torrente Ballester, *Lope de Aguirre, crónica dramática de la historia Americana en tres jornadas* [Lope de Aguirre, a dramatic chronicle of American history in three acts] (1941), he starts to be vindicated as a figure of emancipation, or invoked as the devil. And it is then that *El caballero de El Dorado* [The gentleman of El Dorado] (1942) by Germán Arciniegas and *El camino de El Dorado* [The path to El Dorado] (1947) by Arturo Uslar Pietri appear, followed eventually by *Daimon* (1978) by Abel Posse and *Lope de Aguirre, Príncipe de la Libertad* [Lope de Aguirre, prince of liberty] (1979) by Miguel Otero Silva. Finally, it is worth mentioning José Sanchis Sinisterra's *El retablo de Eldorado* [The portrait of El Dorado] (1985), *Crímenes y locuras del traidor Lope de Aguirre* [Crimes and madness of the traitor Lope de Aguirre] (1986) and *Lope de Aguirre, traidor* [Lope de Aguirre, traitor] (1992), since Saura would later adapt the playwright's *¡Ay, Carmela!*

One of the most successful novelistic treatments has proved to be Ramón J. Sender's *La aventura equinoccial de Lope de Aguirre* [The equinoctial adventures of Lope de Aguirre] (1964). Saura's film is both based on it and directly inspired by the chronicles which lie behind this narrative. Sender's book derives from *La expedición de Ursúa al Dorado y la rebelión de Lope de Aguirre* [The expedition of Ursúa to El Dorado and the rebellion of Lope de Aguirre], published by Emiliano Jos in Huesca in 1927, which was the first modern attempt to approach Lope de Aguirre in a rigorous and dispassionate way. Sender's novel draws considerably on the wealth of documentation in Jos's work, even though his main contribution lay in the portrayal of the main character, with all its attendant ambiguity.

And yet, for spectators, the single most unavoidable film reference to the subject was *Aguirre, der Zorn Gottes/Aguirre, the Wrath of God* (Werner Herzog, 1972), whose influence has been recognised by other filmmakers such as Francis Ford Coppola, when he made *Apocalypse Now* (1979). There is much to admire in the opening of Herzog's film as several cannons and Doña Inés's bunk-bed are carried down the precipices of the Andes: lasting five minutes, the sequence gives a very good idea of the hardships and the harshness of the elements in which the film's adventure evolves. But from that point onwards, and in order to remain faithful to his obsessions, the filmmaker did not hesitate in intentionally mixing up Aguirre's life with that of the discoverer of the Amazon, Francisco Orellana, or in introducing Gonzalo Pizarro and Fray Gaspar de Carvajal into the narrative, knowing full well that the former was already dead and the latter never accompanied Aguirre.

Anyone with the slightest knowledge of the historical facts will find it impossible to believe what the German filmmaker depicts. Fray Gaspar is portrayed in the light of the crudest anti-clericalism. Fernando de Guzmán behaves more like a swineherd than a nobleman from Seville, and his defining characteristic is diarrhoea (perhaps Atahualpa's revenge!). On the other hand, when Herzog casts as noblemen actors who look more like criminals than Aguirre does, an essential contrast is lost: Ursúa and Guzmán were counterweights to Aguirre's persona: young, successful, good-looking noblemen, at times even refined and cultured.

In an interview conducted in 1988, when I asked Carlos Saura about this, he admitted:

> Yo tengo un gran respeto por Herzog, que me parece un tipo muy interesante … Cuando vi *Aguirre, la cólera de Dios* ya tenía la idea de hacer esta historia y me quedé deslumbrado por la primera parte de la película y frustrado por la segunda. Porque la primera parte no tiene nada que ver con Lope de Aguirre, es casi una antología de la conquista de América. Es de una gran belleza y nos descubrió a los españoles algo que deberíamos haber hecho nosotros. Pero, en cambio, cuando la película se centraba en Lope de Aguirre yo ya había leído cosas sobre él (la novela de Sender, alguna crónica …) y veía que eso era un desastre, que era todo mentira, que Klaus Kinski era un Aguirre sobreactuado haciendo el loco desde el principio en una pésima actuación y que estaban desvirtuando una historia maravillosa. (Sánchez Vidal 1988b)

> [I have a great respect for Herzog, I think he is an interesting guy … When I saw *Aguirre, the Wrath of God* I already had the idea of doing this story, and I was dazzled by the first part of the film and frustrated by the second. Because the first part has nothing to do with Lope de Aguirre, it is almost a compendium of the conquest of America. It is a thing of great beauty and it revealed to Spaniards something we should have done ourselves. But, by contrast, when the film centred on Lope de Aguirre, I had already read so many things about him (Sender's novel, the odd chronicle …) and I saw that it was a disaster, that it was all a lie, that Klaus Kinski was overacting, playing Aguirre as mad from the beginning, through some very bad acting too, and that they were distorting a wonderful story.]

It is therefore not surprising that Saura should have approached his subject so differently. He based his project around a very complete and rigorous body of research carried out by the film's historical adviser, his son, Antonio Saura Medrano, who had written his doctoral thesis on Lope de Aguirre. And it was very clear from the beginning for Saura where he was going to put the emphasis. What most concerned him was the confrontation between Spaniards, and he would not have been interested in the story in the least if it had merely been about a confrontation between them and the Amerindians, which is the *raison d'être* of Herzog's film, where, true to his obsessions, the director explores the clash between Nature and Civilisation.

Given this clarity of purpose, everything else in *El Dorado* recedes into the background: weather, mosquitoes, swamps. Even the river is reduced to a mere backdrop:

> Si bien el paisaje sorprende y fascina, rápidamente la costumbre, el hábito, hace que perdamos esa fascinación por lo nuevo y desconocido … Por eso, en *El Dorado* no se debe abusar ni de la selva ni del río ni de los animales salvajes … Eso sería otra película. Lo importante es lo que les ocurre a estos españoles que se matan entre ellos. La selva, las bestias que hay en ella, la monotonía del río, forman parte del fondo del decorado. Conclusión: ¡Hay que dosificar el paisaje y utilizarlo sólo en el momento oportuno! (Saura 1987: 212)

> [Even though the landscape is amazing and fascinating, we get used and accustomed to it very quickly, so that it no longer strikes us as new and unknown … This is why, in *El Dorado,* the forest, the river or the wild animals must not be given too prominent a role … That would constitute a different film. What is important here is what happens to these Spaniards who are killing each other. The jungle, the beasts in it, the monotony of the river, they all constitute the background of the mise en scène. The conclusion that follows is: be sparing with the scenery and use it only at the right moment!]

This decision brings with it some of the unsolved problems with historical cinema that had arisen in *Lament for a Bandit*. If one decides to tell the story of a confrontation and struggle for power in a given time and place, it does not seem right to sever the link between what happened and the circumstances where the events took place. Narrative and drama work better with specifics, and what is interesting is the singularity of a case, not the abstract scheme or the merely geometrical struggle for power. And these failings hinder the next stage in the story's development, which is its transformation into tragedy.

Carlos Saura's project takes for granted a displacement that was well conceived in principle: since El Dorado never appears, the shared adventure and obsession take on another meaning. Aguirre's practical intuition helps him sense that something that probably does not exist cannot be projected towards the future. On the other hand, it can acquire institutional form in something more concrete, the independence and creation of a new kingdom:

> De ese modo llega hasta a enfrentarse con Felipe II, lo que en esa época era una barbaridad, claro, porque dominaba el mundo entero. Eso a mí me parece un disparate fantástico y es lo que más me atrae de Aguirre: el sentido práctico por un lado y, por otro, su locura y sentido de lo quimérico … Se podrían trasladar los problemas de Aguirre a cualquier político actual. La diferencia es que entonces se solucionaban estas cosas con un acto de violencia brutal y ahora los métodos son más sutiles. Pero la mecánica para llegar al poder es la misma. Con la diferencia de que la de Aguirre

es la historia más nítida de pugna por el poder, más todavía que en Shakespeare.
(Saura, cited in Sánchez Vidal 1988b)

[This way, he even goes as far as challenging Philip II, something which at that time
was outrageous, because the King exercised power over the whole world. This for
me is a wonderful, crazy thing to do and it is what most attracts me to Aguirre: his
practical sense on the one hand, and his madness and sense of the fantastical on the
other ... Aguirre's problems could apply to any politician in our time, the difference
being that back then, these things were dealt with through a brutal act of violence
and now people's methods are subtler. But the machinations to achieve power are
the same. The difference is that Aguirre's story is the clearest instance of the struggle
for power, more than in Shakespeare, even.]

Almost half a century ago, Ignacio Zumalde remarked (1963: 61) apropos
Aguirre: 'Shakespeare ignoró la existencia de este hermano de Macbeth'
[Shakespeare did not know of the existence of this brother of Macbeth]. The
tragic dimension of Aguirre's character gives rise to a set of questions and
problems that are no less acute: what happens when a person, who is by now
exhausted, has to give up on his dreams and resign himself to something more
immediate, such as power in the here and now? What kind of sacrifices and
compromises must he be ready to make for this end, and what mechanism
has to be set in motion in order to preserve it? Significantly, the symbol of the
Golden Fleece hangs from Philip II's neck, as the camera takes care to highlight
when it shows his portrait as if it were a sort of anatomy of power. It is worth
noting that the title of *El Dorado* appears in print exactly above the Golden
Fleece.

There is also the vital feminine counterpoint, the parallel trajectory that is
hinted at, from Elvira's innocence to the compulsive use that Inés de Atienza
makes of sex. This double process of initiation effectively frames what functions most powerfully in Saura's film: the movement from the dreams and
fantasies of men to the political calculations of power; from female desire to the
purely mechanical workings of sex as a tool for dominance and annihilation.
Nevertheless, perhaps Saura had too much of a sense of modesty when it came to
building emotional bridges between his film and the spectator.

With regard to the figure of Lope de Aguirre, instead of justifying or con-
demning him, the film tries to understand him. The portrait presented in the
chronicles is that of a madman and a dangerous and quarrelsome traitor, along
with every possible perversity of character. This was effectively based on the declarations of those who tried to justify their own attitude before Philip II, putting
all the blame on the ringleader in order to escape punishment.

Another linchpin in the film is Inés de Atienza, who is dealt with in the
chronicles in a few words, but who proved a key figure in the expedition. We
need to imagine the most beautiful woman in Peru surrounded by a horde of

adventurers and moving from one bed to another following a series of men who fell foul of Aguirre:

> Es una mujer que tiene sangre india, además de una mentalidad pseudo-europea no muy asentada. En el fondo, pienso que conservó su gran amor hacia Ursúa durante toda su vida, y que fue cumpliendo su venganza de manera silenciosa, lenta y tenazmente. El único que se dio cuenta de su tragedia fue Aguirre, que hizo bien en no tener *tratos* con ella. Por eso, creo yo, terminó matándola; si no, no se justifica su acto. (Calleja 1988)

> [(She is) a woman with Amerindian blood, as well as a pseudo-European way of looking at things. Deep inside, I think that she carried on loving Ursúa all her life, and that she exacted revenge on those around her, in a silent, slow and tenacious manner. The only person who was aware of her tragedy was Aguirre, who rightly refused to have anything to do with her. This is the reason why, I think, he ended up killing her; otherwise his action is unjustifiable.]

With all of these considerations in view, the structure of *El Dorado* is relatively simple. Its 151 minutes are distributed by assigning an hour to Ursúa's mandate, another to the 'reign' of Fernando Guzmán and the final half-hour to the direct exercise of power by Aguirre. Overall, the film traces a spiral of violence and descent into chaos that uncoils in the manner of a spring, expanding progressively towards a fatal denouement.

This framework is reinforced by the presence of two leitmotifs. The first of these is visual and appears in the form of the portrait of Philip II by Antonio Moro which is evoked later on in the film, but in a debased light, in the 'kingly' proclamations made by Guzmán and by Aguirre. The other motif is auditory: the *recercada* or variations for harpsichord and viol by the Renaissance musician, Diego de Ortiz of Toledo.

As mentioned previously, the opening credits of the film appear over the painting by Moro, which the camera breaks up into different segments, paying special attention to the insignias of power. Amongst these is the Golden Fleece, a symbol of another mythical expedition – that of the Argonauts – in search of the metal that crystallises power and government. The adventure of El Dorado will come into conflict with that tangible reality principle embodied in the person of the monarch.

The overall structure of variation in the film accommodates patterns of duality which Saura highlighted in his shooting diary. The characters form complementary pairs, as if they were heads and tails. In the case of Ursúa and Aguirre – both Basque – one is noble and successful, the other second-rate and unsuccessful, or Inés and Elvira – both *mestizas* – the former a widow and woman of the world, the latter an innocent virgin. In addition, there are two slaughters (that of the Amerindians by the Spaniards, and the other of the Spaniards by the

Amerindians), two 'coronations' (Guzmán's and Aguirre's), etc. But, above all, there are two dreams that frame the whole film: Elvira's about the golden Indian at the beginning, and Aguirre's nightmare at the end, where the murder of his own daughter destroys the whole fantasy. The expeditionary interlude is therefore located halfway between reality and unreality, between myth and nightmare, like an impossible *sueño de libertad* [dream of freedom] – the phrase featured as the advertising slogan for the film in Spain.

Even though the progression may not always work in terms of narrative, the journey towards destruction is implacable. After the introductory prologue, the action gets under way with the first slaughter half an hour into the film. It starts with the Spaniards killing the Amerindians; then the Amerindians the Spaniards; then, the leader is eliminated; after that, the violence is directed down the scale as shots are fired against Amerindians allied to the Spanish, and against the black slaves; finally, it is everyone against everyone else.

The episode of Guzmán's enthronement with an improvised baldachin and coat of arms offers a crude replica of the portrait of Philip II seen earlier, and it takes place to the musical accompaniment of the *recercada* by Diego de Ortiz (a further variation on a theme that is musical, visual, political, etc.). But after this absurd act of protocol – in the middle of the jungle! – the harshness of reality imposes itself: there are men that need to be fed. Aguirre refuses to kill the horses. We see him climbing to the top of a hill from where he surveys the never-ending jungle interrupted, in its monotony, only by the river: there, the men's horses are completely worthless, and Aguirre has to admit that the best solution is to sacrifice them. This is a key sequence. Once the slaughter has been carried out, with no El Dorado on the horizon and with all hope abandoned, we know that Aguirre will be capable of anything.

The die is cast, even if there are still some occasional respite and alternatives to the fatal violence that has been unleashed. An example is Aguirre's relationship with Inés, of whom he is almost as terrified as he is of the jungle. Or Guzmán's brazen confession of homosexual love for his assistant Duarte when the latter is gunned down with a harquebus. There is also the note of sardonic humour in the impossible dialogue between Father Henao and the recalcitrant cannibal to whom he shows a big crucifix, urging him in the name of this bleeding Christ to stop devouring his fellow man. The Indian appears to examine the ribcage of the crucifix with thoughts that are more gastronomic than religious.

Some of the most searching questions raised by the film are summed up in the proclamation of Lope de Aguirre as Prince of Freedom, in a thatched hut that no one has bothered to deck out with any trappings of authority. Surrounded by Indians, blacks, *mestizos* and the most motley of troops, Aguirre proceeds to make formal declarations of appointments and to write a letter of open insubordination to Philip II. As he hesitates over the use of certain terms and words, the episode dramatises another of the paradoxes of the present adventure: what can one do with the freedom that one has granted to oneself, when this involves breaking all ties from authority?

Lope's nightmare about stabbing his own daughter to death rounds off the film as it fades to black against the density of the jungle, after gliding down that river that flows, never-ending and without points of reference, like life itself: '¿De qué sirve la vida' [What is the point of living] – asks Aguirre – 'si no hay un fin que la justifique? [if there's no end to justify it?]

The publicity campaign for *El Dorado*, based on economic criteria ('La película más cara del cine español' [The most expensive film in Spanish cinema, ever]), and the numerous reports of the difficulties of shooting in the jungle, surrounded it with the halo of a blockbuster and a great adventure spectacle that had a negative effect on public expectations. Once these misunderstandings are put to one side, the structural inadequacies that were the initial subject of critical attention are replaced by a focus on the group of human beings around which the film articulates all its events and concerns.

El Dorado would not have the same meaning were it not for two background factors that constitute – perhaps not by chance – the two most ambitious projects in Carlos Saura's filmography at the time: a film about Philip II and another on the Spanish Civil War. Regarding the former, the director confided to me:

> He leído muchas cosas de Felipe II. Voy acumulando material y voy guardando cosas porque realmente es un personaje fascinante, con unas contradicciones enormes. Un hombre al que le gustaba El Bosco, pero cuyo pintor preferido era Tiziano. Muy delicado, sensible, que promueve, por ejemplo, toda la música cortesana. Era realmente refinado en todos los sentidos, pero también un tipo capaz de matar a quien fuera. Para hacer este Felipe II me gustaría algo que no tuviese una textura realista. No lo veo en ningún escenario concreto. Quizá El Escorial, pero no el edificio que hay ahora, sino a base de proyecciones en un estudio gigantesco, estilizándolo en varios cicloramas. No vale la pena una historia realista, a diferencia de Lope de Aguirre, donde es fundamental la selva, la propia Naturaleza. (Sánchez Vidal 1988b)

> [I have read many things about Philip II. I have been accumulating material and I am storing things, because he really is a fascinating character, with huge contradictions. A man who liked Bosch, but whose favourite painter was Titian. Very cultured and sensitive, he promoted, for instance, all the music of the court. He was indeed refined in all senses, but he was also capable of killing anyone. For this Philip II, I would like to avoid anything with a realist texture. I don't see him in any concrete setting. Maybe El Escorial, but not the current building, rather one constructed by using projections in a gigantic studio, stylising it with several cycloramas. A realist story would not work, unlike with Lope de Aguirre, where the jungle is essential, Nature itself.]

With regard to the second project, the outline of *¡Esa luz!* [That light!] has so far been published in two versions: a film script and a novel. It is based on the situation of a couple who find themselves separated by the outbreak of the Spanish Civil War in July 1936, each on a different side. She is a pianist, like Saura's own mother, Fermina Atarés, and he is a writer, like Ramón J. Sender. Indeed, the story is inspired, on the one hand, by the real experiences of the latter and his wife, Amparo Barayón. But it is also a hypothesis or speculation about the relationship, not-quite that of boyfriend and girlfriend, that Sender and Carlos Saura's mother had when they were both young, in Huesca, and to which the author alludes in his story 'Un poema de amor' [A love poem], published in Huesca in 1922.

It may not be a coincidence that the next two films shot by Saura after *El Dorado* – with Andrés Vicente Gómez as producer once more, and bringing the decade of the 1980s to a close – were *The Dark Night* and *¡Ay, Carmela!* The former is set in the reign of Philip II and centres on San Juan de la Cruz, a dissident figure who, unlike Lope de Aguirre, does not need the expanse of virgin forest to express the freedom of his spirit and for whom a half-lit cell is enough to let his imagination take flight. And the second, which is set in the midst of the Spanish Civil War, and no less germane to *El Dorado*.

While academic study of Saura's post-Franco trajectory has concentrated primarily on his extensive engagement with the politics and aesthetics of reworking flamenco for the screen, the present discussion of *El Dorado* demonstrates a strong degree of political engagement that crucially links the film to his earlier *oeuvre*. Saura was perceived on the international film circuit as a (if not *the*) dissonant filmmaker of the Franco era. Sociopolitical inquiry has remained central to his filmmaking. *El Dorado* is a polyvalent work that combines historical revision of Spain's imperial past with considerations of a broader cultural legacy that has resonances and implications for mid-1980s Spain (and indeed Europe). Longstanding personal preoccupations, including some of a very intimate kind, also lie behind the film. The keys to appreciating *El Dorado* are therefore multiple, ranging from the historical and cinematic traditions to the contemporary moment, and Saura's own family history.

Bibliography

Aguirre, Lope de (1981) *Crónicas 1559–1561*, (eds) Elena Mampel and Neus Escandell, Barcelona: Ediciones Universidad de Barcelona.
Calleja, Pedro (1988) Interview with Carlos Saura, *Fotogramas*, 1741 (May), 57–8.
Caro Baroja, Julio (1983) *El señor Inquisidor y otras vidas por oficio*, Madrid: Alianza.
Collar, Jorge (1988) '*El Dorado*, entre el frío y la pasión', *Heraldo de Aragón* (15 May), 43.
Fernández de Oviedo, Gonzalo (1959) *Historia general y natural de las Indias*, Madrid: BAE.
Gandía, Enrique de (1929) *Historia crítica de los mitos de la conquista americana*, Buenos Aires: Juan Roldán.

Gil, Juan (1989) *Mitos y utopías del descubrimiento. I: Colón y su tiempo; II: El Pacífico; III: El Dorado*, Madrid: Alianza Universidad.

Hemming, John (1984) *En busca de El Dorado*, Barcelona: Ediciones del Serbal.

Jos, Emiliano (1927) *La expedición de Ursúa al Dorado y la rebelión de Lope de Aguirre*, Huesca: Imprenta V. Campo.

Lacarra, M. Jesús and J. Manuel Cacho Blecua (1990) *Lo imaginario en la conquista de América*, Zaragoza: Comisión Aragonesa Quinto Centenario.

Llopis, Silvia (1988) '*El Dorado* irritó a la prensa latinoamericana', *Diario 16* (15 May), 60.

Matamoros, Blas (1986) *Lope de Aguirre*, Madrid: Ediciones Quorum.

Ramos, Demetrio (1973) *El mito de El Dorado: Su génesis y proceso*, Caracas: BANH.

Sánchez Vidal, Agustín (1988a) *El cine de Carlos Saura*, Zaragoza: CAI.

—(1988b) An interview with Carlos Saura (unpublished).

Santo Job, El (1988) 'Tal cual', *ABC* (22 April), 86.

Saura, Carlos (1987) *El Dorado: Guión, fotogramas, documentos e historia de mi película*, Barcelona: Círculo de lectores.

—(1995) *¡Esa luz! (Guión cinematográfico)*, Huesca: Instituto de Estudios Altoaragoneses.

—(2000) *¡Esa luz!*, Barcelona: Galaxia Gutenberg/Círculo de Lectores.

Southey, Robert (2010) *La expedición de Ursúa y los crímenes de Aguirre*, with a prologue by Pere Gimferrer, trans. Soledad Martínez de Pinillos, Madrid: Ed. Reino de Redonda.

Vázquez, Francisco and Pedrarias de Almesto (1986) *Jornada de Omagua y Dorado: Crónica de Lope de Aguirre*, Madrid: Miraguano Ediciones.

Triviños, G. (1991) *Ramón J. Sender: Mito y contramito de Lope de Aguirre*, Zaragoza: Institución Fernando el Católico.

Zumalde, Ignacio (1963) *Lope de Aguirre descuartizado*, San Sebastián: Auñamendi.

5

El sol del membrillo/*The Quince Tree Sun* (Víctor Erice, 1992): moving pictures – painting, drawing and filmmaking

María José Martínez Jurico and Stephen G.H. Roberts

El sol del membrillo/*The Quince Tree Sun* follows the Spanish painter Antonio López (b. 1936) as he paints and then draws the quince tree growing in the garden of his Madrid studio during the autumn of 1990. It shows how López uses his painting to try to capture the autumn sun on the upper branches of the tree but is forced to renounce this project in late October due to the inclement weather. He then undertakes a drawing that lasts until the first fruit fall from the tree in early December. As he works on both the painting and the drawing, we also meet his wife and his lodger and see the artistic works that they are involved in; three Polish bricklayers who are working on the house that contains his studio; and a series of visitors, including his two daughters, the Chinese artist Fan Xiao Ming and her interpreter, and, above all, his old friend and fellow painter Enrique Gran, with whom Antonio López reminisces and discusses art. We also see images of the world that surrounds the studio: the railway lines, the skyscrapers and the blocks of flats dominated at night by the light of the television sets. The completion of the drawing leads into a sequence in which López recounts a dream that features rotting quinces, and the film ends with images of the renascent tree in the following spring.

Palacio, buen amigo,
¿está la primavera
vistiendo ya las ramas de los chopos
del río y los caminos? En la estepa
del alto Duero, Primavera tarda
¡pero es tan bella y dulce cuando llega! …

[…]

Con los primeros lirios
y las primeras rosas de las huertas,
en una tarde azul, sube al Espino,
al alto Espino donde está su tierra ...[1]

Antonio López, the artist at the centre of Víctor Erice's *The Quince Tree Sun*, said in one of the very few interviews he and the director have given together that he did not experience or view the film as a documentary. He called attention instead to just how *constructed* the film appeared to him, from the way it was staged and filmed to the way it was edited and assembled. It was more like a feature film, he suggested, a film that follows an artist as he paints and draws a quince tree in the garden of his studio in Madrid and that ends with the retelling of a dream.[2]

There is no doubt that the film does accompany a real and well-known artist through six months of his life and work, and Erice himself, in the same interview, went out of his way to emphasise the naturalness of the performances and of the dialogues, which were sometimes prompted but never scripted. He also stressed that the whole experience of making the film and of observing how the painter related to the quince tree had made it necessary for him to learn again how to look. Echoing López's point that it was the Impressionists who finally broke free from the tyranny of commissions and managed to create a private space for their art, Erice claimed that cinema is very gradually conquering a similar space for itself, one where the filmmaker is concerned more with the experience of observing reality than with the final product, the film itself. One has to have faith in reality and know how to wait, he claimed, since 'hay ciertas cosas que sabemos que están en la realidad pero la realidad no te las entrega si no sabes esperar y muchas veces si no sabes renunciar' [there are certain things that we know exist in reality but reality will not hand over to you if you do not know how to wait and often if you do not know how to renounce]. It was in the interests of waiting, observing and looking anew that the director decided to accompany the artist over those six months during the autumn of 1990 and the spring of 1991.

Antonio López himself experienced this 'accompaniment' as a form of violence, he told the interviewer, since, in order to observe him and what he himself was observing, the filmmaker and his crew had had to invade and violate the artist's space. The cameras had to be set up at specific angles to their subjects, framing them and isolating them from the rest of the world, and the boom microphones had to be strategically placed so as to record the sound that would accompany the images. Erice agreed with López, explaining that cinema, the offspring of a technological age, is a cruel and invasive medium that has no choice but to employ artifice in its attempt to reproduce reality. It was in recognition of this fact, he added, that he had decided to allow the camera to appear by itself towards the end of the film, when it is caught on screen recording the gradual putrefaction of the fallen quinces through the use of time-lapse photography.

And yet the position, posture and gaze of the camera that we see in these closing scenes quite deliberately echo those previously adopted by Antonio López himself as he painted and drew the quince tree. At one point in the film the artist tells his Chinese visitors, the artist Fan Xiao Ming and her interpreter, that his pleasure, his work, derives from being close to the tree, from accompanying it through all its changes. In order to achieve these things, however, as the film graphically shows, the painter also needs to make use of all the machinery of his art and to invade the space of his own chosen 'model'. For the first 14 minutes of *The Quince Tree Sun*, we watch him constructing his canvas, surrounding the tree with poles and stretching nylon thread horizontally and vertically between them, placing his easel at an angle to the tree, driving metal rods into the earth to fix the position of his feet, painting horizontal lines around the walls behind the tree, drawing horizontal and vertical lines on his canvas, preparing the paints on his palette, and then daubing white vertical lines on some of the leaves and on the trunk and branches of the tree. Only then, only when he is finally able to line up his eye with what he wishes to observe, only when he has measured out both his model and his canvas and used the laws of geometry to work out the exact relationship between the two, is he able to start the mysterious process of translating the tree from the language of nature into the language of art.

López's invasion of the tree's space and Erice's invasion of López's space reveal a central tension and paradox at the heart of all forms of art that set out to observe and capture reality: that the very acts of observation and capture are acts of invasion and violence that distance the artist and the filmmaker from the objects that are being observed and captured at the same time that they make that observation and that capture possible. This paradox is the paradox of *logos* itself, whereby knowledge of an object can only occur within and through the specific language that is allowing that knowledge to take place.[3] To accompany is to invade. To perceive is to affect the object of perception. To know is to denature. To represent is to transfer an object from its natural position into an artistic space, to transform it into a different object altogether.[4] López and Erice are busy recording their knowledge of the tree or of the artist and the tree, respectively, and that means no more and no less than that they are giving expression to that knowledge in and through the language of painting or the language of film. It is those particular forms of knowledge, limited though they may be, that slowly and patiently unfold in front of López, of Erice, of the spectator of the film. And, as they do so, they set up a profound and challenging dialogue between the artists and their respective art forms, encompassing not only painting and cinema but also drawing. Art forms which are quite discrete and yet related in subtle and complex ways.

This chapter sets out to examine that dialogue between painting, drawing and cinema. Many critics have considered certain aspects of that dialogue, looking especially at the relationship between the language of painting and the language of film.[5] But none has focused in detail on the fact that *The Quince Tree Sun* observes an artist first painting and then drawing the quince tree, the change of medium being seen more often than not simply as a response on the part of López and Erice to the poor autumn weather that made it impossible for the artist to continue with the painting. In their interview, by contrast, both men emphasised that the move from one medium to the other was not actually a failure or a defeat but simply a renunciation and 'una suerte de desenlace' [a sort of denouement]. The painting and the drawing are given similar weight and importance in *The Quince Tree Sun*, as is evidenced by the fact that the changeover from the one to the other occurs at almost exactly the mid-point, the temporal centre, of the film. And the way in which each is handled and presented implies that they are both parts of the same project, even if their specific aims and emphases vary. What we shall now do, therefore, is to consider the painting and the drawing in turn, identifying the specific aims of each and also the relationship of each with the art of cinema.

The painting

What Antonio López sets out to do on 30 September 1990 is to create a portrait of the quince tree in his garden. The tree is already there – surrounded by walls, by the house containing López's studio, by his wife, his lodger and the Polish workers, all getting on with their own work, by the houses and flats of northern Madrid, by the more distant railway station and skyscrapers – but the artist needs to appropriate it, to capture it, to transform it into something else. What we are about to see is the magic of representation, as Antonio López starts to re-create the tree in a different form, one that may even outlast the tree itself. To do this, to be as exact as possible in his representation, he surrounds the tree with the paraphernalia of his art. He will now be able to establish the angle of his relation-ship with the tree, and then frame it and scale it down so that trunk, branches and leaves can be transformed into two-dimensional shapes made of oil paint that can fit on the canvas. The artist will use delicate and broad brushstrokes both to fix outlines and to shade them in, giving a sense of colour, texture, proportion and depth.

But the artist quickly decides that his painting should pursue a particular effect. Antonio López's work has often been referred to as hyperrealist,[6] as his paintings of people, rooms, nature or cityscapes are characterised by an extreme, almost obsessive, attention to detail. One of the best known of these, *Gran Vía* (1974–81), depicts the traffic lanes and buildings of the usually busy Madrid thoroughfare at an indeterminate time of day, perhaps dawn, and does so without any sign of life: cars, buses or passers-by. The painting was executed over many days, months and years, and provides a finely honed view of a living but seemingly deserted corner of the centre of the city.

Shortly after starting his painting of the quince tree, López decides that he will take a similar approach to this new portrait. On 1 October, just 24 hours after setting up his canvas, he tells his wife, Mari, that the tree is particularly beautiful during the one or two hours in the morning when the upper branches and fruit are bathed in the golden light of the autumn sun. The sun returns to illuminate the tree for a short period in the afternoon too, but the light is not so golden then. 'Tengo que pintar el sol ... Yo creo que lo debo pintar con sol' [I have to paint the sun ... I feel I must paint it with sun], he declares. And that is what he will set out to do. Over the following three weeks, from 1 to 23 October, Antonio López will attempt to catch the autumn sun on the quince tree at a particular time of day, with the camera filming him at work on five of these days and returning on a further six days to capture the changing shape of the painting.

The undertaking therefore involves the control of light. The control of light is essential for all painting, although for some artists this matter seems to become an explicit and conscious challenge and theme. Over the course of filming, Víctor Erice captured Antonio López and his painter-friend Enrique Gran standing in front of and discussing reproductions of just two works of art, Michelangelo's *Last Judgement* (1537–41) and Velázquez's *Las Meninas* (1656), with only the former discussion making it into the final cut.[7] Although the two painters' discussions are mainly thematic – Michelangelo's brooding, heavy sense of good and evil and Velázquez's enigmatic relationship with his sitters –, there is no doubt that the film is also aware of the formal relevance and significance of both these works. In the case of the *Last Judgement*, the initial close-up on the upper central part of the fresco, with the upright figures of Christ and the Virgin surrounded both above and to the sides by the figures of the saved, offers a striking formal echo of the shape of the tree on López's canvas, with the vertical trunk surrounded by the branches, leaves and fruit.

As for *Las Meninas*, the unspoken theme is that of light, indirectly introduced into their discussion through the painters' interest in the size of the canvas and the existence of a seemingly unfinished dark strip at its very top. In reality, Velázquez's masterpiece can be seen to be a meditation on light: its source, its effects, and its relationship with colour and with shade. The painting itself suggests that the main source of light are the unseen windows to the right, which bring in the daylight that illuminates the main sitters in the foreground and places the figures in the midground – the painter himself and the chaperone, Doña Marcela de Ulloa, and her unidentified companion – in a respectful place somewhere between the light and the shadows.[8] But the eye of the spectator is constantly drawn to the other source of light, the open doorway that lies just off-centre in the background of the painting. This doorway, a source of fascination for Picasso, who gave it great prominence in most of the reworkings of *Las Meninas* that he carried out in the autumn of 1957,[9] sends a shaft of light across the floor and directly towards the figure of Velázquez himself, who is standing,

9. Antonio López, with the tree and his painting.

10. The detail of Michelangelo's *Last Judgement* that introduces López's and Gran's discussion.

paintbrush in hand, in front of his huge canvas. The figure who stands in the doorway, José Nieto, the Queen's Chamberlain, holds open a curtain, thereby allowing the light to flood towards Velázquez, and it is tempting to see him responding to the artist's needs and controlling the flow of light into the room. That room, as a result, becomes a huge camera obscura, almost a camera *avant la lettre*, where the sudden influx of light has allowed Velázquez to illuminate and capture an instant in the life of the Spanish Court.

While Velázquez was controlling the light in a closed and confined space, Antonio López is attempting to do the same thing out of doors. He waits each day for the same moment, the same sun, the same light and the same effects to appear, so that he can continue the task of capturing and recording a particular moment in the life of the tree. As with all portraits, therefore, his painting will offer us the tree at a particular moment that is not in fact single and unique, as would be the case with a photograph, but is rather made up of and forged out of many similar moments. The artist enriches the painting day by day, adding layer after layer to it, refining its representation of the quince tree under the autumn sun. The result will be a tree that exists in an ideal present moment composed of many present moments; the painting will give expression to a deep and layered present that will transform the tree into a symbolic and yet still real and fleeting presence.[10]

Antonio López's painting will present us with a smoothed, limned, layered moment made out of many different moments. But it is only cinema that reveals this fact fully to us. By filming day by day, cinema allows these many moments to be recorded and renders them visible to us. What the film does is to uncover the layers of the final painting, to show the process by which that painting has come into being. The work that is finally put away on 24 October – and, indeed, each separate moment or stage of it that we have witnessed on six separate occasions

Martes 23 de Octubre

11. The final version of Antonio López's painting of the quince tree.

over the previous three weeks – is like a single still image, and *The Quince Tree Sun* not only records those stills but puts them back into the rich context of the particular moments that produced them, a context that includes the changing weather, visiting friends and family, the sounds of the radio, of church bells, of trains and planes, and the surrounding world of flats, streets and urban life. Everything that exists as no more than a suggestion in the final version of the painting is unravelled and revealed to us as a sequence of events; the film uncovers the duration and the sequentiality of the painting.

Each version or moment of the painting acts like a single still image. Film itself, of course, is made up of 24 frames per second, 24 still images that succeed each other to create the illusion of change and movement. At certain moments, *The Quince Tree Sun* seems deliberately to contrast the vertiginous succession of images in cinema with the slow succession of the images that will, together and in layers, make up the painting. On three separate occasions, on 8 and 9 October, 12 and 15 October and 18 and 23 October, it allows a close-up of the painting as it was on the first of each of these pairs of days to dissolve gradually into a close-up of the painting on the second of each pair of days, in what appears to be a slow-motion demonstration of the way in which the fundamental building blocks of film work together. But these moments are not designed to imply that cinema is in any way superior to painting. If anything, Erice seems to be suggesting here that witnessing the process by which Antonio López went about capturing the tree on his canvas has allowed him to slow down the filmmaking process itself and taught him, as he puts it, to wait, to be patient and to see anew. For both men, it is the process of looking, and the knowledge that derives from that process, that has come to the fore; and the process of looking at López's way of working seems to have confirmed Erice's belief in a cinema that has more to do with slow and careful observation than with a final product.

The drawing

In the end, of course, it is the poor weather – the torrential rain and the lack of any sun on the quince tree – that causes Antonio López to renounce the painting and to store it away in the basement of his studio on 25 October. But, as both men made clear in their interview, that renunciation was by no means a failure or a defeat; rather, it marks the start of another moment in the same project.

This time, however, the medium will be different and, just as we witnessed López preparing his canvas in readiness for the painting at the beginning of the film, we now see him and Mari, almost exactly half way through the film, preparing the paper on which he will execute his drawing of the tree, gluing it to a stiff board and leaving weights on top in order to prevent the paper from buckling. On 26 October, Antonio López starts the drawing. The easel is in exactly the same position it had occupied for the painting, the artist's feet are placed up against the same metal rods in the earth, López has once again drawn vertical and horizontal lines across the centre of his paper, and he also continues to use the daubs of paint that he has applied to the tree to measure his gaze, adding many more as the days go by.

The instruments and measuring techniques are the same but the medium is different. When he meets his Chinese guests, López explains that he can no longer aim to capture the light in the same way as he had done in the painting, since drawing is in that sense a more limited medium: 'Se trata únicamente de reflejar el límite de las formas y a través del límite de las formas representar el árbol' [It's just a matter of reflecting the limit of the forms and, through the limit of the forms, represent the tree]. He holds a pencil with at least two centimetres of the lead exposed and uses the sharpened point to 'reflect the limit of the forms', that is, to fix the outlines of the trunk, the branches, the leaves and the fruit. But he also uses the sides of the exposed lead to shade in and around the forms, producing as he does so a vivid sense not only of depth but also of the different textures of the objects that make up the tree. There is no doubt, too, that the shading suggests that some of the leaves and fruit are more exposed to the light than others.

With the change of medium, though, has come a change in the nature of Antonio López's project. His aim now is not to capture one particular moment in the life of the tree, the moment when the autumn sun hits its crown, but rather to capture the changes that the tree is going through as autumn gradually

12. Antonio López working on his drawing of the quince tree.

turns into winter. He explains this once again to his Chinese visitors, who ask him about the nylon thread that he has hung around the tree and the marks that he has made and continues to make on the leaves and the fruit. López answers by referring first to his love of symmetry and to his desire to centre the tree on the paper and thereby treat it with the same solemnity with which he would treat a human sitter. Then he adds that the multiple horizontal marks on many of the fruit hanging on the tree reveal that the quinces are slowly getting heavier and moving earthwards – some five centimetres or so over the month since he started to paint and then to draw the tree. 'Voy corrigiendo, voy corrigiendo', he explains, 'voy acompañando el árbol. Siempre, siempre voy paralelo al desarrollo del árbol' [I keep on correcting, keep on correcting, keep on accompanying the tree. I always, always, keep parallel to the development of the tree].

López's striking claim is borne out by the film itself. Over the period between 26 October and 10 December, we see him drawing, rubbing out and drawing again, almost day by day, as he constantly adapts his work in order to capture the changing state of the tree. This means, in one sense, that the final version of the drawing that we see on 11 December contains within it, just like the painting before it, the invisible marks of the many different moments that make it up, moments that only remain because of the testimony of the film camera. But it also means that the processes involved in the drawing are much closer to the processes involved in filmmaking itself. In the first half of the film, Víctor Erice had adapted his filmmaking techniques so as better to follow and understand

Antonio López's painting techniques, above all the process of turning many different but similar moments into one deep and layered moment. Here, by contrast, Antonio López has moved into a medium whose workings clearly echo those of cinema, as it is perfectly suited to capture passing time and, at least in the way that López himself employs it, forever needs to move into the future, to change and evolve. Each moment in the drawing's history is a single and unrepeatable image that records its unique and fleeting moment in time and is then erased and replaced with the following, unrepeatable image. In this sense, it is like each successive frame in a film and, as in cinema, the succession of the images creates a sense of continuity that is reinforced in the case of the drawing by the fact that López, as Erice (cited in Arocena [1996: 302]) once made clear, does not completely rub out all his corrections, allowing some of the past marks to exist as actual physical traces in the drawing alongside the new ones, and thereby to act as a visible and visual reminder of the changes that have taken place. Víctor Erice uses the drawing in order to meditate upon both its and his own art's relationship with change and movement and the way in which each sets out to depict change and movement. At this stage in *The Quince Tree Sun*, therefore, the rhythm of the drawing comes to work in consonance with that of the film, creating a sense of synchrony, of direction, and also of open-endedness.

The coda

For Antonio López's drawing and Víctor Erice's film could in truth have gone on forever. *Nulla dies sine linea.*[11] In the end, it was the laws of nature that brought the drawing and ultimately the film to an end. The first fruit falls to the ground on 3 December and, by 10 December, the tree is surrounded by fallen quinces. It is at that moment that, Prospero-like, Antonio López breaks the thread that hangs between the poles, picks some of the quinces himself, takes the drawing inside, and then removes the poles and the easel, leaving the tree free once again. It has returned to its natural state, and the fruit can now be picked and consumed by family and friends.

And yet the drawing, which, by centring itself on the inexorable passing of time, has synchronised its rhythm and language with those of cinema, leads seamlessly into the last section of the film, which will be dominated by the recounting of Antonio López's dream. It is here that the film not only becomes more akin to a feature film, with staged and scripted scenes accompanied by music, but also reverts to a language that has been at the heart of cinema since its remotest origins, that is, the language of the unconscious. As if to signal this change in language, the preparatory scenes leading up to the dream include the shot of the camera that now stands alone and records the tree without the presence or guidance of either Antonio López or Víctor Erice. It is the camera, and not the artist or the filmmaker, that will now capture a series of separate images of the quinces over a period of days and weeks that, together – and in a way that directly echoes the process at the heart of López's drawing – will reveal the gradual putrefaction of the fruit, their own personal return to nature. And, just as we move from this sequence into the dream sequence proper, we are invited into the realm of the unconscious by a shot of the moon uncovered and then covered by clouds that directly recalls the opening of Luis Buñuel's dream-laden *Un Chien Andalou/An Andalusian Dog* (1928).

It is Antonio López himself who recounts his dream as a voice-over, accompanied by Pascal Gaigne's haunting music and by images of the artist's sleeping face, of the rotting quinces on the ground, and of the shadow of the lonely camera that is filming those quinces at night. The dream itself takes place in López's native village of Tomelloso and in the presence of his parents and other acquaintances. He sees quinces hanging from a tree, and it seems that only he realises that they are all rotting: 'Nadie parece advertir que todos los membrillos se están pudriendo bajo una luz que no sé cómo describir – nítida y a la vez sombría, que todo lo convierte en metal y ceniza. No es la luz de la noche; tampoco es la del crepúsculo ni la de la aurora' [No one seems to notice that all the quinces are rotting under a light that I don't know how to describe – sharp yet also dark and sombre, that transforms everything into metal and ash. It is not the light of the night; nor is it that of dusk or of dawn]. The dream appears to give visual, plastic and tactile form to an encounter with, perhaps a first revelation of, death, an encounter and a revelation that will forever after, the sequence implies, inform Antonio López's relationship with quince trees and may also help to explain his desire to bathe his own quince tree, not in the sharp yet sombre light of his existential dream, but rather in the golden and vital light of the autumn sun.[12] But what is most striking in this sequence is the interaction between word and image, between the story of Antonio López's dream and the film of the fallen quinces that is used to accompany or illustrate it. Those real, rotting quinces that we are shown are the same ones that the artist has captured in all their colourful plenitude in the painting and in all their changeful decadence in the drawing. The painting has removed them from the stream of time in order to make them inhabit an ideal present moment, while the drawing has immersed them once more in that unceasing stream. And it is the film that brings together both these movements, that gathers together the energies of both of Antonio López's artistic undertakings, by presenting us at the last with quinces that are, at one and the same time, filled with symbolic significance and yet fully and vulnerably real.

The coda to the film takes place several months later and shows us the scene in the early spring of 1991. We see the rotten quinces on the ground, still sporting some of Antonio López's white marks but now almost indistinguishable from the earth that surrounds them. And then we are shown the tree itself, full of the new, budding quinces shining in the sunlight. The artist can be heard humming in the background, perhaps planning new paintings. A sense of rebirth and new possibilities cannot hide the sense of loss, however, and the words 'A Paco Solórzano, in memoriam', a homage to Erice's recently deceased friend and fellow director, appear superimposed on the closing image of the tree. It seems entirely appropriate that a film that has engaged so directly with passing time, observing the painting's seeming ability to lift the tree out of time and the drawing's capacity to place it back into the flow of time, should, like the words from the elegy by Antonio Machado that opened this chapter, end with such a powerful and moving reminder of the contrast that exists between the repeated cycles of nature and the single cycle of an individual human life.

Notes

1 'Palacio, good friend, / is spring already dressing the branches of the black poplar trees / along the rivers and the roads? On the high plain / of the River Duero, spring takes its time / but is so beautiful and sweet when it arrives!... [...] With the first irises / and the first roses in the gardens, / on a blue evening, go up the Espino hill, / the high Espino where her land and her earth are found ...'. Fragments from Antonio Machado's poem 'A José María Palacio', from the collection *Campos de Castilla* (1912).

2 'Conversación Víctor Erice/Antonio López', an interview conducted by the actress Cayetana Guillén Cuervo for the programme *Versión Española*, was broadcast on TVE2 on 16 November 1999, and is reproduced on Disco 2: 'Material adicional', Erice (2004).

3 For an extended discussion of *logos* and of the philosophical implications of the film, see Martínez Jurico (1994).

4 In his 'Presentación', released at the same time as the film, Erice said that painters and filmmakers share the same impulse to 'reemplazar el mundo exterior por su doble' [replace the outer world with its double]. The text of the 'Presentación' is reproduced in the booklet that accompanies Erice (2004).

5 See, for example, Morgan (1993); Smith (1993); Arocena (1996: 275–331); Ehrlich (2000); Giavarini (2000); Saborit (2003: 10–14, 25–7, 85–95, 122–4); Moral (2004).

6 Erice himself questions this term, since, he claims, López, unlike most hyperrealists, does not work from photographs. The director prefers the term 'new realism' to refer to his friend's style of painting (see Arocena [1996: 283]).

7 The discarded footage of the discussion on *Las Meninas* can be found on Disco 2: 'Material adicional', Erice (2004).

8 On the identities of the sitters and the significance of the composition, see Brown (2007).

9 These reworkings are displayed in the Museo Picasso in Barcelona. Reproductions can be found in Rafart Planas (2001).

10 To use Erice's own words, López's painting will provide us with not so much a *testimony* as a *revelation* of reality. See 'Cómo surgió *El sol del membrillo*', reproduced in the booklet accompanying Erice (2004: 12).

11 Antonio López once said that no one, not even the artist, can ever be sure if a work of art is finished or not: 'Es una aventura, como un camino por el que no puedes continuar y te paras' [It's an adventure, like a path along which you can no longer continue and you stop]; cited in Calderón (2008: 14).

12 Víctor Erice also made clear, in his interview with Cayetana Guillén Cuervo (Erice 2004), that Antonio López's dream was one of the main factors that inspired him to make *The Quince Tree Sun*.

Bibliography

Arocena, Carmen (1996) *Víctor Erice*, Madrid: Cátedra. Signo e Imagen/Cineastas.

Brown, Jonathan (2007) 'Sobre el significado de "Las Meninas"', in Svetlana Alpers *et al.*, *Otras Meninas*, Madrid: Ediciones Siruela, 67–91.

Calderón, Manuel (2008) 'Entrevista con Antonio López: "Soy una excepción en el arte español"', *La Razón* (13 April), 14–15.

Ehrlich, Linda C. (ed.) (2000) *An Open Window: The Cinema of Víctor Erice*, Lanham, MD, and London: Scarecrow Press.

—(2000) 'Víctor Erice's *Dream of Light* and the *Bodegón* Tradition', in Ehrlich (ed.), 192–205.

Erice, Víctor (2004) *El sol del membrillo (1992). Edición coleccionista*, Rosebud Films DVD, CAMM CINCO.

Giavarini, Lawrence (2000) 'Projected Shadow (Ombre portée)', in Ehrlich (ed.), 188–91.

Martínez Jurico, María José (1994) *Art as a Process: Víctor Erice, Antonio López and 'The Sun on the Quince Tree'*, dissertation, West Surrey College of Art and Design (Farnham).

Moral, Javier (2004) 'Mostrar o dejar ver: *Le mystère Picasso* frente a *El sol del membrillo*', *Archivos de la Filmoteca*, 47 (June), 143–57.

Morgan, Rikki (1993) 'Víctor Erice: Painting the Sun', *Sight & Sound*, 3:4 (April), 26–9.

Rafart Planas, Claustre (2001) *Las Meninas de Picasso*, Barcelona: Editorial Meteora.

Saborit, José (2003) *Guía para ver y analizar: 'El sol del membrillo'*, Barcelona: Ediciones Octaedro.

Smith, Paul Julian (1993) 'Whispers and Rapture', *Sight & Sound*, 3:4 (April), 28–9.

6

Vacas/Cows (Julio Medem, 1992): from Goya's dining room via *Apocalypse Now*

Jo Evans

Vacas/Cows follows the development of a feud between two families who live on a Basque hillside separated by a mysterious forest. The film is divided into sections with on-screen headings. In the first, 'El aizkolari cobarde' [The cowardly woodcutter] (1875), the theme of the blood feud is established symbolically when the 'cowardly' Manuel Irigibel daubs his face with the blood of his dying neighbour, Carmelo Mendiluze, to fake his own death and escape the trenches of the Third Carlist War. Manuel is thrown onto a cart full of dead Carlists, and his subsequent escape is observed by the mysterious cow that will reappear at various points during the narrative. The second section, 'Las hachas' [The axes], opens in spring 1905. Manuel is now an old man, who paints cows obsessively and makes traps for wild boar. He shares the house in the valley with his son Ignacio, Ignacio's wife Madalem, and their three daughters. Juan, the son of their dead neighbour Carmelo, lives in the house on the hill with his mother and sister. The rivalry between the families continues in the local tradition of wood-chopping competitions. Ignacio becomes the local champion and begins an affair with Juan's sister, Catalina. In the ten-year gap between this and the next section, 'El agujero encendido' [The burning hole] (spring 1915), their illegitimate son, Peru, has formed a close friendship with his half-sister, Cristina and his grandfather, Manuel. All three have become attached to a hollow tree stump in the forest that Manuel credits with supernatural powers. Peru's uncle Juan is increasingly disturbed by Ignacio's relationship with Catalina, and the couple decide to emigrate to the USA, taking Peru with them. Manuel has died by the beginning of the final section, 'Guerra en el bosque' [War in the forest] (1936), when Peru, who has become a press photographer, returns to the valley to cover the Spanish Civil War. He and his half-sister Cristina become caught up in fighting in the forest. Peru is captured, but he is saved from a firing squad by his Uncle Juan. He returns to the forest to look for Cristina, and in the enigmatic concluding sequence the half-siblings take a horse belonging to a dead Nationalist soldier and ride off towards France. As they leave, cinematography appears to contradict the concluding words, 'Estamos llegando' [We're getting there] with a slow zoom back into the hollow tree trunk and fade to black.[1]

El peor fascismo es el interno … . Por eso en la película no se ve nunca al enemigo, éste casi no existe, porque lo que me interesaba era la tensión entre los propios vascos.

[The worst form of fascism is internal … . That's why in the film you never see the enemy, it barely exists, because what interested me was tension between the Basques themselves.] (Medem, cited in Heredero 1997: 570)

Vacas was released in 1992, to mixed critical response. While some welcomed the film's complex visual symbolism, others responded more cautiously to the self-reflexive cinematography, the enigmatic title, the cyclical narrative structure, and the fact that the same actors play different members of the feuding families. In spite of this, *Vacas* went on to win numerous awards including the Goya for 'Best New Director', and it is now regarded as one of the most important films released in Spain during the 1990s (de Ros 1997; Stone 2007: 51; Evans 2009). The work of this 'cinéaste of subjectivity' (Smith, 1999: 11) has continued to divide critics, and the discussion that follows uses Goya's paintings, *Saturn* and *Leocadia*, and Coppola's *Apocalypse Now* (1979/2001) to re-examine two of the more confusing aspects of this film: the self-reflexive cinematography that is epitomised by the zoom through the cow's eye, and the reappearance of the same male actors in different generations. This intertextual rereading should also shed light on Medem's controversial comment that I am using as an epigraph: that the 'worst form of fascism is internal'.

There are two reasons for proposing that *Vacas* might usefully be reread via Goya and Coppola. In relation to Medem's comment about internal fascism, it is striking that all three of these artists/directors represent violence as a process of symbolic self-destruction, or self-consumption. In Goya's painting, Saturn is consuming one of his sons; in *Vacas* paternal/filial self-consumption is indicated in the reappearance of the same actors, and the extraordinary final sequences of *Apocalypse Now* show that Willard (Martin Sheen) has been consumed, symbolically, by Kurtz (Marlon Brando). The second reason for comparing these texts is that all three offer useful insight into the role of gender in iconic representations of violence.

Vacas and *Apocalypse Now*: 'Horror has a face and you must make a friend of horror'

A number of important studies have already established the link between gender and violence in *Vacas*,[2] and Medem's rich symbolism has also encouraged critics to seek out a range of visual intertexts. Medem has acknowledged the influence of Goya on the opening and closing sequences of the film,[3] and connections have also been made to painters like Picasso, El Greco and Zuloaga (Cerdán 1997: 921–3). The black humour that is epitomised by the zoom through the cow's eye has been linked to the aesthetic tradition of the *esperpento* (Ramón del Valle-Inclán's aesthetic of grotesque tragicomedy). This role of black humour provides further intertextual links with Goya, as well as with Spanish filmmakers such as Luis García Berlanga, Pedro Almodóvar and Álex de la Iglesia. Medem's work has also been compared with that of directors like Buñuel (again, because of the dramatic significance of the close-up of the cow's eye), as well as Resnais, Bergman, Kieślowski and Lynch (Cerdán 1997; Martínez Expósito 2004; Stone 2007). Rob Stone has provided the most detailed intertextual account of *Vacas* to date. He examines the influence of Surrealism, Romanticism and Magic Realism (2007: 40–5), and suggests parallels with other films whose protagonists are 'bullied by expectations of masculinity' and that focus 'on the forging of a modern national identity during warfare' (2007: 44–5). However, despite the close attention Stone pays to the construction of masculinity in the context of war, no one has to my knowledge so far examined intertextual links with *Apocalypse Now*.

There are a number of potential points of comparison: the sound of the buzzing fly that disturbs Kurtz during his famous 'hollow men' speech could be compared with the repeated and amplified use of the same sound in *Vacas*; the lines Kurtz is quoting, from T.S. Eliot's 'The Hollow Men' (1925) ('We are the hollow men / We are the stuffed men / Leaning together / Headpiece filled with straw') could be compared with the enigmatic straw figures Manuel creates in the forest to kill wild boar. There is also the symbolic use of cows in both films (and, of course, in Medem's title): both *Vacas* and *Apocalypse Now* include the ritual sacrifice of a cow that in Coppola's film is surely a homage to Eisenstein's *Strike* (1924).[4]

All these points of comparison would provide an interesting focus for intertextual readings, but the one I want to concentrate on here is the striking similarity between the close-up of Manuel's face raised to look up at the white cow, and Willard's face, raised to look up at Kurtz. Willard's camouflaged face accentuates his wide, staring eyes in the same way that Carmelo's blood accentuates Manuel's. Like Manuel, Willard's face is framed as if in supplication: it is daubed with camouflage, raised, and in close-up, but it is cross-cut to show that the 'other' who returns Willard's gaze and who will define him from this point

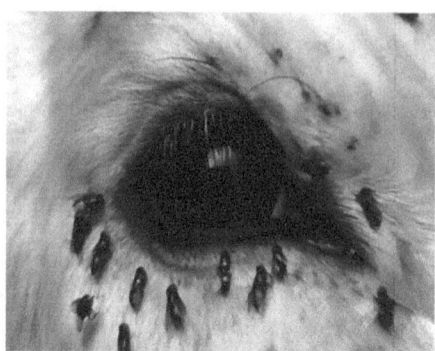

13. The Metonymical Cow's Eye, or first incarnation of the peripheral female gaze
in *Vacas*.

onwards is the terrifying, and terrifyingly similar, face of his victim and nemesis, Kurtz. And these contrasts and comparisons could be extended. In *Apocalypse Now*, this sequence marks the prelude to the climactic destruction of Kurtz that is cross-cut with footage showing the violent ritual slaughter of the caribou. In *Vacas* it is the prelude, on the contrary, to what appears to be the miraculous survival of the white cow that will reappear at various points over the 51 years of the film's narrative.

These sequences are vital to both narratives and I shall return to them below, but as my reading is influenced by psychoanalysis it is worth reminding ourselves of the importance of point of view and the representation of the psychoanalytical 'other' to Medem's filmmaking (Gabilondo 2002). Medem would probably regard Víctor Erice as his most important intertextual precursor. He describes wanting to emulate the 'womb-like' gaps of Erice's narrative ellipses (Heredero 1997: 554), and this emphasis on meanings reproduced in symbolic gaps signals the importance, for Medem, of psychoanalysis and surrealism (Heredero 1997: 553; Stone 2007: 40). Medem's psychoanalytical influence is Freudian rather than Lacanian, and I am reliably informed that Medem has not read Lacan,[5] but the editing of *Vacas* clearly indicates that he shares with the French psychoanalyst an understanding that human consciousness is a process of *méconnaissance*, and that human perception is limited to the elusive meanings that can be deduced from gaps that represent what Lacan calls the gaze. This space, or 'gaze' that we cannot see but that defines our identity is represented from the outset in *Vacas* by the zoom through the cow's eye: a zoom that establishes Manuel's symbolic 'rebirth' as a coward then moves the narrative 30 years into the future to confirm that he has become a mildly deranged old man obsessed with painting cows.[6]

As this sequence is so fundamental to the connection I am making here with *Apocalypse Now*, it is worth describing the similarities between the two films in some detail. Both begin with shots that emphasise the horror of war in the context of the natural landscape. Medem's iconic Basque woodcutter (Carmelo Gómez) is shown chopping a felled tree against the green backdrop of the forest. The only sound heard initially is the amplified noise of the axe slicing through the air. Alberto Iglesias's score then incorporates this chopping sound into the melancholic theme tune as the location moves to the Carlist trenches. The first shot is dominated by the close-up of a dead cow's head and a jawbone. The focus then widens to contrast the smoke rising from the trenches with the calm, green, Basque mountain ranges. The sequence that follows establishes the rivalry between Manuel and Carmelo. Extreme close-ups of Manuel's clenched and trembling hands show us that he is terrified, while Carmelo is calm. When the shooting begins, Carmelo puts his arms around Manuel to steady his trembling hands and arms, but Carmelo is shot in the neck and the two rivals are then framed in medium close-up, lying in the trenches, as Manuel puts his fingers to the blood pulsing from Carmelo's jugular and daubs it over his own face.

Coppola's film[7] opens with a static long shot of the dense green foliage of palm trees. The sound of helicopter rotors can be heard. Surreal fragments of helicopters can be seen, enhancing the aural impact of helicopters 'chopping' through the air, and almost immediately the sinisterly melancholic opening bars of the Doors' song, 'The End' are heard. At the first line, 'This is the end', the palm trees burst (silently) into orange flames. The camera tracks right and smoke fills the screen. Helicopters can now be seen flying in front of the burning palms. Willard's face, upside down and in close-up, is then superimposed over the left-hand side of the screen and, momentarily, the iconic stone mask that will come to symbolise his encounter with Kurtz matches Willard's ghostly face on the right-hand side of the screen. This stone mask is the counterpoint to the cow's eye in the Medem film. It establishes Willard's relationship to the 'other' who will define him in a similar, but also, I argue, crucially different way. And it is the crucial difference in the way these two films represent the 'other' that makes Coppola's film an iconic representation of the 'horror' of war and Medem's an enigmatic, blackly humorous exposition of the psychoanalytical processes that reproduce this kind of horror.

Coppola's opening establishes that Willard is already suffering from what we would now call post-traumatic stress. The sound of the helicopter rotors is echoed visually in the fan spinning on the ceiling as the focus moves to the bedroom where we see Willard as a man fatally divided: when he is in the jungle he wants to be at home, and when he is at home he wants to be in the jungle. The one point of visual calm in the room is the black-and-white photograph of a smiling young woman, but Willard's noir-esque voiceover tells us they have separated: 'I hardly said a word to my wife until I said "yes" to a divorce.' The opening sutures us with Willard (we can only sympathise with a man so trau-matised and so divided from this smiling woman he once loved). This opening also establishes the perverse attractions of war ('Saigon, shit, I'm still only in Saigon. Every time I think I'm gonna wake up back in the jungle'). The Doors' song begins again and Willard starts to move, performing drunken martial arts manoeuvres against invisible 'Charlie'. Clenching his fist towards the camera, a reverse shot shows that we were looking at him from the point of view of a full-length mirror. Willard punches the mirror, cuts his hand, rolls across the blood-spattered white sheets on the bed, collapses, rubs his hands together, then spreads his own blood slowly over his face.

Both these (anti-)war films open with the image of their traumatised protagonists camouflaging their own faces with blood: Manuel with Carmelo's, Willard with his own. There are no women in the opening of *Vacas*, but there is a symbolic female presence that has the effect of distancing us from Medem's critical representation of Basque masculinity. Santaolalla (1999) and others have noted the vaginal symbolism of the felled log that the iconic woodcutter is chopping into, as well as the hollow log to which the film narrative compulsively returns, and Carmelo's reference to his wife in this opening sequence is violently dismissive: 'Esa bruja ha parido un chaval' [That witch has had a son]. In *Apocalypse Now*, on the other hand, the black-and-white photograph of the wife in medium close-up does not distance, but draws us closer to Willard. The similarities and differences in these openings also draw attention to the differences in narrative development: *Vacas* begins with an image of mythical Basque masculinity that the spiralling narrative and the return of the male actors will gradually deconstruct. *Apocalypse Now* opens with a dramatic shot in close-up of the upside-down face of a fatally divided man who will gradually become subsumed by the myth of Kurtz. This close-up of Willard's face is, of course, also a prelude to Brando's famous 'horror' speech: 'Horror has a face and you must make a friend of horror. Horror and mortal terror are your friends, if they are not, they are enemies to be feared.'

The 1979 version of *Apocalypse Now* is iconic in its depiction of the 'horror' of men consumed by territorial violence. However, the 2001 *Redux* version includes 49 extra minutes, the most extended sequence of which involves the romantic encounter between Willard and the French widow at the plantation. This version divided critics, and I tend to agree with those who did not feel it improved on the original. The power of both lies in the gradual and horrific fusion of Willard and Kurtz that is symbolised in the close-up shots of camouflaged faces and the stone icon. In the original, the only memorable sequence involving women was the attack on the bunny girls that establishes the perverse attraction to violence that is also contained in Kilgore (Robert Duvall)'s infamous napalm speech. In the *Redux* version the extended, 'wordy' episode at the French plantation reiterates the perverse attractions of war, but adds nothing useful. The ghostly French widow, shrouded by a mosquito net, explains to Willard that he is divided ('one of you loves, one of you kills'), but her words are banal in the context of the extraordinary formal complexity of the original exposition of this divided man, and this distracting footage reminds us that women are redundant to iconic representations of conflict as 'internal fascism', because their presence threatens to detract from the intensity of the symbolic 'horror' of men consuming men.

Vacas, *Saturn* and *Leocadia*: black humour and peripheral Jocastas

The second iconic intertext I want to consider is Goya's *Saturn* (1821–23). Like Coppola's film, this painting has also been permanently altered by its repositioning in relation to a woman. *Saturn* used to hang alone on the walls of the Prado until the decision was taken to re-hang all the disturbing, so-called 'Black Paintings' that Goya produced towards the end of his life according to what is known of their original layout. A visitor's note tells us that *Saturn* was painted on the wall of Goya's dining room opposite a portrait of Leocadia, the woman who was Goya's housekeeper, and who may have been his lover. The experience of standing in the gap between these two paintings for the first time is striking. This painting of Saturn is, of course, identical to the one that used to hang alone, but the presence of Leocadia changes the iconography, and the iconicity of Saturn. His infamous violence becomes more *esperpento*, more blackly comical in the context of her domestic charm and mildly ironic gaze. Foucault (1966) famously read into the presence of Velázquez in *Las Meninas* the representation of a certain reciprocity in the act of looking (at a painting, or a film, or a work of art). For Foucault, the presence of Velázquez in his own court portrait highlights the infinite slip that exists between word and image, representation and object. And what I am proposing here is that something about a certain reciprocity in the representation of women and 'horror', with a similar scope for slippage, can be read in the gap between these two paintings by Goya and the two versions of *Apocalypse Now*. *Saturn*'s iconic status is reduced by the gaze of *La Leocadia* (1821–23), and it is this 'reduction' in his status that is so relevant to the *mise en scène* of war in *Vacas* and to Medem's statement that he wanted, in this film, to show that 'the worst form of fascism is internal'.

The four 'chapters' in *Vacas* have on-screen headings with dates that are significant to the portrayal of war, but this 'wordy' chronological signposting is disrupted by a *mise en scène* that privileges the visual and accentuates the role of the unconscious. The film is 'casi muda' [almost silent] (Medem, in Angulo and Rebordinos 2004: 215), and the silence adds to the dreamlike spread of the imaginary. Fragments of dialogue are repeated by different characters (White 1999: 10), and words recur in threefold repetitions. The first and most significant of these is the line: 'I'm not dead', which is uttered three times by Carmelo in the opening sequence analysed earlier. This is a form of disavowal (he is not dead yet, but he is dying) and it could be regarded as a metonym for the film's representation of human ontology as a cyclical process of disavowal and projection whose uncanny repetitions reproduce violent conflict.

Chion (1999) uses the term the *acousmêtre* to describe the effects of sound-track and dialogue in film as an aural entity produced in the sounds, silences, projections and disavowals of a film's acoustic rhythm. Like the effect of the helicopters, The Doors' song, and voiceover in the opening of *Apocalypse Now*, the soundtrack in *Vacas* creates the impression of a particularly spectral 'acousmetric body', and it is one that reinforces the representation of masculinity trapped by cyclical wars. The enigmatic sound of Iglesias's score and the repeated sound of the axe chopping wood are echoed, as the film progresses, in the visual repetition of unexplained shots of Manuel's straw figures and the hollow tree trunk in the forest that separates the rival family homes. Although both Medem and Coppola represent violence as inescapable, unlike *Apocalypse Now*, in which the *acousmêtre* sutures us with the characters into the increasingly claustrophobic narrative momentum, these unexplained aural and visual repetitions help to distance us. They reinforce the oneiric tone of Medem's spiralling narrative that is extended in the return of the same three male actors in the roles of sons and grandson.

The reappearance of these actors in different roles emphasises the impression conveyed by the film's ghostly *acousmêtre* that the only thing fixed about human identity is the process of disavowal, or *méconnaissance*, necessary to maintain the illusion of an essential self. The actors recur in subsequent generations like eruptions from a kind of temporal unconscious, and it is a satisfying irony that the uncanny nature of their return is conveyed in their 'familiarity'. For Freud the uncanny is 'something that was once familiar and then repressed' that has become associated with a ghostly sense of 'the return of the dead' (2003: 153). Freud suggests that the artist can use the uncanny to

> intensify and multiply this effect far beyond what is feasible in normal experience; in his stories he can make things happen that one would never, or only rarely, experience in real life. In a sense, then he betrays us to a superstition we thought we had 'surmounted'; he tricks us by promising everyday reality and then going beyond it. We react to his fictions as if they had been our own experiences. By the time we become aware of the trickery, it is too late: the writer has already done what he set out to do. (2003: 157)

In Medem's fiction, the familiar actor becomes 'unfamiliar' in his return as the son, highlighting, self-reflexively, the role of disavowal in film-viewing. Despite what we know about actors (which is that they act), we are 'tricked' by the return of the same person as a different character. For the first-time viewer, it produces what Lacan would call an effect of 'anamorphosis', a visual slip in the field of perception that reveals the wider (unknowable) field of the gaze (1991: 79–90). This is a deliberate slip. The uncanny returns of actors Carmelo Gómez, Kándido

Uranga and Karra Elejalde are the visual exposition of Medem's comment that 'the worst form of fascism is internal'. Like Goya's *Saturn*, they conjure up the notion of men consumed by their fathers in a process of symbolic Oedipal and generational recycling. And if Medem's self-consuming men recall Saturn, his peripheral women recall Leocadia.

Vacas re-enacts this ongoing patriarchal struggle in the context of a peripheral female gaze and, between them, Medem's female characters reflect the enigmatic expression of Leocadia in Goya's painting. Leocadia could be described as looking flirtatious or resigned, depending on your point of view, and Medem's women are similarly split between the flirtatious (the unmarried Catalina) and the resigned (the married Madalem). Characterisation in *Vacas* is reinforced by exchanged glances and dissolves, and the most memorable of the sexually charged glances is exchanged between Catalina and Ignacio. Ignacio is returning, triumphant, from a wood-chopping competition and their (shot/reverse) shared gaze ruffles Catalina's hair and reconstructs her as a pagan goddess of fertility, holding an enormous piece of wood (see de Ros 1997: 232). This construction of Catalina invokes (comically) the gap that stimulates what psychoanalysis calls the scopic drive: a gap that is caught between 'the eye and the gaze ... the split in which the drive is manifested at the level of the scopic field' (Lacan 1991: 73). This sequence also links sexual desire to the notion of a gap caught between 'the eye and the gaze' with the cutaway to the scythe-wielding straw figure that functions as a slowly spinning symbol of death. Catalina's reconstruction in the overloaded zoom that ruffles her hair frames her as a product in Ignacio's (rather partial) gaze. Holding her enormous log, she could be read as a caricature of Lacan's view of woman's relationship to the symbolic phallus (2006), or as a particularly humorous illustration of the fact that we perceive our 'others' from our own limited perspective (in this case, the vision of an object of desire in the eyes of a champion woodcutter).

Magdalena's character is also portrayed in shot/reverse exchanged glances. As the cuckolded wife, her glances express resignation and suppressed rage, and her position in the symbolic order is revealed most clearly in the staging of a photographic *mise en abîme*: the family portrait Manuel takes with his stolen camera. Madalem initially stands near Ignacio, her head dangerously close to the underside of his raised axe. Manuel (as if conscious that her symbolic position in this patriarchal family order is so perilous) asks her to move over and stand next to the family cow. For Medem, the cow's-eye metonym for point of view that is reflected in iris shots of Manuel (looking through his camera and insisting it is 'very important' to look at the small things) has a symbolic value, but it also has a touch of *esperpento*. It is a bit of a black joke (Medem, in Angulo and Rebordinos 2004: 199). As in his other films, these cod-Freudian jokes (about men, fallen logs and axes) overlay more serious insight into Lacanian lack and the struggle to control point of view in the Oedipal battlefield of the gaze. There is comic value in the representation of the two women (Catalina on the haystack and Madalem moving over to stand next to the cow), but there is also a serious side to Medem's irony.

Medem has noted that the theme of 'looking' represents Manuel's guilt and the need to 'look harder' (Angulo and Rebordinos 2004: 199). Manuel's photographs represent his attempt to interrogate the field of the 'gaze'. The iris shots of insects and wildlife highlight, within the wider symbolic Basque order, the value of the 'small things' that, like women and cowards, are sidelined. And yet at the same time, the iris shot of Manuel's eye recalls the Lacanian warning that

> the eye is only the metaphor of something that I would prefer to call the seer's 'shoot' (pousse) – something prior to the eye … . I see only from one point, but in my existence I am looked at from all sides. (1991: 72)

Manuel's focus on the small things only magnifies the 'seer's "shoot"', reminding us of the vastness of the field of the gaze. The stolen camera gives him a certain agency, but the extreme close-up of his eye trapped in an iris shot reminds us that he is himself still sidelined along with the women. So that, although Beck is right to remind us that *Vacas* functions as a 'critique of the male-centered "gaze"' (2000: 159), the film also reminds us that we are always confined by our partial and gendered visions, and that there is in fact no space outside from which to reflect a different symbolic order.

This *mise en scène* of men engaged in intergenerational strife and women (and 'cowards' like poor Manuel) who watch brings us back to Goya's incongruous *mise en scène* of cyclical, male violence in the context of an intimate, but peripheral feminine gaze. At first sight, the painting of Saturn devouring his offspring opposite a portrait of the woman who was the mother of Goya's favourite, although maybe not his biological daughter, seems *unheimlich*, to say the least. Looked at more closely, however, this 'unhomely' hanging is just the standard Oedipal text. It is, however, an enlightening Oedipal paradigm in the context of the discourse of war. The symbolic mother is normally more clearly disavowed in representations of Oedipal conflict. In the myth Freud uses as his metaphor, Oedipus could not 'see' his mother and when he could, he put out his own eyes. In Goya's dining room, on the other hand, the woman normally disavowed in the symbolic contract/Oedipal text is, as it were, dis/avowed: there is still a gap between her and the Oedipally challenged Saturn, but Leocadia is hanging on the other wall. The initial jolt of surprise caused by seeing that Goya originally painted his terrifying *Saturn* opposite this gently domestic portrait of Leocadia is in fact simply an effect of the uncanny that lies, like the return of Medem's male actors, in its familiarity. Read as a symbolic paradigm, it represents the fact that we know it's all about Jocasta, but we expect her to be disavowed. We don't expect her to turn up on the opposite wall, leaning on a grave that looks (uncannily) like a bedstead, looking on.

14. The Camouflaged Self, or first incarnation of the self-consuming Irigibels (Carmelo Gómez) in *Vacas*.

Conclusions

This relationship between Leocadia and Saturn brings us back to the previously omitted 'domestic' footage that was inserted into the *Redux* version of *Apocalypse Now*. The sequence with the French widow complicates the iconography of the original film, just as *La Leocadia* 'complicates' the iconography of *Saturn* (his violence becoming slightly comical in the context of her gaze). Nothing useful is added to what we know of Willard by his romantic encounter with the widow. *Vacas*, on the other hand, is less concerned with the 'horror' of war than with the unconscious drives that reproduce it. So Medem's exposition is assisted by the gazes of his peripheral 'Leocadias'.

Vacas opens with the last of the nineteenth-century Carlist wars. This was a series of wars that the Carlists lost, which have been cited as a source for ongoing separatist violence in Spain (Richardson 2004: 195). The historian Raymond Carr describes the Carlists as 'the prisoners of an intransigent ideal' (1986: 185), and Medem's psychoanalytical *mise en scène* clearly invites more 'transigence', more flexibility in the field of the gaze. For Medem, *Vacas* is about conscience and consciousness. The cow's-eye zoom represents a tantalising, if impossible, way out for Manuel Irigibel, 'que no es un hombre de guerra' [who is not a man of war] (Medem, cited in Ángulo and Rebordinos 2004: 199). According to Medem, once Manuel has dishonoured his family name by faking his own death with Carmelo's blood, 'sólo le queda meterse dentro del ojo de la vaca' [the only thing left for him to do is to get inside the cow's eye], from which he can focus on the 'important things', which are the meanings in the gaps (Angulo and Rebordinos 2004: 199).

Medem's focus on consciousness and conscience and his statement about internal fascism draw attention to the fact that there is nothing more likely to reproduce a violent political regime than a totalitarian gaze that cannot bear to look at itself. And he was clearly taking a risk when he said that the 'worst form of fascism was internal', and that the feuding families in *Vacas* are a metaphor for a self-destructive Basque society that has become locked in cyclical combat with a rival Medem describes as a paranoid fantasy (Heredero 1997: 569). But this complex film, with its recurring male actors, also reminds us of the need to 'repeat'. As the Spanish Civil War exile and concentration camp survivor, Jorge Semprún, points out, the role of the artist is to repeat:

> We have to repeat endlessly so that successive generations do not forget. Historical memory is crucial because the experience of evil is not transferable. The possibility of evil is inherent in the possibility of freedom. (1993: 11)

For psychoanalysis, repetition is about the meanings that keep falling into the gaps. When Medem says that the worst fascism is internal, he is acknowledging the desire to look away from the perverse signifiers in our own psychic gaps, and the danger implicit in any symbolic order that avoids gazing too closely at itself.

In Medem's film, Manuel is brought down, figuratively, in the cow's-eye zoom that represents the 'seer's "shoot"'. In Coppola's, Willard is brought down, figuratively, in the process of killing Kurtz. The 'Other' in Coppola's film is the invisible American state that has reproduced these two broken men. The 'Other' in Medem's film is represented by the zoom through the cow's eye and fade to black. Both films are remarkable for the way they confront the subterranean forces of what Medem calls 'internal fascism'. When he deserts the trenches, Manuel is reborn as a 'coward' under the gaze of the cow's-eye-representative of 'the field of the Other' (Lacan 1991: 246). Willard, on the other hand, remains confined by his (symbolic) reflection in Kurtz's gaze. Willard's consciousness, or rather his *méconnaissance*, is confined by Kurtz, the 'Other' he must destroy, but who will consume him in the process. Reading these two very different war films with the Goya paintings in mind demonstrates that the inclusion of women can have a 'deflating' effect on the representation of male violence against other men. Exploring the similarities and dissimilarities between these two films with the

Goya paradigm in mind also helps to clarify why it is, ironically, that the most famous line from Coppola's film is still Kilgore's 'I love the smell of napalm in the morning.' And if Coppola's terrifyingly claustrophobic *mise en scène* of self-consuming men is summed up by the uncanny returns of the line that could be read as the film's 'real' signifier, it is also not surprising that the enigmatic shot of a cow's eye has come to function as a metonym for *Vacas'* attempt to expose the 'horror' of men consuming men, by widening the focus to expose the futility of territorial violence in the context of the field of the 'gaze', or the 'seer's "shoot"' (Lacan 1991: 72).[8]

Notes

1 Synopsis adapted from Evans (2007). The film was released in the English-speaking world with its Spanish title, and this is the title that is used through the chapter.
2 Santaolalla (1998) examines the representation of gender and territorial rivalry. Sánchez analyses the representation of women in relation to the 'symbolic re-enactment' of war and 'hierarchical male violence' (1997). Richardson (2004) explores the links between reproduction and nationalism. Beck concludes that the enigmatic cow's-eye viewpoint 'radically restructures the visual regime of "looking" and offers a critique of the male-centered "gaze"' (2000: 159), and Stone, who is less convinced, suggests that Medem's 'typical indulgence towards the cowardly male protagonists' is indicated by the fact that 'all end up with gorgeous and adoring young women' (2007: 55).
3 In conversation with Andrew Graham-Dixon for BBC4's *The Art of Spain* (unused footage, series broadcast 2008). I have examined conscious 'quotation' of Goya in *Vacas* elsewhere (Evans 2009).
4 The chapter headings in the DVD copy of *Apocalypse Now Redux* tell us the animal is a caribou, but for symbolic and visual purposes the effect is the same – we watch the ritual sacrifice of a passive, bovine animal cross-cut, in the Eisenstein film, with the mass slaughter of the workers, and in the Coppola film, with the slaughter of Kurtz.
5 My thanks to Silvia Gómez at Alicia Produce for relaying this question to Medem for me.
6 This zoom could be also read as a visual reminder of Lacan's point that 'the relation of the subject to the Other is entirely produced in a process of gap' (1991: 206).
7 The DVD copy I have used for this comparison is the *Redux* (2001) version.
8 I am grateful to the British Academy for funding research towards this chapter.

Bibliography

Angulo, Jesús and José Luis Rebordinos (2004) *Contra la certeza: El cine de Julio Medem*, Huesca: Festival de Cine de Huesca, Filmoteca Vasca.
Beck, Jay (2000) 'Mediating the Transitional in Contemporary Spanish Cinema: Pedro Almodóvar and Julio Medem', *Torre de papel*, 10:1 (Spring), 134–69.
Carr, Raymond (1986) *Spain 1808–1975*, Oxford: Clarendon Press.

Cerdán, Josetxo (1997) '*Vacas*', in Julio Pérez Perucha (ed.), *Antología crítica del cine español 1906–1995*, Madrid: Cátedra/Filmoteca Española, 921–3.

Chion, Michel (1999) *The Voice in Cinema*, New York: Columbia University Press.

de Ros, Xon (1997) '*Vacas* and Basque Cinema: The Making of a Tradition', *Journal of the Institute for Romance Studies*, 5 (1997), 225–34.

Evans, Jo (2007) *Julio Medem*, London: Grant & Cutler.

—(2009) 'Foundational Myths, Repressed Maternal Metaphors and *Desengaño* Iconography in *Vacas*', *Hispanic Research Journal*, 10:2, 122–40.

Foucault, Michel (2007 [1966]) *The Order of Things*, London and New York: Routledge.

Freud, Sigmund (2003 [1919]) *The Uncanny*, trans. David McLintock, London: Penguin.

Gabilondo, Joseba (2002) 'Uncanny Identity: Violence, Gaze, and Desire in Contemporary Basque Cinema', in Jo Labanyi (ed.), *Constructing Identity in Contemporary Spain*, Oxford: Oxford University Press, 262–79.

Heredero, Carlos F. (1997) 'Julio Medem: la imagen conmovida', in *Espejo de miradas: Entrevistas con nuevos directores del cine español de los años noventa*, Alcalá de Henares: Edición del Festival de Cine de Alcalá, 547–87.

Lacan, Jacques (1991 [1964]) *The Four Fundamental Concepts of Psycho-analysis*, trans. Alan Sheridan, London: Penguin.

—(2006 [1958]) *Écrits: A Selection*, trans. Alan Sheridan, London and New York, Routledge.

Martínez Expósito, Alfredo (2004) 'Julio Medem y la poética del compromiso', *Alpha Revista de Artes, Letras y Filosofía*, 20, 121–34.

Richardson, Nathan E. (2004) 'Animals, Machines, and Postnational Identity in Julio Medem's *Vacas*', *Tesserae: Journal of Iberian and Latin American Studies*, 10:2 (December), 191–204.

Sánchez, Antonio (1997) 'Women Immune to a Nervous Breakdown: The Representation of Women in Julio Medem's Films', *Tesserae: Journal of Iberian and Latin American Studies*, 3:2, 147–61.

Santaolalla, Isabel C. (1998) 'Far from Home, Close to Desire: Julio Medem's Landscapes', *Bulletin of Hispanic Studies*, 75, 331–7.

—(1999) 'Julio Medem's *Vacas* (1991): Historicizing the Forest', in Peter Evans (ed.), *Spanish Cinema: The Auteurist Tradition*, Oxford: Oxford University Press, 310–24.

Semprún, Jorge (1993) 'Against Oblivion', interview with Julie Flint, *Guardian* (23 September).

Smith, Paul Julian (1999) 'Between Heaven and Earth: Grounding Julio Medem's *Tierra*', *Bulletin of Hispanic Studies*, 76, 11–25.

Stone, Rob (2007) *Julio Medem*, Manchester: Manchester University Press.

White, Anne M. (1999) 'Manchas blancas, manchas negras', in Rob Rix and Roberto Rodríguez-Saona (eds), *Spanish Cinema: Calling the Shots*, Leeds: Trinity and All Saints, 1–14.

7

Tesis/Thesis (Alejandro Amenábar, 1996): delights and follies in filmic discourse

María Donapetry

Tesis/Thesis takes place in contemporary Spain. Ángela (Ana Torrent) is a student in the Facultad de Ciencias de la Información [Faculty of Media Studies] at the University of Madrid, where she specialises in film. She approaches Professor Figueroa (Miguel Picazo) with the request that he supervise her thesis on real violence in film and he agrees to do so. While watching a snuff film which he had come across in the School's video library, he dies of a heart attack. Ángela discovers his body in a classroom and steals the film. She takes it home and, afraid of what she may see, listens only to the soundtrack. Later on she enlists the help of another student, Chema (Fele Martínez), to find out who made the snuff video. Chema recognises the girl who is being tortured and killed in the video as a fellow student at the University and a former girlfriend of another student, Bosco (Eduardo Noriega). Professor Castro (Xabier Elorriaga) takes over the supervision of Ángela's thesis. He delivers a public lecture in the School addressing the troubled state of Spanish cinema. In order to be successful, he explains, film-makers need to make what the public wants, since cinema is an industry. In the course of investigating who made the snuff video, Ángela is caught by Professor Castro, who tries to film himself killing her. Chema fights with the Professor, who accidentally shoots himself. In the meantime, Ángela feels intensely attracted to Bosco while suspecting either he or Chema could be the author of the snuff video. In spite of her fears, she continues her search and visits Bosco in his house on the outskirts of the city. Once there, and after a fist-fight between Chema and Bosco, the latter ties her to a chair, prepares a camera and explains in horrifying detail what he is going to do to her. In spite of being his captive, Ángela manages to undo her ties and

> shoots Bosco. The last scenes occur in hospital where Ángela visits a conva-
> lescent Chema. A TV programme announces the discovery of the corpses
> of Bosco's victims and is about to show the snuff film. Ángela and Chema
> decide to leave the hospital and not to watch the programme.

Bénie soit la raison! Il m'arrive de penser qu'il faudrait promouvoir et inculquer sans
trêve un système éthique fondé sur le sens commun pour que nous disposions d'une
référence morale en assumant l'existence nécessaire d'une morale dans notre vie
sans avoir à nous raccrocher à la morale religieuse, sans avoir besoin de cette idée –
qu'en tout cas, moi, j'ai definitivement écartée – du châtiment ou de la recompense,
comme si notre vie était un match de foot. En d'autres termes, je crois que si l'on
ne doit pas nuire à son voisin, c'est pour une raison absolument intrinsique et très
claire … et pas du tout parce que les Dix Commandements disent: 'tu ne tueras' …
Non, je veux penser que c'est quelque chose qui naît de l'individu même; la volonté
de faire le bien naît de l'individu même.

Alejandro Amenábar (Berthier 2007: 205–6)

[Blessed be reason! It occurs to me that it would be necessary to constantly promote
and teach an ethical system based on common sense, so that we might have at our
disposal a moral compass assuming the necessary existence of a moral code in our
lives without having to adhere to religious morals, without having the need of this
idea – which in any case I have definitely discarded – of punishment or reward, as
if our lives were a football match. In other words, I believe that if one should not
harm his neighbour, it is because of an intrinsic and very clear reason … and not
because the Ten Commandments say: 'thou shall not kill' … No, I want to think
that there is something that springs from the individual; the will to do good springs
from the individual.][1]

In the epigraph to this chapter, Amenábar discusses his ethical understanding
of violence as spectacle in regard to his debut film, *Thesis*. From start to finish,
Thesis plays with the ambiguous allures of images that are meant both to attract
and repel, in order to make an ethical point: the individual is free to choose
and is responsible for his or her choices. Ambiguity is essential to ethics. As
Fernando Savater puts it: 'In the field of ethics, everything whose reading tries
to be univocal is ecclesiastic dogma or penal code' (2002: 101); therefore, what
is worth pursuing from the point of view of ethics is that which is intrinsically
ambiguous and involves freedom of choice. *Thesis* revolves precisely around
moral choices, around the alibis the individual keeps producing in order to
exonerate himself from responsibility precisely because he is afraid of his own
freedom. This freedom is articulated throughout the film in terms of watching
and being watched, filming and being filmed. As spectators, we are aware of our
position since we also have chosen to watch because watching gives us pleasure.
What we and the characters both desire is pitted constantly against what we
need, although the desires in question are just as constantly justified either by

economic needs or by the unbiased and 'objective' eagerness to know. Desire seems always to demand more than need.

Nothing could signal more clearly a scientific and philosophical endeavour than the title of the film: 'thesis' – Amenábar's subsequent film, *Abre los ojos/ Open Your Eyes* (1997), similarly announces its thesis to both the characters embroiled in the action and viewers who stand outside it. However, and since *Thesis* is a thriller about violence in film, it is quite clear that Amenábar is fully conscious of the irony embedded in his work. As Slavoj Žižek remarks, 'there is a sense in which a cold analysis of violence somehow reproduces and participates in its horror' (2009: 3). In other words, violence affects not only the perpetrator and the victim, but also whoever approaches it either 'objectively' or seeking to derive pleasure from it. Of course, Amenábar makes a distinction between performed violence and real violence. Everything in the film is indeed fiction, but the director seems concerned with the fact that 'the overpowering horror of violent acts and empathy with the victims inexorably function as a lure which prevents us from thinking' (Žižek 2009: 3). Amenábar wants us to be terrified or to feel sympathy for the victims, but he also wants to make us aware that, because of those feelings (consistently tied to our desires), we may lose sight of what is behind the acts of violence. We will later see how his film intertwines subjective violence, objective violence and symbolic violence. Subjective violence is the concrete act or series of acts of violence performed by one subject on another. In *Thesis* we hardly see any of these acts, although we are invited to imagine them. On the one hand, this concealment of subjective violent acts frustrates our expectations but, on the other, it also maintains narrative suspense. Objective violence is what produces the acts of violence. That is, the concrete acts are symptoms of a violent system which endorses and justifies them. Symbolic violence is the visual and verbal form of representing either or both types of violence thus understood.

There are several possible antecedents to this scenario of filming within a film in the suspense genre. Michael Powell's *Peeping Tom* (1959) and Roberta and Michael Findlay's *Snuff* (1976) come to mind. But both seem to deal in the replacement of orgasm's 'little death' by real death.[2] *Peeping Tom*, for instance, stresses the sexual charge of filming as raping/murdering. The protagonist in this film actually attaches a knife to his camera and kills while filming his terrified victims. *Snuff* (1976) comes perhaps closer to *Thesis* in the theme of snuff movies, but it concentrates on the dismemberment and opening of female bodies as a source of pleasure both for the filmmaker within the film and for a possible male audience. *Thesis* departs from both precursors in different ways: the filmmakers within Amenábar's film are not so much pathologically as commercially interested in their filmmaking (even if *Thesis* has in mind a particular kind of capitalist pathological behaviour), and what we see is not scenes of gore, even if we are invited to imagine what they could be like. The pathological aspects in *Peeping Tom* and in *Snuff*, perhaps for the sake of maintaining a specific sort of suspense and thrill, are obvious and constitute the central characteristic of the protagonists, with a consequent blurring of the idea of their freedom of choice. Freudian hang-ups and blind greed respectively are the pathologies affecting the characters in Powell's and Findlay's films. As Žižek declares: "What is truly traumatic for the subject is not the fact that a pure ethical act is (perhaps) impossible, that freedom is (perhaps) an appearance, based on our ignorance of the true motivations of our acts; what is truly traumatic is freedom itself, the fact that freedom *is* possible, and we desperately search for some 'pathological' determinations in order to avoid this fact" (2009: 166, emphasis added). In both *Peeping Tom* and *Snuff* the characters are presented as pathological cases and, therefore, not like us. *Thesis* tries to do something else altogether: it presents its characters as perfectly identifiable and recognised as 'normal', just like us.

Some reviewers have considered Amenábar's casting of Ana Torrent as the female lead as adding an intertextual dimension to *Thesis*. Dominique Russell, for instance, identifies Torrent as 'the little girl from Víctor Erice's *El espíritu de la colmena/The Spirit of the Beehive* (1973), whose eyes were to mark Spanish cinema' (2006: 81). Others also remember Torrent's intense gaze in Carlos Saura's *Cría cuervos/Raise Ravens* (1976). I am sure Amenábar chose Ana Torrent, among other things, because there was something to be said and to be done about the lingering spectre of her gaze in her work with Saura and Erice. If in *Raise Ravens* and *The Spirit of the Beehive* Ana's gaze encapsulates the intensity of total innocence when facing the monster (cinematic, symbolic or real), in *Thesis* that innocence is no longer possible. The actress is an adult woman and, as such, she has to identify the monster inside herself as well as outside.

Amenábar's film opens with a black screen and a voice-over coming from a crackling microphone. The viewer wonders who is speaking and where the characters are; we may even wonder if the projection of the film is working properly. Our frustration at not being able to see or even to understand what is happening only intensifies our desire to see and to know. We are soon appeased by the appearance of the first character in *Thesis*, Ángela, sitting in an underground carriage which she is shortly asked to leave, along with all the other passengers. The opening of the carriage doors marks the beginning of the action: there has been an accident (someone has jumped onto the rails and has been cut into two by the wheels of the train). Ángela, along with the spectator, who is aligned with her, wants to see the body of the dead man. This morbid curiosity, while recognisable as common, gives us a hint of what the film is going to be about: the thrill of viewing violent deaths at close quarters. The setting, the use of space, the attitudes of the characters and their apparent normality encapsulate Amenábar's *Acheronta movebo*.[3]

At the start, Ángela's slim and feminine but unassuming appearance and love for classical music seem to accord perfectly well with her name. However, Amenábar is deliberately playing with our expectations; indeed, he will continue

15. Ángela tied to a chair in the basement of the School is going to be killed and filmed by Professor Castro.

to do so throughout the film, where the actions of his characters pointedly and systematically do not correspond to the symbolic value either of their appearance or their names. Ángela is writing her thesis on violence in films because she wants to treat violence from an 'objective' and 'scientific' point of view, keeping a distance from the acts of violence which eventually and by proximity will turn her into a participant and even victim of the same violence. There may be an objective or scientific vocabulary to deal with violence; however, the motives, the attraction, the desire to see and be thrilled will be absolutely subjective. This is where Ángela embarks on a discovery of her true feelings and an acquisition of conscience, a descent into her own underworld in which we also will be involved.

In this descent, Ángela relies on the collaboration of another student, Chema. He is well known for his collection of films related to violence (mainly gore and porno) and is characterised as a dishevelled fan of heavy metal music and a rude and ugly loner. The School is the setting where the search, first for a film with real violence and then for the author of that film, is going to take place. We begin in the common spaces – the cafeteria and the classrooms – where the characters meet and eye each other up. The video-library, a dark maze of shelves in the depths of the building, is unsurprisingly called the *depósito* ('morgue' in Spanish) and is where evil resides. But Ángela and Chema's search is not depicted as just an adventure of two heroes fighting evil. Both of them, particularly Ángela, will have to come to terms with their own collaboration with evil, however passive it may be. Our moral alignment as spectators with the characters is stressed throughout the film. Ángela's squeamishness about not watching the snuff video but listening to it instead resonates with our own feelings; we share her curiosity and are as reluctant as she is to be tainted by what we may see. Later on, when she shares the video with Chema but watches it only through her fingers, our identification with her is further deepened. What we see there is a mirror image of ourselves: we watch Ángela and Chema's faces and reactions as they watch the video. Yet, in another scene, we will see Ángela through a camera's viewfinder, in black and white. She is facing the camera and looking directly at us. Professor Castro is about to kill her on film. She speaks to the camera, saying, 'Soy Ángela y me van a matar' [I am Ángela and someone is going to kill me]. The interpellation functions as a definite reminder of our involvement. On the one hand, we may wish to see the violent images the characters are watching and we are made aware of our own desires; on the other, the direct way in which Ángela identifies herself and the threat she is facing are appeals to acknowledge and feel for a fellow human being. However passive our position as spectators may be, we have to choose between identifying ourselves with Ángela or giving free rein to our desire to see the violence implied. If we choose the latter, we will be avoiding any thinking and opt for a complete disavowal of our involvement in violence.

The third member of *Thesis*'s trinity, Bosco, in open contrast to Chema, always looks perfectly groomed and in command of his every move. In their first encounter, Ángela identifies Bosco's camera as the one used to film the snuff movie and feels herself both attracted to and afraid of him. While in a public space, she makes a point of being literally in Bosco's field of vision (Bosco is filming a female friend). Ángela wants to be seen and to be filmed. Fear is strongly attached to sexual excitement, to the point that, later on, Ángela dreams that Bosco comes to her bedroom to seduce and kill her. In her fantasy she finally crosses the line between being a terrified spectator and being the protagonist of a sexualised violent encounter. Dreams are not the product of one's will but, in this case, they become a symptom of Ángela's own 'underground' desires and, perhaps, ours. The fact that she is in her own home, surrounded by what is familiar to her in all senses, gives us and her a feeling of being in a comfort zone, a normal space where normal people live normal lives. What we have to acknowledge, then, is that the mind is perfectly able to create pleasurable horrors in the safety of our own bedrooms.

When Chema and Ángela descend to the basement of the School and are trapped in the underground corridors, he tells her a version of Oscar Wilde's story 'The Birthday of the Infanta' in order to calm her nerves. The dwarf in this story entertains the princess by dancing and jumping. While looking for the princess one day, he sees himself in a mirror, realises he is a hideous monster and dies of a broken heart. One could see how Chema might identify with this hideous monster, since he tells the story with a strong feeling of sympathy for the dwarf. Moreover, he feels he is competing with handsome Bosco for the attention of princess Ángela. However, we could also understand the story as a process of self-recognition that also affects Ángela and us. Ángela will have to follow her curiosity and basic instincts in order to realise that the satisfaction or the pleasure she might have derived from her pursuit of knowledge will reveal the monster within. In the case of the good-looking Bosco, it is not till the end that we recognise him for what he is: a monster who does not simply enjoy watching violence but who produces that violence as spectacle and commodity for others to consume and enjoy. Our participation as spectators is what reveals the monster within: we enjoy and consume, thus validating the violence and its conversion into spectacle. Not all monsters, though, are of the same quality. While Chema and Ángela will learn and mend their ways, Bosco is irredeemable. We, as spectators, are forced to think where we stand not only with respect to the subjective violence but also with respect to the pathologies of a consumerist regime.

In an ethical sense, Amenábar's choice of names for the protagonists is significant: Ángela is the innocent soul whose desire to know leads her to plumb the darkest depths of violence; Chema, an abbreviated form of the combination of the Christian names José and María [Joseph and Mary], evokes the role of humans in the divinity made flesh; and Bosco, the handsome student to whom Chema refers consistently as a *pijo* ['upper-class prick'] – indeed, actor Eduardo Noriega brings a history of such roles to the character. This third name does indeed suggest the young man's class and mannerisms, since it became fashionable in Spanish society in the late 1970s precisely amongst the (aspiring) members of the capital's upper bourgeoisie. But, given the religious overtones of the other two names, it could also refer to the patron saint of that name – St John Bosco (founder of the Salesians) – or to the Dutch painter Hieronymus Bosch, known in Spain as El Bosco, whose main works are located in the Prado Gallery in Madrid. I believe Amenábar is yet again playing with the ambiguity of the name of this character and with our expectations. Given that his film is about the creation of images, I am inclined to see a reference to the painter, and more precisely to the triptych *The Garden of Earthly Delights* (1503–04). In this triptych Bosch, in a similar vein to Bosco in *Thesis*, creates images directly related to the seductive power of the sources of all sins: lust and, above all, stupidity.[4] This particular painting by Bosch provides us with some of the cultural clues to understand or, at least, to approach an ethical understanding of Amenábar's film.

What leads me in this direction, besides the choice of names, is the narrative structure of *The Garden of Earthly Delights* (the painting in its entirety looks like a book of illustrations with special covers), the concentration on the figures looking and being looked at, the ambiguity of the images in the central panel, and the representation of hell as *locus stultitia*. Amenábar creates his work within an artistic culture that in Spain is associated with the Christian tradition. Bosch's

16. The exterior shutters of Bosch's *The Garden of Earthly Delights*.

iconography is definitely Christian in theme and symbolism. Amenábar, on the other hand, not only is not Christian but in fact is highly critical of the history and dogma of Christianity. *Agora* (2009) attests to his opinion about early Christians, their principles and behaviour; and in *Mar adentro/The Sea Inside* (2004), the Spanish director supports unambiguously the ethical decision of its protagonist against one of the major tenets of Christian doctrine. And yet, his use of Christian cultural references pervades *Thesis*. Both Bosch and Amenábar tackle the folly (i.e. the condition of not thinking when overpowered by horror, empathy or desire) behind acts of sinful behaviour, whether purely sexual in appearance or mainly violent for sexual pleasure, and they play with the para-doxical binary of their images: attraction/repulsion. While the ethical endeavour of Bosch's painting is understood within the belief in a god who is guarantor of eternal bliss or condemnation,[5] Amenábar's film, as the epigraph to this chapter indicates, espouses and promotes the idea that individuals are the sole guarantors of their choices as to what they want to be and how they want to behave: this is evident also in both *The Sea Inside* and *Agora*, which similarly revolve around issues of ethical choice and religious (in)tolerance.

As can be seen, the exterior panels of Bosch's triptych are like two black doors with a divided image of the world created by God before the introduction of human beings. The structure of the painting, then, is like a book: a narrative in images where we will have to move the covers and start reading from left to right. *Thesis* begins and finishes with the opening and closing of doors: when Ángela emerges from the underground carriage and, at the end, when she and Chema together enter a lift to leave hospital while a TV programme is showing the snuff film to an audience of mesmerised patients. In between these two movements of

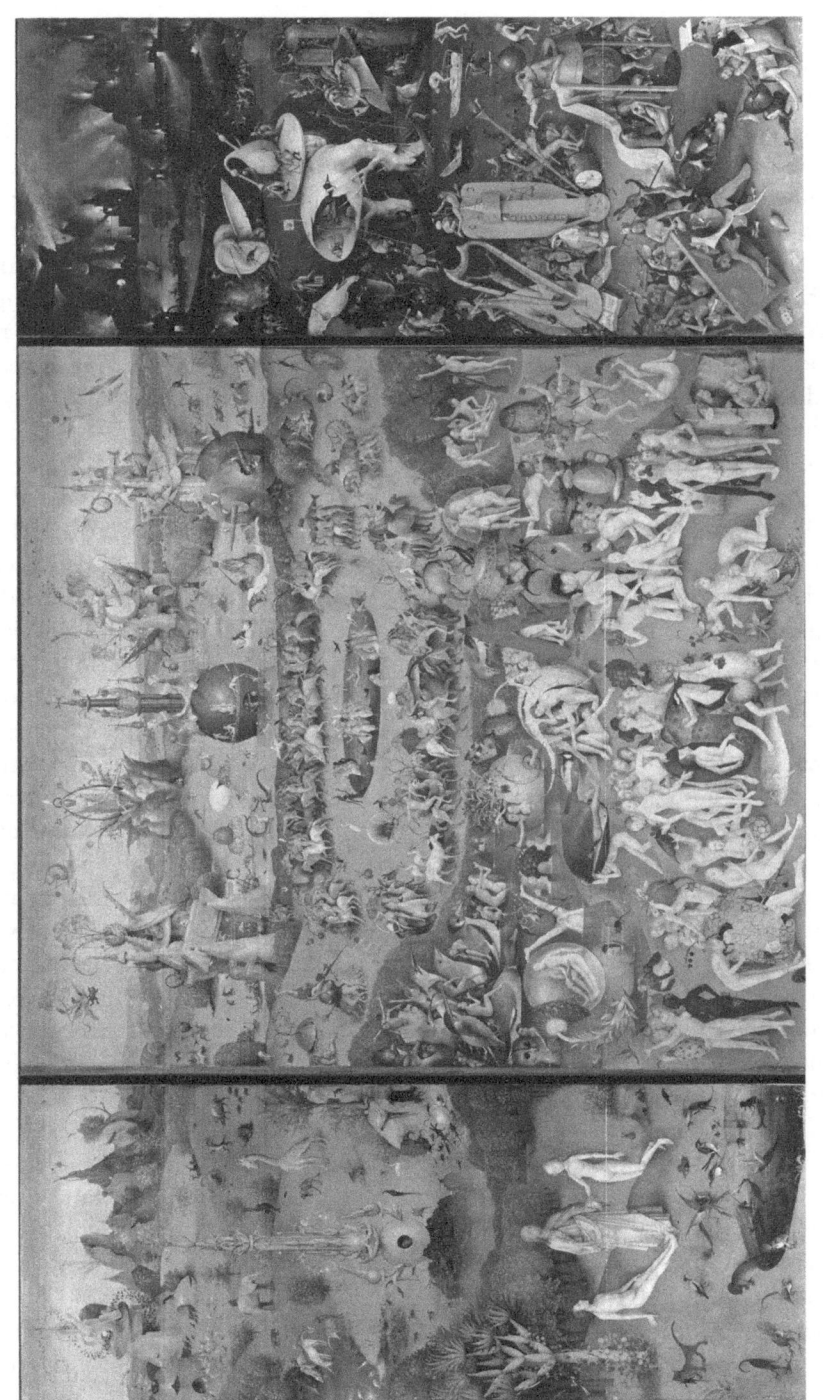

17. The tryptic of Bosch's *The Garden of Earthly Delights.*

the doors, there is a process of learning about temptation, about our own desires and the consequences of our acts.

The first of *The Garden*'s three panels illustrates how the divine creation was before the fall of Adam and Eve. Significantly, some signs of evil are already lurking at the bottom right of the panel, as if to prevent observers from revelling in the sight of all the prelapsarian goodness. What interests me the most, and what I think is relevant to Amenábar's film, is the figures' gazes: God (or Christ) is looking towards the observer of the painting while holding Eve's hand, and Eve is lowering her eyes as if averting Adam's gaze who, in turn, is looking directly at her. There is a latent awareness of what looking and being looked at implies, and the observer is forewarned about the pleasures derived from looking. The directness of the male figures' gazes and Eve's coyness remind us of the ways in which characters in *Thesis* – and even Amenábar with his camera – relate to each other and to the spectator.

In the second and central panel (twice as big as those on either side) the individual human beings, according to Walter Bosing, 'far from dominating the earth, are eclipsed, in fact, by the giant birds and fruits. Thus, the garden does not show the compliance with the divine command Adam and Eve received, but its perversion; from the Fountain of Life they went on to drink from the fountain of the senses, which intoxicates and takes them to death' (2000: 57). We may well believe this is the case but, whether the observer is Christian or not, the fact remains that we are being seduced by colourful images of naked bodies frolicking and apparently enjoying themselves. Most experts on Bosch agree on the ambiguity of the panel: 'to one author, the scenes in the centre panel are depictions of Paradise, while to another they illustrate vice. Mutually exclusive though they are, there is something to be said for both these readings, leaving us to wonder whether Bosch's fantastic scenes are insolubly ambiguous' (Koldeweij, Vandenbroek and Vermet 2001: 102). Whatever the reading, we are still offered a spectacle of lust in the name of art and knowledge. The central scene is supposed to be morally edifying but the excitement of the observer cannot be controlled from the painting itself. Only the third part of the triptych will determine the outcome of the pleasures observed and/or felt by the observer. In *Thesis*, when Professor Castro argues that films should give the audience what they like, he advocates the kind of pleasure this middle panel in isolation from the third one could afford: a thrill-producing image in which the spectator participates passively and, therefore, theoretically will come to no harm. But in *Thesis* and in the triptych we get to know better. Professor Castro is more than willing to kill Ángela to make a snuff film giving some audiences what they want and, in his folly, ends up dead. Ángela, for her part, doggedly follows Bosco to his home and, for the second time, ends up tied to a chair and about to become the protagonist of another snuff film. What is relevant in the relationship between the central panel in *The Garden* and *Thesis* is the inherent ambiguity of

18. 19. Details of the third (right-hand) panel of Bosch's *The Garden of Earthly Delights.*

the images. The delights enjoyed by the figures in the painting, the characters in the film and the observers/spectators within and without both works, however, have consequences.

The right-hand panel depicts chaotic asymmetries and interactions between beastlike figures and humans. The profoundly dark background is illuminated by flashes of light that shine through the gates of a city on fire. The visual metaphor for hell here, though, is compounded by quasi-surreal and particularly disproportionate elements: first, two giant ears are pierced by an arrow with the blade of a knife in between them resembling an erect and lethal penis; and second, the head of a monster-man looks back towards, although not at, the observers. His 'body' is a hollow and broken shell perched on two hollow trunks that support themselves on two boats floating on a mud-like substance. On top of his head there is a flat, round surface on which a bright pink, swollen bagpipe sits.

These images conjoin the symbols of lust (the bagpipe reminds us of the male organs) with stupidity (the almost beatific smile of the face is set in the midst of chaos, monstrosity and darkness). The painting seems to be telling us that the sinner is sinking in mud, he is destroying himself and does not even know he is sinking. In making the human face and the subject's features so noticeable by their size and by his peculiar way of looking and smiling amongst such horrors, one can only conclude that this human being is incapable of recognising his situation and, therefore, unable to extricate himself from it. Somehow it is his very stupidity which makes damnation and hell as eternal as death, hence the consideration of hell as *locus stultitia*. In *Thesis*, and for a variety of reasons, each of the main characters believes himself or herself to be in command of the situation, until they die or kill. Although Ángela's lack of self-awareness takes her perilously close to Bosco's own hell, it is Bosco who will remain there, with a smile not dissimilar from that of the man in the third panel of *The Garden*.

The last part of the film brings to the fore the acquisition of awareness and the choice to act accordingly. Ángela literally and figuratively breaks the ropes that bind her and then kills Bosco. At last both Chema and Ángela are capable of stepping backwards and making moral and aesthetic considerations. At least momentarily, they have to leave aside their 'natural' instincts and reflect on ways of looking at violence and their feelings about it. Immediately after the scene where Ángela kills Bosco, we see her visiting Chema in hospital. The episode in the hospital also seems to echo the third panel of Bosch's triptych. The chosen location signals without a doubt a place of sickness. On the screens of every television set a newscaster can be seen and heard announcing the discovery of Bosco's victims. Of course, the presenter cautions the audience about the horrible images they are going to see and about the sensitivities those images might hurt. What they are going to show is one of Bosco's snuff films. The patients look at the screens, not only unafraid of what may happen to their sensitivities but as if their lives depended on watching the programme, all except Chema and Ángela who refuse to be taken once more into this cycle of violence and horror. Again, the faces of this captive audience remind us of the one that stares out in *The Garden*'s third panel: they are utterly unaware of what they are seeing, seduced by 'real' violence. The irony cannot escape us: the making and exhibiting of snuff films is a crime but, under the pretext that the public has the right to be informed, the exhibition of such films is sanctioned by a public medium. I think Amenábar's point here is that the mass media exploit people's stupidity and proclivity to spectacles of violence but also that the individual has the option of not participating, of not looking.

What do we make, then, of the unsolvable paradox that is manifest both in Bosch's painting and in Amenábar's film? The two artists create perverse images in order to dissuade the observer from being seduced by their allure, while making them particularly alluring. It is clear that one of the obvious differences between *The Garden* and *Thesis* is that in the painting the images are eminently allegorical and are very far from representing a palpable reality. The painter and the observer are fully aware of the highly stylised and symbolic quality of the painting, while the film counts on the willing suspension of disbelief on the part of its spectators. The asymmetry of relations between the observer and the ones observed – those who suffer in the images – is of a different quality in each work. Even so, the consideration of *stultitia* as the real source of evil is paramount in both works. Those of us unable to step back and keep a distance from 'temptation' (be it as a religious concept or as a basic instinct), even after or while being tempted, will collaborate in our own self-destruction. This is, of course, a thematic further developed in *Agora*, where the fourth- to fifth-century mathematician-astronomer Hypatia engages in a series of scientific and theological debates on the nature of faith.

Beyond this quasi-religious and immediate consideration, I believe Amenábar is also making a point about the pathologies of capitalism with regard to art as consumption, particularly in the case of cinema – concerns picked up and elaborated in his subsequent work, especially *Open Your Eyes* and *The Others* (2001). The concrete acts of violence we see or imagine are not there to ideologically displace the real culprit. Amenábar leaves no doubt that the ultimate culprit is a society in which commodities substitute or aim to substitute for art. It might seem ironic that the Spanish director makes a thriller about the making of an extreme kind of thrillers even if, as Carlos F. Heredero concludes, '*Tesis* se mantiene en la antesala reflexiva sobre el ejercicio y la representación de la violencia' [*Thesis* remains in the reflexive anteroom about the exercise and representation of violence] (1999: 37). There is nothing cold or objective in *Thesis*; it is not a clinical study of violent films but a violent film itself somehow 'contaminated' by the tendencies and desires of its characters and our own. And it could not be otherwise: the truthfulness of the subject matter of the film is signalled by the contamination of the manner of representing it (Žižek 2009: 3).

In *Thesis* Amenábar makes explicit his rules of engagement with the spectator, the spectator he seeks and interpellates, and these rules include an understanding of what cinema can do to us, not what cinema should or should not do. His ambition with this film centres around symbolic violence as the prime focus of *Thesis*. As a director, Amenábar aims at making his best film from the start and, as Truffaut says, 'Le meilleur film est peut-être celui dans lequel nous parvenons à exprimer, volontièrement ou non, à la fois nos idées sur la vie et nos idées sur le cinéma' [The best film is perhaps the one in which we get to express, voluntarily or not, simultaneously our ideas about life and our ideas about cinema] (1987: 271). Any film that matters must matter to somebody. Amenábar makes sure that it matters to us and that, beyond being entertained, excited or terrified, we can see ourselves or our possible selves in his film. By giving visual expression to our underground desires, he acknowledges them, and makes us acknowledge them so that we avow them and move on in that knowledge. Against convention, *Thesis* has no other hero than the thinking individual. There is an ethics of seeing which affects the film-maker and audiences alike. There is no gap between the aesthetic experience and the thinking experience. When there is, folly has won.[6]

Notes

1 All translations from French as well as Spanish throughout the chapter are mine.
2 Here I paraphrase Linda Williams (1999: 192) writing about *Snuff*.
3 'Flectere si nequeo superos, *Acheronta movebo*' [If I cannot move Heaven, then I will stir up the underworld; emphasis added] is used by Sigmund Freud as an epigraph for

one of the chapters in his *Interpretation of Dreams*, and is taken from Virgil's Aeneid, Book VII, 312.

4 Walter Bosing (2000) puts forward this interpretation of the images in *The Garden of Earthly Delights*.

5 Here I paraphrase Slavoj Žižek, who observes: 'some beliefs always seem to function "at a distance": in order for the belief to function, there *has to be* some ultimate guarantor of it, yet this guarantor is always deferred, displaced, never present *in persona*' (2009: 82–3; emphasis added].

6 This chapter expands substantially on a lecture first delivered in the Cátedra Jovellanos (University of Oviedo) in July 2001 and later at Cinelit (Portland State University of Oregon) in March 2003, under the title 'Delicias visuales: *Tesis* de Amenábar y *El jardín de las delicias* del Bosco'.

Bibliography

Berthier, Nancy (ed.) (2007) *Le cinéma de Alejandro Amenábar*, Toulouse: Presses Universitaires du Mirail.

Bosing, Walter (2000) *La obra completa. Pintura: El Bosco*, Madrid: Taschen.

Heredero, Carlos F. (1999) *20 Nuevos directores del cine español*, Madrid: Alianza.

Koldeweij, Jos, Paul Vandenbroeck and Bernard Vermet (2001) *Hieronymus Bosch: The Complete Paintings and Drawings*, New York: Harry N. Abrams.

Russell, Dominique (2006) 'Sounds like Horror: Alejandro Amenábar's Thesis on Audio-Visual Violence', *Canadian Journal of Film Studies* 15:2, 81–95, http://findarticles.com/p/articles/mi_qa4092/is_200610/ai_n17195481/ [accessed 23 September 2010].

Savater, Fernando (2002) *Pensamientos arriesgados*, ed. José Sánchez Tortosa, Madrid: La esfera de los libros.

Truffaut, François (1987) *Le plaisir des yeux*, Paris: Flammarion (Cahiers du cinéma).

Williams, Linda (1999) *Hard Core*, Berkeley, Los Angeles and London: University of California Press.

Žižek, Slavoj (2009) *Violence*, London: Profile Books.

8

Un instante en la vida ajena/A Glimpse of Other Lives (José Luis López-Linares, 2003): domesticating the documentary archive

Kathleen M. Vernon

Drawing on over 150 hours of footage recorded by amateur filmmaker Madronita Andreu, beginning in the 1920s and continuing until her death in 1982, *Un instante en la vida ajena/A Glimpse of Other Lives* provides a glimpse into the life and times of a most untypical Spanish family. The daughter of a famous and wealthy Barcelona physician, Dr Andreu, famous for his cough remedies, Madronita took full advantage of the privileges afforded her to pursue her passion for home movies, producing an account of the *buenos momentos* [good moments] of family life, dinners, dancing, weddings and frequent travel abroad and to other regions of Spain. Shaped and edited by director José Luis López-Linares into an 80-minute documentary, Andreu's footage invites the spectator to reflect at the same time on what it excludes – direct evidence of the Civil War and postwar hardship and repression – as well as what it includes: a chronicle of the cosmopolitan modernity of the Catalan upper classes during the early decades of the twentieth century and their continuing mobility under the Franco dictatorship. In its creative appropriation of domestic cinema as archival source, *A Glimpse of Other Lives* represents a first for Spanish documentary and reflects the growing interest in the form among film scholars, social and cultural historians and filmmakers.

If 'film beget films', as pioneering historian of the archive-based documentary Jay Leyda observes in the title of his 1964 study of the genre, then López-Linares's 1996 reconstruction of the life and times of Trotsky's notorious assassin Ramón Mercader, *Asaltar los cielos/Storm the Skies*, is the immediate and literal forebear of *A Glimpse of Other Lives* (henceforth *A Glimpse*), whose images were discovered by the director in the Filmoteca de Barcelona during the course of research into the life of Mercader's mother, Caridad del Río. Before abandoning Barcelona for Paris, the Soviet Union and radical Communist politics, del Río would have crossed paths with other members of Catalan high society and *alta burguesía*, including the family of Madronita Andreu, the subject and originating source of *A Glimpse*. Drawing on material filmed by Madronita over some 50 years and consisting in over 150 hours of 16mm film housed in 90 canisters in the Barcelona archive, López-Linares has created a unique contribution to contemporary documentary film practice and a fascinating counter-narrative of recent Spanish history.

Documentary cinema in Spain, nearly dormant during the years of the Franco dictatorship when non-fiction filmmaking fell under the control of the organism created to produce the official newsreel, the NO-DO, has seen a rebirth that has, if anything, accelerated since the year 2000. The work of López-Linares and collaborator Javier Rioyo, who specialise in archive-based compilation films, in many ways looks back to important films from the first years of the transition to democracy. The revival of Spanish documentary in the post-Franco era begins with the clandestine productions of Basilio Martín Patino, whose *Canciones para después de una guerra/Songs for After a War* (completed in 1971 but not released until 1976, after the dictator's death) and *Caudillo* (1973, released in 1977) make use of a myriad of textual sources, Civil War-era documentaries, Spanish fiction features, comic books and the NO-DO itself to produce the first of an ongoing series of dialogic re-encounters with official Spanish history. Other compilation films would follow, such as *Raza, el espíritu de Franco/Race, The Spirit of Franco* (Gonzalo Herralde, 1977), which stages a confrontational dialogue with the 1942 film *Raza/Race*, the Franco-scripted, mythified retelling of the Civil War through the fictionalised version of the dictator's own family. Both compilation films and the other important documentaries of the period, like *El desencanto/The Disenchantment* (Jaime Chávarri, 1976) and *La vieja memoria/The Old Memory* (Jaime Camino, 1977), draw heavily on the role of expert witnesses and participants, so-called talking heads, that lend both subjective immediacy and evidentiary weight to the proceedings. López-Linares's and Rioyo's previous documentaries, *A propósito de Buñuel/Speaking of Buñuel* (2000) and *Extranjeros de sí mismos/Aliens to Themselves* (2000), as well as *Storm the Skies*, apply the established techniques of the form, designed to 'interrogat[e] the fracture between archival history and personal memory' (Zimmerman 2008: 10), to a biography of a delightedly self-contradictory Luis Buñuel, the contrasting and complementary stories of Spanish volunteers from the notorious División Azul fighting for Germany in the Second World War and Italian soldiers sent by Mussolini to support Franco, and the elusive life of Trotsky's murderer Ramón Mercader, respectively.

For all its historical significance and critical esteem, however, until recently documentary film in Spain, as elsewhere, has faced many obstacles in reaching beyond a minority audience of festival-goers and specialists. The year 2001 marks something of a breakthrough, with the success of José Luis Guerín's *En construc-ción/Work in Progress*, winner of the first annual Goya Award for a documentary feature, which charts the transformation of the working-class Raval neighbour-hood in Barcelona as seen through the construction of a luxury apartment build-ing.[1] The achievements of *Work in Progress* coincide with an upward rise in the absolute number and proportion of documentary features vis-à-vis fiction films produced in Spain, as charted by Javier Marzal Felici: from 4 in 2000 (versus 209 fiction films) to 12 in 2001, 44 in 2004 (versus 144 fiction) and 50 in 2006 (compared to 127 fiction), the last year covered in his study (2008: 176). *A Glimpse* also took home the Goya for Best Documentary Feature in 2003, a surprise winner over Julio Medem's *La pelota vasca/ The Basque Ball*, a thoughtful survey of different attitudes toward the Basque 'problem' and ETA set against the framing device of that quintessential Basque sport. A major factor in the creative ferment generated by these new documentaries in Spain was the found-ing in 1998 of the Màster en Documental de Creació [Master's programme in Creative Documentary] at the Barcelona-based Universitat Pompeu Fabra, where Guerín is a professor.[2] Although López-Linares is not formally associated with the Pompeu Fabra project, *A Glimpse*, with its innovative form and engage-ment with broader transnational trends, can surely be said to participate in the spirit of 'creative documentary'.[3]

Archives and authors: Madronita as filmmaker

From the first images projected on screen, the film embraces its dual authorship, positioning Madronita Andreu at the centre of the frame. The looped footage depicts a matronly Andreu literally setting the stage for a filmed self-portrait, fussing over the position of flowers on a table in front of a sofa on which she briefly alights and then leaves, only to return again and again in succession. We also see the traces of the second and definitive enunciation, the manipulation of original footage through editing, selection and ordering. This first sequence like-wise introduces us to the film's dramatised narrator, identified through super-imposed titles as 'Salvador Guardiola, montador de cine y televisión' [film and television editor]. In contrast to both the omniscient 'voice of God' narrator dear to traditional documentary conventions and the talking-head witness-participant of the compilation film, *A Glimpse*'s narrator speaks from an artfully delineated middle ground between intimate family knowledge and distanced expertise. In fact the fictional projection of a real archivist who worked with Andreu in her later years, played here by Els Joglars actor Jesús Angelet (Savall 2003), the figure of the narrator functions first to situate and confirm the location of Madronita Andreu's remarkable corpus of home movies in geo-cultural terms. At the same time this device confirms the film's positioning at the intersection of what

Patricia Zimmerman, perhaps the best-known scholar of amateur film in all its dimensions, identifies as 'a series of transversals, translations and transcriptions between history and memory, text and context, ... the public and the private' (2008: 9).

Any analysis of *A Glimpse* must take into account the growing attention being paid to domestic cinema as a genre on the part of film scholars, social and cultural historians, archivists and filmmakers. In Zimmerman's 1995 book, *Reel Families*, she argues for the value of amateur film in general as an alternative to Hollywood commercialism and aesthetics, but is largely critical of home movies for their grounding in 'familialism ... an ideology and social practice that emphasized familial relations above other kinds of social or political interactions [and] wedded amateur film to ... the most important and consuming narrative of all – the grand, happy epic of the nuclear family' (1995: 132, ix). By the time of the publication of the edited volume *Mining the Home Movie* in 2008, in conjunction with curator and documentarian Karen Ishizuka, Zimmerman's views had evolved considerably. In the introduction she links the revalorisation of home movies to larger developments in historiography, to the growing concern with popular memory and the notion of plural histories and 'polyvocalities', and the need to 'interrogate the function of the archive itself as a machine of selection and privileging of discourses that requires expansion into new territories' (2008: 10). As both *Mining the Home Movie* and the 2010 Spanish critical anthology *La casa abierta: El cine doméstico y sus reciclajes contemporáneos* [Open house: domestic cinema and its contemporary recycling] recognise, these investigations are currently being shaped by the work of filmmakers like Ishikuza, Alan Berliner, Péter Forgács and now López-Linares, among scores of others,[4] whose excavations and reappropriations of home movies offer a glimpse into the underside of history, the micronarratives, everyday activities and rituals of ordinary, if often economically advantaged, individuals.

In watching and analysing the film we can only speculate on the distance and differences between the 150 hours of raw material and the finished 80-minute documentary. One thing that is clear is that López-Linares intended to maintain our awareness of the original domestic character of the films, their 'home movieness', even while exercising authorial power in the selection of scenes and storylines he chooses to pursue.[5] First among these is a mediated autobiography of Andreu herself, like Caridad del Río Mercader a daughter of privilege who made unorthodox life choices, marrying first a Colombian and then an American Jew, which led her and her children far afield from Barcelona, if not from the values and customs of her wealthy upbringing. But her initial claim on our attention lies in her role as an amateur filmmaker, a 'pioneer', according to the narrator. For him, her films mark 'la primera vez que alguien ha rodado su propia vida en imágenes, de principio a fin' [the first time anyone has filmed his or her own life, from beginning to end]. Her recording of bullfighter Manolete's second to last *corrida* in 1948 is the first colour film shot by a Spaniard. And he returns again and again to her sense of herself as a kind of documentarian, although perhaps not in so many words, to her understanding of the role of cinema to 'captar y preservar buenos momentos' [to capture and preserve good moments], and her drive to film as much of life as possible and preserve her work for the future, because 'la gente pasa pero las películas quedan' [people disappear but films remain].

Such self-awareness raises the issue of the artistic dimension of Andreu's films. Although the question of aesthetic quality is generally dismissed as a red herring when speaking of domestic cinema – Roger Odin takes care to distinguish the enunciative particularities of home movies from the 'torpezas, errores y fallos' [clumsiness, errors and mistakes] of 'mal cine' [bad filmmaking] (2010: 41–4) – it would be wrong to overlook entirely the visual flair and ambitions of Madronita's work. A product of her time and place, Andreu grew up, the narrator observes, in an atmosphere of 'euforia modernista' [modernist euphoria], fascinated with all manner of 'aparatos, cámaras fotográficas y, después, de cine' [mechanical devices, cameras and, later, movie cameras]. While Spanish scholars Nogales Cárdenas and Suárez Fernández are dismissive of her efforts as those of 'una mujer de la alta burguesía barcelonesa, casada en segundas nupcias con un millonario americano, que hizo sus pinitos en el cine *amateur*' [a woman from the Barcelona gentry, married for the second time to an American millionaire, who dabbled in amateur filmmaking] (2010: 101), it is also clear that the advantages of her milieu gave her access to the technological and familial support that allowed her to move beyond what Zimmerman has characterised as the traditional constraints of amateur film, 'very much feminized within women's cultural practice and neutralized within the family' (1995: xvii).

Surely one potential effect of what Odin identifies as the 'deframing' and resulting shift from familial to cultural readings (2008: 262) that occurs when home movies are reactivated into the work of documentary or feature filmmakers is a heightened attention to the visual character and contexts of the images. For example, early on in *A Glimpse* spectators may be struck by the allusive cinematic quality of a series of scenes drawn from the years 1928–30, following the death of Andreu's first husband when the American Max Klein was courting the widow with three children. In one sequence, coming after shots of Max dancing the Charleston, Madronita mugs for the camera in medium close-up, crossing her eyes and twisting her rubbery features in the manner of Hollywood comediennes of the era. These cinematic influences (or associations) recur at various moments, most immediately in a section of footage shot on the Costa Brava in 1930, that invokes contemporary film conventions of slapstick and physical comedy in its depiction of adults at play engaged in a game of hide-and-seek. At the same time, not content to simply film the everyday activities of family and friends, the narrator informs us, Andreu cajoled them, especially the children, into dressing up and performing in pageants, processions and plays she produced and directed for the camera.

Later her artistic aspirations found expression in filmed travelogues, especially of the two cities she returned to again and again, Seville and New York. Beginning with the family's departure from Spain after the outbreak of the Civil War, the film devotes an extended central segment to a period of travel between Europe and the USA. After initially taking refuge in Switzerland, the family moved to the States in 1942 – urged by Max, who feared that Franco would enter the war on Hitler's side – returning to Barcelona in 1948. But all three daughters were educated in the USA, only coming back to Spain during school holidays. The counterpoint between New York and Seville proves an especially effective structuring device, providing a pretext for some of the most visually striking moments in the film while provoking a range of reflections on the sociological and ethnographic implications of the contrasting material. A series of nocturnal views of the New York skyline and neon marquees of Times Square dating from 1948 are at once strongly evocative of a romanticised, urban-noir landscape and the obvious appeal of this icon of mid-twentieth-century modernity. Tellingly, while Andreu's three daughters appear out of focus in several of the shots, we can clearly read the names, titles and advertising messages blazing from the billboards above their heads. Cutting directly from the colourful night-time scene, the next sequence carries us to Seville and to successive images of well-to-do women dressed in black, Holy Week penitents in their purple robes and peaked hoods and religious-themed *pasos* [floats] passing through the streets. There a well-framed overhead shot depicts the surging crowd held back by uniformed police and then pans closer in slow motion to the massed bodies moving in waves as if part of a single organism. Although it is not at all clear that the artistic impression produced by these scenes is owed exclusively to Andreu, the narrator is keen to signal her artistic accomplishments, attributing her eye for formal composition to the inheritance of her maternal uncle, the painter Francisco Miralles. The smoky haze of a New York wrestling match from the same era, shot in atmospheric black and white, forms the backdrop for his evocation of the incongruous image of the indomitable and elegantly dressed Madronita who went wherever she wanted and filmed whatever she wanted, pulling out her Bell and Howell camera from the ample sleeve of her mink coat. 'Esta época supone el colmo de su técnica de cámara' [This era marked the high point in her camera technique], he informs us.

As deployed in *A Glimpse*, Andreu's travel films effectively straddle the boundary between home movies, with their emphasis on the pleasure to be derived from seeing familiar faces in new and unfamiliar settings, and the early amateur ethnographies characterised by Zimmerman as a cross between 'ingenuous anthropology and a Sears catalog' of the marvels of the Other that 'trace the encounters between privileged and mobile First World people who control technology (cars and cameras)' and those who do not (1995: 80). Of course,

20. The ethnographer's eye: St Patrick's Day Parade, New York City, 1955.

one of the important differences is that Madronita trained her lens primarily, if not exclusively, on the members of closely related 'tribes'. Clearly the family's extended periods of residence abroad shaped the way she saw her native country and the rest of the world, in particular, New York. The juxtaposition of material shot in 1948 and 1955 in Seville and New York highlights the multiple frames of vision wielded by the cosmopolitan observer. The Seville footage depicts the pageantry of the April *Feria* with shots of women on horseback in typical Andalusian folkloric dress, among them Madronita's Catalan daughters. Back-to-back New York scenes portray the participants in the St Patrick's Day and Easter parades on Fifth Avenue in Manhattan, with their marching bands, Irish flags and green shamrocks, in the case of the first, and showy Easter bonnets, in the second. The representation of both secular and religious rituals, processions and parades, whether the Holy Week processions and the Andalusian pilgrimage to the Virgin of the Rocío or the patriotic, anti-Axis floats in 1942 New York, constitute a recurring motif that conveys the unsettling combination of familiarity and strangeness communicated by the film.

Two further sequences resemble more closely Zimmerman's vision of the travelling eye of the mobile First World tourist. During the 1950s, with their children grown, we are told, Max and Madronita undertook a number of car trips, taking advantage of the presence of visiting Americans to explore different regions of Spain. In these segments, shots of country roads with few cars give way to images of Andalusian villagers of all ages. This is the Spain of postwar underdevelopment, ripe for a soon-to-be unleashed tourist boom, where untrammelled natural beauty and poverty coexist, their picturesque effects punctuated by the presence of a pair of *Guardia Civil* on bicycles. The camera takes it all in, then settles on small groups of children or mothers and babies, later lingering on individual faces. The children and older men stare and then smile for the camera and the women perform, striking *sevillana* dance poses on the spot. Little wonder that the visitors are received as foreigners, as the camera pulls back to reveal their enormous Cadillac automobile with its small American flag fluttering on the bonnet.

Several years and some 25 minutes of screen time later, the couple are shown on a 1967 trip to Kenya. As they travel by car through the savannah, we are treated to predictable shots of animals, a zebra, monkeys, an elephant and lions drowsing in a field. The camera also captures images of people passing by the side of the road, including colourfully dressed women accompanied by children. Other scenes are set in centres of population or marketplaces where the white tourists seem to outnumber the native inhabitants. Indeed, at moments the film would seem to seek to elude the innocent yet imperious gaze of the First World tourist to show the Other looking back: in the image of a Masai warrior casually smoking a cigarette at the side of the road; a freeze-frame that captures the angry gesture of a Kenyan woman towards the camera; or the densely populated shot of the inside of a bus full of camera-wielding tourists clamouring for position at the windows. The emblematic, concluding scene of the segment suggests that perhaps the principal object of the camera's marvelling gaze is the then 72-year-old Andreu herself. Filmed at the side of the road, Madronita first stands to the right of a sign stating in English, 'Do not walk beyond here'. Looking at the camera, she turns, shrugs, and walks past the sign and straight ahead.

Regarding history

La película es como un álbum de fotos. Los personajes miran a la cámara de una forma especial porque pensaban que sólo verían las películas ellos el fin de semana en el salón de los Andreu. Me gustaba la idea de ser un voyeur que se cuela en esas reuniones sin que nadie le haya invitado.

[The film resembles a photo album. The characters look at the camera in a special way because they thought that the films would only be seen by themselves at the weekend in the Andreus' sitting room. I liked the idea of being a voyeur who managed to slip in to those family occasions unbeknownst.] José Luis López-Linares (Otero 2003)

Many Spanish commentators on *A Glimpse* have concentrated on the apparent absence of historical awareness in the film. The editor of *La casa abierta*, Efrén Cuevas Álvarez, while recognising the film's pioneering standing as 'el primer – y hasta la fecha último – largometraje [español] que ha reivindicado el material doméstico como registro sociohistórico' [the first – and to date only – (Spanish) feature-length film to make use of home-movie footage as part of the socio-historical record], remarks on what he deems the predominant tone of *alegría* [happiness] in the film and its central character 'que no sufrió la Guerra Civil ni la Segunda Guerra Mundial pués se alejó primero de España y luego de Europa' [who did not suffer the effects of either the Civil War or the Second World War, since she first abandoned Spain and then Europe] (2010b: 134–5). Miqui Otero, writing in *El Mundo*, is harsher still: 'Las bonitas imágenes recogidas por López-Linares no transcienden la crónica social de una familia rica, o del encanto de la vida acomodada en una época difícil, con un valor acaso antropológico' [The lovely images reproduced by López-Linares convey nothing more than the social chronicle of a wealthy family, or the charms of the easy life during hard times, with a perhaps anthropological value] (2003). There is no doubt that Andreu's films, as home movies everywhere, worked to memorialise 'el lado amable de la vida' [the pleasant side of life], as the narrator observes, and it would be misleading to speak of her perspective as representing 'history from below'. Beyond the self-portrait of Andreu as filmmaker, explored in the previous section, the anthropological dimension common to domestic films as 'auto-ethnographies', or what George Perec terms 'endotic', as opposed to exotic anthropology (Zimmerman 2008: 20; Odin 2008: 263), is amply represented in the depiction of the social customs of Andreu's native socioeconomic-ethnic class: from festive dinners and family weddings to games of golf or charades, car-racing and informal Olympics at the family country house in Puigcerdà, and the beach holidays on the Costa Brava or the newly 'discovered' fishing village of Cadaqués in the company of its most famous resident, Salvador Dalí.

In some respects these complaints seem to misunderstand in fundamental ways the nature of home movies in their original incarnation. As Odin reminds us, history and even temporal references are missing from domestic cinema, which is characterised by a 'temporalidad indeterminada ... sin pasado ni futuro ... No tiene necesidad de producir una estructura narrativa ni una construcción coherente porque éstas preexisten en la memoria de los participantes' [indeterminate temporality ... without past or future ... It has no need to produce a narrative structure nor a coherent construction because those pre-exist in the memories of the participants] (2010: 41, 45). In the absence of those family memories and that initial audience invoked above by López-Linares, of course, other concerns and contexts obtain. The lives portrayed in *A Glimpse*, 'nada corrientes en un tiempo nada corriente' [anything but ordinary in an extraordinary time] in the words of the narrator, acquire larger referents and invite broader meanings, notable as much for what they exclude – direct evidence of the Civil War and postwar hardship or repression – as for what they include. Indeed, anticipating the discomfiture felt by the spectator who intrudes, like the voyeur, on what is in effect a private party as well as the shift in vision required to make sense of what he or she sees, the film has the narrator himself give voice to a certain uneasiness. Because of Andreu's films' avowed focus on 'buenos momentos', he observes: 'sus imágenes tienen algo de extraño y llegaron a inquietarme. Estoy acostumbrado a ver en la pantalla todo tipo de conflicto. No estoy acostumbrado a tanta felicidad. ¿Quiénes eran todas esas personas? ¿Eran realmente así de felices?' [their images have something strange about them and I came to find them disturbing. I'm used to seeing all kinds of conflict on screen. I'm not accustomed to such happiness. Who were all these people? Were they really as happy as they look?]

The absence of conflict, and especially of the central conflict of twentieth-century Spanish history (and historical cinema), the Spanish Civil War, hangs over *A Glimpse*. In this respect López-Linares's film invites comparison with the work of Hungarian documentarian Forgács, best known for documentaries like *Meanwhile Somewhere* (1994) and *The Maelstrom: A Family Chronicle* (1997), which incorporate recently recovered home movies and amateur footage that chronicle the everyday lives of ordinary citizens in Germany and Eastern Europe before and during the Second World War. Speaking of *Meanwhile Somewhere*, William Wees signals the awareness of the war and history that shadows the film: 'Conforme la película progresa, la ausencia de la guerra en las películas domésticas se convierte de forma creciente en una presencia poderosa. Resulta imposible mirar incluso las más inocentes y jugetonas escenas del día a día de la vida familiar sin tener conciencia de que algo más está sucediendo en una sociedad europea transformada por la guerra' [As the film progresses, the absence of the war in the home movies increasingly is transformed into a powerful presence. It becomes impossible to watch even the most innocent and playful scenes of everyday family life without being aware that something more is happening in a European society altered by the war] (2010: 203–4). This double consciousness pervades *The Maelstrom,* which makes extraordinary use of a cache of home movies shot by Max Peerebom, the wealthy head of a Dutch Jewish family, that shows them, among other scenes of everyday life, preparing for a holiday in Paris the day before the Nazi invasion of Poland, or sewing and packing for their departure for what will be their final journey to the Auschwitz death camp. In the home movies deployed by Forgács's films, as in those of López-Linares, history occurs largely offscreen. As Michael Renov notes in his study of *The Maelstrom,* 'Nosotros (la audiencia) sabemos peligrosamente más que los creadores de los imágenes' [We (the audience) know dangerously more than the creators of the images] (2010: 178). Cuevas Álvarez highlights the audience's potential response to this gap between micro- and macro-historical perspectives in the home movies appropriated by Forgács that show a family life 'aparentemente ajena a la creciente persecución judía de aquellos años y la guerra que luego estallará, en un aparente conformismo que puede resultar frustrante para el espectador' [apparently oblivious to the growing persecution of Jews during those years and to the war about to explode, in an apparent complacency that may end up being frustrating for the spectator] (2010a: 131).

Such is the impact of Forgács's work that three articles treating his films (from which I cite above) and an interview with the director himself are included in *La casa abierta.* Given the parallels between his films and that of López-Linares, why is the latter received so differently? Certainly there are important formal and rhetorical differences between their construction that condition the contrasting responses. Renov describes Forgács's creative method as a 'reorchestration' of the original images in a process that entails the application of colour tints and slow and fast motion effects, along with freeze-frames (2010: 176–7). And unlike *A Glimpse*, where every frame of the film derives from the camera of Andreu, Forgács does not hesitate to include material from other archival sources that provide what he calls a 'hidden dramaturgy' to the documentary (2010: 362).[6] In this regard the Hungarian's work seems much closer to that of Basilio Martín Patino in his groundbreaking compilation films, *Songs for After a War* and *Caudillo*. However, another source of divergence, I suggest, is owing to the 'fact' or judgement that the unsuspecting protagonists of Forgács's films, seen in retrospect, are victims of the war and history, while in the still predominant Manichaean view of Spain's recent past, the Andreu–Obregón–Klein family is not.

Still, as we have seen, the very privileged nature and exceptionalism of Andreu and her family's life experience offer us an angle on mid-twentieth-century European history seldom associated with Spain and a generally supposed Spanish insularity. Among critics and reviewers of the film there has been a failure to recognise that some of the same factors that contributed to the family's unique financial and cultural capital and afforded them protection from the ravages of the Spanish Civil War and the Second World War in Switzerland and, later, New York, were also the source of the fears of persecution that sent them there in the first place. Against images depicting the family's journeys by ocean liner, the narrator contrasts Madronita's daughters' bookish inclinations with their mother's preference for constant action and movement. Here travel is tied to the opportunity provided by Andreu's marriages to foreigners that opened the family's horizons and made possible her children's escape from the oppressive atmosphere of postwar Spain. All three daughters studied in US universities, as the narrator explains, where they took full advantage, coming in contact with political exiles, 'los grandes maestros' [the great teachers and thinkers], from the Nazis as well as Franco's Spain.[7]

Finally, while no doubt falling short of the profound sense of historical irony generated by the work of Forgács, *A Glimpse* also carries its own melancholy awareness of the mortality of individuals and nations. To that extent, and following Michael Renov, the film participates in that 'most elemental of documentary functions, familiar since the Lumières' *actualités,* traceable to the photographic antecedent ... the desire to cheat death, stop time, restore loss'. In this, he notes, 'ethnography and the home movie meet insofar as both seek out what Roland Barthes has termed "that rather terrible thing which is there in every photograph: the return of the dead"'(1993: 25). The allusion to Barthes's *Camera Lucida* is especially relevant here. With its fusion of the family *albúm de fotos* [photo album] with a social and historical chronicle, López-Linares's film traverses an ever-moving terrain located between the two ways of seeing photographs described by Barthes, the objective, anthropological attitude that characterises the *studium* and the more personal engagement with the image viewed provoked by the 'prick' or 'wound' of the *punctum*. While acknowledging *A Glimpse*'s function in relation to the *studium*, most Spanish critics would seemingly restrict its access to the *punctum*. For example, fixing on the insistently upbeat tone and content of the images of the film, Santos Zunzunegui describes it as 'un espacio utópico hecho visible a través de unas imágenes de las que se ha extirpado de raíz cualquier conciencia del dolor, de la desigualdad, de la muerte' [a Utopian space made visible through a collection of images from which all traces of suffering, inequality and death have been thoroughly eliminated] (2003: 42).

I would argue, on the contrary, that the effects of death, loss and ageing increasingly stalk the film and are felt most deeply in the final segment as López-Linares's editing foregrounds a temporal order and chronology that matches biographical time to a larger historical referent. Opening with an extended sequence devoted to the June 1968 funeral of Bobby Kennedy as experienced on the same Manhattan streets that witnessed the earlier shots of festive St Patrick's Day and Easter celebrations, the film shifts to a sombre tone as the camera roams the crowd. Live footage of the assembled mourners on the sidewalks near St Patrick's Cathedral alternates with Andreu's second-hand recording of the television coverage of the event. The scene observed on Fifth Avenue reflects a changed New York, with notably more black faces glimpsed among the children, adults and even police officers gathered to pay their respects to the victim and his family. Whatever their original purpose or audience, read chronologically, Andreu's films cannot help but bear witness to the changes that shaped the world she lived in. At the same time, in reproducing the forward march of the family album, *A Glimpse* invites us to contemplate the seemingly incompatible nature of historical versus personal time: agent of progress or harbinger of death? A recurring editing trope in the film juxtaposes portraits of the adult family members with their child selves. More poignant still is the suturing effect produced by the image of a matronly Madronita in a feathered hat during the era when the narrator-archivist claims to have met her, contemplated in reverse angle by a 20-ish Max Klein. Ticking down to its conclusion, the film returns once more to footage of a lanky Max dancing the Charleston, but the final word or image on these *vidas ajenas* is left to a lingering shot of lower Manhattan that slowly zooms in on the Twin Towers, suggesting a resonant *memento mori* that implicates us all.

Notes

1 The first Goya Awards took place in 1987. It seems notable that the first prize for documentary short was not awarded until 1993, while the prize for documentary feature had to wait eight years, until 2001.
2 Guerín, whose fiction film *En la ciudad de Sylvia/In the City of Sylvia* is the subject of

Chapter 12 in this volume, is probably the best known director associated with the Pompeu Fabra Master's. Other filmmakers who have worked with the programme include the late Joaquim Jordà, Marc Recha, Isaki Lacuesta and Mercedes Álvarez.

3   In a 2003 article, Marsha Kinder links Guerín's 1997 film *Tren de sombras/ Train of Shadows*, based on the ghostly remains of the faux home movies shot by a fictional French lawyer and amateur filmmaker, Gérard Fleury, with López-Linares's *Storm the Skies* in light of their experimental documentary practice and formulation of an increasingly transnational projection of Spanish identity. This pairing also argues for their shared parentage as inspirations for *A Glimpse*.

4   See the selected filmography and videography complied by Czach in Ishizuka and Zimmerman (2008: 289–97).

5   Not least in the intermittent projector noise that accompanies the initial frames, recurs at various moments in the films and seems designed to evoke the typical intimate viewing setting of the family film. Roger Odin picks out this feature as one that differentiates the viewing experience for traditional film from that of home movies, also suggesting that it exercises a kind of Brechtian function on the spectators. '[L]a presencia insistente del ruido del proyector … nos mantiene despiertos, evitando que nos dejemos capturar por las imágenes … nos obliga a adoptar una posición productiva en relación a lo que estamos viendo' [The insistent presence of the projector noise keeps us awake and prevents us from being fully taken in by the images … it obliges us to adapt a productive position with respect to what we are watching] (2010: 54).

6   See Forgács's comments on what he judges his overuse of contextual material and historical explanation in his film devoted to the Spanish Civil War, *El perro negro/ The Black Dog* (2010: 365–7).

7   There is a suggestive parallel here with the Mercader clan's nomadic existence, where a cosmopolitan education in Paris and the Soviet Union led to a very different outcome for Caridad's children.

Bibliography

Barthes, Roland (1981) *Camera Lucida*, trans. R. Howard, New York: Hill & Wang.

Cuevas Álvarez, Efrén (2010a) 'De vuelta a casa: variaciones del documental realizado con cine doméstico', in Cuevas Álvarez (ed.), 121–66.

—(ed.) (2010b) *La casa abierta: El cine doméstico y sus recliclajes contemporáneos*, Madrid: Ocho y Medio.

Czach, Liz (2008) 'Selected Filmography and Videography', in Ishizuka *et al.* (eds), 89–97.

Forgács, Péter (2010) 'Entrevista', in Cuevas Álvarez (ed.), 359–67.

Ishizuka, Karen L. and Patricia R. Zimmerman (eds) (2008) *Mining the Home Movie: Excavations in Histories and Memories*, Berkeley: University of California Press.

Kinder, Marsha (2003) 'Uncanny Visions of History: Two Experimental Documentaries from Transnational Spain: *Asaltar los cielos* and *Tren de sombras*', *Film Quarterly* 56:3 (Spring), 12–24.

Leyda, Jay (1964) *Film Beget Films: A Study of the Compilation Film*, New York: Hill & Wang.

Marzal Felici, Javier (2008) 'Avatares de la mirada: estrategias enunciativas del cine documental español contemporáneo', *Hispanic Research Journal* 9:2, 165–80.

Nogales Cárdenas, Pedro and José Carlos Suárez Fernández (2010) 'Evolución histórica y temática del cine doméstico español', in Cuevas Álvarez (ed.), 89–117.

Odin, Roger (2008) 'Reflections on the Family Home Movie as Document: A Semio-Pragmatic Approach', in Ishizuka *et al.* (eds), 255–71.

Odin, Roger (2010) 'El cine doméstico en la institución familiar', in Cuevas Álvarez (ed.), 39–60.

Otero, Miqui (2003) 'El color de una vida fotosensible', *El Mundo*, 23 August, http://e-barcelona.org/index.php?name=News&file=article&sid=1443 [accessed 19 February 2011].

Renov, Michael (2010) 'Discursos históricos de lo inimaginable', in Cuevas Álvarez (ed.), 167–86.

Renov, Michael (1993) 'Toward a Poetics of Documentary', in Michael Renov (ed.), *Theorizing Documentary*, New York: Routledge, 12–36.

Savall, Cristina (2003) 'El legado de Madronita Andreu viaja a Venecia', *El Periódico de Aragón*, 24 August, www.elperiodicodearagon.com.noticias/noticia.asp?pkid=73028 [accessed 19 February 2011].

Wees, William C. (2010) '"Cómo *era* entonces": el cine doméstico como historia en *Meanwhile Somewhere …*', in Cuevas Álvarez (ed.), 187–206.

Zimmerman, Patricia R. (2008) 'Introduction. The Home Movie Movement: Excavations, Artifacts, Minings', in Ishizuka *et al.* (eds), 1–28.

—(1995). *Reel Families: A Social History of Documentary Film*, Bloomington: Indiana University Press.

Zunzunegui, Santos (2003) 'La vie en rose', *Blanco y Negro cultural* (15 November), 42.

9

Ninette (José Luis Garci, 2005): Paris revisited

Sue Harris

Fue a Paris para buscar la aventura y encontró más de las que esperaba. [He went to Paris in search of adventure and found more than he bargained for.]
(intertitle from the original theatrical trailer for *Ninette y un señor de Murcia/Ninette and a Gentleman from Murcia* (Fernando Fernán-Gómez, 1965)[1]

Ninette begins in Murcia in 1959, with religious shop-owner Andrés Martínez (Carlos Hipólito) and his friends talking about the romantic successes of an acquaintance, Armando (Enrique Villen), who is currently living in Paris. Andrés goes on holiday to Paris, but is disappointed to find that Armando has secured him lodgings with exiled Republicans Don Pedro (Fernando Delgado) and Madame Bernarda (Beatriz Carvajal), whose nostalgia for all things Spanish (music, food, wine, furnishings) rules their life. Furthermore, Armando has an entirely negative view of Parisian pleasures, and thwarts all Andrés's plans to enjoy the city and its potential for romance. Andrés finds solace with Ninette (Elsa Pataky), the precocious daughter of Pedro and Bernarda, who seduces him in secret, and persuades him to feign illness so that he can remain in the apartment with her while her parents are out at work. As a result of this subterfuge, Andrés never leaves the apartment and never gets to visit the city. The relationship is ultimately exposed when Ninette announces her pregnancy to an astonished Andrés and her incredulous parents. The couple marry and return, along with Armando and the parents, to Murcia, where we learn that there was in fact no pregnancy. Ninette and her mother go into business selling lingerie and fashions imported from Paris, while Armando finds romance with Andrés's assistant Maruja. The proposed conversion of the religious artefacts shop into a car showroom completes the transformations set in motion by the Parisian holiday.

In the inaugural decade of the twenty-first century, with Hispanic film at the forefront of postmodern experimentation and genre hybridity, José Luis Garci's *Ninette* (2005) seems an anachronistic production; a determinedly old-fashioned film in style, tone and content, more in the vein of Frank Capra, George Cukor or Billy Wilder than the hip Almodovarian avant-garde. A wistful, sentimental comedy of manners, featuring a range of gentle caricatures of stock Spanish types, *Ninette* is a script-driven, highly polished studio production, in which the political and social realities of the Franco era are reduced to a set of comic markers. Set in Paris in 1959, among a family of Republican exiles, the film wears its history lightly, using exile and censorship as the driving mechanisms of a frothy comedy of frustrated sexual desire.

The action of the film is entirely taken up with the intriguing predicament of the hapless protagonist, Andrés Martínez, a naive provincial shop-owner, who sets off for a Parisian holiday with high hopes of sexual adventure; Andrés's fate is to find himself confined within the four walls of a gloomy apartment building, with all the attractions of the city tantalisingly out of reach, unable to escape the clutches of the sexy, sultry daughter Ninette. The dramatic organisation revolves around imprisonment, a comic variation of the familiar 'enclosed house' setting, identified by Paul Julian Smith as a key trope of post-Franco filmmaking. But where Smith notes that imprisonment as used by Carlos Saura, Eloy de la Iglesia and Iván Zulueta privileges 'four walls set against the urgent demands of a changing world outside that had become – all too suddenly – fascinating, changing, terrible' (2011: 11), Garci uses enclosure to confront the protagonist with a threat relocated *within* the domestic environment. *Ninette* thus functions according to the conventions of classic farce: the spatial layout of the 'closed house' with its various doors, bedrooms, corridors and common spaces creates a less thematically menacing, but equally tumultuous 'other world' that also speaks of rapid social change. The core notion of entrapment is of course a ludic device, playfully reinforced in the film's decor: a manifestly artificial set of domestic interiors which suggests the modern sitcom setting, while pointing to the film's origins as a 1960s stage play. But while the specificities of context – temporal, spatial, political, historical – relative to the setting in Paris in 1959 are thereby neutralised, the film's achievement is in the way in which it renders the prospect of change fabulous, marvellous and joyful, and thereby offers a new perspective on the critical potential of popular comedy.

Ninette is a modern remake of a much loved popular hit of the 1960s, *Ninette y un señor de Murcia/Ninette and a Gentleman from Murcia* (Fernando Fernán-Gómez, 1965), itself an adaptation of the award-winning stage play of the same name by Miguel Mihura (the play received the Calderón de la Barca prize in 1964). As Douglas R. McKay notes, the play – first produced in September 1964 – ran for some 2,000 performances, and gave rise not only to a film treatment, but also to a sequel, *Ninette, modas de Paris* [Ninette, Paris fashions] in

21. Ninette and Andrés meet for the first time in the distinctly un-French Paris apartment.

1966 (McKay, 1977: 124). The original film portrays Paris as a modern, vibrant city, and is shot partly on location, in a realist style akin to the (then recent) films of the French New Wave. The patriarch Don Pedro and his wife are convincing Parisian residents, attracted to a city with a long tradition of commitment to civil liberties and Republican ideals, and at home with the political ethos and international complexion of the capital. Their daughter Ninette (Rosanda Montaros) is an equally convincing Parisian figure: a thoroughly modern young woman, who is seen shopping and frequenting cafés with various boyfriends. Her elfin physique, short, dark hair, cropped trousers and bare feet position her as a contemporary cinematic female type in the mould of Jean Seberg, Anna Karina or Audrey Hepburn – a worldly, liberated young woman, at ease in a busy European capital. The film's comedy derives from Ninette's seduction of Andrés (Fernán-Gómez), who finds her sexual liberty and permissiveness disconcerting and compelling in equal measure. The erotic pleasures she promises are distinctly at odds with the reality of his life as a bachelor in provincial Murcia, and Andrés's experience – which results in the marriage of the lovers and their proposed return to Murcia – is framed as a carnivalesque moment: a transgressive interlude in his life, in which Paris serves as a safe space of sexual development that is a historical impossibility on home territory.

The original film is in many ways typical of its time period and circumstances of production. As Barry Jordan and Rikki Morgan-Tamosunas note of the comedy films of the era:

> Under the dictatorship, the narrative structure of most mainstream comedies offered the spectator excursions into temporary social chaos, mixed with gentle titillation and emotional excess, but all safely contained within conservative resolutions which reinforced notions of patriotism, patriarchy and unassailable Catholic morality. (1998: 64)

Paris here – in both its geographical distance and its alternative cultural complexion – clearly intensifies the possibilities of a temporary escape from the prevailing social norms of provincial Spain, before the reassertion of a status quo that will contain the libidinous excesses of the young transgressors once they are safely removed from its influence. But as Jordan and Morgan-Tamosunas suggest, such formulaic practices in 1960s cinema nevertheless afforded the opportunity for social commentary and critical reflection, in this case on the nature of both moral censorship and Iberian masculinity. Here, all patriarchal authority is undermined by a cast of suitors, friends and parents who are powerless when faced with the independence and sexual assertion of the young woman in their midst. The film is thus a sharp satire on masculinity and national identity, darkly critical of the impotence of what is shown as an inactive, quasi-bourgeois political exile.

Ninette, directed by Oscar-winning director Garci, was released in 2005 to mark the centenary of playwright Mihura's birth. Garci was one of the first notable figures to emerge in the post-dictatorship production vein that would be termed the *tercera vía*, or third way: a large corpus of middlebrow, well-produced, largely comic films aimed at the mass market in Spain as well as international audiences. As the first Spanish recipient of an Academy Award for Best Foreign Film (*Volver a empezar/ Begin the Beguine*, 1982), with four subsequent Oscar nominations to his name, Garci is one of the country's most high-profile directors on the global stage.[2] Born in 1944, with a scriptwriting and directorial career under way from the early 1970s, he is an emblematic example of Spanish cinema's *niños de la guerra* [children of the war] whose careers began in the Transition period, and who have returned again and again to the post-Civil War years as a period setting in their films. Early critical successes such as *Asignatura pendiente/ Subject Pending* (1976), *Solos en la madrugada/ Alone in the Dark* (1978) and *Las verdes praderas/ The Green Meadows* (1979) are set in the Franco years, and offer what has been described as a melancholic 'reclaiming of an emotional past denied [to them] by Francoist repression' (Jordan and Morgan-Tamosunas 1998: 69). *Ninette*, from the director's mature career, provides a useful platform to consider the development of a discourse of reminiscence in modern popular Spanish filmmaking, and the ways in which this has been treated in popular cinematic modes. As this chapter will show, Garci's project is multiply nostalgic

– first, in its reinvestigation of the critical potential of Spanish genre film in the late Franco era; second, in its harnessing of the visual and performative codes of classic theatre and cinema; and third, in its revisiting of the city of Paris as a signifier of political freedom, sexual identity and modern cosmopolitanism, as well as cinematic escapism. These three priorities will be outlined and evaluated in the discussion that follows.

Ninette remade: the comic framework

Garci's *Ninette* announces itself from the outset as a tribute to Miguel Mihura, both by its abbreviated title and by the inclusion in the opening montage of a black-and-white photograph of the playwright, framed by the dates 1905–2005. The audience's complicity is immediately solicited in a brief moment of animation, in which Mihura's photograph winks at the camera: for a mainstream Spanish audience, Mihura's direct appeal to their prior recognition of his work (in the form of both film and stage play), and to the historical relevance of these texts to popular Spanish culture, is unambiguous. The voyage to Paris to be undertaken collectively in this remade film is thus signalled as an explicitly nostalgic one, leading not to discovery of somewhere new, but to a warm and familiar cinematic space in which the simplicity of life, relationships and political affiliations is set against the 'already known'.

Unsurprisingly, then, the film retains much of the light tone and structure of the original, most importantly the narrative premise of Paris as an exotic, semi-magical destination, replete with the promise of sexual adventures. From a street view of Murcia, with its religious artefact shop and a bugle sounding the end of the day at the army barracks opposite, church and military are established as local points of reference for provincial Spain in 1959. The action shifts to the cramped back room of the *Fuensanta* shop, where a half-hearted card game is under way between Andrés Martínez and three local friends. The conversation comes round to an acquaintance, Armando, who 'saw how things were' and went off to Paris where, as the friends enviously note, he has had an unexpected degree of success with French women. Paris, as they imagine it, is a place of endless opportunities ('liberté, fraternité, charcuterie …' [freedom, brotherhood, cold meats]), a place where people kiss in the street, and on public transport. Aroused by their own imaginations, the friends imagine Armando (whom they admit is 'no Marlon Brando') speaking to a woman on the rue Saint-Honoré and asking her what colour underwear she has on. 'Estas cosas allí son normales' [That's normal there], they conclude; but as they go on to note ruefully 'allí es allí y aquí es aquí' [there is there, and here is here] – and here in Murcia, none of them has ever 'scored' with a woman. Paris, then, is a place that strikes them with awe, a subversive space of distinctly feminine pleasures, from the pious Notre Dame, to the sinful Moulin Rouge, via the '*dames*' they dream of meeting in the streets. Paris exists for them as a forbidden playground: a place of easy seduction, insouciant behaviour and elegant forms, and this idealised vision of the city is immediately confirmed for the viewer in a series of naive illustrations that comprise Andrés's dream of the adventure to come: barges nestling on the Seine beneath the Eiffel Tower; besotted lovers on a nocturnal café terrace, and a brazen couple kissing on the square in front of the Hôtel de Ville.[3]

Andrés's arrival in Paris proceeds via a series of encounters with a cast of comic figures who – with the exception of Ninette – are the antithesis of the stylish Parisians that inhabit his dream. There is a grotesque quality to the characterisation consistent with the tone of the original film: Madame Bernarda[4] is loquacious and overbearing, never allowing her reluctant lodger a word as she guides him post-haste through the disappointingly shabby bedroom and explains the intricacies of the use of the shared bathroom on the landing. Don Pedro, known also as Monsieur Pierre, is a corpulent, uncommunicative figure, who enters the apartment only to take a glass of Valdepeñas before leaving as mysteriously as he arrived. And the much-vaunted Armando (Enrique Villén) is a gloomy pessimist – a cross-eyed polar opposite of the Hollywood matinée idol – who finds Paris wearisome and 'caro' [expensive]. Andrés's repeated pleas for alternative lodgings (a hotel with a view of the Seine) and dinner in a fancy Parisian restaurant – where there might be girls – are met with flat refusals. Instead, beer, an obscure Russian film and an early night are advised. Andrés's first experience of Paris is thus a comic blend of familiarity (Spanish is spoken, Spanish wine is consumed, images of Spain decorate the walls of the apartment) and intense dislocation – a sense of profound detachment from the place in which he expected to find himself, and on which his desires converge. This dislocation is intensified on first sight of the portraits of left-wing political figures – Pablo Iglesias, Vladimir Lenin and Don Alejandro Lerroux – that hang in pride of place in the apartment. A print of Picasso's *Guernica* (1937) goes unremarked in the background. With Ninette's arrival in the flat, Andrés's confusion is complete: young, beautiful and uninhibited about her body, Ninette is an equally 'alien' figure to Andrés; but she is also the concrete manifestation of his formerly abstract dreams of Paris. Through an open bedroom door, he watches her in a mirror as she undresses, Paris completely forgotten in the spectacle of her erotic display. When she returns from her bedroom and asks him his opinion of the as yet unseen city, his breathy response is a dazzled 'precioso' [beautiful].

The collapsing of the character of Ninette and the city of Paris into a single spectacle is at the heart of the film's reworking by Garci: the renowned visual pleasures of the 'City of Light' are effectively transposed onto a screen siren in the classical mode – a female 'site of visual pleasure' in the Mulveyian sense of the term. In the original film Paris is an unambiguously real site: a modern city, whose narrative relevance is as a political refuge as well as tourist destination. The film thus documents Paris as a dynamic urban space, blending location shooting (railway stations, streets, landmark buildings) with studio set pieces. Ninette is seen shopping in the Galeries Lafayette department store and at newspaper kiosks, and flirting with a boyfriend on a café terrace. A panoramic tracking shot of the Place Pigalle recalls Jean-Pierre Melville's innovative treatment of the same site in *Bob le Flambeur/Bob the Gambler* (1955), while a montage of tourist sites adds to the veracity of Andrés's adventure. He even meets actual Parisian women, chatting amiably with some young French sculptresses whose balcony adjoins that of Ninette's family. Additional scenes of Armando in his workplace confirm the film's attention to a concrete world that exists beyond the confines of the apartment. In the 1960s, this realist approach to setting would have reinforced the film's topical relevance, suggesting that the experiences depicted – although comically loaded – were anchored in the reality of a life lived outside the Spanish homeland. Paris in Fernán-Gómez's film is a space whose cosmopolitanism, modernity and absence of censorship coexist with the social experiences of contemporary domestic audiences. Thus, although the slight narrative tale is limited in terms of political insight, the vision of an alternative European experience – conducted in relative geographical proximity – resonates deeply throughout the film.

In *Ninette,* this material reality of Paris is excised, and throughout the film, the city remains a 'site unseen'. Early on, Madame Bernarda and Ninette both describe to a frustrated Andrés what they see from the apartment windows. But the lodger (and by extension the viewer) sees nothing more than a dank wall outside his bedroom. Like Andrés, we would love to believe that the apartment in Les Halles offers views of both the Place Pigalle and the Seine, as Madame Bernarda energetically insists; but the most basic geographical knowledge of the city points to this as a flawed mapping of space. To see both from the same window would be a geographical impossibility. Of course, we cannot be entirely sure, because, like Andrés, we never leave the apartment. But the dramatic reduction of the city to four interior walls immediately neutralises Paris as a known and penetrable cinematic space. Indeed, the Paris of *Ninette* is not the Paris we know (or think we know), but a dream space, as unreal and fantastical a space as Pan's haunting labyrinth (*El laberinto del fauno/Pan's Labyrinth*, Guillermo del Toro, 2006). The diegetic invisibility of one of the world's most iconic cities transforms Paris into an idea, an idea that varies according to each character's desires: for Madame Bernarda, Paris is a place of social elevation, a place in which she is not simply a *verdulera* but a more exotic *marchande de légumes*[5] who wears a hat to work. For Armando, it is a sanctuary, a deception he can hide behind, far from the scrutiny of his old friends back home – at least until Andrés's visit threatens exposure. For everyone contained within the four walls of the apartment, Paris is already a place of enchantment, in which lives are transformed and identities reinvented. And as the exotic Ninette bewitches her hapless suitor, and weaves a web of playful deceit around her parents, so the apartment becomes the magical core of the intangible idea of Paris: a spatial distillation of the transformative possibilities of the city in which all obstacles are eventually overcome, in which love flourishes and in which social harmony prevails. Significantly, the remade film's narrative and formal celebration of escapism serves both a nostalgic and a political function: escapism as historical literalism (the flight from dictatorship), but also as creative force – reminding us of the comfort and pleasures to be found (and surely found by Fernán-Gómez's audiences) in the comic narrative.

Ninette performed: classic antecedents

By eliminating the familiar, identifiable city of Paris from the spatial framework of the film, Garci brings new momentum to the dramatic possibilities of farce in the Ninette story. Comic dilemmas – a tourist who never visits the city, a virginal daughter who seduces a lodger under her parents' noses, and a relationship that must be kept secret at all costs – multiply in the film, and each stage in the narrative intensifies the predicament of the protagonist. The restricted spaces of the apartment alternately separate and unite the various parties, and physical and verbal humour play an important role in advancing events: Andrés feigns first injury, then interest in Pierre's food and dreary Asturian bagpipe music in order to be near his beloved Ninette, while Armando's distinctive cross-eyes seem to swivel in his head as he attempts to unravel the mystery of his friend's sudden desire to be housebound. Of course, Armando initially suspects a liaison with the imposing Madame Bernarda, a misunderstanding that cannot be tolerated by Andrés, and which brings the subterfuge to an end. This, however, is symptomatic of the climate of transgression that prevails throughout: rules and codes of behaviour are broken within the family home, as well as in terms of the national cultural norms of the era. The first film concludes with the announcement of Ninette's pregnancy to her astonished parents – from which there is no way back other than marriage. Garci's *Ninette*, however, sees the new family unit (newlyweds and parents) return to resume their lives in Murcia.

Nostalgia is formally written into the film at the level of the complexity of cinematic referencing, an approach that speaks of the international outlook in Garci's career, as well as post-Franco cinema generally. In visual terms, the design of *Ninette* recalls the sets of the French poetic realist films of the 1930s. The films of the era are recognisable for their privileging of working-class Paris, and the life of the inhabitants of its close-knit apartment buildings. Marcel Carné's *Le Jour se lève/Daybreak* (1938), starring the legendary Jean Gabin, is perhaps the most emblematic film of this type, with the entire story told in flashback from an apartment under siege at the top of an imposing tenement. But films from across the decade, beginning with *Sous les toits de Paris/Under the Rooftops of Paris* (René Clair, 1930), showcase the apartment building, with its ironwork banisters, communal landings, bare floorboards and peeling walls, as a key action space in the era's production. Billy Wilder's *Irma la Douce* (1963), also set in the Les Halles area, and designed in Hollywood by one of the most celebrated art directors of the poetic realist movement, Alexandre Trauner, shows how enduring this image has become in international screen representations of Paris. When Andrés and Ninette dance to accordion music ('le piano du pauvre' [the poor man's piano]) on the darkened landing, looking out at the city beyond, it is as if they have been preserved in aspic: haunting shadows from the lyrical world of French poetic realism.

The French New Wave also offers a clear intertext for Garci's film. Photographs of Jean-Paul Belmondo and Jean Seberg in *A bout de souffle/Breathless* (Jean-Luc Godard, 1960) adorn Ninette's bedroom walls.[6] A second image, evoking François Truffaut's teenage rebel Antoine Doinel (*Les 400 coups/The Four Hundred Blows*,1959) walking hunched up through the streets of Paris, is also visible, an image that resonates in terms of the film's contemporaneous setting in a cramped family residence in a working-class area of the city. But it is in its suggestion of women as magical, unfathomable creatures that the parallels are most evident.[7] Indeed, Ninette's first appearance in the film directly evokes one of Truffaut's signature shots: that of a woman's stocking-clad legs and high heels, filmed in close-up at ground level. The broader action of this scene plays out unseen as the camera remains fixed on the shapely lower legs, black high heels and red skirt hem of Ninette ascending the staircase on which Andrés so recently sat awaiting entry to his lodgings. The voyeurism is explicit, both from the camera and the unseen observer, an artist who lives upstairs, and who is to lose his footing – and his dignity – every time Ninette comes into view. Ninette, then, is immediately coded as enigmatic, an object of fascination and desire; as such she conforms entirely to the template of the female that informs many of Truffaut's films (Claire Maurier as Madame Doinel; Fanny Ardant and Catherine Deneuve in *Vivement Dimanche/Confidentially Yours* [1983] and *Le Dernier Metro/The Last Metro* [1980], respectively). Her physical representation once inside the apartment – sultry, curvaceous, with long, loose blonde hair, and a naked body draped in silky fabrics – powerfully recalls the more exotic 'sex kitten' figure of Brigitte Bardot, an image deconstructed by Godard in *Le Mépris/Contempt* (1963).

The third level of nostalgic cinematic reference relies on Hollywood, and particularly the screwball comedy. The same basic elements are in place: the ostensibly mismatched couple, the secret relationship, and the triumph of the independent woman who ultimately gets the outcome she desires. Films like *It Happened One Night* (Frank Capra, 1934) and *Bringing Up Baby* (Howard Hawks, 1938) are classics of the genre, structured around the conceit of courtship, with the relationship advanced by female autonomy. An escapist genre *par excellence*, the format allows for a measured 'battle of the sexes' in which issues of class, gender – and by implication sex – can be circumvented and a new model of male–female cohabitation established. The screwball comedy is of course a variant on farce, with roots in classical theatrical forms from *commedia dell'arte* to Shakespeare to Oscar Wilde. The universality of the dilemmas and the timeless appeal of comedy as a social safety valve are highlighted in an ironic moment of self-referentiality in *Ninette*: Bernarda and Pierre announce they are going to the cinema to see a Marilyn Monroe film, and to participate in a public discussion about 'La comedia como escapismo en el cine de Hollywood' [comedy as escapism in Hollywood cinema]. Andrés and Ninette greet this news with genuine puzzlement.

Ninette: Modas de París

Where Garci's film differs substantially from the original is in the incorporation of a long segment adapting the second Mihura play, *Ninette: Modas de París*. This serves various purposes: on the one hand it extends the tribute to Mihura and his work, bringing to the screen the story of Ninette and Andrés's marriage following the Paris romance. Second, it allows the story arc to reach a more satisfying conclusion in terms of the secondary characters, in ways consistent with the multiple resolutions of traditional farce, as well as screwball comedy: the reaffirmation of the social order clearly necessitates much more than the unification of the central loving couple. Finally, the addition enables a more extensive critical reflection on the era, by allowing us to witness the impact of the transformations set in place by Paris back in provincial Spain. The formal priorities of the earlier segment are, however, retained, in the attention to interior settings, which are limited to the shared spaces of the marital home and the religious artefacts shop.

Ninette and Andrés resume life above the *Fuensanta* shop, where we learn there was no pregnancy. Away from Paris, Ninette remains the focus of the tensions associated with the city episode, but seems a more transgressive figure in her relocation to conservative, traditional Spain. She is first seen sunbathing topless on her balcony, in full view of the military barracks, and we are immediately aware that she will no more concede her identity to the national patriarchal model than she will to her new husband; his protestations about her 'indecorous' behaviour fall on deaf ears, and the acidic disapproval of Andrés's female assistant Maruja is coolly ignored by Ninette. But just as the encounter with Ninette has been a transformative experience for Andrés, so her presence in Murcia is a catalyst for change: Ninette's function is to bring something of Paris back to Francoist Spain – on the one hand her formerly exiled parents, and on the other a commercial project in the form of a lingerie shop, called 'Ninette: Modas de París'.

The setting-up of the lingerie shop, selling imported underwear from Paris, is an effective vehicle for bringing together many of the film's narrative strands: in particular it enables the implantation of symbols of Parisian exoticism and eroticism in the Murcian community. Inasmuch as it exceeds its functionality, lingerie can be understood as a decadent object, an extravagant indicator of female sexuality. The implied sanctity of the religious environment (*Fuensanta*) is therefore compromised, not by the political threat of Don Pedro's unwavering communist beliefs, but by something potentially much more contaminating: the erotic imagination. Ninette's entrepreneurial success is a comic extension of the libidinous energy she embodies: unsentimental about the commercial demise of the sleepy *Fuensanta*, confident about the prospect of new markets, Ninette is more than a purveyor of 'scandalous' products (Andrés begs her not to put her name to the shop). Indeed, she is the film's principal motor of social change – bringing urban, liberal modernism to Spain in the form of commerce and luxury. It is significant that she is aided in her venture by her mother, Madame Bernarda, whose social and professional elevation (set under way in Paris) are made complete as she assumes the role of a modern business director.

Like Bernarda, the other secondary characters are implicated in the transformations of the Murcia segment, as each of them brings a little of their Parisian experience back to the homeland. Don Pedro remains an ardent communist, but finds an intellectual equal and social companion in the figure of the rational, chess-playing priest who regularly visits the family. The marriage of communism and capitalism symbolised in the parental couple (the original exiles), as well as the alliance between Republicanism and Church in the Pedro–priest alliance, suggests a tolerance of political positions that would have been inconceivable to the characters pre-Paris. Indeed, it is significant that the exiles do not return to Spain as penitents or converts to the old regime; rather they remain 'intact' – true to the political positions and character traits established in the Parisian episode. The trope of enforced cohabitation elaborated in the farce of the first part of the film is here translated into something more Utopian, but also more sustainable: the essence of this renewed Spanish community is the compatibility of all the different figures and factions, and the productive interaction of what should be (and have been) polar opposites. Even love rivals Ninette and Maruja are eventually reconciled, as the latter falls in love with a newly confident Armando. 'Rosa' [pink], she declares, in answer to an unspoken question about the colour of her underwear, confirming the influence that Paris has had, even on those who have not travelled to the city.

Garci's exiles return, of course, to pre-Transition Spain, and the narrative trajectory they undertake is an expression of comic fantasy rather than historical possibility. But the picture of a 'new' Spain that is painted here – a Spain already in a process of transition – suggests an embryonic optimism that would come to fruition in cinema after Franco's death and the end of dictatorship. In its accumulation of commercial activities, culminating in the proposal that *Fuensanta* be refurbished as a car showroom, run by Don Pedro, a former employee of the Citroën firm in Paris, it is clear that this is a society in full flow of the experience of *la apertura* (the 'opening up' to new influences that took place in the final decade of the Franco era). Patriarchy, in the figures of Andrés, Pedro and Armando, is visibly overwhelmed by the pace of change; but the male characters are ultimately well served by the innovations and assertive modernity of their female partners. And it is the experience of Parisian otherness that gives momentum to the tentative reconciliation of opposing elements (tradition/

modernity; provincial/urban; conservative/liberal) in advance of the historical establishment of a new social framework. Of course, this promise of change, and of a recalibration of the structural inequalities of Spanish life, is only possible from the vantage point of the future: while Fernán-Gómez in 1966 could not know for sure what was ahead, Garci has the historical advantage of knowing that the end of dictatorship is only a decade away.

This redemptive quality to Garci's film is made explicit in the film's final scene, which sees Andrés and Ninette – now successful international business people – return to Paris to spend a belated honeymoon in one of the city's most elegant hotels. The elevation of all the characters is completed by the revelation that the hotel concierge is none other than the artist so frequently dazzled on the tenement stairs by Ninette in the first part of the film. Andrés finally looks out of the hotel window and sees Paris stretching before him: from the Seine to the Eiffel Tower, at last the sights of Paris are within his reach. But Ninette, once again assumes authority over the city, usurping its visual pleasures and replacing them with her own. Faced with the choice between visiting the city and making love to his awaiting wife, Andrés' Parisian fate is sealed; the city is destined to remain unseen.

Notes

1 I am grateful to John Shanks, a former student of Peter Evans at Queen Mary, University of London, for introducing me to both films discussed in this chapter, in the course of my MA module 'Paris on the Screen'.
2 Garci's star has waned somewhat in the noughties, and his films are increasingly perceived as dated within the mainstream of Spanish filmmaking.
3 The latter is a clear copy of Robert Doisneau's celebrated photograph of *Le Baiser de l'Hôtel de Ville* [*The Kiss*, 1950].
4 The name and behaviour suggest a playful nod to Bernarda, the overbearing mother of Lorca's *La casa de Bernarda Alba* [*The House of Bernarda Alba*, 1936].
5 Both terms translate as the rather pedestrian 'greengrocer'.
6 This is anachronistic, as the film in question had not yet been released in 1959.
7 The character Alphonse in Truffaut's *La Nuit Américaine/Day for Night* (1973) famously asks the question, 'are women magic?', a question that has since heavily informed scholarship about the representation of women in the director's work.

Bibliography

Jordan, Barry, and Rikki Morgan-Tamosunas (1998) *Contemporary Spanish Cinema*, Manchester: Manchester University Press.
McKay, Douglas R. (1977) *Miguel Mihura*, Boston: Twayne.
Smith, Paul Julian (2011) 'Spanish Spring: Spanish Cinema after Franco', *Sight & Sound*, 21:7 (July), 34–7.

10

El laberinto del fauno/Pan's Labyrinth (Guillermo del Toro, 2006): Spanish horror

Paul Julian Smith

El laberinto del fauno/Pan's Labyrinth takes place in 1944, the fifth year of peace following the Civil War, and recounts the exciting journey of Ofelia (Ivana Baquero), a young girl of 13, who along with her mother, Carmen (Ariadna Gil), whose condition is frail because of her advanced state of pregnancy, moves to a little village where Vidal (Sergi López) is based. He is a cruel captain in the Francoist army and Carmen's new husband, for whom Ofelia feels no affection. Vidal's mission is to finish off the last traces of Republican resistance, hidden in the forests of the region. Also in the village stands the mill that serves as Vidal's headquarters and where Mercedes (Maribel Verdú), the young head of the household, and the doctor (Álex Angulo), who will take charge of Carmen's delicate state of health, are awaiting the family. One night Ofelia discovers the ruins of a labyrinth in which she meets a faun (Doug Jones), a strange creature who reveals something incredible to her: Ofelia is really a princess, the last of her line, whose family have been waiting for her for a long time. In order to return to her magical kingdom, the girl must undergo three trials before the full moon. During this mission, fantasy and reality join hands to give free rein to a marvellous story where the magic that surrounds Ofelia transports us to a unique universe, one that is full of adventures and charged with emotion. (Clubcultura 2006; my translation)

There seems little doubt that *El laberinto del fauno/Pan's Labyrinth* (Guillermo del Toro, 2006) is one of the greatest critical and popular successes of its decade. It was the winner of seven Goya awards in Spain (including best original screenplay, best cinematography and best new actress), nine Ariels in Mexico (including best picture, best director and best actress), and three Oscars (best cinematography, once more, and best art design and make-up). And it was seen by 1,682,172 viewers in Spain, thus making it the third and ninth most popular local feature in 2006 and 2007, respectively (Ministerio de Cultura 2010), while its cumulative gross of over $37 million made it one of the most popular foreign-language films ever at the US box office. The UK total of £2,723,276 was also unprecedented (Gant 2009). Uniquely, for a Spanish-language fiction feature, it has also inspired a large bibliography in specialist journals of psychology and psychiatry (see Cook 2009; Rohde-Brown 2007; Segal 2009).

Yet beyond these bare facts, *Pan's Labyrinth* exhibits continuing contradictions. Although the Spanish Ministry of Culture website defines it simply as a 'drama', the film was generally received as a horror title; and IMDb (2010) lists its multiple genres as 'drama, fantasy, mystery, thriller, war ...'. Conversely, director Guillermo del Toro was clearly identified as *Pan's Labyrinth*'s auteur, a filmmaker with a personal style and vision uniquely capable of crossing national frontiers and generic borderlines (in an interview included with the UK DVD extras, he claims that it is his 'most personal' film). Accepted as a Spanish film in Spain and a Mexican movie in Mexico (hence its eligibility for both Goyas and Ariels), it is in fact a co-production between del Toro's own Tequila Gang and Picasso Studios, the successful feature-making arm of Spanish television broadcaster Tele 5.

While the Spanish Ministry of Culture website is enviably precise about the proportion of the film that can be allotted to each country (based on the budget, 78 per cent of the credit goes to Spain and 22 per cent to Mexico), the cultural allegiance of *Pan's Labyrinth* is more difficult to apportion. Indeed the fact that del Toro had already made an earlier feature charting the Civil War through the eyes of a child (*El espinazo del diablo/ The Devil's Backbone*, 2001), and presented this second film as in some way a sequel to the first, could be seen as making *Pan's Labyrinth* yet more markedly his own cinematic property. And in an interview del Toro admitted to risking cliché by connecting the violence in his film to a 'Mexican sensibility' (Kermode 2006). Yet by locating a genre film for the second time at a precise and traumatic moment in Spanish history, del Toro encouraged spectators to read the fantasy format that generally transcends time and space within a very particular context. And by making his young protagonist female in this second film, del Toro also raised the question of gender (claiming *Pan's Labyrinth* as a 'sister' to the 'brother' movie of *The Devil's Backbone* [Kermode 2006]), a question that, as we shall see, has transformed academic understanding of horror film in recent years.

Genre, then, as a set of formal characteristics that function as triggers of recognition for competent audiences, intersects in complex and unstable ways with a number of different factors: nationality, history, industry and sexuality. In this chapter I argue that *Pan's Labyrinth* deserves to be read within a particularly Spanish context. Beginning by raising the question of whether there is a specific kind of horror in the Spanish audiovisual sector (both cinema and television), the chapter then makes reference to varied and influential precursors in the field (including Narciso Ibáñez Serrador's *Historias para no dormir*/*Stories to Keep You Awake* [1964–82], Víctor Erice's *El espíritu de la colmena*/*The Spirit of the Beehive* [1973] and del Toro's own *The Devil's Backbone*) and places *Pan's Labyrinth* within that context. Particular attention should be paid here to *Pan's Labyrinth*'s principal production companies, mentioned earlier, the transnational specialist film enterprise Tequila Gang and Spanish national TV channel Tele 5, whose Estudios Picasso was at the time the most successful audiovisual producer in Spain. The chapter finally offers a close textual analysis of *Pan's Labyrinth* itself, calling attention to the points at which it coincides with and those at which it diverges from the transnational tradition of horror and its unique Spanish variant.

To begin, nomenclature is not simply a question of classification but also of production and reception. In Spain (where the English 'horror' is in any case normally translated by 'terror'), the requisite term, irreducible to foreign taxonomies, is *cine fantástico*. Vital for the understanding of the genre in Spain is the International Festival of that name held in Sitges since 1968. A leaflet published for that founding event, grandly titled *Índice analítico del cine fantástico* and written by the festival's first director Antonio Cervera (1968), attempts to set out the parameters for a body of previously neglected films. Yet, as in IMDb's description of the many genres of *Pan's Labyrinth*, categories proliferate. The leaflet lists no fewer than 42 variants or sub-genres of the 'fantastic': from vampires, werewolves and witches, through myths, dreams and fantasies, to 'personification of the abstract', the 'incarnation of death' and 'the invented past'. Signalling the open ended nature of the account and the impossibility of fully encompassing the genre, the final category reads simply 'Y … [*sic*]' [and …].

Modern scholars of this wide and indefinable field are indebted to one Spanish researcher, who, uniquely, has championed what he has baptised *Cine fantástico y de terror español* [Spanish fantasy and horror film]. Carlos Aguilar's invaluable collection of that name is divided into two volumes (1900–83 and 1984–2004), each prefaced by an excellent introduction (1999, 2005). And what is most significant here is that, going well beyond the taxonomic remit of Sitges, he links formal characteristics to the historical, political and industrial factors that inform and constrain them. Aguilar begins his account of the 'hot, black blood' of Spanish *fantasía* with an unequivocal assertion that a specifically Spanish *cine fantástico* definitely exists. The latter encompasses its own multiple conceptions of the genre, its more or less specialised auteurs, its high and low points, and its masterpieces and minor works (1999: 11). Aguilar estimates the corpus of such films as 200, with fully half of them released in the period 1968–74 (after Sitges was set up as a genre showcase) (1999: 13).

Two factors mark Spain's 'anomaly' in the field. The first is a characteristic belatedness. In literature, Romanticism, the origin of terror narratives, took (weak) root in Spain only in 1830, when it was already on the way out in Britain and France (1999: 14). Stymied by the strength of the Catholic Church, film horror, with its typical archetypes and obsessions, did not reach Spanish film until the 1960s, decades after such pioneers as German Expressionism and the 'splendour' of Lon Chaney and Todd Browning (1999: 15). And the Francoist regime allowed the shooting of supernatural stories only if they took place outside Spain.

The second feature of Spain's 'anomaly' for Aguilar is its crudity. From genre specialists Jess Franco and Narciso Ibáñez Serrador to (the unexpectedly cited) Álex de la Iglesia and Alejandro Amenábar, Spanish auteurs embrace the putrid, sickly and sordid, having little taste for science fiction and pure fantasy (for speculation and wonder) (1999: 16). The interaction between eroticism and violence or sex and death is thus held to be the most recognisable characteristic of Spanish horror (here rendered as 'terror') in all periods of film production.

In the introduction to his second volume Aguilar historicises this broad model, asking what happens when the Spanish fantastic genre becomes 'modern'. Ironising at the expense of the PSOE [Spanish socialist workers' party] government, which came to power in 1982, Aguilar lauds the Socialists for downgrading the influence of the Church and armed forces and liberalising access to pornography, but attacks the new cultural policy imposed by the *finos* [refined] politicians (2005: 12). The effect of the subsidy regime of the Miró Law of 1983 was, he writes, to abolish the middle ground in which fantasy film had thrived: now there were only the two irreconcilable currents of expensive 'important' films (financially backed by officials and benefiting from the best technical facilities and most prestigious casts) and despised 'sub-products' (made by tiny crews and professionals out of sync with modern trends and destined for straight-to-video distribution). The continuity and renovation of the horror genre thus proved impossible during the lengthy PSOE era.

For Aguilar the sad fate of fantasy is no accident. The Socialists hated anything that fell outside pure rationalism and, encouraged by the awards won by 'important' films at foreign festivals, cultivated the rural drama and social realism (preferably in plots adapted from classic novels) as new stereotypes for a dignified national cinema (2005: 13). Ironically coinciding with their Francoist predecessors, then, the PSOE proved that the Spanish 'contempt' for the fantastic genre is 'impermeable', irrespective of varied political positions.

Fortunately, the genre revived in the 1990s. And for Aguilar one then recent film project that transcends persistent Spanish binaries and preconceptions is precisely del Toro's *The Devil's Backbone*: a co-production between Spain and Mexico that fuses historical realism with traditional fantasy (2005: 41). Another is a cross-media hybrid: *Películas para no dormir/ Films to Keep you Awake* (2005) is a series of six feature-length episodes made for TV (like *Pan's Labyrinth*, by Estudios Picasso, based on classic television drama by Ibáñez Serrador but helmed by cinematic auteurs such as de la Iglesia [2005: 42]). This hybridity or difficulty in firmly locating horror within a single genre, territory or medium is confirmed by an idiosyncratic feature of Aguilar's style: his frequent appeal to foreign loan words or phrases such as 'fantastique', 'wonder sense [*sic*]', 'soft core' and 'ghost story'. This suggests that the films he treats are not quite Spanish, even as he insists on the unique characteristics of the nation's form of *terror*. (For the same reason, a later, less magisterial study written in Castilian is actually given the English-language title of *Spanish Horror* [Matellano 2009].)

Aguilar, sympathetic to his chosen subject, offers the opportunity to reread a genre much despised in Spain in a way he himself defines as artistic-historical-industrial (2005: 13). And he establishes a broad canon of Spanish directors that range from those firmly pigeonholed in a neglected genre to the most respected in general filmmaking: thus in the second volume Julio Medem is included on the basis of his propensity towards 'real' dreams (2005: 199–218). And there is little doubt that del Toro is a significant figure in this context and one who benefits from this new form of analysis. As mentioned earlier, *The Devil's Backbone* receives close study by Aguilar who, always sensitive to hybridity, praises its status as a co-production (a phenomenon to which other Spanish scholars are often hostile) and its fusion of painful Spanish reality (the Civil War) with the ghost-story format that is held to be of Anglo-Saxon origin (2005: 503). The film's creative process is equally impure, based as it is on the fusion of two separate narratives: a Spanish-set story of an unexploded bomb and an originally Mexican project located in a boarding school (2005: 504).

Clearly, although Aguilar does not state it explicitly, it is del Toro's foreign status and financial independence that make him immune to the 'impermeable' Spanish contempt for the genre in which he specialises and render him undeterred by the artistic-historical-industrial complex that has hitherto hobbled Spanish filmmakers drawn to the genre. As an outsider, del Toro can also bridge the divide established in a previous decade between the 'important' films that monopolised big budgets and technical and artistic talent and the straight-to-video 'subgenres' that (barely) preserved the anarchic vitality of sub-genres such as horror movies.

It is a bridging function of which del Toro makes good use in promotion, as well as production, in a range of countries: as *Sight & Sound* wrote, *Pan's Labyrinth* 'charmed both the hardcore horror … fans at [specialist festival] FrightFest in London … and the upmarket critical cognoscenti who snapped to attention following his Palme d'Or nomination at Cannes' (Kermode 2006). In *Pan's Labyrinth* horror motifs typical of the subgenres are thus combined with technical mastery (the Oscar-winning prosthetic make-up of Catalans David Martí and Montse Ribé) and prestigious casting (respected thespians Maribel Verdú, Ariadna Gil and Sergi López). The participation of such technicians and artists serves to underwrite the 'importance' of a film that was claimed by its auteur as the first over which he had complete artistic control.

Del Toro also embraces multiple 'variants' of the fantastic, beyond the stricter definitions of Anglo-American 'horror', diverse elements that were already proposed in Sitges in 1968. *Pan's Labyrinth* thus encompasses revamped versions of traditional monsters (a hideous toad, the 'Pale Man' with eyes in the palms of his hands), mythical creatures (the Faun and fairies) and more abstract 'personifications' (Captain Vidal as the embodiment of sadistic machismo and the incarnation of death), all set in an 'invented past', del Toro's brilliantly stylised re-creation of a corner of Spain in 1944.

In spite of the breadth of his definitions (and his inclusion of auteurist directors such as Medem in the canon of the *fantastique*), Aguilar does not mention the clearest Spanish antecedents of del Toro's twin Civil War-set dramas, art movies with genre influences that view 'Spanish reality' through the eyes of a child. Erice's *The Spirit of the Beehive* not only incorporates a fragment of James Whale's *Frankenstein* (1930) as a basis for its own haunting narrative, but also offers clear precedents for scenes in *Pan's Labyrinth*. As I have written elsewhere, del Toro's child heroine, Ofelia, replaces a missing piece (the eyes) in the face of a figure, just as Erice's did some 30 years earlier (in *Pan's Labyrinth* it is a stone image of the faun Ofelia will soon encounter, in *The Spirit of the Beehive* it is the wooden 'Don José', used to teach anatomy lessons) (Smith 2007: 5).

Likewise in del Toro, as in Erice, it is the status of the monster that is at stake. For Peter Evans (1982), Frankenstein's monster is associated with Ana's somewhat distant father (Fernando Fernán-Gómez), a reading later contested by Jo Labanyi (2010), who associates the monster rather with the 'living dead', forgotten victims of history. Likewise the Faun is the object of the child's fascination, but also of her fear, as Ofelia finds herself, like Ana (and following Evans's title), 'growing up in the Dictatorship'. It is a reference not lost on the film critics of the Spanish press: the reviewer in national daily *20 Minutos* (2006) claimed that *El laberinto* had more in common with the 'regresiones infantiles' [childhood regressions] of Erice than with recent 'mágico-mitológico' [magical-mythological] spectacles like the *Harry Potter* and *Chronicles of Narnia* franchises.

Significantly the several and less haunting films on this theme that followed *The Spirit of the Beehive* and preceded *Pan's Labyrinth* employ not girls but boys as uncomprehending witnesses to historical horror, boys whose sense of loss is often focused on father figures. In Montxo Armendáriz's *Secretos del corazón/ Secrets of the Heart* (1997), 9-year-old Javi explores a haunted house in the Basque Country in which the voices of the dead (including his father) can still be heard, while in José Luis Cuerda's *La lengua de las mariposas/ The Butterflies' Tongue* (1999) it is Galician schoolboy Moncho who sees his Republican teacher (Fernán-Gómez once more) taken away to his death. In Cuerda's subsequent *Los girasoles ciegos/ The Blind Sunflowers* (2008), also Galicia-set, child Lorenzo witnesses his father's suicide when the latter's hiding place is revealed to the Francoist authorities. Only in this last film is there a link between the small corpus of 'important' (self-important) films on childhood and dictatorship and the still underrated genre movie: Roger Príncep, the fearful son of *The Blind Sunflowers*, had recently featured as the vulnerable child in the hugely successful horror hit *El orfanato/The Orphanage* (J.A. Bayona, 2007), a feature for which del Toro himself took a high-profile producer credit as 'presenter' of the film.

For Spanish audiences, however, the most pervasive horror strand is one derived from television: Narciso Ibáñez Serrador's *Stories to Keep You Awake* are low-budget studio-set dramas (now re-released on DVD) whose grainy black-and-white photography and claustrophobic sets (so different to the expert production design of del Toro) no doubt heightened the horror they instilled in faithful Francoist audiences. The fact that, as mentioned earlier, the *Stories* were later remade by cinematic auteurs, proves that they remain essential as a context within which Spanish audiences view the genre. Ibáñez Serrador's one-off dramas show their allegiance to the 'Anglo-Saxon' roots of the ghost story in the same manner that Aguilar suggests by employing foreign settings (the creator himself, who regularly introduced the episodes, is like del Toro of Latin American origin, in his case Uruguayan).

Just as important as this pervasive sense of foreignness attached to the fantastic genre is the fact that the *Historias* sometimes featured child protagonists, early precursors of del Toro's tortured infants. Thus in one tale (*El muñeco/The Doll*, 1966), loosely alluding to Henry James's *The Turn of the Screw* (1898), a disturbed girl in Edwardian England ecstatically communes with her dead governess before murdering her father by sticking pins into a doll. Ibáñez Serrador's few feature films (generally held to be less compelling than his work in television) also focus on minors: in *La residencia/The House that Screamed* (1969) girls mysteriously disappear from their boarding school, while in *¿Quién puede matar a un niño?/Island of the Damned* (1976) a murderous band of children terrorise an adult couple. Such works thus create a context for del Toro's more prestigious but still genre-based works.

But it is in his focus not only on a child but on a female heroine (relatively rare in Spain) that del Toro coincides with academic trends that have vindicated the role of young women in the horror genre. As is well known, Carol Clover's *Men, Women, and Chainsaws: Gender in the Modern Horror Film* (1993) seeks to refocus attention from sadism to victimhood as sources of pleasure for young (and mainly male) audiences. Beginning with an account of Brian de Palma's *Carrie* (1973), which was based on a novel by Stephen King, Clover suggests that, first, the central figure (a schoolgirl who wreaks havoc after she is bullied on first getting her period) is at once victim, hero and monster; and second, that the intended viewers of this female-focused narrative (who King claims 'had their gym shorts pulled down' as kids) are clearly male (1993: 5). For Clover, slasher and rape-revenge movies provide strong yet ambiguous heroines for boys to sympathise with in a form of identification different from (and hostile to) the sadistic-voyeuristic and fetishistic-scopophilic looks that were previously attributed by feminist film theorists to male spectators (1993: 8). In this newly slippery film world 'we are both Red Riding Hood and the Wolf; the force of the experience in horror comes from knowing both sides of the story' (1993: 12).

Clover suggests that the horror that harks back to an archaic 'one-sex' model of physiology, in which male and female cannot clearly be separated (1993: 13), is sensitive nonetheless to changes in historical circumstance. Indeed she cites Stephen King himself on *Carrie* as a fearful response to the challenge posed to men by feminism in the 1970s (1993: 5). This challenge is embodied in the figure famously dubbed by Clover the 'Final Girl' (1993: 35), the distressed female who fights back against the monster. What Clover offers us here, then, is a chance to reread both gender and history in a filmic genre often considered to have its roots in misogyny and myth.

We have seen thus far how genre intersects in complex and changing ways with such factors as nationality, history, industry and sexuality. And we have addressed the question of the specific kind of horror in the Spanish audiovisual sector (both cinema and television). We can now go on to carry out a textual analysis of *Pan's Labyrinth*, informed by the historical and theoretical debates outlined above.

Pan's Labyrinth begins with titles over a black screen, clearly specifying the film's time, place and historical situation (the struggle of the *maquis* against victorious Francoist forces). The opening sequence, however, works to unsettle that specific setting. Anticipating the final shot of the film (and reversing chronological time), blood flows back into the nostril of heroine Ofelia (newcomer Ivana Baquero). Guillermo Navarro's camera, in the first of many physically impossible shots, penetrates her eye to reveal a fantasy location, reinforced by voice-over: in a vast palace set (actually an expert miniature made by Spanish special-effects veteran Emilio Ruiz del Río), Ofelia is a princess in exile who must return to her father the King. The cinematography remains unusually mobile and fluid as we cut to the first sequence proper in the real world: Ofelia's arrival with her sickly pregnant mother Carmen (Ariadna Gil) at the mill where she will meet her brutal stepfather Vidal (Sergi López). The camera soars over the spectacular ruins of a devastated village, cuts in close to see Ofelia replace the missing piece in the Faun's monolith, and flies behind the insect following the family's car, which will metamorphose into one of Ofelia's 'fairies'.

From the very beginning of the film, then, fantasy and reality are inextricable and we are provided with no clues, either narrative or visual, as to which of the elements we see are to be read as part of the child's imagination. What I would suggest, however, is that this unique film, which has already established itself in a generic hinterland between drama, fantasy, mystery, thriller and war movie, re-creates in its fluid diegetic and filmic texture that national and generic border crossing held to be so typical of its auteur.

However, nationality is inseparable from history. And *Pan's Labyrinth's* vision of Fascist violence, embodied in López's terrifying Captain Vidal, was read in Spain as an intervention in the debate on historical memory that had dominated contemporary Spanish politics in recent years. Thus while foreign viewers will find the film's hostility to the dictatorship uncontroversial, some local spectators read it as supporting the PSOE's policy of promoting awareness of the continuing legacy of the Civil War. One hostile conservative viewer (Rodríguez Pardo 2010) branded the film 'inverosímil' [unrealistic] not because of its appeal to fantasy, but for its hostility to a regime for which he clearly remained nostalgic. While it is easy to dismiss such views as marginal in democratic Spain, the important point is that the discursive context in which *Pan's Labyrinth* was received was more urgent and precise than outside its country of origin, namely what this writer brands 'el pensamiento Zapatero' [the philosophy of [Socialist President] Zapatero].

If *Pan's Labyrinth* is a historically specific intervention in Spain, it is also industrially anomalous within the Spanish tradition of the fantastic. I have already suggested that its melding of quality production values and generic narrative formulae would have been inconceivable under an earlier Socialist cultural policy. And *Pan's Labyrinth* puts to rest the two charges laid against Spanish 'terror' by its champion Aguilar. Hardly belated, it employs the most up-to-date technical effects (albeit as often animatronic as digital) to give an impression of modern professionalism as perfectly realised as any Hollywood blockbuster. And rejecting the 'crudity' also held to be typical of Spain, *Pan's Labyrinth's* vision of the erotic is subtly displaced into disturbing elements of *mise en scène*: Vidal's fetishistic love of his black leather boots and gloves or the pure Ofelia's repeated immersion in the abject fluids of mud and blood.

If sex does indeed lead, in traditional style, to death (Ofelia's mother will die giving birth to the baby fathered by the monstrous Vidal), then that sex remains off-screen. Ironically, then, *Pan's Labyrinth*, which rejects the rationalism or realism of an earlier mode of Spanish quality cinema, is in part a re-creation of the refined rural drama that was the favoured format of the 1980s. The Goya-winning film was thus acceptable to the Spanish cinematic establishment, as it appeared to reconcile social or historical realism with fantasy in a way anticipated to some extent by the 'real dreams' of such iconic auteurs of the 1990s as Julio Medem and Alejandro Amenábar.

This supposed 'Spanish reality', familiar since at least the time of Erice, is of course seen through the eyes of a child, in this case a girl, whose perspective is consistently privileged throughout the film. As I have written elsewhere (Smith 2007: 8), the main technical devices of *Pan's Labyrinth* are the masked cut (where the fluid shift between real and fantastic locations is achieved by such

22. Reconciling social or historical realism with fantasy: Ofelia in the forest.

techniques as the camera passing behind a tree) or the sound bridge (where the same movement is effected by the audio of one space, such as the clicking of the fairy-insect, merging with that of another, such as the ticking of the Captain's stopwatch).

But this expert blurring of boundaries is based on our identification with Ofelia's point of view as internal narrator. For example, it is only when we hear her tell her unborn brother the tale of a magical flower that the camera penetrates the mother's womb to show us that brother and flower. Or again, the most generic sequences (such as the child's encounter with the monstrous toad and Pale Man) are filmed using the most classical point-of-view shooting style which sutures our look in with that of the terror-struck, yet plucky, protagonist.

As is revealed by Ofelia's response to her three trials, she is as much heroine as she is victim. And the male viewers who, still, make up the majority of horror fans are encouraged to identify with her in her distress, rather than taking voyeuristic pleasure in her sadistic treatment at the hands of the Captain. But although Ofelia dies protecting her baby brother, the avenging force of the Final Girl is projected on to another major female character who does indeed survive: Maribel Verdú's steely housekeeper Mercedes slashes Vidal's face, saying he is not the first pig she has gutted. If, as Clover suggested, horror comes from knowing both sides of the story, then those two sides (victim and heroine) are distributed by del Toro between his twin active female protagonists. Archetypal characters and situations (fauns and fairies, dreams and trials) thus come up against a modern conception of feminism that has, since the 1970s, threatened some men with their worst fears. And in spite of its physically immature heroine, *Pan's Labyrinth*, like *Carrie*, is haunted by the prospect of menstruation: shot in the belly in the final sequence, Ofelia drips blood on to the full moon that is reflected in the puddles deep in the labyrinth.

The film thus clearly follows classic horror in its enduring attachment to the archaic 'one-sex' model: a bifurcated, curving design, based on the Fallopian tubes, recurs throughout the *mise en scène*. The faun and his attendant fairies are sexless, as is the pre-pubescent Ofelia, who scorns the feminine fripperies of pretty dresses and shiny shoes. The narcissistic Captain, who prefers not to sleep with his wife, holds a lavish dinner for local worthies such as the priest, who have sublimated erotic pleasure into gluttony. Although one critic (Edwards 2008) has claimed that Ofelia's assumption of the maternal function is 'conventional' (unlike Lewis Carroll's Alice, whom he claims as her sister), del Toro's plot strips horror of its classic misogyny and mythical trappings, reinscribing gender roles into a challenging and troubling historical context.

Moreover, *Pan's Labyrinth* avoids the focus on father figures that so preoccupies the strand of Spanish cinema in which children bear traumatised witness to the legacy of the Civil War. Ofelia repeatedly insists, at the start of the film, that the Captain is not her father. And only at the end will she return to the fantasy realm where her real parent (Federico Luppi, a ghostly revenant from *The Devil's Backbone*) is barely glimpsed. Distancing himself from the father fixation of earlier films on the violent legacy of the dictatorship, del Toro also takes care to cut quickly away from scenes of surgery or torture in *Pan's Labyrinth*, images on which recent body horror, in Spain as elsewhere, dwells at considerable length.

Beyond the changing taxonomies of film genre and their academic re-readings, however, *Pan's Labyrinth* is also a cross-media hybrid. One telling detail for older Spanish audiences is that Francisco Vidal, the actor playing the minor role of the gluttonous priest was, a lifetime ago, the kindly padre in one of the most celebrated series in the history of Spanish television, *Crónicas de un pueblo/ Chronicles of a Village* (Antonio Mercero, 1971). Likewise Álex Angulo, who plays the larger part of the doctor, has been a popular regular in high-profile TV fiction for some 20 years and remains best known for over 100 episodes of Tele 5's groundbreaking workplace drama *Periodistas/Journalists* (1998–2002). Given these triggers of televisual memory, it would thus seem appropriate that *Pan's Labyrinth* was mainly funded by Tele 5, under the Law of Cinema that requires TV stations to subsidise the loss-making feature-film sector. And media cross-fertilisation works both ways: it is no coincidence that the most innovative television format to première in 2007, the year after *Pan's Labyrinth*'s high-profile success, was a mystery-horror title which is rare in that medium. *El internado/The Boarding School* (Antena 3) boasted a cast of teens and infants terrified by the monsters that lurked in the forest that surrounded their school and in the 'labyrinth' of tunnels beneath it. *El laberinto* is thus not simply a prestigious feature film; it is also a prime example of the newly converged Spanish audiovisual sector.

In 2009 Kim Newman, the best-known horror critic in the UK (perhaps the British equivalent of Carlos Aguilar), wrote that amidst the 'localized, nationally distinctive' scenes in Europe 'only in Spain is the horror film simultaneously thriving in its classic and modern forms, delivering gruelling ordeals of survival and pointed ghost/fantasy stories' (2009: 38). Industry commentator Charles Gant also noted in the same year that Spanish horror films have a unique 'track record' in the UK in bringing together arthouse audiences and genre fans. In the light of J.A. Bayona's *The Orphanage* and Paco Plaza and Jaume Balagueró's [*REC*] (both 2007), more recent and no less successful than *Pan's Labyrinth*, it might perhaps be better to talk of a Catalan connection: there now exist a cluster of specialist directors and technicians based in Barcelona. Whatever the case, it is clear that as a Spanish horror film, *Pan's Labyrinth* engages with a special matrix of nationality, history, industry and sexuality that is found only in its home country. But the masterpiece of del Toro, the Mexican nomad, not only refers, as we have seen, to the rich and complex cinematic legacy of the past. It has also established a unique and invaluable model for the future of Spanish genre film.

Bibliography

20 Minutos (2006) 'El laberinto del fauno', www.20minutos.es/cine/cartelera/pelicula/28455/el-laberinto-del-fauno/ [accessed 19 August 2010].

Aguilar, Carlos (1999) *Cine fantástico y de terror español: 1900–1983*, San Sebastián: Donostia Kultura.

—(2005) *Cine fantástico y de terror español: 1984–2004*, San Sebastián: Donostia Kultura.

Cervera, Antonio (1968) *Índice analítico del cine fantástico*, Sitges: Semana Internacional de Cine.

Clover, Carol (1993) *Men, Women, and Chainsaws: Gender in the Modern Horror Film*, Princeton: Princeton University Press.

Clubcultura (2006) 'El laberinto del fauno: sinopsis', www.clubcultura.com/clubcine/clubcineastas/guillermodeltoro/ellaberintodelfauno/sinopsis.htm [accessed 19 August 2010].

Cook, Beverley Richard (2009) 'Jungian Archetypes in Guillermo del Toro's *El laberinto del fauno*', http://congreso.cgjung.cl/pdf/cursos/mesas_redondas_congreso/C12%20Cook,%20B.%20R..pdf [accessed 19 August 2010].

Edwards, Kim (2008) 'Alice's Little Sister: Exploring *Pan's Labyrinth*', *Screen Education*, 49, 141–6.

Evans, Peter W. (1982) '*El espíritu de la colmena*: The Monster, the Place of the Father, and Growing up in the Dictatorship', *Vida Hispánica*, 31:3, 13–17.

Gant, Charles (2009) 'Do the "Right" Thing: European Horror at UK Box Office', *Sight & Sound*, 19:6 (June), p. 9.

Internet Movie Database (IMDb), 'Pan's Labyrinth', www.imdb.com/title/tt0457430/ [accessed 19 August 2010].

Labanyi, Jo (2010) 'Coming to Terms with Ghosts and Spectrality in Contemporary Spanish Culture', http://arachne.rutgers.edu/vol1_1labanyi.htm [accessed 19 August 2010].

Kermode, Mark (2006) 'Girl Interrupted', *Sight & Sound*, 16:12 (December), www.bfi.org.uk/sightandsound/feature/49337/ [accessed 19 August 2010].

Matellano, Víctor (2009) *Spanish Horror*, Madrid: T&B.

Ministerio de Cultura, 'Base de datos', www.mcu.es/cine/CE/BBDDPeliculas/BBDDPeliculas_Index.html [accessed 19 August 2010].

Newman, Kim (2009) 'Horror will Eat Itself', *Sight & Sound*, 19:5 (May), 36–8.

Rodríguez Pardo, José Manuel (2007) 'El inverosímil *Laberinto del fauno*', www.nodulo.org/ec/2007/n067p14.htm [accessed 19 August 2010].

Rohde-Brown, Juliet (2007) Review of *Pan's Labyrinth*, *Psychological Perspectives*, 50:1 (January), 167–9.

Segal, Timothy (2009) '*Pan's Labyrinth*: A Subjective View on Childhood Fantasies and the Nature of Evil', *International Review of Psychiatry*, 21:3 (June), 269–70.

Smith, Paul Julian (2007) '*Pan's Labyrinth* (*El laberinto del fauno*)', *Film Quarterly*, 60:4, 4–9.

11

La noche de los girasoles/The Night of the Sunflowers (Jorge Sánchez-Cabezudo, 2006): palimpsests of genre, palimpsests of violence

Tom Whittaker

Angosto, a tiny Castilian village, the present. A woman has been found raped and murdered in a field of sunflowers. The killer, a travelling salesman (Manuel Morón), drives through the countryside, searching for his next victim. Esteban (Carmelo Gómez), a speleologist who lives in Madrid, arrives in Angosto to inspect a cave which one of its residents has discovered. Eagerly awaiting his arrival, the community hope that the cave can be turned into a tourist attraction. Esteban's partner, Gabi (Judith Diakhate), and a photographer, Pedro (Mariano Alameda), join him. As Esteban and Pedro inspect the cave, Gabi finds herself alone in the countryside, where the salesman attempts to rape and murder her. Traumatised, Gabi confuses her attacker with Cecilio (Cesáreo Estébanez), an elderly resident who lives in an abandoned village nearby. Esteban and Pedro enter into a violent confrontation with Cecilio, which results in his murder. Realising they have made a grave error, they call the police. A policeman, Tomás (Vicente Romero), arrives, drunk, and offers to hide all knowledge of Cecilio's death in exchange for money; they then hide his corpse in the cave. Cecilio's elderly neighbour, Amós (Walter Vidarte), who found the corpse shortly after he was killed, reports his discovery to the police station. The chief of police, Amadeo (Celso Bugallo), who is also Tomás's father-in-law, finds that the body is not there, and the police at first do not take his claim seriously. However, Tomás's plot slowly unravels as Amadeo begins to investigate what really happened to Cecilio.

Jorge Sánchez-Cabezudo's directorial debut, *La noche de los girasoles/The Night of the Sunflowers*, was both a critical and commercial hit in Spain. As Carmen Herrero has observed, the film was among the Spanish feature films with the highest box-office takings of 2006 (2010: 126). Set in the heart of rural Spain,

The Night of the Sunflowers explores the fading legacy of the Spanish countryside in an age of increasing urbanisation and global flows. The writer Julio Llamazares, whose novels often focus on the rural Leonese landscape of his childhood, has said that Spain is an urban country with a rural memory.[1] Sánchez-Cabezudo's film similarly provides an archaeology of Spain's rural memory, where the rural emerges as traces of a violent and monstrous nightmare, which haunt the urban consciousness. As I will show, this tension is played out in the complex representation of landscape in the film. The landscape is primarily one of loss, trauma and fragmentation: not only does it register a nation unable to reconcile itself with its recent rural past, but it articulates a greater desire to nurture and preserve a way of life that is fast disappearing in the present. In examining the various surfaces and meanings that have been erased and overwritten on the landscape, my discussion of *The Night of the Sunflowers* contributes towards our understanding of the contemporary shifting structures of rural Spain, and its increasingly complex location in the national imaginary.

Geography and genre

In spite of the film's rural setting and concerns, it was primarily conceived and distributed as a Spanish *noir* thriller – a genre that is most associated with the dark and labyrinthine streets of the city. This tension is played out in the film's UK, French and Italian poster, whose stark minimalism alludes to the iconic designs of Saul Bass, who created the promotional material and credit sequences of several films in the 1950s by Otto Preminger, Billy Wilder and, most famously, Alfred Hitchcock. Like Bass's designs, which according to Pat Kirkham were able to capture the essence of the film through an 'aesthetics of reduction and fragmentation' (Kirkham, 1994: 16), the poster similarly condenses the film's complex geography into one striking image. A silhouette of a woman's body, prostrate and bleeding, is superimposed onto a brilliant backdrop of golden sunflowers. The poster points to a violent appearance of the urban within the rural: while the woman's dark shadow gestures towards the aesthetic of *noir*, it lies incongruously against a pastoral oasis of flowers and light. If the image eloquently summarises the dislocation of city folk within the country, it also illuminates the contradiction which lies at the very heart of the film's title, *The Night of the Sunflowers*. The aesthetic of *noir* conceals more than it reveals through its expressionistic nocturnal shadows, while sunflowers turn their heads to follow the sun during the hours of daylight. The flowers, however, are first seen in the film's opening sequence which takes place at night: they are the blind witnesses of the rape and murder of a young woman, whose inert body has been abandoned in an isolated field.

An antagonistic duality between night and day is also keenly felt in the film's original title, *Angosto*, which is the fictional name of the crumbling village in

23. Poster for *The Night of the Sunflowers*.

the film. Significantly, *angosto* also means 'narrow' or 'tight' in Spanish, and thus vividly conjures up landscapes that are simultaneously both material and interior. For it points to the submerged cave into which Cecilio's body is lowered – a space to which Esteban, the speleologist, refers earlier in the film as 'no encontrarás nada más oscuro' [you won't find anything as dark], and which later emerges as the dark centre around which the film's intrigue of duplicity and denial is spun. But it might also gesture more generally towards the spatial structures of noir, whose labyrinthine forms and oblique angles are as much an expression of the city as they are of the psyche. Again, darkness is thematically imbricated with light: Angosto also resembles the word *agosto* (August), and the oppressive and asphyxiating Castilian heat of the summer. Indeed, the actor Carmelo Gómez has commented on the difficulties the crew faced when making the film, pointing to the 'calor terrible' [awful heat] and having to shoot some scenes from within a cave as significant setbacks (Domínguez 2006: 12–13). The titles and the poster, therefore, possess a *mise en abyme* quality which holds in tension both the city and the country, night and day, and the unseen and the seen. Most crucially, these work together to throw light on the geographical anxieties that are at the very heart of *The Night of the Sunflowers*.

Like so many villages in central Spain, the community of Angosto (actually the villages of San Bartolomé de Béjar and Becedas in the Castilian province of Ávila) struggles to survive. Its smaller neighbouring village, located further within the lower reaches of the valley, has all but been deserted, save for its two remaining elderly inhabitants, Amós and Cecilio. The presence of time is palpable everywhere in the neighbouring village: an extreme long shot shows weatherbeaten buildings, whose stones have crumbled into the surrounding landscape; a camera elegantly tracks across a ramshackle graveyard, an indication of the once thriving community that Amós and Cecilio have since outlived. Its very stillness recalls earlier Spanish films such as *Las Hurdes/Land Without Bread* (Luis Buñuel, 1932), which was filmed close to the location of *The Night of the Sunflowers* and *La aldea maldita/The Cursed Village* (Florián Rey, 1942), whose landscape, according to Requena, has 'ciertos valores zurbaranianos: un estatismo casi absoluto y, sobre todo, intemporal, denso e inmune al paso del tiempo' [certain Zurbaranesque values: an almost complete sense of stasis and, most of all, eternal, dense and immune to the passing of time] (González Requena 1998: 25). Village life is far from idyllic, as we see Cecilio and Amós locked in a bitter feud that has presumably lasted for years. Cecilio vehemently accuses Amós of trying to steal the church bell, an important symbol of communal identity that once marked the occasions of weddings and christenings, but has now fallen silent. They are both figures within a landscape of loss, where the memories of the past inexorably intrude into the present, and the present bears the weight of ghosts of the past. Indeed, Amós is frequently beset by spectral visions of his dead neighbours; after discovering Cecilio's corpse, he is even led to believe that he is responsible for his death, as during a bitter argument he tells him that he wishes he were dead. Significantly, however, it is the city folk who kill Cecilio. A protracted and unflinchingly violent scene sees Cecilio defend himself with his rifle, while Juan takes Cecilio's pitchfork and charges towards him, stabbing him in the stomach; a few moments later, Esteban then shoots him with a rifle. Killed in part by his own tool, his death more widely suggests the greater implosion of rural Spain. As Jorge Sánchez-Cabezudo has commented in an interview in *Sight & Sound*, 'the old rural way of life is disappearing now, and the death of one of the characters is a symbol of the death of this way of life' (Macnab 2007: 12).[2]

As is well known, Spain was only until relatively recently an agrarian economy. Accelerated modernisation, which began in earnest in the late 1950s, led to far-reaching geographical change, where the burgeoning growth of Spanish cities coincided with a massive exodus from the countryside. According to Caro Baroja, while during the 1950s nearly half of Spain's population was employed in farm work, by the 1980s only 15 per cent worked on the land (2002). The social cost of migration was nothing short of disastrous: as Eduardo Sevilla-Guzmán has shown, the Franco regime failed to take sufficient measures to help ailing village communities sustain themselves, and many were left crippled, with the regions of Extremadura, Andalusia and, most crucially, Castile most affected (1976: 118). Indeed, it was in Castile that depopulation was most keenly felt: Shubert demonstrates that in the Castilian provinces of Palencia, Segovia, Soria, Zamora and Ávila, where the film is set, the population by 1975 dwindled to less than it had been some 75 years earlier (1990: 92). But just as these rural communities continue to erode and disappear, they also appear to weigh more heavily on Spanish consciousness. To this effect, *The Night of the Sunflowers* can be seen as part of a greater trend in contemporary Spanish cinema in which rural space is not just the setting but the subject of films. In the recent thrillers *El rey de la montaña/King of the Hill* (Gonzalo López-Gallego, 2007), *Bosque de sombras/The Backwoods* (Koldo Serra, 2006) and *Hierro* (Gabe Ibañez, 2009), remote rural settings are presented as an impenetrable and foreboding Other to urban outsiders, while the more gentle dramas *Cenizas del cielo/Ashes of Heaven* (José Antonio Quirós, 2008) and *La vida que te espera/The Life That Awaits You* (Manuel Gutiérrez Aragón, 2004) and the poetic documentary *El cielo gira/The Sky Turns* (Mercedes Álvarez, 2004) register the changing face of rural communities within a context of global flows. According to the geographer Keith Halfacree, this contradiction can be found in many contemporary representations of local rurality. As the author puts it: 'We may have to recognise that whilst the referent – the rural locality – may be withering away in respect to its causal significance and distinctive-ness, its nominally associated social representation may well be flourishing and evolving' (1993: 34). This absence/presence is strikingly played out in contemporary Spanish cinema, where the centrality of the rural landscape responds to a wider social anxiety in the face of geographical change.

Fractured landscapes

Significantly, *noir* is a genre or aesthetic that similarly concerns itself with space – or rather, more specifically, the very fragmentation of space. Edward Dimendberg shows that many classical films *noir* sought to capture a vision of the American city that, during the 1940s and 1950s, was in decline. With the flight of the American middle classes to the suburbs, and the postwar clearouts of the city, film noir emerges 'as a social memory bank that provides a means for the film spectator to remember disappearing urban forms' (Dimendberg 2004: 10). The production of rural space in *The Night of the Sunflowers* appears to display a similar dynamic. It is a landscape of anxiety, whose violent fragmentation simultaneously responds to an underlying desire to preserve Spanish rural culture, to nurture it and to keep it intact. Indeed, the camera, in its frequent tracking shots and establishing shots, seeks to capture the landscape in its totality. Despite the paranoia and moral turpitude of several of the film's characters, the cinematography lovingly emphasises the pictorialism of the landscape, with its fields, trees and buildings bathed in the brilliant light of midsummer. Moreover, the film's narrative arc concludes by keeping the rural and urban apart as two autonomous and discrete spaces: Gabi, Esteban and Juan return to Madrid, traumatised and some €80,000 poorer; Tomás is forced to stay in the village and remain faithful to his pregnant wife; and despite the wishes of its inhabitants, neither the village nor its caves will be opened up to the global flows of ecotourism. The landscape can therefore be seen as an elegiac document: it simultaneously laments and preserves a way of life that is fast disappearing, and articulates Spain's alienation from its recent rural past.

One of the film's most striking features is its fractured narrative, which like Akira Kurosawa's *Rashomon* (1950), is organised into six different 'chapters', each focalising the story as it unfolds through the eyes of different characters.[3] Again, in common with *noir*, the complication of story and plot contributes towards the film's web-like structure of fate, where the predestined courses of the characters gradually emerge as enmeshed and interconnected in one another. Its narrative structure also throws light on the complex structures of space produced in the film. As Dimendberg has suggested, the fragmented narration of film *noir* 'remains well attuned to the violently fragmented spaces and times of the late modern world' (2004: 6). Correspondingly, the different viewpoints simultaneously bring into focus the making and unmaking of the landscape, illuminating it as a complex and unstable social space. For instance, in the second chapter, 'los espeleólogos' [the potholers], rural space is refracted through the urban gaze of Pedro, Esteban and Gabi – an effect which is created through a conspicuous use of eye-line matches and point-of-view shots. In particular, Pedro's camera emphasises their location as outsiders, and in one scene he takes a photograph of two elderly villagers in traditional clothes, going about their everyday business. In literally 'framing' the village with his camera, his camera freezes the image into a flat spectacle, an exotic Other to their urban gaze. Their way of looking conforms to what John Urry has famously called the 'tourist gaze', in which the landscape is consumed for its visual pleasure. According to John Urry, 'the tourist gaze is directed to features of landscape and townscape which separate them off from everyday experience. Such aspects are viewed because they are taken to be in some sense out of the ordinary' (2000: 3). The urban outsiders' adoption of the tourist gaze clearly signals their separation from the rural land: it is frequently presented as *beyond*, rather than part of themselves. As with the American eco-thrillers *Deliverance* (John Boorman, 1972) and *Straw Dogs* (Sam Peckinpah, 1971) – films which were made amid the growing environmental tensions generated by the world oil crisis, and which the director cites in the DVD interview as key influences on his film – the rural in *The Night of the Sunflowers* emerges as an unrepresentable and untamed force, a sublime and atavistic Other which the urban outsiders try – and fail – to contain and repress. To frame the landscape is therefore to draw reassuring boundaries around it, to make order out of the chaos, and regain control of space. To this effect, Susan Sontag has famously written that photographs 'help people to take possession of a space in which they are insecure. Thus photography develops in tandem with one of the most characteristic of modern activities: tourism' (2008: 9).

It is the potential extraordinariness of the local landscape that Julián (Enrique Martínez), the village mayor, seeks to promote. As Esteban is officially introduced to the excited villagers in the town hall, the mayor tells him that they hope that their discovery might lead to 'una de esas cuevas espectaculares' [one those spectacular caves] with cave paintings, the likes of which were recently found in rural Galicia. A little later on, from a high vantage point looking down on the abandoned village, he explains to Esteban that the caves will attract tourists, and will therefore be pivotal to the survival of their community: '"Turismo rural". Ésa es la palabra. Resulta que está de moda. La gente viene a pasar su tiempo libre' ['Rural tourism'. That's what they call it. It's all the rage. People come here to spend their free time]. Unlike the homogenised *turismo de sol y playa* [sun and beach tourism] holiday resorts, rural tourism promises a more 'authentic' cultural experience. Rural tourism, which as Afinoguznova and Martí-Olivella note, first emerged in Spain in the late 1980s (2008: xxii), aims to showcase the regional particularity, or what geographers refer to as the 'localisation', of a specific place. But in opening up villages like Angosto to the global flows of capital and people as a site of consumption, their authenticity is potentially threatened.

If in the chapter of the potholers the landscape is framed from without, the chapters 'El hombre del camino' [The man on the road] and 'Amós el loco' [Amós the crazy] offer the 'insider's' perspective of Cecilio and Amós, respectively. Their relationship to the land can be further illuminated through the writing of the Spanish ruralist writer, Miguel Delibes. In an interview, when asked his opinion of Emile Zola's famous assertion 'los campesinos no ven el campo' [peasants don't see the countryside], Delibes responds, 'Sí ven el paisaje, naturalmente que lo ven, pero no desde un punto de vista estético sino económico' [Of course they see the landscape, but from an economic point of view rather than an aesthetic one] (García de León 1996: 243). Correspondingly, for Amós and Cecilio, the landscape is primarily a site of capital, territory and survival, a space of production rather than visual consumption; as such, it is not so much experienced as landscape, as it is *land*. John Berger writes that landscape can often conceal the land: 'Landscapes can be deceptive. Sometimes a landscape seems to be less a setting for the life of its inhabitants than a curtain behind which their struggles, achievements and accidents take place' (1976: 13, 15). A 'curtain' similarly conceals the social reality of the rural community from the urban outsiders, holding in antagonistic tension a conflict between landscape and land. The film's distinctive formal structure thus not only serves to fragment the narrative, but to vividly convey the fragmentation of space. The various viewpoints in the film therefore act as framing devices, each simultaneously providing different evocations of and cultural negotiations with the same space.

Palimpsests of violence

In the DVD interview, Jorge Sánchez-Cabezudo says that although he intended to make a *noir*, and had not originally thought of making the film in the Spanish tradition of the rural film, 'es algo que queda en el subconciente, y a la hora de hacer la película todo eso vuelve' [it is something that remains in the unconscious, and it all returns when making the film]. Indeed, the legacy of the rural genre appears to haunt the film and to find its most vivid expression in its representation of violence and landscape. Key rural films include *La caza/ The Hunt* (Carlos Saura, 1965) and *Los santos inocentes/ The Holy Innocents* (Mario Camus, 1984), which Sánchez-Cabezudo cites as influences, as well as *Pascual Duarte* (Ricardo Franco, 1976) and *Los desafíos/ The Challenges* (Víctor Erice, José Luis Egea and Claudio Guerín, 1969).[4] These films were known for their *tremendismo*, a style of heightened realism that reveled in the gruesome, violent and often irrational aspects of human experience. Correspondingly, these were elements that Spanish critics were quick to observe in *The Night of the Sunflowers*. According to *Fotogramas*, 'la violencia pura y dura, irracional y salvaje, instintiva e irrefrenable es la gran protagonista del primer largometraje de Jorge Sánchez-Cabezudo' [an unvarnished violence, irrational and savage, instinctive and uncontrollable, is the great protagonist of Jorge Sánchez-Cabezudo's debut film] (Anon. 2008) while Javier Ocaña of *El País* writes that the film exhibits 'una violencia tan seca como inesperada' [a violence that is as brusque as it is unexpected] (2006: 34). Significantly, *irracional, salvaje* and, in particular, *seco* (which can be translated also as 'dry') are words that could be equally used to describe the oppressive landscape in the rural film. Indeed, in these films, violence is most often intimately bound up with the rural milieu in which it unfolds. The harsh and barren land is presented as a corrosive influence on its inhabitants; it is an overwhelming and unforgiving force, which appears to nurture the most irrational and primal impulses in its people.

John Hopewell has perceptively recognised the importance of the setting in many Spanish films: 'Actions … seem under-motivated … the driving force of conduct lying outside the film is Spanish history itself. Hence the extreme importance of background detail and secondary characters in Spanish films' (1986: 28). As we have seen, space in *The Night of the Sunflowers* is similarly central to understanding the actions and motivations of its characters. It is as if the violence lies hidden or dormant within the immediate environment, ready to find its sudden expression in those who pass through it at any moment. Indeed, the critic of *Fotogramas* has observed, 'es, quizás, más salvaje la violencia de la que habla el film por su entorno' [the violence in the film is perhaps more savage because of the setting] (Anon. 2008). Again, the location of the cave is pertinent here: the potential discovery of prehistoric cave paintings, whose most prevalent theme are depictions of men hunting bison, deer and other animals, provides an ironic reflection on the predator–prey relationships in the film. Even the most 'civilised' people, the film suggests, can fall prey to primitive and instinctual impulses when faced with extraordinary situations. This blurring of predator and prey, animals and humans, is similarly prevalent in the rural film, where people are inexorably driven by brute forces. To this effect, Hopewell has commented that '(Spanish) film-makers return time and again to the brutality of the Spaniards, their residual animality of conduct, with an insistence even on the same broad metaphor – human relations as a hunt' (1986: 27). Like Buñuel, Sánchez-Cabezudo follows the fateful movement of his actors through the dispassionate lens of an entomologist. In an (accidental?) homage to Buñuel's *Land Without Bread*, the film closes with the serial killer, as he returns to his house and sits down to watch a television documentary on beekeeping in Extremadura. The scene in some ways thematically echoes the film's opening sequence: an aerial shot scrutinises the killer from above, as if looking down on an insect, as he furtively forges a path through the sunflowers to his car.

If the cave at the beginning of the film is hoped to be the potential lifeblood of the village's ailing economy, by its close it can be seen as an allegory for its violent demise. Not only does it not contain the cave paintings, but it hides the evidence of a brutal murder of Cecilio deep within its cavities – and, by extension, the agrarian way of life which he symbolised. The archaeology of the cave therefore emerges as a metaphor for the unconscious mind: hidden but not forgotten, the unspeakable horror of the rural Other will haunt Esteban, Juan and Gabi for years to come. In its geological layers of hidden violence, the cave mirrors the historical production of the Castilian landscape which surrounds it – a type of landscape which Maria Tumarkin has called a 'traumascape', which she defines as a geography that has been 'transformed physically and psychically by suffering' (2005: 13). In the official geography of the Franco regime, Castile was projected as the ideological heartland of National Catholicism. Hidden behind the construction of 'la España eterna' [the eternal Spain], however, lay a regime of violence. Although the hard-working Castilian peasant embodied the values of Francoism, and exemplified the Spanish 'caste' in its purest form (Blanco Rodríguez 1998: 368), he was often compelled to work under the most brutal and exploitative conditions, most often under the sway of unscrupulous landowners (Sevilla-Guzmán 1976: 103–4). The historical reality of a fragmented nation, reeling from the trauma of the Civil War, exhausted and hungry, was overlaid with the official geography: a Castilian idyll of community and social cohesion. Significantly, the rural films mentioned above ran counter to this vision, and depicted the dark underside of rural life on the Castilian *meseta* (or the Extremaduran *meseta*, in the case of *Pascual Duarte*), reconfiguring the region as a space of exploitation, sickness and oppression. As in *The Night of the Sunflowers*, the landscape in these films emerges as a traumascape, which Tumarkin describes as being able to 'catalyse and shape remembering and reliving of traumatic events. It is through these places that the past, whether buried or laid bare for all to see continues to inhabit and refashion the present' (2005: 13). Like the cave, then, the landscape can be read as a palimpsest: it is haunted by the immaterial traces of a violent past that resounds in the present.

Conclusion

The symbolic 'burial' of Spain's rural past within a national consciousness that is now overwhelmingly urban is as poignant as it is urgently relevant. As we have seen, Sánchez-Cabezudo's film concerns itself with the archaeology of Spain's rural memory. And as rural Spain continues to buckle under the weight of globalisation and geographical change, it is a memory that resonates with increasing urgency. In holding in thematic tension both the *noir* and the rural genres, the city and the country, and night and day, the film articulates a wider social anxiety in the face of a rapidly vanishing way of life. Sánchez-Cabezudo's film would therefore appear to call for a long overdue reconciliation with rural Spain, and a closer understanding of its land, its culture and its people. Although the film successfully refrains from casting moral judgements on its characters, it nevertheless provides a cautionary tale. As the monstrous secret buried deep within the cave would appear to suggest, to ignore, misunderstand or repress Spain's recent rural past comes at a heavy price.

Notes

1 See, for instance, te Riele (2002).
2 Terrified of getting caught out, Tomás pretends to Amadeo that Cecilio has moved to the city, claiming that a witness saw him at the bus station carrying a suitcase – an ironic nod to Paco Martínez Soria and his iconic suitcase, in his famous role as a *paleto* [country bumpkin] migrant in *¡La ciudad no es para mí!*/ *The City is Not for Me!* (Pedro Lazaga, 1966).
3 Unlike Kurosawa's film, however, the chapters do not offer subjective and contradictory accounts of the same event; rather, each picks up where the previous one ended, and contributes towards the progression of the narrative.
4 With the exception of *The Holy Innocents*, these rural films were all produced by the dissident Spanish producer Elías Querejeta (Whittaker 2011: 45–70). For more information on the representation of rural landscape and violence in *Pascual Duaete*, see Faulkner (2004: 54–9).

Bibliography

Afinoguznova, Eugenia and Martí-Olivella, Jaume (2008) *Spain Is (Still) Different: Tourism and Discourse in Spanish Identity*, Lanham, MD: Lexington Books.

Anon. (2008) '*La noche de los girasoles*', *Fotogramas.es* (25 June), www.fotogramas.es/Peliculas/La-noche-de-los-girasoles/La-noche-de-los-girasoles [accessed 3 June 2010].

Berger, John (1976) *A Fortunate Man*, London: Writers' and Readers' Publishing Cooperative.

Blanco Rodríguez, J.A. (1998) 'Sociedad y régimen en Castilla y León bajo el primer Franquismo', *Historia Contemporánea*, 17, 359–87.

Caro Baroja, Julio (1992) 'Introduction', in Cristina García Rodero, *España oculta*, Barcelona: Lunwerg Editores, i–iii.

Dimendberg, Edward (2004) *Film Noir and the Spaces of Modernity*, London and Cambridge, MA: Harvard University Press.

Domínguez, E. (2006) 'Carmelo Gómez: "Deberíamos hacer un estatuto para el cine español"', *ABC Madrid* (25 August), 12–13.

Faulkner, Sally (2004) *Literary Adaptations in Spanish Cinema*, London: Tamesis.

García de León, María Antonia (1996) *El campo y la ciudad*, Madrid: Centro de Publicaciones; Ministerio de Agricultura, Pesca y Alimentación.

González Requena, Jesús (1998) *El campo en el cine español*, Madrid: Banco de Crédito.

Halfacree, Keith (1993) 'Locality and Social Representation: Space, Discourse and Alternative Definitions of the Rural', *Journal of Rural Studies*, 9:1, 23–37.

Herrero, Carmen (2010) 'Edgy Art Cinema: Cinephilia and Genre Negotiations in Recent Spanish Thrillers', *Studies in European Cinema*, 7:2, 123–34.

Hopewell, John (1986) *Out of the Past: Spanish Cinema after Franco*, London: BFI.

Kirkham, Pat (1994) 'Looking for the Simple Idea', *Sight & Sound*, 4:2 (February), 16–21.

Macnab, Geoffrey (2007) 'Country and Eastern', *Sight & Sound*, 13:6 (June), 12.

Ocaña, J. (2006) 'Magnífico debut', *El País* (25 August), 34.

Sevilla-Guzmán, Eduardo (1976) 'The Peasantry and the Franco Regime' in Paul Preston (ed.), *Spain in Crisis: The Evolution and Decline of the Franco Regime*, Hassocks, Sussex: The Harvester Press, 101–24.

Shubert, Adrian (1990) *A Social History of Modern Spain*, London: Unwin Hyman.

Sontag, Susan (2008) *On Photography*, London: Penguin.

te Riele, Dorothée (2002) 'The Metaphorical Landscape of the Spanish Author Julio Llamazares', *European Studies*, 18, 199–213.

Tumarkin, Maria (2005) *Traumascapes: The Power and Fate of Places Transformed by Tragedy*, Melbourne: Melbourne University Press.

Urry, John (2000) *The Tourist Gaze*, London: Sage.

Whittaker, Tom (2011) *The Films of Elías Querejeta: A Producer of Landscapes*, Cardiff: University of Wales Press.

En la ciudad de Sylvia/In the City of Sylvia (José Luis Guerín, 2007) and the *durée* of a *dérive*

Rob Stone

On the days between three nights in a European city, a sensitive young man finds a café on a map, observes and sketches the patrons and follows one beautiful young woman when she leaves. He pursues her through the city, unaware that she is trying to evade him. He approaches her on a tram and asks if she is Sylvia, a woman he met six years ago in a bar called *Les aviateurs*. She says no and berates him. He apologises. She gets off the tram, ordering him to stay, and wishes him luck in his quest. That night he goes to *Les aviateurs* and picks up another beauty. The next day he returns to the café and follows another woman.

On its drift around the film-festival circuit *En la ciudad de Sylvia/In the City of Sylvia* provoked what David Bordwell diagnosed as 'the jubilation you feel in the presence of calm, precise artistry' (2007). Although devoid of plot, this observational and reflective essay on the constructed nature of memories and myths posited a sense of cinema in which, as Lee Marshall observed in *Screen International*, its maker José Luis Guerín 'created pure drama without recourse to story' (Marshall 2007). Yet, in addition to its more formalist experimentation, *In the City of Sylvia* also operates in relation to various industrial and critical contexts and in terms of specifically European, but increasingly transnational philosophies of time and its expression on film. This chapter begins by surveying the work of Guerín and contextualises his career, his films and their reception within arguments relating to the relationship between local, European and world cinema. Thereafter, a revision of his earlier, complementary works leads to an analysis of *In the City of Sylvia* and its construction, deconstruction and reconstruction of memory and myth by allusion to Henri Bergson's theory of an intuitive sense of the *durée* [duration] of time and its relevance to Gilles Deleuze's theory of the time-image, as well as the affined philosophies of the *flâneur* and the psychogeography of the *dérive* [drift] as practised by Guy Debord and the Situationist International. The aim is to delineate not just a textual analysis of a peculiar example of the contemporary Spanish art-house but also to reveal a progressive, modernist, even Cubist notion of cinema that is exemplified in this film's elaboration.

Born in 1960 in Barcelona, José Luis Guerín is an idiosyncratic figure in contemporary European cinema because his films are exploratory, experimental essays that share a professorial concern with the limits of the medium. The academic basis of his work is literal, for Guerín teaches at Barcelona's prestigious Universitat Pompeu Fabra, where he encourages his students to experiment and innovate rather than conform or copy. Leading by example, moreover, Guerín makes films that exist in the overlap of fiction and documentary and offer digital media and its apparatus as an intermediary between film and photography. *Innisfree* (1990), *Tren de sombras/ Train of Shadows* (1997), *En construcción/ Work in Progress* (2001), *Unas fotos en la ciudad de Sylvia/ Some Photos in the City of Sylvia* (2007), *In the City of Sylvia* (2007) and *Guest* (2010) often infuriate audiences by very slowly undoing the distinctions between fact and fiction, befuddling narrative and documentary traditions and subverting conventions of filmmaking and film-watching. Instead of story, structure and sentiment, his films are intellectual assemblages based more on ideas of collage than montage, on the association of images and sounds rather than their juxtaposition. They are tapestries of ideas threaded through a sense of time that purposefully interweaves reality and myth and inspires a process of reception and perception that is both radical and meditative. In addition, if one has the patience, his films are also seductive and rewardingly playful. His closest forebear is perhaps Chris Marker, writer-director of *La jetée/ The Pier* (1962) and *Sans soleil/ Sunless* (1983), who in the latter admits that 'I will have spent my life trying to understand the function of remembering, which is not the opposite of forgetting, but rather its lining.' Guerín is also concerned with the malleability of memory, history and myth. His tools and tricks include the presentation of *cinéma vérité* as a record of reality and its rug-pulling reveal as artifice, the similar revelation of subjectivity as formalism, and the consequent admission that the suspended timelessness of a long take is actually artfully calibrated. Moreover, Marker's dictum, 'we do not remember, we rewrite memory much as history is rewritten', inspires an appreciation of *In the City of Sylvia* as a palimpsest of Guerín's previous films. Although they all threaten to dissolve into shapeless sketches, they are each products of exquisite framing and judicious sleight of hand in the editing, which suggests a revealing paradox – that Guerín's apparently cold dissection of the mechanics of filmmaking and film-watching disguises a romantic, even passionately hands-on love of film.

Any attempt to contextualise Guerín and his films within the history, industry and thematic and aesthetic traditions of regional or national cinema in Spain is problematic. The *El Mundo* newspaper gives up and describes him simply as 'una "rara avis" en el panorama nacional e internacional' [a 'strange bird' in the national and international panorama] (I. M. 2007), while *El País* declares that 'Guerín es el maestro. Después han venido muchos otros, por supuesto, pero el primero fue Guerín' [Guerín is the master. Many have come along afterwards, of course, but Guerín was the first] (Belinchón 2010). First what? The national newspaper does not say, and this inability to situate Guerín within the national panorama also afflicts international critics, who locate *In the City of Sylvia* within a European art-house tradition instead. *Variety* deems it 'ultra-Gallic' (Holland 2007) and *The New York Post* describes it as 'Alain Resnais' "Last Year in Marienbad" filtered through the senses of Eric Rohmer' (Musetto 2008). Only the Harvard Film Archive recognises that confusion over Guerín may be because he 'occupies a unique place in the vibrant and still largely underappreciated history of Catalan cinema' (2008). On the one hand, it is precisely because *In the City of Sylvia* is so difficult to categorise within Spanish cinema that a reacquaintance with Catalan cinema and a vague echo of the experimentation of the Barcelona School may be posited and supported by reference to Guerín's dayjob. Yet beyond the Gallic influence there may be nothing particularly Catalan about his films, which he has made in Ireland, Normandy and Strasbourg. For all its solipsism, *In the City of Sylvia* expresses a transnational sense of cinema as an evolving art form with as yet unexplored potential. Because his films find their audiences through festivals, art-houses and rare, plush DVDs, so Guerín is labelled an *auteur* filmmaker and subject to the kind of global reception that he studies by turning the camera on the festival audiences and venues for *In the City of Sylvia* in *Guest*. The ruse is typical, for his films commonly explore complex issues of viewing and reviewing, of seeing and believing and rarely, if ever, find these terms synonymous.

Innisfree, for example, is seemingly a scrapbook of images and interviews that attests to Guerín's fanboy-pilgrimage to the Irish town where John Ford shot *The Quiet Man* (1952). But this is only a 'seeming,' because Innisfree only exists in the W.B. Yeats poem 'The Lake Isle of Innisfree', as a tiny island in Lough Gill in Sligo, and in that Technicolor romantic comedy of 'Oirishness' starring John Wayne and Maureen O'Hara, which was actually shot in Connemara and Cong. *Innisfree* therefore effects an exploration of myth and the collusion of film in something that 'is neither a lie nor a confession; it is an inflexion' (Barthes 1973: 129), in which Guerín gradually elides any distinction between the signifier (*The Quiet Man*) and the signified (the romantic myth of Ireland as envisioned in an emigrant's nostalgic memory of the old country). Although the film begins with the humourless subtitle promising 'things seen and heard in and around Innisfree between 5th Sept. and 10th Oct. 1988', the punchline comes in the final disclaimer that reveals the workings of the cinematic machine: 'Innisfree is based on a small village in western Ireland, Cunga St Feichin, Co. Mayo. The identity of its inhabitants is in no way implied in that of the characters, which are the result of a free cinematographic treatment.'

In fact, seen from the perspective of any year since its release, the film not only allows for a revisiting of the 1927 in which *The Quiet Man* is set, but also the 1951 of its Hollywood re-creation and the 1988 of Guerín's return journey to a place that he (like John Ford) had never been. These superimposed pasts are initially revisited in clips from Ford's feature, footage and photographs of its production, archival material of the time of its making and travelogue of sight-seeing around its supposedly surviving sets. Yet the film is a palimpsest, reworking itself as it goes along like a poet revising his scribbles. Subject to collage, the past is illustrated in film clips, remembrances and re-enactments that mix memory, history, imagination and reality as well as classical narrative cinema and modern observational documentary. The tale of *The Quiet Man* is recounted piecemeal by children who aid the mix of myth and history by using the names of the actors instead of the characters and Guerín adds to the confusion by interspersing excerpts so that John Wayne/Sean Thornton and Maureen O'Hara/Mary Kate Danaher appear to be waving at these kids. Memory of the film is not simply reclaimed but fought over in the local pub: 'I filmed with Maureen O'Hara!' claims one Guinness-drinker, while two more dispute ownership of the collie that herded her sheep. Film clips, photographs and newspaper clippings are produced and folk are cajoled into testifying for whatever the collective and individual imagination of these people offers as a preferred, improved truth. Furthermore, such purposeful mischief perpetuates the tradition it espouses, for these people in the pub are just as full of 'blarney' as those in *The Quiet Man* and, as shall become apparent, the makers of *Innisfree*. While driving along country lanes and filming through his windscreen, Guerín passes a young female hitchhiker, brakes and reverses to pick her up. An apparently off-the cuff interview takes place, with the young woman recounting her experiences as an au pair in America before Guerín (who never appears on camera) drops her off at her destination and the vehicle and his filming continues. Later she reappears, selling entrance tickets to gullible tourists wishing to enter a cottage that has been similarly 'reconstructed' in faux-nostalgic fashion reminiscent of the fondly remembered 40–year old film. And finally, the 'actress' appears again, made up as Maureen O'Hara and cycling against an off-camera wind machine in front of a stormy Technicolor backdrop. Like *Innisfree*, she is a palimpsest, an imitation of a mock-up of a myth: an actress playing a common Irish girl impersonating an actress pretending to be a common Irish girl.

Such overlapping versions of truth and fiction, memory and myth are an essential element of Guerín's collages by association. In symmetry with the theories of Bergson, the truths are times that are not remembered as static or immutable but so subject to the invention, manipulation and illusion of memory that they are ever-becoming, incomplete and evolving. Guerín concurs with Bergson in rejecting any rigid, intellectual understanding of time being subject to clocks and calendars in favour of an intuitive sense of time that is subject to memory and association. Consequently, film form and content fuse in the films of Guerín in correlative opposition to Eisenstein's theories of intellectual montage, whereby film was constructed as a linear series of calibrated images that were to be rationally understood in conflict with each other. Instead, Bergson maintained that intuition senses time in the flow of life. 'To think intuitively is to think in duration' (1992: 34), he wrote, and further argued that the perception of this *durée* negated any static measurement of anything subject to man-made time and inspired reflection upon its evolution instead. Thus, visual and aural collages in *Innisfree*, like that of the quaint Irish jig dissolving into a shot of head-banging kids, conflate the ages and speak not of any artificial conflict but of an authentic, eternal becoming because 'it is flux, the continuity of transition, it is change itself that is real' (Bergson 1992: 16). What is more, the collage of past and present provides evidence of a Cubist perspective on an object (whether the perfect Ireland of *The Quiet Man* or, as shall be seen, the ideal woman of *In the City of Sylvia*) that supposedly exists in memory rather than any specific place. Correlatively, in contrast to Eisenstein's theories of intellectual montage, there arises the notion of intuitive collage by association in the work of such filmmakers as Godard, Marker and Guerín, whose films do not offer any objective notion of truth as fixity but present an unruly flow of images and sounds instead. Just as Bergson implored his audience to 'restore to movement its fluidity, to time its duration' (1992: 17), so these filmmakers allow the association of ideas to guide their creativity. The assemblage of footage is thus subject to intuitive links in fulfilment of Bergson's prediction that the cinema is 'an apparatus whose function would be to record the parts of the past capable of reappearing in our consciousness' (1992: 153). For all its 'seeming' artifice, *Innisfree* is a 'valid' memory of the film that Guerín must have often thought of making. Such remembering also resembles a Cubist approach to the past because memories are not static, but mobile and liable to mutation, with the result that any distinction between what is remembered, what is imagined and what is *imagined as remembered* is impossibly elusive.

Perhaps surprisingly, Guerín trades subjectivity for formalism in order to transpose the effort of examining memory to film. The paradox may rankle, but works such as *Innisfree* and *In the City of Sylvia* disable critical or popular disdain for their lack of 'action' because they are experimental films that respond to nothing less than their own criteria. Even more hermetic is *Train of Shadows*, for the film-within-a-film that is ostensibly its subject is not a Hollywood confection like *The Quiet Man* but the silent, scratched and soiled home movies that, the subtitle explains, a Parisian lawyer named Gérard Fleury shot at Le Thuit in Normandy between 1928 and 1930. Yet again however, the footage presented as authentic is a fabrication. These damp and scratched images of a well-off family that flicker between the shadow-play of sprockets and the crackle of damaged film may resemble the work of the Lumière brothers, but they are bespoke antiques. Guerín uses the 'found' footage to construct a family portrait reminiscent of Renoir (both father and son), but this only illustrates the paradox that although the purpose of such movies is to 'remember' reality, their structuring as a narrative turns such memories into fiction. He exaggerates this paradox by treating the footage as vital evidence in an imagined family melodrama that may have resulted in Fleury's disappearance on 8 November 1930. Film form becomes the message. Rewinding footage, freezing frames, zooming in on details and repeating images begin to denote an obsessive search for clues: did Uncle Étienne dally with a maid, and was there a child witness? Eventually, inevitably and purposefully, Guerín replaces investigation with the 'remembering' of events that never happened by simply manufacturing them in the editing. Like the Zapruder film of the assassination of John F. Kennedy, the footage becomes subject to all manner of analysis and, consequently, the stuff of conspiracy-thriller cliché. Yet *Train of Shadows* only masquerades as a crime-scene investigation in order to illustrate an academic thesis. In his conclusion the footage runs out, and Guerín cuts to contemporary colour reconstructions of the events of 1928–30; but with the same actors. Once again, these are palimpsests, reworked copies of copies. Figures posed like still photos re-create the now discredited footage and even speak in order to resolve the plastic mystery set up in the fake film's first act. Like *Innisfree* and *In the City of Sylvia*, *Train of Shadows* is an essay on film *on film* instead of on paper.

Guerín characteristically revisits his thesis on the constructed nature of memory and film in *Work in Progress*, which appears to record the destruction of a block of slums in the El Xino quarter of his native Barcelona and the construction of a building of condominiums. The degraded slum is like the found footage in *Train of Shadows*, the Ireland encountered in *Innisfree* and the young woman in *In the City of Sylvia*, being seemingly unchanged for many years, yet actually in a state of constant flux and evolution. The construction works are, like the editing of film in *Train of Shadows* and *Innisfree* and the sketching and stalking in *In the City of Sylvia*, an attempt at structuring, improving, even fashioning a reality that conforms to a fixed ideal; but irony undermines all these attempts at constructing a myth out of reality because it becomes necessary to destroy the truth in order to save it. Thus, Guerín manufactures *cinéma vérité* techniques and stages episodes featuring prostitutes, layabouts and immigrant bricklayers, who are replaced by skilled tradesmen, estate agents and prospective new tenants. By these means he also reveals the overlapping of history, film and memory in a cycle of construction, destruction and reconstruction that suggests the complex and treacherous, potentially Cubist layering of time and all things subject to it that informs *In the City of Sylvia*.

The notion of the female muse is ancient and mythic and its stimulant is the memory of an unreachable woman that has haunted many men, particularly artists, poets and filmmakers such as Orson Welles, whose *Citizen Kane* (1941) shares with *In the City of Sylvia* its theme of a search for the validation of a memory that will attach meaning to the present. As the aged Bernstein (Everett Sloane) states:

> A fellow will remember a lot of things you wouldn't think he'd remember. You take me. One day, back in 1896, I was crossing over to Jersey on the ferry, and as we pulled out, there was another ferry pulling in, and on it there was a girl waiting to get off. A white dress she had on. She was carrying a white parasol. I only saw her for one second. She didn't see me at all, but I'll bet a month hasn't gone by since that I haven't thought of that girl.

Thus the artist is haunted by the memory of a girl whose perfection is both inspirational and confounding. *Some Photos in the City of Sylvia* is Guerín's essential companion work to *In the City of Sylvia*, and this photo-essay explains how the memory of an unattainable woman who embodies an illusory ideal has haunted many writers and artists, including Goethe, Poe, Dante and Petrarch. Cinematic counterparts include the aforementioned Bernstein, and Scottie (James Stewart) in Alfred Hitchcock's *Vertigo* (1958), who attempts to re-create his ideal dead woman (who never existed) from a flawed real woman (whom he kills). In Spanish cinema there is the ultimately murderous attempt of Antonio (Antonio Gades) to create the myth of Carmen from a real woman named Carmen (Laura del Sol) in Carlos Saura's *Carmen* (1983) and the refashioning of Lisa out of Sofía (Emma Suárez) by Jota (Nancho Novo) in Julio Medem's *La ardilla roja/ Red Squirrel* (1993). In each case, real women are denigrated in comparison with a fabricated memory in order to protect the immature, sexist, self-deluding and masturbatory fantasy of males who see this ideal woman as a Lacanian mirror-image of their own precious wonderfulness. Nevertheless, the male's enslavement to this idea, his pursuit of its possibility and the eventual disintegration of the dream forms the basis of both *In the City of Sylvia* and *Some Photos in the City of Sylvia*.

Some Photos in the City of Sylvia presents itself in explicitly autobiographical terms as an attempt 'intentar dar cuenta de una experiencia' [to try to express an experience] that supposedly occurred to Guerín in Strasbourg in 2004, namely his searching for a woman who resembled his memory of an 'ideal' he had met there once as a youth, some 22 years previously. His only clues are her name, her sketch-map of how to find a bookshop and a matchbox from a bar called *Les aviateurs* where they met. He claims to recall she spoke some words in Castilian during a conversation 'de la que apenas recuerdo nada' [that I can barely recall], in which she said she was a nurse who liked the sound of her name in Spanish and had studied for a few months in Salamanca. Beginning with shots of his room in the seventeenth-century Hotel Patricia near the Conservatory of Dramatic Arts, his search for her is reconstructed out of thousands of photographs that warrant the feature's inclusion in the miniscule genre of the photographic essay approximating imagistic poetry that includes Marker's *La jetée* and Jonás Cuarón's *Año uñal Year of the Nail* (2008), and is mostly restricted to art galleries. Although the figure of Sylvia has long since disappeared, her ghost still haunts the present. Like Scottie in Hitchcock's oneiric San Francisco, Guerín follows a woman in Strasbourg, loses her, and her loss reveals the city as the city reveals her lack. The search is locked to his obsessive gaze, but the memory of the ideal woman disperses in the crowd of faces on people and posters. When the search coincides with that for a missing girl announced on flyers, the film becomes peripatetic as Guerín shifts from Strasbourg to an international, even universal quest. Obsession even resembles madness as any and all women are lost in a torrent of photographs that flicker by so quickly that the work becomes a motion picture. And thus the search ultimately becomes metaphysical: what is sought and found is not just the idea of a woman, but of a film.

In the City of Sylvia is this film, which was made without a screenplay. 'Hacer una película significa un proceso de adaptación constante' [Making a film requires a process of constant adaptation], says Guerín. 'Como, finalmente, nos dieron una cuarta parte de lo previsto, de presupuesto y de días de rodaje, se tuvo que reinventar el film' [As they only gave us a quarter of what was expected in terms of budget and shooting days, the film had to be reinvented] (Anon. 2008). It begins with three nights in the same Hotel Patricia of *Some Photos in the City of Sylvia* in which the play of light, shadow and sound from passing cars reveals the room and the re-created clues of a matchbox and a map of how to find a bookshop. Sitting cross-legged on the unmade bed, the artfully dishevelled young man identified in the credits as the Dreamer (Xavier Lafitte) searches in vain for words to add to his book of scribbles and sketches, but is clearly lacking a muse. This shot lasts for several minutes and only his occasional blinking marks the difference between this and a photograph, but unlike 'the photograph's freezing of reality [which] marks a transition from the animate to the inanimate, from life to death' (Mulvey 2006: 15), this crucial factor marks the long take as a Deleuzian time-image that expresses a vital, ever-becoming sense of time. Indeed, to impose a narrative on this film is to elide its evocative temporal gaps and thereby ignore its meaning. In the following static shot from one end of the street, for example, the Dreamer leaves the hotel, consults his map and hurries off camera, but instead of cutting to follow what passes for action, Guerín holds the take for several minutes, observing passers-by that promise a multitude of alternative narratives in a shot that denies them all. There is an absence, a void, at the heart of Guerín's films that may be mistaken for a missing narrative, but this is only what Deleuze called the eruption of 'a little time in its pure state' (2005: xii) in time-images that render the audience subject to their *durée*.

The next morning the Dreamer occupies a table outside the conservatory café and allows his gaze to wander and alight on the patrons who frequent the place. The collage of lengthy shots effects a reflective, even meditative mood; yet, crucially, the subjectivity of the camera that Bordwell recognises 'may or may not be the Dreamer's POV' (2007) is not explicitly substituted for his. The Dreamer is often revealed to be on the opposite side of the tables from the camera and is therefore subject to its gaze. If anything, the subtle camera movement and its angles, the teasing and revealing use of framing, the expository but misleading use of deep focus and the artful sound editing adopt the strategy of imitating his purpose but making him victim of it too. Thus, although the film was the target of feminist criticism at the Venice Film Festival, the constantly shifting perspective complicates the accusation of being shot from the Dreamer's point of view. As always with Guerín, the subject here is film: a blonde beauty scribbles postcards, giggles and is cut to a shot of a handsome young man that changes focus to reveal that the object of transient desire is the person sitting at the table behind him, while a shot of a woman and two men sitting side-by-side but not communicating inspires, even demands the imposition of a narrative that reframing confidently dismantles. A collage of faces is made and unmade in the filming and editing, but true connections adding up to narratives are a matter of perception.

The Dreamer, too, shifts his gaze, but is more appreciative than predatory. He sketches details of the women that are incomplete, overlapping, merging with each other and never able to cohere into that of a single female, thereby creating a Cubist sense of a woman. He writes 'Dans la ville de Sylvie' above the temporal portrait and writes '*elle*' upon the sketch, only to add an '*s*' that indicates the familiar universal quest for '*elles*'. Thereafter, the collage of patrons chatting, thinking, ordering and drinking is built up in edits that function as synaptic responses to new stimuli. As people shift position and the angle and focus change, other patrons are revealed as the object under scrutiny and ownership of the gaze is only aligned with that of the Dreamer by the audience's expectation of narrative. In fact, the camera never surrenders control of this gaze but rather observes the Renaissance beauty of Lafitte with equal interest. If anything, therefore, Guerín deploys the camera as a substitute for the audience rather than the ostensible protagonist, in order to make a film about film-watching and a search for aesthetic pleasure in which both the ideal woman and the film itself are projections. The Dreamer is obsessed with the memory of a girl whose lack, whose absence, is discovered in the presence of everyone else. Like Scottie in *Vertigo*, he fixates upon the knot of hair on the back of one girl's head, but like Judy (Kim Novak) in Hitchcock's film about obsession her beauty fails to match up to his remembered ideal. Instead, her movement in the frame and a subsequent change of focus reveal Pilar López de Ayala inside the café, her features fragmented and dissolving amongst the many reflections of the women upon the window in an explicitly Cubist manner (see Figure 24). As Bordwell recognises, 'as he gapes

24. Cubist collage in *In the City of Sylvia*.

at the woman inside, layers pile up, creating a cubistic climax of all the optical obstructions we've encountered' (2007), but Bordwell mistakes the image for a spatial representation of the female rather than a temporal one. This collage of feminine features resembles the sketch-filled pages of the Dreamer's notebook but also reveals the film's particularly intuitive sense of time because this mobile, ever-becoming image of a changing, evolving woman (that no still can replicate) is not spatially determined but temporally indefinable. This billiard-break of an idea of a woman expresses observation (the present), memory (the past) and potential (the future) and it embodies the Cubist notion of overlapping or super-imposed expressions of time.

The moving image of this woman is equivalent to Pablo Picasso's and Georges Braque's multi-angled re-creations of objects as being subject to time in their Cubist works. In *Les Demoiselles d'Avignon* [The young ladies of Avignon] (1907), for example, Picasso produced a painting of five female figures that was a 'perpetual motion machine that never loses its vitality. Actually looking at the picture means moving constantly from one facet to another; it never lets you settle on one resolved perception' (Jones 2007). Instead of measuring and locating the female in space, the spectator's intuition is liberated to consider an infinite number of ways in which she may be changing. In the same way, Braque's *Violon et palette* [Violin and palette] (1909) fragments its still life by rendering the objects in time instead of according to the rules of perspective that govern spatial representation. In other words, because no single perspective is dominant, what is rendered is the objects' *durée*. The Dreamer shifts in his seat to get a better view as Guerín cuts between different angles, but their attempts are frustrated because Cubism always rejects any fixed viewpoint. Instead, this fragmentation of a three-dimensional subject redefines it as a temporalised collage, with the result that this woman is always arriving and forever departing. Moreover, in accordance with Bergson's theories of an intuitive sense of time, it may be recognised that cinematic Cubism explores and expresses her endlessly incomplete *durée* in time-images wherein time 'increasingly appears for itself and creates paradoxical movements' (Deleuze 2005: xi).

When she leaves the café, the Dreamer hurries after her and slows to a cautious pace, yet the gaze of the camera remains independent. Initially, she walks off screen, he enters from camera right or left and the shot is held until long after he too has left the frame. In addition, the camera is mostly just above the ground, which negates any correspondence between its perspective and theirs. Even as the camera progresses through the streets a few inches above the pavement, alternate shots of him and her are entirely subject to the perspective of the apparatus: when she is walking away from the camera, he is walking towards it, and when she is walking towards the camera, he is following behind her. Consequently, accusations of a dominant male subjectivity may be dismantled because the camera's position does not correspond to that of either character or gender but is neutral, even indifferent to their passing. This indifference results in time-images that endure beyond any expectation of narrative progress and offer instead long periods of hanging, hollow time spent observing the streets before or after the characters have passed, with the consequence that the audience experiences all the time left hanging. Subject to the *durée* of the shot, we find ourselves searching the street, following passers-by in vain and receiving nothing in return except the knowledge of our own inability to either affect proceedings or have the film serve our expectations of narrative in any way.

The labyrinth of streets is, of course, a metaphor for how the mind stores memories and retrieves them by the association of ideas. None of these streets are dead ends. Rather, bridges, tunnels, alleyways, squares and corners reveal new (synaptic) connections. The Dreamer gets lost occasionally but he persists because somewhere in this physical and mental maze is the girl (the present), his memory of her (the past) and their possible reunion (the future). As in Christopher Nolan's similarly themed but epic *Inception* (2010), the synaptic links persist and repeat themselves in this metaphysical geography. Previously traversed streets are encountered anew from different angles and characters who were glimpsed earlier (such as the flower-seller) reappear. Most persistently, the omnipresent graffiti declaring 'Laure, je t'aime' adds another layer to this collage of association by reminding the Dreamer that his dilemma is a palimpsest of that suffered by Petrarch, who abandoned the priesthood after seeing a woman called Laura and subsequently sought to capture her in his poetry, which is suffused with the frustration of desiring this unattainable woman. The multilayered transnational and intertextual references in this collage even extend to the profound Petrarchan influences on the courtly love rhetoric that was a prominent feature of Spanish poetry from the fifteenth century, revealed in such elements as the comparison of the beloved to nature. Nevertheless, the impossibility of Petrarch or the Dreamer ever erasing their memory of 'her' is suggested by Guerín's shot of workmen using pressurised water to try and blast away just one instance of the graffiti dedicated to Laura that appears all over the mindful city. In addition, this fusion of form and content by which the physical landscape expresses a mental journeying also suggests the art of psychogeography by which an emotional awareness of the chaos and structure of an urban landscape is experienced by intuitive exploration. The model for this is Guy Debord's *dérive*, which he devised as a strategy of the Situationist International, and which is so determined by intuitive choices and changes in direction that it overlaps with the Bergsonian notion of time and its immediate and evolving *durée*. Furthermore, the expression of the *durée* of the *dérive* in cinematic terms is justified by the use of time-images because they render a temporal portrait of an object that is moving through time and cannot be defined from any one perspective. Consequently, the film's numerous time-images are essential to what may be interpreted as a Cubist strategy.

The Cubist object here is all women as embodied in the one played by López de Ayala, who anchors the flourish of a 360-degree tracking shot in close-up when the Dreamer catches up to her at a tram stop. Only when the tram arrives and she alights does the possibility of romantic cliché arise when he follows through another door and approaches what might pass for a happy ending along the gangway of the articulated tram. 'Sylvia? C'est toi?' [Sylvia? Is it you?] he utters, and she turns; but unlike the previous shots that contained them both, the shot-reverse-shot of their encounter signifies they belong apart. She dismisses his memory of her as false, and Guerín cuts to a medium shot of them both framed by the oblong window of the tram, like a cinema screen, thereby suggesting the opposite of the Kuleshov effect in this apposite thesis, that although they share the cinematic space constructed in the filming and editing there is no connection between them. The girl berates him for following her through the city and the entire *durée* of their cinematic *dérive* is revealed ironically with her exclamation in French: 'Il était si long! Interminable!' [It was so long! Interminable!]. Guerín's alter ego apologises. She tells him not to follow her and disembarks, but blows him a sympathetic kiss. The Dreamer sits and rests his head against the window of the tram, and its reflection provides him with what Lacan might posit as the true objective of this deluded male's quest for the ideal woman: a mirror image of himself.

The dejected Dreamer retraces his steps, and in his isolation he resembles a reflective *flâneur*, who Baudelaire describes as 'distilling the eternal from the transitory' (1972) in his anonymous observation of the city. The contrast between his crumbling ego and the eternal concrete is debilitating, but he responds by relocating his psyche at the centre of an order of things that is so defiantly of his own making that his *flânerie* corresponds to a kind of 'time-space psychosis' (Tester

1994: 77). He should be Baudelaire's 'perfect idler [and] passionate observer' (1972), but his sense of time and place is now so distorted by 'her' absence that it provokes the disintegration of coherent experience. This Chaplinesque *flâneur* should be revelling in the city where Baudelaire supposes he '[sets] up house in the middle of the multitude, amid the ebb and flow of movement, in the midst of the fugitive and the infinite' (1972), but night is falling and the city is emptying. For Walter Benjamin, the *flâneur* 'derives pleasure from his location within the crowd, but simultaneously regards it with contempt' (1983: 35), and to be without a crowd entirely leaves him annulled. The city *of* Sylvia *without* her is like *Innisfree* if *The Quiet Man* had never happened: the knowledge of her absence stalls the ongoing present. To rehabilitate his ego and have a reason to live he must reinstate the myth, which incidentally is the same strategy employed by Leonard (Guy Pearce) in Nolan's *Memento* (2000), another Cubist film about memory.

The Dreamer returns to his sketches, flicking back and forth through pages just as Guerín played and rewound the footage in *Train of Shadows* searching for a paradox: evidence of a myth. Then, as a damp dusk falls across the city, he returns to *Les aviateurs*, where reminders of the eternal female are readily available in such figures as the waitress, who is framed as in Édouard Manet's painting *Un bar aux Folies Bergère* [Bar at the Folies Bergère] (1882). Thus the Cubist collage, which Braque and Picasso developed to incorporate scraps of newspaper and textured material during the Synthetic phase, evolves accordingly as a natural vehicle for intertextuality. Paintings, songs and films that speak of the eternal female all crowd into the frame as the Dreamer watches a drunken beauty dance to 'That Woman' by Migala – 'My ears and eyes are failed … but I want that woman / that I feel near in dreams' – and he spends a fourth night in the city (a reference to Bresson's 1971 film *Quatre nuits d'un rêveur/Four Nights of a Dreamer*), lying naked beside her in room 107. Satisfaction is apparently transitory, however, because he remains addicted to a masturbatory fantasy of a relationship rather than its consummation. The following morning, when fresh graffiti insisting that Laure is loved appear, the Dreamer returns to the café, spies a girl dressed in red and hurries after her. Thus, this perpetual cycle of self-ful-filling pursuit, by which the delusional Dreamer flatters his fragile male ego into believing that no single woman could ever complete him, signifies a 'groundhog day' that maintains the myth that 'the *flâneur* is a multilayered palimpsest' (Jenks 1995: 148), one that illustrates 'a utopian representation of a carefree (male) individual in the midst of the urban maelstrom' (Tester 1994: 67). Yet this myth is so threadbare that the self-conscious stylings of the Dreamer are a mismatch for the authentic, eternal becoming of women that is celebrated in a collage of shots of females milling about at the breezy tram stop, and includes some from the café as well as many that are older, more ethnically diverse and even scarred. Sylvia is all of them and none of them. Instead of rapture, the Dreamer feels only impotence and fails to sketch a single one. And finally, as a tram pulls in, the reflection of Pilar López de Ayala is framed in the cinematic flickering-past of its windows. The shot suggests she is an unreliable memory, insists she is a cinematic construct and allows her to be a real woman as well; for, ultimately, as in all of Guerín's films, meaning is multilayered, time is too, and the possibility of any single viewpoint on a Cubist conundrum is as paradoxical as a camera running, standing still in the city of Sylvia.

Bibliography

Anon. (2008) 'En la ciudad de Sylvia', *Fotogramas* (25 June), www.fotogramas.es/Peliculas/En-la-ciudad-de-Sylvia/En-la-ciudad-de-Sylvia2 [accessed 1 October 2010].

Barthes, Roland (1973) *Mythologies*, trans. Annette Lavers, St Albans: Paladin.

Baudelaire, Charles (1972) '*The Painter of Modern Life*', in *Selected Writings on Art and Literature,* trans. P.E. Charvet, London: Viking, 395–422, www.idehist.uu.se/distans/ilmh/pm/baudelaire-painter.htm [accessed 10 October 2010].

Belinchón, Gregorio (2010) 'El cazador de magia', *El País* (18 July), www.elpais.com/articulo/madrid/cazador/magia/elpepiespmad/20100718elpmad_18/Tes [accessed 29 September 2010].

Benjamin, Walter (1983) *Charles Baudelaire: A Lyric Poet in the Era of High Capitalism*, trans. Harry Zohn, London: Verso.

Bergson, Henri (1992) *The Creative Mind: An Introduction to Metaphysics*, trans. Mabelle L. Andison, Syracuse, NJ: Citadel Press.

Bordwell, David (2007) 'Three Nights of a Dreamer' (5 November), www.davidbordwell.net/blog/?p=1457 [accessed 23 September 2010].

Deleuze, Gilles (2005) *Cinema 2*, trans. Hugh Tomlinson and Robert Galeta, King's Lynn: Continuum Impacts.

Harvard Film Archive (2008) http://hcl.harvard.edu/hfa/films/2008janfeb/guerin.html [accessed 3 October 2010].

Holland, Jonathan (2007) 'In the City of Sylvia', *Variety* (14 September), www.variety.com/review/VE1117934734.html?categoryid=31&cs=1 [accessed 29 September 2010].

I.M. (2007) 'En la ciudad de Sylvia', *El Mundo* (17 September), www.elmundo.es/metropoli/2007/09/14/cine/1189720813.html [accessed 23 September 2010].

Jenks, Chris (1995) 'Watching your Step: The History and Practice of the Flâneur', in *Visual Culture*, New York: Routledge, 142–60.

Jones, Jonathan (2007) *Pablo's Punks* (9 January), www.guardian.co.uk/culture/2007/jan/09/2 [accessed 3 July 2009].

Marshall, Lee (2007) 'Past Perfect', *Screen International* (19 October), 27.

Mulvey, Laura (2006) *Death 24x a Second*, London: Reaktion Books.

Musetto, V.A. (2008) 'Stalking Up Lost Love', *New York Post* (12 December), www.nypost.com/p/entertainment/movies/item_GYuwPHwZFfarmFxpgmTgmM;jsessionid=361EAF83867A5BCDE484D2BAE167B174 [accessed 30 September 2010].

Tester, Keith, *The Flâneur*, New York: Routledge.

13

Vicky Cristina Barcelona (Woody Allen, 2008): Penélope Cruz and Javier Bardem acting strangely[1]

Chris Perriam

Best friends Vicky (Rebecca Hall) and Cristina (Scarlett Johansson), on holiday from West-Coast USA, meet artist Juan Antonio (Javier Bardem) in Barcelona. Although Vicky is engaged to Doug (Chris Messina), the two girls agree to spend a weekend away with Juan Antonio. Cristina eventually moves in with Juan Antonio, who later confesses his continuing love for his ex-wife María Elena (Penélope Cruz), and Doug surprises Vicky by proposing they get married in Barcelona; but María Elena's unexpected arrival, following a suicide attempt, throws everything into confusion, a brief *ménage à trois* being followed by Cristina's departure. Throughout, the action is accompanied by a wry voice-over commentary (by Christopher Evan Welch).

Bardem, Cruz, Barcelona

As is very well known, especially in Spain, Penélope Cruz and Javier Bardem, two members of the 'Hollywood Latin royalty' (Smith 2009: 63), married early in July 2010 in the Bahamas, Cruz having won an Academy Award in 2009 for her role in *Vicky Cristina Barcelona* and Bardem having gained an Oscar a year earlier for *No Country For Old Men* (Joel and Ethan Coen, 2007) (Reuters 2010). During their courtship they had played a married couple who had already split up, tragicomically, in *Vicky Cristina Barcelona*, and an idealised version of the textures of that city had been indelibly added to the connotations of their star personas; in the case of Cruz, reinforcing her association with the city in Pedro Almodóvar's *Todo sobre mi madre/All About My Mother* (1999).

To a large extent this process of addition, this coding, is picturesque. Akbar Abbas, in his discussion of the cinematic city, observes that

The great promise of cinema is that it does not have to give us 'pictures' of the city, although this promise is not always kept. Admittedly, there will always be films that use the city as mere setting and close down the movement of cities and images by drawing on recognisable urban landmarks as stable points of reference. The exorbitant city, though, is neither securely graspable nor fully representable. (2003: 144)

In Allen's film both the city and the actors moving around it revert, enjoyably enough, to the status of pictures. But there is a saving exorbitance – a breaking-out — at the level of performance and in the potential for gently resistant readings of what the film is plotting. This is instigated by the two Spanish actors in particular. They play up the most conventionally obvious traits of their characters and act up to a degree which destabilises the urban and domestic spaces of the Catalan capital as well as playing, via a swift side-trip to Asturias, with more generalised notions of Spanishness, amusingly only half-understood by the director but much better so by the two native stars.

The incidental curiosity of Bardem and Cruz playing in English, mainly, but on home territory, combines with the ambivalent status of Barcelona as Catalan capital and rival cultural capital of Spain to highlight one of a number of delightful and propitious clichés used in the film, in this case that of the city as a stage. Oviedo too, when Juan Antonio, Vicky and Cristina fly there – although it emerges visually as more the city as an archive – is used dramatically, but in a somewhat four-square manner with Juan Antonio's double seduction led a stately dance through the neatly arranged hotel lobby and bedroom (trailer: 00:49–01:02), Romanesque buildings (all apices, and, inside, verticality: 01:11–01:13), and with venerable stone and polished wooden props placed about in such profusion that, were this a late nineteenth-century novel of unhappy adultery, they would of themselves have caused the bout of illness that afflicts Cristina, comically ruining the first night of the adventure. In this section I want to consider the roles played by Cruz and Bardem in maintaining (or, sometimes, not) the fine, ironic balance between critiquing and colluding in North-American cinema's representation of European cities in terms of mere pictures or as 'cities of containment', commodities, 'objects' (Schonfield 2000). Later we shall see that this positioning at a point of ideological ambivalence echoes the patterns of sexual politics in which their characters are enmeshed. As Schonfield suggests:

[E]ach time Hollywood depicts Paris, London or New York, they are presented, by implication, in ossified contrast with Los Angeles. Hollywood visits these other cities in the form of familiar, oft-repeated objects, usually introduced from the air: the Manhattan skyline; the Eiffel Tower, closely followed by Sacré Coeur or Notre Dame; Big Ben, St Paul's Cathedral and the Tower of London. (2000: 134)

The specificity of Barcelona in the film certainly gets erased in the interests of entertainment and commercial and craftsmanlike pragmatism, as Romney has observed (2008: 68). The reason that Vicky has for being in Barcelona is ostensibly in part that she is writing a Master's dissertation on Catalan culture, but her scripted obtuseness is such that, on the same day as she is taken to the highly un-Catalan northern port of Avilés and told by Juan Antonio that it is his birthplace, she justifies her sudden interest in him by saying that 'after all, you are a Catalan painter, and that's my subject'. Comically (or insultingly), to her almost total lack of knowledge of Castilian is added her absolute lack even of an awareness of the Catalan language, part of its glaring absence in the film (as also in *All About My Mother*, pointed up by its use of one of the premier Catalan-language actors, Rosa Maria Sardà).

Of particular note are language and music. There is, as one professional blogger has noted, 'Ni una ratlla de diàleg en català. Ni una' [Not one single line of dialogue in Catalan], so that the film's Barcelona 'es una Barcelona espanyola' [is a Spanish Barcelona] (Montalt 2008). Musically, the effect is similar: the Catalan song 'El noi de la mare' is played during a sequence set in Asturias, and the Spanish guitar (little associated with Catalunya) predominates (Montalt 2008). Isaac Albéniz's 'Granada' is the piece performed on guitar as part of the second evening's entertainment in Oviedo (on screen and off; about 700 kilometres and several national-cultural layers out of sync), while Albéniz's 'Asturias' plays extradiagetically on the seafront breakers at Barceloneta beach (some 900 kilometres wrong) while Cristina contemplates her future. Indeed, the confusions multiply to such a degree that Allen fans at least might benignly suspect as much deliberate farcicality at play as regrettable culture-blindness: but the film's substitution of the international bilingualism of Spanish–English for the true official bilingualism of the city in which the action is supposed to take place most certainly jars, and is surely an embarrassment to two Spanish actors whose careers were launched jointly – in *Jamón, jamón* [Ham, ham] (Juan José Bigas Luna, 1992) – with an ironic exploration, precisely, of 'las estructuras ideológicas de la sociedad española' [the ideological structures of Spanish society] (Evans 2004: 21).

The strangeness of the mix of cultural vagueness and the use of two nationally highly specific actors is worth looking at more closely. Given the care which Allen habitually accords to his narrative and dramatic use of music on his soundtracks (Deleyto 2009: 61–2), it is not out of the question that these crass mismatches are themselves mischievously intentional – indeed, the snatch of 'Asturias', in the scene just alluded to, does resolve across a sound bridge to become signature music for the transplanted artist Juan Antonio himself; and perhaps somebody on the music-design team knew that some of the audience would know that the composer Albéniz was born in the deeply Catalan province of Girona. The characters, and the actors with their highly globalised auras, move around the city contributing to the general haziness, however. As Joan Ramon Resina has observed in relation to different, literary, cases of representation of Barcelona, 'Sites such as the Sagrada Familia ... become the scene for a masquerade of identity [marked by] semantic vagueness' (2008: 167). There is a paradoxical effect in the film's richness and brightness of presentation of the church in construction, of the Parc Güell, or the proudly (if violently) redeveloped marina and beach areas of the urban littoral: their specific meanings get washed out, and socio-cultural intra-images are eclipsed. When Vicky happens upon Juan Antonio one radiant day in the Parc Güell, the much photographed Font del Drac steps are strenuously centrepieced (trailer: 02:00 and 02:04), with Hall and Bardem framing the sculpture. Bardem's cool, easy playing of courteous seductiveness, the light falling on his face and black cotton-clad upper torso from a point behind Hall, and the mise en scène's half-equation of him (sketchbook casually in hand) with the genius designer of the Parc, make the place no more than the pleasant scene of the drama of erotic disappointment (for Vicky) and confident control (in Juan Antonio).

A subsequent sequence of classic shot-reverse-shot sets Hall against the wavering horizontals of a balustraded walkway leading off behind and Bardem against the upward diagonal of a stepped pathway: the site becomes a set. Similarly, the two talking at the balustrade of the Tibidabo amusement park high above the city is shot in four, slow, semi-circular pans which allow the city to be laid out as a picture yet also erased as a signifier (all attention is on the moment of comic misunderstanding being played out in the conversation). The sequence ends its low-key virtuoso movement with the steadicam floating back in on the cue of Vicky's rueful 'I'm an idiot. I don't know what I expected to happen', as she turns her face away, but as Bardem's stubbled face, tousled head and regretful man-of-the-world eyes occupy nearly half the frame. Barcelona is little more, at this moment, than an apricot haze; the historic view out to sea reduced to a proportional horizontal, a pleasing two-thirds up and straight across the frame in the background; it is a portrait of Bardem, here, not a portrait of a city.

However, such real concerns need to be put into perspective. As Celestino Deleyto observes, Barcelona becomes an imaginary place, a magical space with its own (anti-)logic where all are driven by the inexorable impulse of desire (2009: 216–17). Here 'la cruel mezcla de espacio social y espacio cómico' [the cruel mixing of social and comic space] (217) frames the characters in an abstract scheme where neither psychological development nor any real change is readily available to them (216–17). Thus Cruz, for all the energy and changeability put into her performance of María Elena, has this challenge of performing set pieces within a set piece. As part of the making of equivalences between the city Barcelona and the character María Elena (as constructed in the title's substitutional triptych and in the voice-over's suggestion that 'they photographed everything … but the best subject was María Elena herself'), Cruz the actor finds herself increasingly made lapidary or monumental. The would-be iconic shot of María Elena, hair down and cigarette on lips, leaning against a graffiti-inscribed roller-shutter (the first up in the stills gallery at www.vickycristinabarcelona.co.uk – and the cover image of this book) fixes Cruz's body in at least two ways, perhaps limiting the room for histrionic manoeuvre. In one direction she becomes part of the archive of visual memories of the Raval district (where Cristina takes the photo within the diegesis) from the photographs of Joan Colom through to the images of *En construcción/ Work in Progress* (José Luis Guerín, 2001). In another, she becomes Cruz the top-rank pin-up, not exactly but almost advertising the silky, sensuous dress, the handbag, the camera, the cigarette itself, or the hair – so glossy, so carefully unkempt. The voice-over narrator's deadpan, barbed observations about characters taking photographs (in Cristina's case, 'experimenting with her latest passion') draws attention not just intentionally to the disingenuousness of the North American visitors – of the American in Europe – but unintentionally (perhaps) to the ways in which the film objectifies and makes pictures of Cruz, especially, in an extension of the ways which Evans (2004) had already identified as central to her appeal to Hollywood, as feminine, luminous, youthful, Mediterranean (61), and, also, bound up in a long tradition of mythifying construction of images of feminine beauty on screen (62). Bardem, though, is also shamelessly and enjoyably exploited, his dark-shirted, commanding presence in chic corners of prime sites, cycling carefree through the Catalan countryside as if it were the cinematic rural France or Italy of the 1960s, or driving his flash, red car (trailer: 02:02–02:03). It is as if he were playing the now grown-up and more refined version of the character Raúl, in *Jamón, jamón*, whose hyper-sexualised *macho* body (Evans 2004: 77–85) finally seduced Penélope Cruz's Silvia, and whose ambition was a motorbike.

On the other hand, and benefiting also from her appearance in *All About My Mother*, as already mentioned, Cruz's association with the city's marvels on screen enmeshes her star personality in a web of considerable theoretical importance and in a rich strand of cinema history. Already likened to Sophia Loren or Anna Magnani for her role in *Volver* (Pedro Almodóvar, 2002) (Miller 2006), and to Audrey Hepburn in *Blow* (Ted Demme, 2001), Cruz's second Barcelona-set role augments her trajectory away from the dust and open spaces of *Jamón, jamón* and *The Hi-Lo Country* (Stephen Frears, 1998) into glamorous international, urban spaces such as New York (in Cameron Crowe's *Vanilla Sky*, 2001) or Vancouver (in Isabel Coixet's *Elegy*, 2009). While Cruz partakes of the rich codedness of this cinematic city, her character 'becomes the spirit of Barcelona during the photography expedition as she merges, almost literally, into its walls' (Fuller 2009: 27), and the film reflects constantly on visuality.

Resina's warnings about semantic vagueness, alluded to above, certainly apply to the stars of the film themselves, but if their performances blur at the edges at times, framing and lighting unfailingly offer a sharp intertextual enhancement of their status. Javier Aguirresarobe's cinematography not only 'bathes [the city] with a lemon-golden light' (Fuller 2009), which enthrals and sustains the fantasy, but it also identifies the film with other less semantically vague ones for which he was cinematographer, such as *La muerte de Mikel/Mikel's Death* (Imanol Uribe, 1984) and *Secretos del corazón/Secrets of the Heart* (Montxo Armendáriz, 1997) for landscapes and interiors or *La niña de tus ojos/The Girl of your Eyes* (Fernando Trueba, 1998) and *Mar adentro/The Sea Inside* (Alejandro Amenábar, 2004) for arresting images of Cruz and Bardem, and all four films for their addressing of particular social and historical issues meticulously set in period. The two actors are, then, obliquely reinscribed by the cityscape as shot and lit into classic Spanish cultural and cinematic history at its most sharp and poignant. Moreover, they are aurally framed by 'a creakily pedantic voiceover narration' which is 'a knowingly transparent revamp of the age-old Americans-in-Europe story, as perfected by Henry James and Edith Wharton ... providing the appropriate bookish tone' (Romney 2008: 68) – framed, that is, in high transnational culture of a purportedly more elegant, more finely ironic, age.

Sexual politics and the love triangle

Deleyto (2009) draws attention to the extraordinary degree of difficulty facing married couples in Allen's comedies (48) and to the accompanying ideological ambivalence in the sexual politics of the films (221). Here it comes to the fore, for instance, with self-effacing humour and scandalous misdirection, when Bardem's unmistakable, manly bulk first hovers out of anonymity in the corner of a 'little restaurant' on the first night of Vicky and Cristina's stay, to become the extravagantly over-confident Juan Antonio (trailer: 00:25–00:44). Smoothly conflating power, money, sexual adventure and artistic prestige – there is 'a beautiful statue' which needs to be seen (in Oviedo) – he wraps together a seductive but devilishly snob-*machista* proposition. The gentle smile of amusement which breaks across his face from time to time during the exchange is as much Bardem's, enjoying this, as his character's: for example, accompanying the words 'does she always analyse every inspiration until its grain of charm is – errr, ¿cómo se dice ...? – squeezed out?'; or on feigning to get their two names confused. Bardem, Cruz, the other stars and their audiences have to run with the equivocations. As Deleyto points out:

> el humor de las películas de Allen se mueve entre la tendenciosidad patriarcal y la celebración de la igualdad, entre la aceptación a la vez gozosa y resignada de la fuerza del instinto sexual y la sátira de las estructuras opresoras de la sociedad.

> [the humour in Allen's films moves between patriarchal tendentiousness and the celebration of equality, between the glad or resigned acceptance of the force of sexual instinct and satire of society's oppressive structures.]

> (2009: 217)

This particular intersection of sexual politics and comedy, pervasive in *Vicky Cristina Barcelona*, is characteristically focused in Cruz and in the dialogue given to María Elena. When she, Cristina and Juan Antonio all go to visit the latter's father, dressed in gypsy-chic she wanders through the quaint old walled garden with Cristina picking up on an earlier (and similarly parodied) theme, that of her love for Juan Antonio being everlasting, but impossible: romantic. Onto this classic canvas of deterministic coupledom, though, María Elena – and with a now softly sensual and feminist sisterly set of looks and arrangement from Cruz – paints also the beginnings of the brief sexual ménage-à-trois which is to follow. Heteronormativity gives way to bohemian but nonetheless committed emotional radicalism; but the pendulum swings to and fro. Cristina realises that 'she was not as open-minded as she had always imagined herself', but also 'relax[es]', throws herself into it, and talks it through with Vicky and Doug. The same-sex kiss which properly initiates the relationship, so falsified and exalted in the blog-osphere and the popular press,[2] is also on the move ideologically, in Deleyto's terms. The red-lit darkroom in which it occurs removes it into a fantasy realm where it might either signify the sort of anti-bourgeois, anti-heteronormative radicalism we might associate with photo-art and independent filmmaking, or it might signify make-believe, wish-fulfilment, the faux-radical patriarchalism of that very same filmmaking (for example, the French New Wave, on whose sexism see Sellier 2008).

Always hovering over the rebellious ideal – again encapsulated in Cruz's convincing yet parodic interventions as the spirit of unruliness – is the ghost of marriage (Judy [Patricia Clarkson] and Mark's [Kevin Dunn], stifling; Vicky and Doug's, unequally anticipated; Juan Antonio's and María Elena's). When Cristina tells Juan Antonio and María Elena that their three-way relationship cannot go on, it is in the former marital home, at the centre of established domesticity, the kitchen area (trailer: 01:31–01:35). In costume and styling, Bardem and Cruz – he in black polo shirt and she in lace-embroidered night-gown-cum-petticoat – are recapitulating momentarily not only the comfortable casual intimacies of domestic living from their characters' past but also, in the scopic regime imposed upon them, some of the structures of sexual commodifi-cation which sustain such apparent intimacies. At the stove, Cruz in cream looks petite but exorbitant – her hair luxuriantly disarrayed once more, and eroticising the shoulders and collar bones on which it falls – against the handsome bulk of Bardem in black and quarter- and half-profile, stubbled, and with a soigné, masculine, bed-head look to his hair. In this catastrophic end to their experiment in love the two look lovely; their very presence (as stars) makes Cristina's studied reasoning lame and Scarlett Johansson's role the tragically subsidiary one of the about-to-be exiled from the stage of romance.

However, solemn concerns over the equivocal sexual politics of what Bardem, Cruz and Johansson are being asked to do here are deflected by way of the comic deflation yet escalation of the dramatic situation which is Cruz's rendering of the intervention by María Elena. She swivels erratically between the stove and the object of her scorn and disappointment, deploys theatrically conventional angry grins as she delivers her verdicts and diagnoses ('chronic dissatisfaction is what you have, chronic dissatisfaction'), stoops and bends, directing her glares at the two other actors in ways in which the camera delights. Veering between English and a deliberately coarsened Spanish ('¡niñata de mierda!, ¡niñata de mierda!') [spoilt little brat!], María Elena's temper and Cruz's brio in rendering it are a storm into which Bardem injects a calm through Juan Antonio's drawing of the two women to him, enfolding them in a priestly embrace which perhaps he, Bardem, most recently rehearsed in playing the role of the inquisitor priest Brother Lorenzo in *Goya's Ghosts* (Miloš Forman, 2006).

Comedy acting

As actors working in a language other than their first, Bardem and Cruz take up the opportunities afforded to them by Allen's wit and formal brilliance, in particular allowing them to break free of some of the obstacles which had attended even their recent performances in English-speaking roles.[3] Bardem had suffered at the hands of portentousness in the script for *Love in the Time of Cholera* (Mike Newell, 2007), although, in the same year, a certain strangeness of diction had only added to his triumph in his role as the (anyway eerily off-key) killer Anton Chigurh in *No Country for Old Men* (Perriam 2010). Cruz has been dogged by received ideas about a career which habitually mixes success in Spanish productions with 'Hollywood clunkers' (Pierce 2009), as well as by the surely connected notion that she is good in Spanish but poor in English (McCarthy 2008: 39). However, as *Variety*'s reporter suggests, 'Allen even generates affectionate comic mileage from the common [assumption] by having her deliver Maria Elena's colorful tirades in her native language', only to be made to switch to English by Juan Antonio (McCarthy 2008: 39).

During María Elena's first moments in the house (trailer: 01:16–01:18 and 01:22–01:24), following her suicide attempt, Cruz uses the character's disorientation and her dismay at being a guest 'en mi propia casa' [in my own home] to lay down a soft counterpoint of languid beauty-in-distress (during which Cruz seems to be teasingly hiding the fact that it is she, through downcast face, and hands to forehead) to the erotically edgy, jilted jealousy which follows. In both modes, she wittily plays up the imposed switching of languages – with pouting, exhausted or pointed, challenging looks and flicks of the hand – until it becomes the very token of what to her character's eyes is the crass inappropriateness of the amorous substitution Juan Antonio has himself made. Cruz gets and gives much pleasure out of the dialogue's taking up and exaggerating of selected absurd theories of romantic love (as already discussed above), superstitions and xenophobic received ideas. As if suddenly an Andalusian woman of a bygone age, María Elena (in Spanish) expresses her mistrust of Cristina on the grounds that her eyes are of different colours. Coiled in a chair with arms wrapped around her raised knees, or springing lithely across the bed Juan Antonio is making, Cruz's María Elena uses her Spanish to trot out some powerful old clichés about perfect love, and the separated lover being lost and damaged. At the table in the garden (trailer: 01:37), she pours scorn on Cristina indirectly by decrying the ugliness of the sound of the Chinese language that Cristina unguardedly admits to having started to learn (much as one might hear, all too often, unreconstructed Castilians bemoaning the sound of Catalan or German); and by declaring Chinese cuisine 'de lo más desagradable' [the most unpleasant thing you can imagine] (in an echo of a still familiar Spanish chauvinism in matters of food; but also with an edge of racism). Perfect timing, sulky looks and barbed little social challenges keep the adversarial comedy moving: Cruz expresses with perfection the fleeting transition from gleeful malice to apparently friendly overture, at the start of the conversation about Chinese, via a shifting, quiet smile, given perspective and impact by the not incidentally smouldering cigarette she holds in the hand whose arm is leaning on the lunch table, and which will lever her up, triumphant, post-sniping.

The film places its actors, then – at least contingently, and through the magnifying sheet-glass of wry reflexivity – in the frame of the romantic comedy. Deleyto (2009) arrives at a three-point definition (35) of which two are germane here. First, there must traditionally be a narrative structure which takes into account shifts and transformations in social views and critical understanding of love, marriage and sexuality (25–6; 43–4). *Vicky Cristina Barcelona* recapitulates and updates this tradition in toying with a discourse of brittle, polymorphous desire. The Spanish stars enrich the process by bringing oblique associations with other (Spanish) cinematic narrative accounts of this sort. In Bardem's career *Segunda piel/Second Skin* (Gerardo Vera, 2000) in tragic mode and *Entre las piernas/Between the Legs* (Manuel Gómez Pereira, 1999) in more comic mode had already explored the stresses on coupledom caused by the presence of a third lover (Perriam 2003: 96, 113–16). In Cruz's case, the apparent lesbianism of her character (a male spirit in a fallen female angel's body) in *Sin noticias de dios/Don't Tempt Me* (Agustín Díaz Yanes, 2001) had created amusing havoc, and the extreme disruption of the pair-bond in *Abre los ojos/Open Your Eyes* (Alejandro Amenábar, 1997) and subsequently *Vanilla Sky* (2001) had been centrally concerned with shifts and transformations.

Deleyto's second characteristic of romantic comedy is the presence of the protective and transformative fantasy space (2009: 35). Here this is found in the Oviedo and Barcelona dreamscapes, and in the studio house and its darkroom. We have already seen how, in Deleyto's words, Allen's characters move around 'entre el espacio social y el espacio ideal, entre el realismo y la fantasía' [between social space and ideal space, between realism and fantasy] (46). It is Cruz's method of inhabiting these which most emphatically provides the humorous point of view which for Deleyto (35) positions the characters vis-à-vis love, desire and sexuality. She is also central to the lucid considerations of the contradictions and limitations of the romantic comedy which Deleyto sees in the film (218).

Conclusion

As the *Guardian*'s reviewer observed (Bradshaw 2009), the performances of both Bardem and Cruz contrast strongly with those of the rest of the cast, showing as dynamic and energetic against 'Hall and Johansson [who] are slightly subdued and off the beat', in his view: 'Cruz looks as if she has wandered in from a more hefty film entirely', he observes. Similarly, but giving the American actors the benefit of the doubt, *Time* (Corliss 2008) considered that 'Whenever Bardem or Cruz are on screen, [the film] finds its heart. It sees them as fully in tune with their feelings … The Americans are children by comparison, a little stiff.' Cruz is both 'dynamite' (McCarthy 2008: 39) and, if not gravitas personified, at least substantial intensity, elemental, 'una fuerza de la naturaleza' [a force of nature] (Yáñez Murillo 2008).

Both actors parodically reprise their own past iconic performances of Castilian typicality, aware, perhaps, in ways that Allen and his team are not, of the destabilising effects on the performance of identities of superimposing Castilian and Catalan cultures. Acting across English and Spanish, they indirectly draw into frame questions about their own now-powerful presence in English-language cinema, making Barcelona both archaic and quaint and the vivid transnational, photogenic city space. However, this is a cinematic space which threatens to trap and take control of the actors as much as does Allen's light take on the genre. Sensing this, perhaps, Cruz herself is reported as having pressed for a different, subtler rendition of the character and more rehearsal time, but with Allen having insisted on boldness, chaos and spontaneity (Carpenter 2008; Guerrasio 2008: 73). The tensions between these ways into the performance are among the features which lift it above some of the rest of the film.

Both Bardem, especially (Perriam 2010), and Cruz, to a lesser degree (supporting, for example, the ONE campaign and Global Green), are manifestly and publicly sensitive to many manifestations of injustice, hegemonic exclusions and circumventions of rights in the world outside the sexual politics of comedy. Although equally manifestly on holiday from such issues in Allen's film, these two hugely photogenic and still emphatically Spanish stars play up their transnational glamour, irony and iconicity in ways which accord the film – and the heterogeneous Barcelona it displays – a certain real point. Given performances with an edge, the loss of definition which can be imposed on the city by its image, as well as the potential semantic vagueness of the American Europhile film, can both be countered. The attractive oddities in both can turn out to be those, rather, of the stars themselves.

Notes

1　Note on illustrations: the discussion of individual scenes in this chapter is best illustrated by reference to the official UK trailer of the film, which is to be found at www.
imdb.com/video/imdb/vi388104985. Timings are given where appropriate to the
discussion. Additionally, the stills gallery at www.vickycristinabarcelona.co.uk will
help readers to situate the discussion.
2　The kiss between Johansson and Cruz had scored 894,933 hits at www.youtube.com/
watch?v=Sal6XacQRp4 when accessed on 12 November 2010; and another 81,981
at www.dailymotion.com/video/x8jv8l_penelope-cruz-and-scarlett-johansso_short-
films, accessed on the same day. Referred to as 'Lesbian lip-lock' at www.garagetv.be/
video-galerij/celebritywatch/scarlett_johansson_penelope_cruz_kiss_penelope_cruz.
aspx [also accessed 12 November 2010], the still image is used, for example, at www.
fotogramas.es/Peliculas/Vicky-Cristina-Barcelona/Scarlett-Javier-Penelope-Woody.-
Juntos-y-revueltos/Joven-americana-busca-emociones-fuertes; www.thesun.co.uk/sol/
homepage/showbiz/bizarre/article1309355.ece; and http://lesbicanarias.es/2008/05
/18/el-beso-entre-scarlett-johansson-y-penelope-cruz [all accessed 12 November
2010]: 'es repetida millones de veces en blogs y web sociales del mundo gay' [is
repeated millions of times on blogs and social networking sites in the gay world]
(Diario Femenino 2010).
3　In an interview in London in 2006, for instance, Cruz refers to the tension arising from
working in English as 'not a friend of acting' (Delgado 2006).

Bibliography

Abbas, Ackbar (2003) 'Cinema, the City, and the Cinematic', in Linda Krause and Patrice
Petro (eds), *Global Cities: Cinema, Architecture, and Urbanism in a Digital Age*, New
Brunswick, NJ and London: Rutgers University Press, 142–56.
Bradshaw, Peter (2009) '*Vicky Cristina Barcelona*', *Guardian* (6 February), www.guard-
ian.co.uk/film/2009/feb/06/woody-allen-vicky-cristina-barcelona-scarlett-johansson-
penelope-cruz [accessed 15 November 2010].
Carpenter, Cassie (2008) 'Who's in the Running: Film: Double Featured: Once
Considered Just a Pretty Face, Penélope Cruz Shows Her Range in *Elegy* and *Vicky
Cristina Barcelona*', *Back Stage* (11–17 December 2008), A15.
Corliss, Richard (2008) 'Cannes: Vicky, Cristina, Barcelona and Woody', *Time* (16 May),
www.time.com/time/arts/article/0,8599,1807381,00.html [accessed 15 November
2010].
Deleyto, Celestino (2009) *Woody Allen y el espacio de la comedia romántica*, Valencia:
IVAC/Generalitat de València.
Delgado, Maria M. (2006) 'The *Guardian* Interview with Pedro Almodóvar and Penélope
Cruz', London, National Film Theatre, 4 August, www.bfi.org.uk/features/interviews/
almodovar.html [accessed 28 December 2010].
Diario Femenino (2010) 'Penélope Cruz, ídolo homosexual en Estados Unidos', www.
diariofemenino.com/actualidad/famosos/articulos/penelope-cruz-gay-estados-unidos
[accessed 12 November 2010].
Evans, Peter (2004) *Jamón, jamón*, Barcelona: Ediciones Paidós.

Fuller, Graham (2009) 'No City for Old Men', *Sight & Sound*, 19:2 (February), 24–7.

Guerrasio, Jason (2008) 'The 18th Annual Gotham Independent Film Awards: Penélope Cruz', *Filmmaker – The Magazine of Independent Film*, 17:1, 72–4.

McCarthy, Todd (2008) 'Woody Revels in Sex and the Spanish City', *Variety*, 411:3 (2–8 June), 31, 39.

Miller, Gerri (2006). 'Penelope Cruz Makes a Welcome Return in *Volver*', hollywood.com (8 November), www.hollywood.com/feature/Penelope_Cruz_Makes_a_Welcome_Return_in_Volver_/3580210 [accessed 20 November 2010].

Montalt, Salvador (2008) 'Apunts des de Canes', Club 7 Cinema Blog (16 May), http://blocs.mesvilaweb.cat/bloc/view/id/5631/cat/3958 [accessed 23 December 2010].

Perriam, Chris (2003) *Stars and Masculinities in Spanish Cinema: From Banderas to Bardem*, Oxford: Oxford University Press.

—(2010) 'Javier Bardem: Costume, Crime, and Commitment', in Ann Davies (ed.), *Spain on Screen*, Basingstoke: Palgrave Macmillan, 114–28.

Pierce, Nev (2009) 'Pretty, Gifted', *Empire*, 236 (February), 86.

Resina, Joan Ramon (2008) *Barcelona's Vocation of Modernity: Rise and Decline of an Urban Image*, Stanford, CA: Stanford University Press.

Reuters (2010) 'Actors Javier Bardem and Penelope Cruz wed in Bahamas', *Independent* (14 July), www.independent.co.uk/news/people/news/actors-javier-bardem-and-penelope-cruz-wed-in-bahamas-2026400.html [accessed 20 November 2010].

Romney, Jonathan (2008) 'Vicky Cristina Barcelona', *Film Comment*, 44:4, 68–9.

Schonfield, Katherine (2000) *Walls Have Feelings: Architecture, Film and the City*, London and New York: Routledge.

Sellier, Geneviève (2008) *Masculine Singular: French New Wave Cinema*, trans. Kristin Ross. Durham, NC: Duke University Press.

Smith, Paul Julian (2009) 'Film Culture in Madrid', *Film Quarterly*, 62:4, 63–8.

Yáñez Murillo, Manuel (2008) 'Woody Allen nos explica las claves de *Vicky Cristina Barcelona*: Maestro de la comedia busca explicar el amor', *Fotogramas* (4 September), www.fotogramas.es/Peliculas/Vicky-Cristina-Barcelona/Scarlett-Javier-Penelope-Woody.-Juntos-y-revueltos/Maestro-de-la-comedia-busca-explicar-el-amor [accessed 23 December 2010].

14

La mujer sin cabeza/The Headless Woman (Lucrecia Martel, 2008): silence, historical memory and metaphor

Maria M. Delgado

Argentina. The present. Three children and a dog play close to an isolated country road. Middle-aged dentist, wife and mother Verónica (María Onetto) – known by all as Vero – is driving home. Distracted by the ringing of her mobile phone, she hits something or someone but doesn't leave the car to discover who or what she has collided with. Dazed and confused, she goes to hospital but walks out prematurely, checking into a hotel where she bumps into and then sleeps with her cousin's husband, Juan Manuel (Daniel Genoud). Returning home, she remains in a daze, barely connecting with her husband, Marcos (César Bordón), or her colleagues at work. When she confesses to her husband that she fears she may have hit a person, they return to the scene of the crime, but her husband insists that she only hit a dog. Her husband speaks to well-connected friends to try and discover if there are rumours of any hit-and-run accident. News circulates in the community that a child has disappeared. Vero continues with her social engagements – visits to her elderly aunt Lala (María Vaner) and cousin Josefina (Claudia Cantero), whose teenage daughter, Candita (Inés Efron), recovering from hepatitis, writes Vero love letters. Vero's husband liaises with family and friends in the town to ensure that all traces of the accident – her visit to the hospital, damage to the car, her stay at the hotel – are removed. The child is discovered, presumed drowned, in the canal.

Transnational cinema and historical memory

Recent scholarship on transnational cinema has questioned long-held understandings of what might be termed an 'authentic' national film. For Elizabeth Ezra and Terry Rowden, the transnational – 'understood as the global forces that link people or institutions across nations' – itself announces 'the decline of national sovereignty as a regulatory force in global coexistence' (2006: 1). The currency of funding film features in an age of high capitalism necessitates a culture where monies are raised from a range of sources based on economic (rather than national) priorities. Migration, exile and internationalism have all served to interrogate established understandings of what constitutes 'the national' and how it is articulated in a world order where the global exchange of capital and information effectively reterritorialises both the First and Third Worlds. While English as a second language may be the *lingua franca* of advanced global capitalism, the growing economic might of Latin America has rendered it an attractive partner for a Spanish state struggling within the precarious situation of a boom-and-bust economy. Spain's ex-Prime Minister José María Aznar may have opted to affiliate himself with the economic might (and right-wing credentials) of George Bush's USA, but his foreign investments were firmly located in Latin America (Martín and Toral 2005). His successor, José María Rodríguez Zapatero, chose to publicly associate himself with its southern neighbours, *el cono sur*, citing a shared neocolonial linguistic heritage – *la hispanidad* – (rather than a problematic colonial past) in which discourses of origins and purity have no part. As political researcher Susanne Gratius recognised in *El País* in 2010, 'Más que ser una prioridad de política exterior, América Latina es un asunto interno' [More than a foreign policy priority, Latin America is an internal matter]. Investment in Latin America remains an economic necessity for global Spanish brands such as Telefónica and Banco Santander, seeking to emerge from the economic crisis that generated a central deficit gap of €99,785 billion in 2009 and took Spain's unemployment from 8.3 per cent in 2007 to 24.4 per cent at the end of March 2012 (Anon. 2011; BBC 2012).

Spanish cinema has long recognised the potential and possibilities of the Latin American film market. Spanish America is a lucrative economic marketplace for the exchange of cultural wares – with expanding populations having access to both increased disposable income and modes of representation – and equally an attractive potential investor in the manufacturing process.[1] Films that have benefited from enhanced production investment, high production values, star actors and conspicuous marketing and distribution budgets are able to circulate more effectively across national borders. This is evident in the trajectories of *Vicky Cristina Barcelona* (Woody Allen, 2008) and *Biutiful* (Alejandro González Iñárritu, 2010). Indeed, both these films indicate that, in order to compete more aggressively in a market where it is the mainstream (genre-driven cinema with familiar plots and actors) that has habitually performed at the box office,[2] Spanish producers have strategically opted to put together their own superproductions. The refashioning of genre pics against the 'exotic' landscapes of Spain – picture-postcard Barcelona in the case of *Vicky Cristina Barcelona* and the gritty, dangerous 'other' of the city in *Biutiful* – has certainly been one approach. *Vicky Cristina Barcelona* works within the paradigms of the genre pic; *Biutiful*, on the other hand, proffers a take on the Odysseus myth as a contemporary Ulysses wanders through an urban metropolis, both the agent and victim of his own misfortune.

Both films, like Guillermo del Toro's *El laberinto del Fauno/Pan's Labyrinth* (2006) and *Los abrazos rotos/Broken Embraces* (2009), also provide further evidence of the status of Spanish as a major world language (no longer the case with French, Italian or German, the traditional stalwarts of European arthouse cinema). Spanish-language culture is a marketable commodity and the wave of co-productions that have accommodated popular genres (as with the Spanish-set horror features of Guillermo del Toro and Rigoberto Castañeda's *KM 31* [2006]), romantic comedies (Juan José Campanella's *El secreto de sus ojos/The Secret in Their Eyes* [2009]), thrillers (Marcelo Piñeyro's *Las viudas de los jueves/Thursday's Widows* [2010]) and road movies (Steven Soderbergh's *Che* [2008]) point to a greater confidence in the mobility of Spanish-language products across the global economy.

As a general rule, since 2000, about a quarter of the films produced in Spain have been co-productions with Latin America.[3] The attractions of such co-productions are evident: potential audiences across Spanish America, the possibility of planting high-profile Latin stars who can help sell a feature, the exchange of technical crews and specialist expertise. While a significant number of the examples I have drawn on above are Mexican–Spanish co-productions, it is Argentina that has proved Spain's most conspicuous partner in the area of two-way and three-way co-productions since the turn of the century. In 2009 Spain and Argentina were involved in 7 of the 30 two-way co-productions realised that year and a further 6 of the 16 three-way co-productions. In 2008 this figure was 13 of 39 and 1 of 3, respectively. In 2002 Argentina already led the way, with 9 of the two-way co-productions made that year: in 2003 the figure was 6 of the 25 two-way co-productions between both countries.

These figures are significant in that they testify to the growing importance of Argentina as a co-producing partner on a breadth of commercial Spanish features, from Carlos Saura's *Tango* (1998) to Ramón Costafreda's *Abrígate/Wrap Up* (2007). Significantly, Spain has also come on board as a co-producer on projects that do not necessarily feature Spanish characters or a Spanish locale but rather 'invest' in a trend, such as the New Argentine Cinema – the generation of film school-educated independent filmmakers whose poetic, neo-realist aesthetic and move away from the studio-bound, magic realist whimsy and/or political didacticism of their predecessors marked a decisive shift in Argentine filmmaking.[4] This was an enterprising 'poor' cinema with a pseudo-documentary feel (including a recourse to non-professional actors) and a reliance on handheld camera work. Grouped under the title New Argentine Cinema, the filmmakers who emerged in the years between 1995 and 2002 embraced a variety of styles and genres, from the black, droll humour of Martín Rejtman's *Silvia Prieto* (1999) to the austere black-and-white long single takes and sparse narrative of Trapero's *Mundo grúa/Crane World* (1999). Their playful games with genre – the con movie in Fabián Bielinsky's *Nueve reinas/Nine Queens* (2001) and the road movie in Diego Lerman's *Tan de repente/Suddenly* (2002) – offered new possibilities for invigorating well-worn formulas. Spain wanted to 'buy into' the kudos around the New Argentine Cinema and moved in to invest in a number of productions directed by the most conspicuous brand names of this new 'national' cinema.[5] The minimalist environmental films of Lisandro Alonso have found Spanish support through Luis Miñarro, Spain's most adventurous independent producer,[6] who had a 20 per cent stake in *Liverpool* (2008). Fabián Bielinsky's follow-up to *Nine Queens, El aura/The Aura* (2005), was funded by a 43 per cent Spanish stake from Tornasol. Tornasol also enjoyed a 54 per cent investment in the Oscar-winning *The Secret in Their Eyes*.

Certainly, while economic interests are paramount in film investment, I would argue that further factors may perhaps account for the particular thematics that have dominated a number of the most conspicuous Spanish–Argentine co-productions of recent years. Co-productions, made possible through globalisation, have also taken globalisation as a central motif – as with Gerardo Herrero's *El corredor nocturno/Night Runner* (2009). The legacy of recent dictatorships has also proved a potent subject for nations negotiating the move to democratic structures. In 2007, the then Spanish Prime Minister José Luis Rodríguez Zapatero introduced the contentious Law 52/2007, *Ley de Memoria Histórica* [law of historical memory], in the face of vociferous opposition from right-wing interests fronted by the Partido Popular [PP or People's Party]. After decades of the *pacto de olvido* [pact of silence] that effectively suppressed discussions of the Republican dead in the years after democracy was restored to Spain, the law allows for a confrontation of the more uncomfortable legacies of the Civil War and its aftermath.[7] It is thought that 100,000 dead lie in mass graves across Spain, victims of nationalist aggression in the Civil War and its aftermath.

Spain has not been alone in introducing legislation that has sought to come to terms with a dictatorial past and its human rights violations. Argentina, too, has its own quota of *desaparecidos*, who were eradicated by the military *junta* that seized power in 1976. Between 1976 and 1983, when Raúl Alfonsín's civilian government came to power, over 30,000 Argentines were aggressively detained by the military regime and never seen again. Alfonsín and his successor Carlos Menem effectively introduced a *pacto de olvido* of their own, offering only the most cursory recognition of the atrocities committed by the four generals – Jorge Videla, Roberto Eduardo Viola, Leopoldo Galtieri and Reynaldo Bignone – who headed the *junta*, and effectively introducing legislation to protect both the police and military who had executed the country's 'Dirty War'.

President Nestor Kirchner (2003–07) and his wife and successor Cristina

Fernández de Kirchner (2007–), however, have offered no such impunity to those responsible, allowing for the systematic introduction of a new national discourse of human rights that has at its centre an embracing of historical memory as a cornerstone of governmental policy. Like Zapatero – whose grandfather was a Republican executed by nationalists – Kirchner was directly affected by the *junta*'s crackdown on political dissent and opposition and imprisoned twice in the 1970s for his political opinions. His desire to affiliate himself as an heir to the Madres de la Plaza de Mayo [an association of Argentine mothers of those who disappeared], his conspicuous role in mobilising supporters on what remains of the Navy School of Mechanics [ESMA] – arguably the most notorious of the *junta*'s clandestine detention centres – and his pledge to convert it into a museum to honour the victims of the dictatorship, as well as the trial of 13 ESMA officers in 2009 have effectively positioned the Kirchners as visible advocates for a politics grounded in the need to come to terms with past human-rights atrocities.[8]

It is perhaps not surprising, therefore, that in two nations where political leaders have positioned themselves in close relationship to public accountability for historical crimes, issues of historical memory should prove an influential trope in contemporary filmmaking. In Argentina, Albertina Carri's *Los Rubios/ The Blonds* (2003), Nicolás Prividera's *M* (2003), Lucía Cedrón's *Cordero de dios/Lamb of God* (2008), Israel Adrián Caetano's *Crónica de una fuga 1977/ Buenos Aires 1977* (2006) and Jonathan Perel's *El Predio/The Lot* (2010) have all gravitated around the terrain of the disappeared. In Spain, there have been biopics revisiting victims of Francoism – Manuel Huerga's *Salvador* (2006), the treatment of the arrest and garrotting of anarchist Salvador Puig Antich – and tales of lives truncated by the culture of dictatorship – Ventura Pons's *Barcelona (un mapa)/Barcelona (A Map)* (2007). Unflinching assessments of nationalist atrocities and abuses refracted through horror – *Pan's Labyrinth* – and drama – *Pà negre/Black Bread* (2010) – have also been accompanied by tales of hidden traumas unearthed through the mundane and the worldly – Jordi Cadena and Judith Colell's *Elisa K* (2010) – as well as the other-worldly – Julio Medem's *Caótica Ana/Chaotic Ana* (2007) and J.A. Bayona's *El orfanato/The Orphanage* (2007). Isaki Lacuesta's *Los condenados/The Damned* (2009) takes place in an unnamed country that we presume is Argentina, as two old friends come together to unearth the body of a colleague who 'disappeared' during what is presumed to be Argentina's military dictatorship or the period immediately preceding it. *The Secret in Their Eyes*, a prominent Spanish–Argentine co-production, uses a romance-cum-thriller with the structural conceit of an unsolved murder as the hinge for a probing examination of historical memory, vigilante justice and modes of interrogating the abuses of the past in a country scarred by the collective memory of a brutal military dictatorship.[9]

Even Pedro Almodóvar has acknowledged a political inflection to his recent work grounded in issues of historical memory (see Delgado 2009). The focus on the ghosts of the past that return to haunt the present in *Volver* (2006) and both the issue of amnesia and the relationship between individual and institutional discourses of mourning in *Broken Embraces* articulate a national trauma embedded in the necessity of coming to terms with the abuses of the Civil War and Franco's regime. *La piel que habito/The Skin I Live In* (2011) touches on the theme of the disappeared, as a new identity is imposed on a kidnapped youth by the charismatic patriarch whose veneer of respectability masks a refusal to work within the limits of the law.[10] It is perhaps not insignificant that Almodóvar's production company, El Deseo, was the Spanish co-producer of Lucrecia Martel's *La mujer sin cabeza/The Headless Woman* (2008), the film that I will focus on for the remainder of this chapter.[11] Almodóvar had previously co-produced Martel's second film *La niña santa/The Holy Girl* (2004), having admired the elegant craftsmanship and seductive savagery of her first film, *La ciénaga/The Swamp* (2001) (Almodóvar 2009a).

There are certainly points of contact between Martel's three films: the languid pacing, the attention to frame composition, the camera's role as a microscope that gives us a brutal close-up into middle-class angst and self-destruction, the ominous sense of impending chaos that hovers over the action threatening to unravel at any moment, the stagnating environment (unnamed, but actually Martel's home province of Salta in northern Argentina) in which her characters function, the complex soundscape – evident in the rasping sound of the chairs being dragged across the patio in the opening scene of *The Swamp*. While her first two features had garnered positive reviews when premièred at the Berlin and Cannes Festivals, respectively, *The Headless Woman* attracted more perplexed responses when it was first seen at Cannes in 2008 (Anon. 2008; Romney 2010). The hostile tone of a significant proportion of these effectively delayed the Argentine première of the film (Enríquez 2008). As with Almodóvar's *Broken Embraces,* which similarly disappointed critics on its initial release in Spain,[12] I would argue, however, that the film enunciates a trauma of collective guilt and grief that remains unarticulated in overt narrative terms. A hit-and-run contemporary thriller where plot gradually gives way to metaphor, *The Headless Woman* clinically dissects the mechanisms that operate a culture of the disappeared.

Metaphor and political parable

Two worlds come into sharp contrast at the beginning of *The Headless Woman*. There is the world of Argentina's 'haves' embodied through the film's protagonist – the elegant, disengaged middle-class dentist Vero and the privileged bourgeois society of which she is part. The film's second sequence sees Vero bidding farewell to her family and friends after a lunch party. Small children play obtrusively around the large Volvo and Rover cars – symbols of Western affluence and affiliation – irritatingly refusing to listen to the commands of their elders.

These strident children are contrasted with the 'have-nots', the cleaners and gardeners who labour silently in the background, quietly and efficiently servicing the needs of Vero and her extended family. When Vero fears she may have killed a child from the other side of the tracks – one of the 'have-nots' – the patriarchs of the family close in to protect their interests. Interestingly, the child she may (or may not) have killed, because she was reaching for her mobile phone while driving, is first seen playing with a sibling and a dog at the side of the road – effectively on the margins from the film's opening. Vero is never sure if she has killed a child or a dog – in her world there is something shockingly interchangeable about what they represent. She never approaches the faceless shape on the asphalt – from a distance, it looks like a dog, but the glance is too fleeting to be reliable. The storm that hangs over the early part of the film – and which then keeps Vero within the confines of the hotel where she seeks refuge from the incident – may not have erased all traces of the hit-and-run accident, but the bourgeois family will ensure that any evidence that remains is decisively and definitely disposed of.

The Swamp and *The Holy Girl* can also be read as allegorical tales of domestic decomposition. In the former, two middle-class families now fallen on hard times refuse to face the realities of their shabby estate – brilliantly conceptualised by the dirty, festering pool around which the adults drunkenly congregate in the film's opening scene. In the latter film, a teenage girl's sexual awakening takes place in the context of the run-down hotel – a transient environment – managed by her drunken mother and uncle, where a medical conference is taking place. I would argue, however, that *The Headless Woman* is Martel's most overtly political film to date. Her visual and sonic landscape highlights the social schisms that underpin Argentine society: the poor who wait for treatment at the bleak local hospital, the faceless prisoner shackled to guards in the hospital bathroom, the masseur who visits Vero at home, the boy who cleans the car (seen only as a silhouette by the door), the elderly garden-centre attendant and his assistants who struggle noisily with the large pots Vero purchases to adorn her garden, the shadowy servants with indigenous features only ever partially in view. Martel opts for wide-screen Cinemascope that leaves these toiling figures slightly out of focus. Their stories are filtered through windows, glass doors and water, keeping the primary focus firmly on María Onetto's traumatised Vero.

Vero remains an enigma for much of the film. The viewer discovers that she is a dentist the morning after the accident, when she takes a taxi into work and remains in the waiting room as if killing time waiting for treatment. She refuses to take responsibility for her patients – much as she refuses to take responsibility for the accident.[13] The Vero who emerges post-accident is a dazed being: she commits adultery with her cousin's husband at a hotel in an encounter that

25. The shadowy presence of the 'have nots' in contrast to the prominent Vero
(María Onetto).

appears out of character. She avoids her husband when he returns to the house
from his hunting expedition bringing the bleeding corpse of the *corzuela* (a small
native deer) – a proxy for the victim of the accident – into her domestic space.
She is a woman out of joint, whose visits to the house of her elderly, bedridden
Aunt Lala cause bemusement. She appears to be unsure of who she is or where
she has come from, looking at images from her past – as with her grainy wedding
video – as if they are revealing an 'other' person. 'Tan hermosa estabas. ¿Para qué
arruinarte?' [You were so beautiful. Why let yourself go?], Lala asks the immacu-
late Vero. As such, Lala's comments appear to refer to a moral rather than a
physical decomposition. Significant here is the name Vero – short for Verónica.
In Italian – over half of Argentina's 40 million population are thought to be of
Italian descent – *vero* means truth. Only Vero seems to be unable to cope with
the veracity of the situation in which she finds herself, and allows for a different
'trust' to be constructed.[14] I am not the first to note that it is as if Vero is constructing an identity for herself – an event that can be read against the context of
the 'new' identities constructed for the children of the disappeared, stolen from
their parents and farmed out to affluent families who were compliant with the
authorities during the 'Dirty War'.[15]

   As in *The Swamp* and *The Holy Girl*, the swimming pool emerges as a key
motif in the film: a space of putrefaction, rot and decay.[16] In the former, it is
a metaphor for Mecha's dysfunctional family and their predicament: dirty and
uncared-for. In the latter it is a steamy, humid thermal spa where the adolescent
Amalia and her friend Josefina share sexual and religious complicities and desires.
In *The Headless Woman* it may be a more openly enticing locale but it is nevertheless cast as an arena of social exclusion, associated with moral neglect and
hermetically sealed from the world beyond. The new pool (and the malignant life
that Vero's cousin Josefina – Claudia Cantero – fears will threaten it because of

its proximity to the local vet's) is a hot topic of discussion for Vero's cousins and friends as they discuss who will attend its grand opening.

Water is a conduit in *The Headless Woman*: Vero is dripping wet from the heavy rain when she arrives at the hospital. 'Es una bendición este agua' [This water is a blessing], she is told as she hovers in the doorway of the building; Vero takes a shower on returning home, as if wanting to cleanse and purify her body and so eradicate any lingering evidence of her adultery; a bottle of water is brought to Vero by the kind *mestizo* welder at work as she weeps uncontrollably in the changing rooms and is poured over her in a religious gesture of purification and absolution; water transports the body of the disappeared boy down the canal. Rain doesn't wash away Vero's sin but rather confines her to wander as if suspended in a fish tank. Martel has spoken of the fish tank as an appropriate analogy for the world in which her characters are placed (2008). Vero spends much of the film in a suspended state and the film – placing the viewer in the position of its disorientated protagonist – articulates Martel's view of humanity as consistently dangling within what she terms 'an elastic fluid, it might be water but also air. We habitually forget that we are immersed in air' (2008). In *The Headless Woman* the viewer floats alongside Vero. At the hospital, in the immediate aftermath of the accident, Vero wanders through the corridors and public spaces as if in a trance, and has to be guided through the procedures by overworked nurses. The elderly woman sitting next to her in the waiting room comments to the man with her that 'Se está durmiendo la señora' [The lady is falling asleep] – signalling Vero's sleepwalking state. 'Me parece que estoy medio ... No me siento bien' [I feel a little ... I don't feel well], she confides to her dental assistant the following morning. For much of the film she appears to be moving at a more sluggish pace than everyone else. This sense of an unhinged world is further reinforced by Martel's framing: Vero is often positioned with friends and family members who are captured by the camera in incomplete form. The partially dismembered bodies – sometimes headless, sometimes with arms out of shot – offer the image of an amputated society. Vero's daughters are also significantly absent for much of the film: ostensibly studying law in Tucumán, only one of the two makes a brief appearance in the final sequences.

Even when Vero is able to confess that she might have killed someone, it is a simple statement to her husband in a crowded supermarket. He drives her to the scene of the crime to reassure her. 'No pasa nada' [nothing is wrong], he insists. While he persistently repeats that it was just a dog, however, the implications of the accident resonate through the film. '¿Qué hago?' [What should I do?], she asks him, but he is adamant that it is simply a question of getting some sleep. *The Headless Woman* charts Vero's journey from a shock-induced zombie-like lethargy to a re-engagement with the people and places that surround her as her husband and his accomplices (effectively the powers that be in the town) work behind the scenes to ensure that public records in effect concur that 'nothing' happened.

A society in denial

El proceso voluntario de olvido necesita mecanismos muy complejos y sutiles.
[The voluntary process of forgetting necessitates very complex and subtle mechanisms.]
Lucrecia Martel (Climent 2008)

Like Juan Antonio Bardem in *Muerte de un ciclista/Death of a Cyclist* (1955), Martel uses the hit-and-run narrative to comment on a society in denial. While Vero never treats her servants (notably nameless) with the contempt that Mecha and her cousin Tali reserve for *los collas* – the racist term they use for their industrious domestic help – in *The Swamp*, there is also no evidence provided of a relationship with anyone outside her family that is not based on servicing her needs. This is a film about the unspoken privileges that underpin a society. Jonathan Romney has written of the 'fishtank spaces' where Vero's family congregate in the film (2010). Martel favours cramped interiors that contain the characters and force them to coexist in the same frame. This further accentuates the depiction of social segregation that proved such a hallmark of her two earlier films.

Here, too, sound remains of paramount importance: servants attending to their daily tasks (sharpening knives, ordering taxis, brewing coffee); the noises of the large pots that Vero and her friends use to decorate their gardens being lifted by the elderly owner of the garden centre and his under-age assistants; children playing with their dog around the canal in the film's opening sequence; the acute ringing of Vero's mobile phone; the piercing sounds of the revellers at the pool; the repetitive scanning of items at the supermarket; the downpours of rain and claps of thunder; overlapping conversations at Lala's house where the viewer can never be sure who is speaking. The buzzing sound of the many encounters that take place – some entirely off screen but partially audible – create the sense of a series of insects hovering around Vero. For Martel sound never involves incidental music but rather a heightened aural landscape: 'Sound is the vibration of air. The only thing that physically touches you in the cinema is sound. You close your eyes and you will not see the movie, but sound still touches you, your body, all around' (in Matheou 2010).

The eccentric, bedbound Lala – María Vaner with echoes of Chus Lampreave – a character that might have been lifted from one of co-producer Pedro Almodóvar's early features, recognises that something is amiss. 'Esa voz no parece tuya' [That voice doesn't appear to be yours], she tells Vero, but this is a family haunted by the living dead. The only person prepared to mention it is effectively self-imprisoned within her own bedroom, a madwoman in the attic whose rants and ramblings are dismissed by those around her. Why are there children's clothes in Vero's house when her own daughters are supposedly grown up? What lies under Vero's garden? Are the handprints on Vero's car window those of her friends' children or those of the child she may have killed? Why does a young boy appear as Lala talks of the *espantos* [phantoms] that haunt the house? Is he the son of Lala's cook? Martel provides no concrete answers and opts instead for the systematic mapping of a culture where 'de eso no se habla' [we don't talk about that] (Monteagudo 2008).

It's the moral questions that resonate, repeatedly, through the film. *The Headless Woman* underlines the multiple ways in which a society eschews social responsibility. Vero even avoids discussing the amorous advances of her adolescent, convalescing feverish niece, Candita, whose love letters she ignores. Candita – the name evokes the Spanish *cándida* (candid) – wants direct answers: 'las cartas de amor se contestan o se devuelven' [love letters should be answered or returned], she informs Vero defiantly.[17] Vero, however, appears pathologically welded to the culture of secrecy: there is an adulterous liaison with her cousin's husband, Juan Manuel (Daniel Genoud), to conceal also. Secrets, evasions, denials and lies appear to be a way of life for Vero and much of her extended family. Even her garden appears to have its secrets – a fountain or pool buried beneath it, discovered by the gardener. Is it any wonder that Josefina observes: 'En esta familia todos terminan perdiendo la cordura' [Everyone in our family ends up crazy].

Martel writes of the film having emerged both from her own personal nightmares of having killed someone and the damage that she experienced in the aftermath of a serious accident when she was 5 years old (2010). She visited a faith healer to address the trauma or, as she states it, so that her soul would return to her body: 'me gustó esa idea de cuerpo sin alma' [I liked that idea of the body without a soul] (in Enríquez 2008). I would argue that it is precisely this idea of a collective body without a soul – in effect, historical memory – that the film addresses. Certainly 'the disappeared' remains a resonant narrative device in the New Argentine Cinema and, I would argue, recent Spanish film. Martel's film differs from features like *Buenos Aires 1977* and *Black Bread*, however, in its approach: *The Headless Woman* is rooted in an ostensibly contemporary world – the unnamed north-western Salta landscape of her earlier films – that alludes only obliquely to the *junta* regime and its horrors. For Martel the silence of complicity is far more shocking than torture: 'Entiendo más la impiedad, la muerte y la violencia que la actitud del resto de la sociedad de hacerse la que no sabe, o evitar darse cuenta de lo que está pasando' [I understand cruelty, death and violence much more than the attitude of the rest of the society which makes out as if they don't know, or avoid coming to terms with what is happening] (in Enríquez 2008). *The Headless Woman* delineates how a culture of collective silencing is implemented across society's operational strata. Once Vero has revealed her secret, her husband Marcos (Cesár Bordón) springs into action. Dressed in a camouflage jacket – suggesting an association with the military – he mobilises Juan Manuel, calling on the support of a web of doctors, lawyers and police to erase details of Vero's movements (the hospital X-rays, the hotel registration) on the night of the accident.

The 1970s infiltrates the ostensibly contemporary world of the film largely through a soundtrack where a version of Fernando Arbex Miró's 'Soley, Soley' and Hubert Giraud's 'Mammy Blue' position Vero and her family firmly within the ideology of the dictatorship. 'Soley, Soley' (presented in its 1971 recording by the Scottish band Middle of the Road) is playing on the car radio immediately before, during and after the accident. 'Deja de llorar' [Stop crying], another song by Miró from the mid-1970s, here covered by the Argentine band Los Charros, plays as Candita tries to confront Vero. 'Mammy Blue', sung by Demis Roussos, plays at the family party at the end of the film as Vero receives final confirmation from the hotel receptionist that there is no record of her having stayed there on the night of the accident. Martel has spoken of 'Mammy Blue' as a 'banda de sonido de la dictadura' [soundtrack of the dictatorship], recalling her own soldier uncle playing it on his guitar for her while she was a child (in Enríquez 2008). The songs resonate also across Spain – crooner Julio Iglesias, who represented Franco's Spain in the 1970 Eurovision Song Contest, recorded the latter in 1994. 'Soley, Soley' and 'Deja de llorar' were products of a Spanish songwriter who personified the transnational European easy-listening disco sound of the mid-1970s. Grainy wedding footage that Vero watches at Lala's house shows *Saturday Night Fever* dance routines that recall those re-created by Pablo Larraín in *Tony Manero* (2008). As with Alfredo Castro's deluded disco-dancing obsessive in Larraín's feature, Vero reinvents herself anew by dyeing her peroxide-blonde hair a warm brown, attracting admiring comments from friends and family. By the end of the film – once she hears from her brother, a doctor at the hospital where she was treated, that he has destroyed all incriminating evidence – Vero blends effortlessly into the domestic landscape. In the first half of the film, Vero's haughty demeanour and blonde 'otherness' position her as a figure of allure and fascination. Her cousin's husband is evidently attracted to her, as is his 13-year old daughter, and her hair colour attracts favourable comments from a friend early on in the film. Jonathan Romney views her as a possible 'echo of the once idolised Eva Perón' (2010). I would argue that her synthetic blondeness also offers a link to Carri's *The Blonds*, where the family's 'otherness' is conceived through their artificial peroxide wigs. Vero is emphatically not the *cabecita negra* [little black head] of an Argentine working class made up of immigrants from the northern provinces bordering Bolivia.[18]

The Headless Woman may, on the surface, be the least accessible of Martel's features – a characteristic noted by the majority of the critics in the Spanish press, as well as *Variety*'s Leslie Felperin and the *Guardian*'s Xan Brooks – but it is ultimately the most enigmatic, accomplished and rewarding. Certainly, there is no exposition and very little happens in narrative terms – something that bemused and irritated a significant proportion of the non-Argentine critics[19] – but it is in the build-up of seemingly inconsequential details over the film's 89 minutes that its power ultimately lies. Martel's camera here appears as a further character, a mode of implicating the viewer within the unfolding trauma: a silent witness in the car with Vero; another member of the extended family at the social gatherings – a constant reminder of the absent 'other', the crime that no one will acknowledge. Only at the end of the film does the camera hold back, keeping its distance outside the room as Vero joins in the family party.

Spanish critics seemed wilfully reluctant to accept the film as a parable on the collective history of the disappeared (Rodríguez-Marchante 2008; Boyero 2008), while the Argentine press corps who reported on the film's Cannes première as well as its domestic release in August of that year inscribed a reading centred on the film's circuitous references to the country's military dictatorship (Monteagudo 2008; López 2008). Martel has acknowledged that the film 'no se puede entender sin ciertos códigos' [can't be understood without certain codes] – which might explain the bemusement of the UK's Jonathan Romney and Xan Brooks on first viewing the film (Romney 2008; Brooks 2008). She is also aware of the shared context of military dictatorships and a particular religious education that has facilitated what she terms Almodóvar's empathetic 'lectura cercana' [close reading] of the film (in Enríquez 2008). Perhaps, like Vero and her family, the Spanish critics made a deliberate decision not to engage with a particular set of circumstances presented before them. *Clarín's* Diego Lerer has argued that Argentine history is a history of denials (2008), but I would posit that this is effectively also the case – as the *pacto de olvido* demonstrates – with regard to Spain. Like Bayona's *The Orphanage*, *The Headless Woman* is about the ways in which the repressed returns to haunt the collective psyche. As Romney's and Brook's responses indicate, metaphor does not always traverse national frontiers.[20] However, I would argue that Martel's disturbing film uses shared thematic references and suggestion to offer a commentary on both contemporary Argentina *and* contemporary Spain, as a house full of ghosts.[21] Significantly, however, in confronting those ghosts through its own *mise en scène*, *The Headless Woman* also firmly undermines Lala's conservative advice: 'No los mires y se van' [If you don't look at them, they just go away].[22]

Notes

1 Imperialist prerogatives in the culture of Spanish-Latin American co-productions are directly critiqued in Iciar Bollaín's *También la lluvia/Even the Rain* (2010); see Chapter 17.

2 For details of the top grossing domestic features in Spain, see the Ministry of Culture's

'Boletín Informativo de Cine' 2002–09, 164–5. Annual reports for the years between 2002 and 2009 are available at www.mcu.es/cine/MC/BIC/index.html.

3 In 2000, of the 98 films made in Spain, 34 were co-productions. The figure in 2001 was 40 of 126; 2002, 57 of 137; 2003, 42 of 110; 2004, 41 of 133; 2005, 53 of 142; 2006, 41 of 150; 2007, 57 of 172; 2008, 49 of 173 and 2009, 51 of 186. Data collected from the 'Boletín Informativo de Cine' 2009.

4 On the New Argentine Cinema, see Aguilar (2008); Andermann (2012); Page (2009).

5 It is, of course, possible to present an argument that sees this as a further manifestation of neocolonialism, with Spain seeking to appropriate desirable products from South America.

6 Miñarro's 2010 successes alone include the Cannes Palme D'Or winner Apichatpong Weerasethakul's *Uncle Boonme Who Can Recall his Past Lives* and Kavlovy-Vary's Crystal Globe winner Agustí Vila's *La mosquitera*/The Mosquito Net.

7 See http://leymemoria.mjusticia.es/ [accessed 8 September 2010].

8 For further details on the legislation initiated by the Kirchners, as well as earlier measures such as the 1994 Ley Nacional de Reparación Económica [National Law of Economic Reparation], the problematic Ley de Punto Final (1986) and the Ley de Obediencia Debida [Full Stop and Due Obedience Laws] (1987), see Feitlowitz (2011: 299–366).

9 I proffer a reading of the film through historical memory in Delgado (2010b). This chapter draws on my earlier review of *The Headless Woman* (see Delgado 2010a).

10 For further details on the scandal surrounding the trafficking of children stolen from Spanish hospitals and reallocated to 'approved' Catholic families between 1940 and 1990, see Navarro (2008) and Fopiani (2011). Currently there are 900 such cases under investigation, with lawyers claiming that the total could reach 30,000 (Adler 2011). On the sequestration of the children of Republican prisoners in the aftermath of the Civil War, see Preston (2012: 513–14).

11 El Deseo offered a 25 per cent investment in the film, which also benefited from French (25 per cent) and Italian (10 per cent) co-producers.

12 Hostile criticisms of the film were published by Carlos Boyero and Borja Hermoso (both 2009). Almodóvar responded to the tone of the reviews in a number of outlets, including his blog (2009b), and the spat attracted substantial press attention.

13 Although it is not clear whether the failure to take responsibility is a wider characteristic shared by her social circle and its obsession with drawn-out leisure activities – hunting, banal gossiping and shopping.

14 Vero's family surname is Berardo – a name of Portuguese origin. For further details on the Italian influence in Argentina, see Devoto (2006).

15 This was of course, the subject of Argentina's first Oscar-winning film, Luis Puenzo's *La historia oficial*/*The Official Story* (1984), and remains a sensitive political issue in Argentina. Marcela Noble Herrera and her brother Felipe, heirs to the *Clarín* media group, underwent DNA testing in 2010 to determine whether they were forcibly taken from their parents and handed over to their wealthy, politically compliant mother Ernestina Herrera de Noble. The case attracted considerable media attention because both children were opposed to what they viewed as the state's infringements

of their human rights; it pitted the powerful Herrera family against Cristina Fernández de Kirchner. Spain has its own *niños desaparecidos*, discussed earlier in note 10.

16 Martel has spoken to me of disliking swimming pools, describing them as rancid, unclean spaces (Martel 2008).

17 The jaundiced Candita is recovering from hepatitis – and Martel's choice of this viral infection may well position her as a victim of contamination, 'tainted' by the culture of 'disease' that marks her conservative relatives. Her non-compliance and frankness, however, suggest that she (and perhaps by association her generation) may break with the culture of secrecy that defines these relatives.

18 For further details on the history of the term and its appropriation by Perón, see Sosa (2009: 258, 261). Sosa provides a reading of the film using Judith Butler's discussion of mourning in *Precarious Life* (London: Verso, 2004), and this chapter has benefited from my extensive discussions with Sosa on the dynamics of the film.

19 See, for example, Anon. (2008); Felperin (2008); Boyero (2008). The film has also had vociferous champions, such as *Sight & Sound*'s Nick James and the *Guardian*'s Peter Bradshaw (2010).

20 And while it might be possible to craft an argument that sees the film as ideologically compromised by the ways in which it transforms a very specific national trauma for the international marketplace, I would argue that the film's initial responses at Cannes precisely indicate the problems of assuming that the processes and politics of local meaning-making somehow do not come into play in the process of reading metaphors.

21 Lala's precise words are 'Está llena la casa. Son espantos' [The house is full. They're dead].

22 I am grateful to Margherita Laera for her assistance with research for this piece.

Bibliography

Adler, Katya (2011) *Spain's Stolen Babies* [This World], BBC2, produced and directed by Steven Grandison (broadcast 18 October).

Aguilar, Gonzalo (2008) *New Argentine Film: Other Worlds,* trans. Sarah Ann Wells, Basingstoke: Palgrave Macmillan.

Almodóvar, Pedro (2009a) Interview with the author at the Soho Hotel, 1 May.

—(2009b) 'Notas sobre crítica negra del Festival de Cannes' (25 May), www.pedroalmodovar.es/PAB_ES_11_T.asp [accessed 10 March 2011].

Andermann, Jens (2012) *New Argentine Cinema*, London and New York: I.B. Tauris.

Anon. (2008) 'Las críticas a "La mujer sin cabeza"', *Clarín* (23 May), http://edant.clarin.com/diario/2008/05/23/espectaculos/c-01202.htm [accessed 14 June 2012].

—(2011) 'El paro ha crecido en casi tres millones de personas en solo cuatro años', *El Mundo* (28 January), www.elmundo.es/mundodinero/2011/01/28/economia/1296201852.html [accessed 11 March 2011].

BBC (2012) 'Eurozone unemployment hits record of 5.64 million', *BBC News Business* (27 April), www.bbc.co.uk/news/business-17866382 [accessed 1 June 2012].

Boyero, Carlos (2008) 'El críptico universo de Lucrecia Martel', *El País* (22 May), www.elpais.com/articulo/cultura/criptico/universo/Lucrecia/Martel/elpepicul/20080 522elpepicul_7.Tes [accessed 17 March 2011].

—(2009) '¿Qué he hecho yo para merecer esto?', *El País* (18 March), www.elpais.com/ articulo/cine/he/hecho/merecer/elpepuculcin/20090318elpepicin_2/Tes [accessed 16 March 2011].

Bradshaw, Peter (2010) 'The Headless Woman', *Guardian* (19 February), www.guardian. co.uk/film/2010/feb/18/the-headless-woman-review [accessed 15 March 2011].

Brooks, Xan (2008) 'The Ones That Got Away', *Guardian* (21 May), www.guardian. co.uk/film/2008/may/21/cannesfilmfestival.festivals7 [accessed 13 March 2011].

Climent, María Luz (2008) 'La argentina Lucrecia Martel deja fría a la crítica con "La mujer sin cabeza"', *El Mundo* (21 May), www.elmundo.es/elmundo/2008/05/21/ cultura/1211374909.html [accessed 13 March 2011].

Delgado, Maria (2009) 'Sensory Perception: Almodóvar's *Broken Embraces*', *Sight & Sound*, 19:9 (September), 40–4.

—(2010a) 'The Headless Woman', *Sight & Sound*, 20:3 (March), 64.

—(2010b) 'The Secret in Their Eyes', *Sight & Sound*, 20:9 (September) 76–7.

Devoto, Fernando J. (2006) *Historia de los italianos en Argentina*, Buenos Aires: Editorial Biblos.

Enríquez, Mariana (2008) 'La mala memoria', *Página12 [Radar]* (17 August), http://www. pagina12.com.ar/diario/suplementos/radar/9–4766–2008–08–17.html [accessed 11 March 2011].

Ezra, Elizabeth and Terry Rowden (2006) 'What is Transnational Cinema?', in Ezra and Rowden (eds), *Transnational Cinema: The Film Reader*, Abingdon: Routledge, 1–12.

Feitlowitz, Marguerite (2011) *A Lexicon of Terror: Argentina and the Legacies of Torture*, revised and updated edn with a new epilogue, Oxford: Oxford University Press.

Felperin, Leslie (2008) 'The Headless Woman', *Variety* (21 May), www.variety.com/ review/VE1117937236?refcatid=31 [accessed 1 June 2012].

Fopiani, Ana María (2011) 'El anuncio de la Fiscalía de investigar los bebés robados dispara el número de denuncias', *El Mundo* (4 January), www.elmundo.es/ elmundo/2011/01/04/andalucia/1294154844.html [accessed 30 December 2011].

Gratius, Susanne (2010) 'La vocación iberoamericana en España', *El País* (17 May), www.elpais.com/articulo/internacional/vocacion/iberoamericana/Espana/ elpepiint/20100517elpepiint_2/Tes [accessed 17 March 2011].

Hermoso, Borja (2009) 'Almodóvar, Francia, España', *JamesBlog* (20 May), http:// lacomunidad.elpais.com/james-blog/2009/5/20/almodovar-francia-espana [accessed 17 March 2011].

Lerer, Diego (2008) 'Una serie de eventos desafortunados', *Clarín* (21 August), http:// edant.clarin.com/diario/2008/08/21/espectaculos/c-00701.htm [accessed 10 March 2011].

López, Fernando (2008) 'Contagiosa inquietud: Lucrecia Martel ofrece una perturbadora radiografía humana y social', *La Nación* (21 August), www.lanacion.com.ar/1041645– contagiosa- [accessed 10 March 2011].

Martel, Lucrecia (2008) Interview with Maria M. Delgado following the screening of *The Swamp* at the Discovering Latin American Film Festival, 3 December.

—(2010) 'Director's Notes', Press Book for *The Headless Woman*, New Wave Films.

Martín, Félix E. and Pablo Toral (eds) (2005) *Latin America's Quest for Globalization: The Role of Spanish Firms*, Aldershot: Ashgate.

Matheou, Demetrios (2010) *The Faber Book of New South American Cinema*, London: Faber & Faber.

Ministerio de Cultura, 'Boletín Informativo de Cine' 2002–09, www.mcu.es/cine/MC/BIC/index.html [accessed 15 March 2011].

Monteagudo, Luciano (2008) 'Cuando no se sabe ni tampoco se quiere saber', *Página 12* (21 August), www.pagina12.com.arg/diario/suplementos/espectaculos/5–10992–2008–08–21.html [accessed 16 March 2011].

Navarro, Vicenç (2008) 'Los niños perdidos del franquismo', *El País* (24 December), www.elpais.com/articulo/opinion/ninos/perdidos/franquismo/elpepiopi/20081224elpepiopi_10/Tes [accessed 17 March 2011].

Page, Joanna (2009) *Crisis and Capitalism in Contemporary Argentine Cinema*, Durham: Duke University Press.

Preston, Paul (2012) *The Spanish Holocaust: Inquisition and Extermination in Twentieth-Century Spain*, London: HarperPress.

Rodríguez-Marchante, E. (2008) 'Sin cabeza, pero rubia', *ABC* (28 November), www.abc.es/hemeroteca/historico-28–11–2008/abc/Espectaculos/sin-cabeza-pero-rubia_911566704775.html# [accessed 16 March 2011].

Romney, Jonathan (2008) 'Cannes Roundup: War, Revolution, Love, Death … and Liverpool', *Independent on Sunday* (25 May), www.independent.co.uk/arts-entertainment/films/news/cannes-roundup-war-revolution-love-death-and-liverpool-833848.html [accessed 14 March 2011].

—(2010) 'The Headless Woman', *Independent on Sunday* (21 February), www.independent.co.uk/arts-entertainment/films/reviews/the-headless-woman-lucrecia-martel-87–mins-12a-1905589.html [accessed 14 March 2011].

Sosa, Cecilia (2009) 'A Counter-narrative of Argentine Mourning: *The Headless Woman* (2008) directed by Lucrecia Martel', *Theory, Culture and Society*, 26:7–8, 250–62.

15

Los abrazos rotos/Broken Embraces (Pedro Almodóvar, 2009): talking cures

Marvin D'Lugo

Screenwriter Mateo Blanco is a former film director now known as 'Harry Caine' who was blinded years earlier in a car accident that killed Lena, his leading lady. He is cared for by agent Judit and her adult son Diego. When he learns of the death of millionaire financier Ernesto Martel, Mateo recalls painful memories of the last film he directed, starring Lena and bankrolled by Martel. Martel's gay filmmaker son, Ernesto Jr, proposes that Mateo write a fictionalised version of his father's life, but Mateo declines. Diego asks him why Judit so fears Ernesto Jr, leading Mateo to recount events surrounding his ill-fated last film. Through an elaborate voice-over flashback he recounts how, during the filming of *Chicas y maletas/Girls with Valises*, he and Lena began a torrid affair. The production completed, the couple fled to Lanzarote, where they learned of the film's terrible critical reception in Madrid, the result of Martel's sabotaging of the final cut. Lena died in a car crash which left Mateo blind.

The catharsis from retelling these traumatic events enables the blind filmmaker to reassume his former identity as Mateo. At his birthday party, Judit confesses that, out of jealousy over Mateo's affair with Lena, she facilitated the disastrous re-editing of *Girls with Valises* that wrecked his career. She provides Mateo with the salvaged negatives from the film, which he and Diego re-edit for its long-delayed release as the director envisioned it.

'That only happens in the movies'

At the midway point in the extended flashback sequence in Pedro Almodóvar's *Los abrazos rotos/Broken Embraces* (2009), a brief dialogue between the film's amorous couple, the would-be actress Lena (Penélope Cruz) and filmmaker

Mateo Blanco (Lluís Homar) crystallises essential aspects of the film's complex narrative structure. Lena has been brought in a wheelchair to the movie set to discuss the resumption of the filming of Mateo's film. When the couple are alone in his office, Mateo demands the truth about Lena's injury, presumably an accidental fall down a flight of stairs. In fact, her jealous lover, Ernesto Martel (José Luis Gómez), had pushed her down the stairs. Mateo observes ironically: 'La gente no se cae por la escalera, eso solo pasa en las películas' [People don't fall down the stairs. That only happens in the movies].

Mateo's reaction to Lena's cover-up story of her fall is an acknowledgement of the melodramatic script that their love affair has come to resemble. This lucidity about the staginess of their lives is a crucial but short-lived break in Mateo's self-absorption as scriptwriter and director who otherwise sees the world either as movie dialogue or screen images. His awareness of the force of self-consuming cinematic illusion suggests a tension between lived experience and movies that shapes Almodóvar's conception of his film. At once a celebration of cinematic creativity (Kinder 2010: 28), *Broken Embraces* is also a meditation both on the cinematic artifice and the potential of movies to illuminate the meaning of individual and collective experience.

The film's complex self-referential narrative details the transformation of Mateo, the sighted filmmaker, into his avatar, Harry Caine, the scriptwriter who was left blind after the car accident that killed Lena. Lena's death has so traumatised him that he cannot even speak of it. In this way, blindness and insight are aligned within the very fabric of the plot in important ways. Mateo's recall of these events provides a motivation for the extended flashback of his love affair with Lena in 1994 as evoked from the contemporary vantage of 2008. The process through which this symbolic blockage gradually dissolves parallels the transformation of events from Mateo's past into words through his cathartic voice-over narration. In this strategy of enunciation, the privilege of speech over images underscores the dilemma of characters whose emotional and physical lives are inspired by movie melodrama.

The over-the-top staging of Lena's fall, strikingly emblematised in a stylised close-up of her face that has been widely used as the film's promotional image, recycles the famous moment from John Stahl's noir melodrama, *Leave Her to Heaven* (1945), in which the conniving Gene Tierney throws herself down a staircase to abort a pregnancy in order to retain total possession of her husband, Cornel Wilde. The plot of *Broken Embraces* regenders Tierney's deranged possessiveness into Martel, transforming the graphic image of her self-inflicted violence into words through Lena's retelling of the scene to Mateo.

While underscoring how the artifice of cinema has devoured the life experiences of both characters, Almodóvar's emphasis on speech acts proposes a strategy to counter the force of self-consuming cinematic illusion and to expose the psychological traumas it masks. The key to that deconstructive project lies in foregrounding a cluster of tropes of classical Hollywood noir cinema that emphasises the human voice. These include the prominence of voice-over flashback, the particular privilege given to telephones as auditory props and, finally, the scripting of expositional monologues that recall some of the origins of film noir in radio dramas. James Naremore observes the roots of voice-over in Hollywood noir films of the 1940s in the radio dramas of the period that used complex plot twists 'to motivate retrospective forms of first-person narration' (1998: 259). Almodóvar himself recalls to interviewers how, as a child in the 1950s, he became addicted to serialised soap operas on Spanish radio (Boquerini 1989: 14). The radio-inspired melodrama of his scripts, in which the human voice overtakes cinema's conventional image-based narration, is a long-established feature of his film style. In *Broken Embraces* words have in fact devoured images, just as Harry Caine the screen writer has displaced the director Mateo Blanco.

This verbal dimension of the film expands and intensifies aspects of what Marsha Kinder identifies as the persistent 'audio fetish' in Almodóvar's cinema, 'grafted over the traditional visual fetishes' (1993: 254). In *Tacones lejanos/High Heels* (1991), for instance, the audio fetish is emphasised by what Kinder terms the 'oracular professions' of the two female protagonists, a torch singer and a television newsreader, 'sexual subjects pursuing their desire' (255). In this way, the female voice works as a subversive narrative strategy, challenging the patriarchy that owns the airwaves. In *Broken Embraces* the auditory markers of woman's status as subject are expanded to convey both desire and a more profound lucidity about Spanish cultural and historical consciousness. The key to understanding that new complex paradigm lies in Almodóvar's use of a neo-noir stylistic as both a historically bound cinematic style and a contemporary signifier of social corruption and decay, as with Bardem's *Muerte de un ciclista/Death of a Cyclist* (1955).

In interviews he speaks of the relation between *Broken Embraces* and Spain's Law of Historical Memory reflected in Mateo's relationship with Lena in 1994: 'There's a moment when Mateo has the accident, where in order to survive he has to deny the past … He's already created another identity for himself with the name Harry Caine, so he adopts this name and doesn't allow any discussion of the past … This is exactly what happened in Spain during the transition (to democracy). We were all really pleased to move from a dictatorship to a democracy without the spilling of blood' (Delgado 2009: 44).

Almodóvar's words belie an even more ambitious project in which his own filmography is used as the conduit through which the blocked past is mediated for contemporary audiences. We see this in the interpolation of sequences from his first international crossover hit, *Mujeres al borde de un ataque de nervios/Women on the Verge of a Nervous Breakdown* (1988). Self-referential movie intertexts similarly informed the development of his two preceding films – *La mala educación/Bad Education* (2004) and *Volver* (2006).[1] In all three works, key plot elements are rooted in an implicit retrospective nod to the director's films of the 1980s, suggesting that *Broken Embraces* might be productively read as part of a broader process of Almodóvar's rethinking the decade of his meteoric rise to fame, but also the period of Spain's transition to democracy and modernity.

No mere remake of *Women on the Verge*, cinematic self-reference serves a heuristic purpose as *Broken Embraces* develops an ambivalent relation to personal and collective history, at once evoking a presumably simpler cinematic time, but also questioning the contemporary nostalgia that views the immediate post-Franco decade as a bright and cheerful past. Ultimately, the interpolated film-within-the-film serves as the means to interrogate through a personal focus broader historical relations between the characters and their social and personal past as these are embodied in the play of noir voices.

The particular choice of *Women on the Verge* as the symptomatic text upon which to posit this project appears motivated by a variety of factors: within Almodóvar's canon, this is the director's first international crossover film, an Oscar-nominated work and one of the biggest Spanish commercial film successes of all time (Larrañaga and Ruiz Molina 2010: 301). Its clever use of staged voices, those of two movie dubbers, works self-referentially to convey the cosmetic and mediatised quality of social change in 1980s Spain; finally, the ironic appropriation of *Women on the Verge* in recent years by intellectuals as a demonstration of the country's problematic political transition. Eduardo Subirats, for instance, sees *Women on the Verge* as the crystallisation of tendencies of the ambiguous transition to modernity in Spain, most strikingly the culture of spectacle of social emancipation that belies the persistent mindset of the film's protagonists Pepa (Carmen Maura), Iván (Fernando Guillén) and Lucía (Julieta Serrano). By the end of the first post-Franco decade, these characters still retain regressive sexual and political ideologies (2002: 79–80).

Alberto Medina similarly identifies the film as an exemplary expression of the complex process within which the focus of politicians and political discourse has shifted from the people (*el pueblo*) to the camera lens (2002: 29). Collective experience, according to Medina, was thus transformed into a superficial performance self-consciously emblematised for him by Almodóvar's ironic use of La Lupe's recording of 'Puro teatro' [Pure theatrics] which serves as a musical coda in *Women on the Verge*. In broad terms, this shared view of *Women on the Verge* as a simulacrum of the problematic nature of personal and collective history of which Almodóvar speaks illuminates the filmmaker's particular treatment of *Broken Embraces*.

Historical trauma and talking cures

In *Women on the Verge*, Almodóvar mixed melodrama with Hollywood comedies of the 1950s to produce a particular Utopian effect, a dazzlingly colourful new

Spain of the 1980s that portended a bright future (Smith 2000: 93). These elements are now replaced by emphasis on a slower, more languid pace of action and a shadowy aura in the lighting of key dramatic scenes that connects the film with the narrative design of *Bad Education*, a film that filtered the light and airy *movida* culture of the same decade through a recognisable neo-noir optic. This notable refiguring of period style works as part of the broader project to engage the film's audience in an interrogation of personal and collective manipulation of history and memory (D'Lugo 2009: 361). Here the evoked past is identified in two pivotal flashbacks as 1992 and 1994. These were the years of the 'spectacularisation' of Spain through the Olympic Games, Expo Sevilla and the designation of Madrid as European Cultural Capital. It is also the period of the public culture of political chicanery largely masked by Spain's media-driven spectacle of modernity (Medina 2002: 28–9).

That nexus between melodrama and politics is anchored in the villainous figure of Martel, identified with finances and media through his image as corporate titan and producer of Lena's film debut. We are first introduced to him through Mateo's flashback occasioned by the news of Martel's death. Listening to the artificial voice read the internet obituary from *El País*, Mateo's mind elides the financier's actions in the early 1990s with his memory of Lena's relation with Martel. Lena's story is presented through a series of brief scenes, nearly all of which involve the audio-prop of a telephone, thereby reinforcing the pattern of noir radio dramas. Like Mateo, Lena also has multiple names: her mother calls her Magdalena, a reference to Mary Magdalene, and she works as a call girl under the name Séverine, an allusion to Buñuel's film, *Belle de Jour* (1967). The Buñuel intertext is, in fact, a palimpsest of the scenarios of deceit that are masked by glossy fashion-magazine appearances of characters and their personal and social spaces.[2] The flashback suggests a social and political back-story to the film in which Martel is cast as a cipher of the exploitative entrepreneurial culture that has overtaken the Utopian imaginary of Spain of the previous post-Franco decade. The artist's self-enclosed world, represented by Mateo and Lena and paralleling Almodóvar's own heralded *pasotismo*, his apoliticism during the decade of Felipe González's socialist government, is threatened precisely by the off-screen culture of corruption embodied in Martel.[3]

The emphasis on the staging of story-telling acts suggests an important duality in characters' speech that links the personal with the social. J.P. Tellote, for instance, observes the social underpinning of the fetishised recurrence of voice-over flashbacks in Hollywood *film noir* as 'a need for speaking in a world that already seems narrated' (1989: 222). Citing Lacan's observation that the subject's 'verbalization might hold a "cure" for hysteria and similar psychic ills', he argues that '[i]n trying to articulate our personal and cultural anxieties film noir similarly works out such a "cure", offering us a better sense of ourselves, or at least a clearer notion of who we are individually and socially' (1989: 222). As in the classical Freudian scenario, the function of speech is cathartic and ultimately restorative, proposing through words to illuminate the conflicts that underlie surface symptoms and thereby to effect a 'cure'.

Mateo's narration in particular appears to update and, importantly, regender what Kaja Silverman in a related context identifies as 'the talking cure' in Hollywood's women's films of the 1940s (1988: 59–60). *Broken Embraces* in general and Mateo's speech in particular need to be seen as interrogations of the gendered 'authority' of narrating an individual and collective past. These questions, as Telotte and Silverman suggest, are rooted in social reality and cultural practice. The complex dynamics of the speech act is dramatised in the first post-credit scene which appears to function as a simple film device to introduce the protagonist, Mateo, through his masked identity as the Harry Caine of 2008. An off-screen female voice poses the question: '¿Cómo te llamas?' [What is your name?]; this is followed by an extreme close-up of the female eye and the reflection of a newspaper in her pupil. Next the shot moves to Mateo and his response: 'Harry Caine', therein follows a brief flashback with Mateo's off-screen voice explaining both his double name and his professional identity: a filmmaker a.k.a. Mateo Blanco, whose current identity is that of a blind screenwriter. His voice-over, however, is not heard by the woman but rather supposes a different interlocutor, the audience of the film.

On one level, the staging of this narrowly defined first affirmation of identity is evoked as a contemporary variation of another Buñuelian intertext, this time, the famous eye-cutting scene from the beginning of *Un Chien Andalou/An Andalusian Dog* (1928), which served as an invocation to the story. Tellingly, the sense of the mutilated female eye from the Buñuel film is now transposed to Mateo in the form of his blindness, the first of a series of gender reversals and an opaque reference to the mythical figure of Oedipus. The off-screen female voice and the mutilated eye problematise cinematic sight and sound and their origins: the off-screen and implicit privilege of the female voice that transcends the body and the narration of the male filmmaker, reduced by his blindness to the role of the object of the female glance. Much of what follows in *Broken Embraces* will be an interrogation of Mateo's dual identity emblematised by his two names, and a refutation of the seemingly simple self-affirmation of his restrictive professional identity as filmmaker and screenwriter.

This brief scene is, however, also a cinematic *trompe l'oeil*. After Mateo's initial voice-off to the woman, his subsequent speech is really a voice-over directed not to the woman but to the off-screen spectator of the film. Silverman notes the tension between off-screen voice narration and voice-over, born of the codification of classic Hollywood cinematic tropes of voice-off and voice-over: 'Voice-off exceeds the limits of the frame, but not the limits of the diegesis … The voice-over, on the other hand, is coded as occupying a different order from the main diegesis. When it becomes separated from the fiction, as in documentaries, it becomes a "voice on high", like that of an angel … a voice that speaks from a superior knowledge and which superimposes itself "on top" of the diegesis' (1988: 48–9). It is, in fact, this assertion of the authority in voice-over that is largely in contention in *Broken Embraces,* both as a problem of cinematic storytelling, but also of control of the historical narration to which the film refers.

In his exploration of the voice in cinema, Michel Chion adopts the term 'acousmatic' to characterise a particular cinematic voice-over narration that serves to engage spectators in the search for narrative origins. This is 'sound that is heard without its cause or source being seen' (1999: 18). In describing what is at stake, Chion notes the origins of the term in a Pythagorean sect

> whose followers would listen to their Master speak behind a curtain, as the story goes, so that the sight of the speaker wouldn't distract from the message … This interdiction against looking, which transforms the Master, God or Spirit into an acousmatic voice, permeates a great number of religious traditions, most notably Islam and Judaism. We find it also in the physical setup of Freudian analysis: the patient on the couch should not see the analyst, who does not look at him. And finally we find it in the cinema, where the voice of the acousmatic master who hides behind a door, a curtain off-screen, is at play in some key films. (1999: 19)

The relationship between the acousmatic voice and its observed agent is fluid and ambiguous, 'a relationship of power and possession capable of functioning in both directions; the image may contain the voice, or the voice may contain the image' (Chion 1999: 23). The early textual shift from an explicit voice-off to Mateo's more subtle voice-over is itself the mark of the fictional filmmaker's attempt to control the story of his own identity which, despite his efforts, will be usurped by women.

The sequence following this introductory gesture emphasises voice and dialogue over the merely visual as Mateo asks his unnamed female companion to render her body and appearance in words. In the love-making scene that ensues, audiences might have expected to see more explicit images of flesh and bodies; these hallmarks of earlier Almodóvar films are now replaced by a discreet silhouette image of feet from the back of the sofa and the off-screen sighs of sexual pleasure. This is an opaque reference to the scene of erotic sighs of Buñuel's second film, *L'Âge d'Or/The Golden Age* (1930), which introduced the sexual rapture of Gaston Modot and Lya Lys through the strategic use of off-screen sound.

When we are introduced to Judit (Blanca Portillo), Mateo's former lover, collaborator and manager, in the moments following the love-making scene, she chides him for his casual sexual encounters, thus suggesting a different answer to the question of who is Harry Caine. Her voiced disapproval of his sexual liaison with a total stranger appears to echo the perspective of Pepa the heroine who, at the beginning of *Women on the Verge,* understood the fickleness of her lover,

26. Diego, Ernesto Martel Jr and Mateo Blanco: multiple tales of Oedipal rivalry.

Iván. Unlike Pepa, however, Judit has reached a professional accommodation with Harry beyond any sentimental one.[4]

As we begin to glean from Judit's dialogue with Mateo that follows, the question of his identity necessarily needs to move 'off screen' to his life beyond the mask of filmmaking. That identity bears all the outward trappings of an Oedipal narrative: the master's search for identity in the past that explains his real and metaphorical blindness, and the essential misrecognition of fathers and sons.[5] This narrative thread is first introduced when Judit asks Mateo about his next film script and he tells her of his interest in a version of the story of Arthur Miller's relation to his Down's syndrome son, whom he had essentially abandoned. The story of the father's disavowal of the son, filial misrecognition and the eventual reconciliation of father and son will then be transformed from words to images with the arrival at the apartment of Diego (Tamar Novas), Judit's son who, we only learn later, is also Mateo's biological offspring.

Further framing Mateo's cinematic activity of screenwriting, Diego's arrival is followed by the comments about and the eventual appearance of Rayo-X, Ernesto Martel Jr (Rubén Ochandiano), also a filmmaker, who proposes that Mateo write the script for a fictionalised biopic to express his own hatred of his deceased father. Together these multiple tales of Oedipal rivalry, proposing both murderous desire and an alternative narrative of the son's forgiveness of the father, provide a set of potential resolutions to the violent conflicts that are woven into both the plot of Mateo's own life and the political-cultural back story of *Broken Embraces*. As Telotte suggests, the therapeutic talking cure promises 'a better sense of ourselves, or at least a clearer notion of who we are individually and socially' (1989: 222).

Staging the voice drama

After the initial sequences in Mateo's apartment, which introduce the principal characters and hint at the crisis of Mateo's past, the narrative evolves through three clusters of scenes of embedded voice dramas. The most elaborate of these self-referential sequences is the flashback 'story' Mateo tells Diego to explain why Judit so fears Ernesto Jr. Within this narration we find two other embedded sequences: Ernesto Jr's video surveillance of the lovers that interrupts Mateo's narrative, and a sequence from *Girls with Valises* that contains the six-minute monologue by comic actress Carmen Machi as Chon, the conservative local politician. Finally, there is another extended monologue, this time by Judit, which she presents as a birthday gift to Mateo to explain how the copy of *Girls with Valises* was sabotaged by Martel. These theatrical speeches self-referentially dramatise for the audience the dual acts of speaking and listening, placing cinema's conventional emphasis on seeing at a remove. Also, they provide a symmetrical structure with two scenes in which male characters seek to control the telling (Mateo, Martel), and two by women: the fictitious Chon, and the real-life Judit.

Mateo's story to Diego begins with a voice-over situating the action involving Lena's participation in his last directing role. The first image we see is that of Lena with a youthful hairstyle, looking like Audrey Hepburn as Mateo photographs her in the studio dressing-room. As the camera pulls away, we discover that the image we are viewing is the mirror reflection of Lena, thereby underscoring the indirect and limiting manner in which cinematic sight operates throughout Mateo's narration. Also present in the dressing room are the film's make-up artist, hairstylist and wardrobe designer, as well as Ernesto Jr, who has been sent by his father presumably to shoot a documentary of the film production, but really to spy on Lena and Mateo.

Judit appears in the scene at one point and grimaces to Ernesto, thereby acknowledging his presence in a way that the others in this space do not. In response, he directs his camera to her but she only makes faces at him as if to disavow her presence in the story. The hairdresser provides Lena with a platinum wig which transforms her into a Marilyn Monroe double. The references here to Monroe and Audrey Hepburn, allusions to frothy Hollywood comedies of the 1950s, underscore the patterns of Mateo's imagination as he sees the world almost exclusively through a frivolous movie lens.

The image cuts rapidly to Ernesto senior in his home as he views these scenes as part of his son's surveillance video. Unable to decipher what Lena and Harry are saying, he complains about the poor sound quality. We then cut back to the studio set, where the shooting has begun and Mateo is guiding Lena through a restaging of the memorable moment in *Women on the Verge* when Pepa, here called Pina, prepares soup that will be laced with sleeping pills. Shifting back to

27. Lip-reader (Lola Dueñas) helps Ernesto Martel (José Luis Gómez) continue his acoustic surveillance of Lena.

Martel's viewing of this scene, now as a film within Mateo's story of his own film, we see the jealous Martel accompanied by a lip-reader (Lola Dueñas) who serves as a ventriloquist for the previously undecipherable verbal exchanges between Harry and Lena.

Besides its specular function of dramatising Ernesto Jr's role as surrogate eyes for his father, the sequence emphasises speech as three 'voices' converge: the direct speech of the characters in the spaces of the studio; the distanced ventriloquism of the lip-reader, and the framing voice-over narration of Mateo off screen as he recounts these events of 1994 to Diego. Although Mateo and Martel have presumptions of power through their controlling perspectives on the narrative, it is Ernesto Jr and, eventually, Judit, who by virtue of their acousmatic status, have the power to illuminate Mateo's identity.

This same strategy of competing frames of omniscience will be replayed in the later dramatic scene in which Ernesto Jr has traced Lena to Mateo's apartment and waits outside. In another cinematic reference, this time from Alfred Hitchcock's *Rear Window,* Lena comes out of the apartment building and catches Ernesto spying. We view this scene first from Ernesto Jr's videocam perspective, whose jumpy camera work precipitated by Lena's jostling with her stalker lends a *vérité* quality to the image.

The scene then cuts abruptly to the elder Martel's viewing room. As in the earlier projection of Ernesto's documentary from this same space, the lip-reader provides clarifying dialogue. But the projection is disrupted when Lena enters the room and begins voicing her own words from the video. Standing at the back of the room, behind Martel and the lip-reader, Lena is thus transformed from the object of the double glance of both Martels into the role of the acousmatic source of power and of meaning over the image and, presumably, the story. Importantly, this self-conscious restaging of voice elides into Lena's assertion of control and threatens the privilege of what up to this point had been the naturalised and unchallenged assertion of male mastery over story.

In theorising the problematic nature of woman's voice in Hollywood cinema, Amy Lawrence expands on Silverman's argument about the textual containment of female voice in film (1988: 45–7), observing its potential threat: 'The speaking woman disrupts the dominant order' (1991: 32). It is cinema's broader ideological bias against the female voice as source of narration that is assaulted in Lena's ironic simulation of 'post-dubbing' in this scene.

That assertion of female sexual authority through voice is then picked up within Mateo's film-within-the-film. What we see of *Girls with Valises* appears to be a new version of the sequence from *Women on the Verge* in which Marisa, originally played by Rossy de Palma, has fallen asleep at the kitchen table of Pepa's apartment after drinking a glass of soup laced with sleeping pills. In Mateo's version, Carmen Machi is Chon, a bored local politician from the right-wing Partido Popular [PP or People's Party] (called PAP in the film), who presents a monologue to the sleeping character, Marisa, expressing her views on female desire. She recounts the story of her new lover, whose body she has sexually devoured from big toe to genitals. He has left her a valise containing pure heroin which she has brought to Pina's apartment. This is the valise referred to in the title of Mateo's film.[6]

Chon's spirited comic monologue, a throwback to an earlier Almodóvar, stands, however, in sharp contrast to the sombre world evoked in Mateo's narration to Diego. It has no real equivalent in the original version of *Women on the Verge*. Rather, it recalls Carmen Maura's theatrical monologue in *La ley del deseo/Law of Desire* (1987), the first of Almodóvar's plots to depict a filmmaker as protagonist. Inspired by Jean Cocteau's play *La Voix humaine/The Human Voice*, Maura's monologue is constructed around the radio-melodrama prop of the telephone. Chon's monologue, though not involving a telephone, is, nonetheless, an unbridled expression of female sexual desire, all but absent in the male-driven narrative that frames it. With its subsequent release as a separate film short for Spanish cable television, Chon's monologue suggests a formal as well as thematic challenge to the primacy of the story that Mateo/Harry will tell as *Girls and Valises*. That is, it is both an affirmation of female desire and a text that stands outside the controlling force of the male filmmaker and producer. When the scene reappears at the film's end, discovered by chance by Mateo, it is in a mutilated form; he calls the soundtrack *desentonada* [out of tune], again reminding us of the importance of voice to creativity. Only through the agency of Judit's story and action, in fact, can Mateo's dream of completing the film be fulfilled.

The culmination of these auditory sequences is Judit's confession at Mateo's birthday party that she was Martel's accomplice in sabotaging his film, thereby providing a form of anagnorisis to Mateo's quasi-tragic verbal journey of self-discovery. Unlike tragedy, however, but more in tune with radio soap opera, the confession gives privilege to the female voice, revealing Judit's power to control the destiny of the male's illusion of mastery (Mateo's film). Like Chon, Judit has in effect devoured the 'body' of the male's work. Finally, it is the power of the female voice that reveals to Diego the identity of his biological father.

The monologue, structurally akin to Carmen Maura's extended confession to her daughter at the end of *Volver,* proposes a dramatic telling that supersedes cinema's power to merely 'show'. Judit's story exposes the errors of Mateo's version, ennobles the much maligned Ernesto Jr and facilitates the restoration of Mateo's film. Her revelation facilitates the (re)construction of the new cinematic family (the filmmaker, his son and his spiritual and professional muse, Judit), thereby affirming her acousmatic power over the narration of the individual and collective past.

It also serves a historical function in keeping with Almodóvar's conceptual objective of aligning what appears to be a self-referential celebration of cinema with his broader contemporary Spanish historical project. We may note that in the ambiguous closure to the film, framed from within by the restoration of the *Girls with Valises* and the reconstitution of the family. Mateo's final line of dialogue, 'Hay que terminar la película, aunque sea a ciegas' [The film has to be finished, even blindly], is echoed in the closing music (Miguel Poveda's 'A ciegas'). These final words remind us of how his physical blindness is also metaphoric blindness, that is, his inability to achieve the desired mastery, knowledge and power to realise full control.

It is telling that in the last scene of the restored film-within-the-film that we see, Chon and Pina approach the camera as they go to answer the doorbell. The final image of the opened door in the restored film-within-the-film is motivated through an auditory marker, the ringing of the doorbell. We never see who is at the door. Instead, the image is immediately cross-cut to Mateo and Diego viewing the scene on a Moviola from their contemporary vantage point, 14 years after the sequence was shot. The film appears to have written a dated genre ending: the symbolic open door frames the two women, who embody the 1980s Spanish cinematic convention of female sexual desire. Yet it transposes this scene into the contemporary context, providing the visual and auditory 'open door' to the unfinished business of Spanish modernity. Two women from the past come face to face with two generations of Spanish men, Mateo and his son Diego, as if to initiate the much delayed but crucial dialogue between contemporary Spain and its recent past.

The meditative moment of reflection about the decade of political transition of the 1980s, as Subirats argues, is an antidote to the celebration of Spain's ambiguous modernity. From the vantage of a filmmaker, looking back over a career that spans three decades and the historical trajectory of Spanish modernity and its discontents, Almodóvar's film suggests a similar recognition of the need to engage in a contemporary interrogation of the personal and social underpinnings of a society that otherwise refuses to look beneath the surface of its recent past.

Notes

1 *La mala educación/Bad Education* (2004) returns to the Madrid of 1980 and his first commercial film, *Pepi, Luci, Bom, y otras chicas del montón/Pepi, Luci, Bom*, and *Volver* (2006) bears the conspicuous marks of a reworking of *¿Qué he hecho yo para merecer esto?/What Have I Done to Deserve This?* (1985).
2 The *Belle de Jour* intertext is additionally evocative in that the heroine's husband, Pierre, ends up blind after having been shot by her lover.
3 The view of the film's 'social' anchoring is suggested by Antonio Castro, who sees in the father–son relationship between Ernesto Martel and his son an opaque reference to Enrique Sarasola, the Spanish financier closely aligned to the socialist government of Felipe González, and his openly gay son Quique; see Castro (2010: 290).
4 Despite the star billing for Penélope Cruz in the role of Lena, and of her status in the plot as the object of Mateo's *amour fou*, the centre of gravity of the film's complex plot rests in the structural pairing of Mateo with Judit as they embody the struggle between male and female authority to tell the story of his past.
5 The theme of paternity is, as Peter Evans reminds us, one of the important plot details of *Women on the Verge*, as developed around the twin father–child relationships, those between the mad Lucía and her father, and Lucía's son, Carlos (Antonio Banderas) and his father, Iván. See Evans (1996: 42–8).
6 The sequence was eventually re-edited by Almodóvar into a separate short, *La concejala antropófaga/The Cannibal Deputy*, shown on Spanish cable television with Mateo Blanco credited as director and Harry 'Hurricane' Caine as scriptwriter, further blurring the lines between fiction and cinema in the real world.

Bibliography

Boquerini, Francisco Blanco (1989) *Pedro Almodóvar*, Madrid: JC.

Castro, Antonio (2010) 'Los abrazos rotos', in Antonio Castro (ed.), *Las películas de Almodóvar*, Madrid: JC, 279–92.

Chion, Michel (1999) *The Voice in Cinema,* trans. Claudia Gorbman, New York: Columbia University Press.

Delgado, Maria (2009) 'Sensory Perception: Almodóvar's *Broken Embraces*', *Sight & Sound*, 19:9 (September), 40–4.

D'Lugo, Marvin (2009) 'Post-Nostalgia, Written on the Body of Sara Montiel', in Brad Epps and Despina Kakoudaki (eds), *All About Almodóvar*, Minneapolis and London: University of Minnesota Press, 357–85.

Evans, Peter William (1996) *Women on the Verge of a Nervous Breakdown*, London: BFI.

Kinder, Marsha (1993) *Blood Cinema: The Reconstruction of National Identity in Spain*, Berkeley, Los Angeles and London: University of California Press.

—(2010) 'Restoring Broken Embraces', *Film Quarterly*, 63:3 (Spring), 28–34.

Larrañaga, Julio and Amelia N. Ruiz Molina (2010) 'La aportación de la obra de Pedro Almodóvar al mercado cinematográfico español', in Antonio Castro (ed.), *Las películas de Almodóvar*, Madrid: JC, 295–313.

Lawrence, Amy (1991) *Echo and Narcissus: Women's Voice in Classical Hollywood Cinema*, Berkeley, Los Angeles and Oxford: University of California Press.

Medina, Alberto (2002) 'De la emancipación al simulacro: la ejemplaridad de la transición española', in Subirats (ed.), 23–36.

Naremore, James (1998) *More than Night: Film Noir in its Contexts*, Berkeley, Los Angeles and London: University of California Press.

Silverman, Kaja (1988) *The Acoustic Mirror: The Female Voice in Psychoanalysis and Cinema*, Bloomington and Indianapolis: Indiana University Press.

Smith, Paul Julian (2000) *Desire Unlimited: The Cinema of Pedro Almodóvar*, 2nd edn, London: Verso.

Subirats, Eduardo (2002) 'Transición y espectáculo', in Subirats (ed.), 71–85.

Subirats, Eduardo (ed.) (2002) *Intransiciones: críticas de la cultura española*, Madrid: Editorial Biblioteca Nueva.

Telotte, J.P. (1989) *Voices in the Dark: The Narrative Patterns of Film Noir*, Urbana and Champaign: University of Illinois Press.

16

V.O.S. (Cesc Gay, 2009): from Shakespearean comedy to national identity

Celestino Deleyto

V.O.S. is a romantic comedy about the writing of a romantic comedy set in Barcelona. Clara (Àgata Roca) and Manu (Paul Berrondo) have decided to have a child together, even though they are not partners. Ander (Andrés Herrera), Manu's best friend, is involved with Vicky (Vicenta N'Dongo). They are looking for a place to live although Ander is anxious about commitment. Clara and Ander fall in love, as a consequence of which Ander and Vicky split up and he and Clara get married. Shortly afterwards, Clara and Manu have their baby. The story concerns the four characters but also the four actors playing them. The actor playing Ander is writing the screenplay for a romantic comedy based on their experiences; this screenplay is the film we see, although it also concerns the writing of the screenplay. There is no separation between the two stories, which constantly spill into one another. Most of the remaining characters are members of the crew which is shooting the different scenes, and they all end up at the beach, celebrating the completion of the film.

'No ho entenc. Algú em pot explicar què està passant aquí?' [I don't understand. Can anybody explain what's going on here?], asks a nurse near the beginning of Cesc Gay's *V.O.S.* Clara has just given birth and Manu and Ander are eagerly awaiting the good news outside the delivery room. The two men are thrilled and while trying to decide which one will go in to see mother and baby first, they tell the nurse that one is the father and the other the husband. She is confused, and looks off screen, asking for an explanation. This moment announces both the film's generic affiliation to romantic comedy and its formal conceit: the coexistence in the same diegetic continuum of characters and actors, filmic space and shooting locations. The next scene, a flashback to some ten months earlier, when Manu and Clara reveal to their friends their plans to have a baby together, starts with a shot of the film's script in Spanish on a black screen, as the lines of the dialogue are spoken in Catalan by the characters off screen, before the next shot shows the four friends driving along a road north of Barcelona, with the city in the background. While the city of Barcelona will play a crucial role in the film, Gay does not seem capable of staying within his constructed fictional world for very long, and a few shots later the real background is revealed to be rear projection: when Clara gets out of the car, which was not moving, she is inside an improvised studio rather than in the middle of the road. In the course of the film, a multitude of similar devices are employed in order to break the illusion of reality and to dissolve the boundaries between discrete ontological levels.

There is nothing new in this use of metafictional devices, nor is the film attempting to break new ground in deconstructive terms. In fact, it could be argued that in collapsing the two levels the film is moving in the opposite direction. In the very long final scene of Shakespeare's *A Midsummer Night's Dream*, once the action has been resolved with various weddings and reconciliations, Bottom and his crew of artisans perform the play *Pyramus and Thisbe* for the aristocratic lovers. The production is very poor, the actors very bad, and the action of the play-within-the-play is interspersed with the very disparaging comments of the on-stage spectators. Hippolyta, the Queen of the Amazons, is particularly critical: 'This is the silliest stuff that ever I heard' (V.i.207). Yet before long even the Queen has fallen under the spell of the story: 'Beshrew my heart, but I pity the man' (V.i.279). In this play, a story which deconstructs and almost dismantles itself continues nevertheless to do its work and engage its spectators. Shakespeare both taps and derides our unquenchable desire for stories. Even as we know that we are being mocked, we continue to fall prey to their power. The metafictional framework of *V.O.S.* fulfils a comparable function: rather than spoil our fun or distance us from its fictional world(s), it appeals to us even more strongly by advocating the ultimate inability of the frame-breaking devices to overcome our desire for narrative. This desire for narrative is in fact one of several forms of desire which structure Gay's film and make it a relevant instance of contemporary Spanish cinema and, more specifically, a privileged space for the exploration of the uncertain and slippery concept of Catalan cinema. This chapter attempts to identify those forms of desire and the links between them.

The box office for *V.O.S.* was very modest. If we compare its little more than 30,000 spectators in 2009 with the 3.5 million of Alejandro Amenábar's *Agora* (2009), the more than 2 million of *Celda 211/Cell 211* (Daniel Monzón, 2009), the million who saw *Que se mueran los feos/To Hell with the Ugly* (Nacho G. Velilla, 2009) or even the relatively disappointing almost 700,000 of Almodóvar's *Los abrazos rotos/Broken Embraces* (2009), the movie hardly made any impact at all. Gay's earlier films, while still unimpressive in commercial terms, had been considerably more successful at the box office. For every spectator who went to see *V.O.S.* in Spain in 2009, 300 saw *Avatar* in the same year (Ministerio de Cultura 2010). These figures are symptomatic of the commercial problems of Catalan cinema, a situation which, as I shall try to argue below, is closely linked to its cultural and, more specifically, linguistic contradictions. *V.O.S.* is from the beginning, even from its title, aware of those contradictions and limitations and turns them partly into the motor that activates its deepest form of desire. The film is not only a romantic comedy, but also a text about national and transnational identity, one which self-consciously pits its own desire against the institutional and industrial barriers that keep Catalan cinema in a state of permanent crisis.

Scenarios of desire

In *A Midsummer Night's Dream*, desire for narrative is indissolubly linked with sexual desire. The various sexual permutations, betrayals, infidelities and arbitrary changes of object of desire constitute the core of the play's structure and lead us not only to a longed-for denouement but also to the re-enactment of sexual scenarios which seek to arouse the spectator. In the final scene, the artisans' performance finishes with Theseus's exhortation: 'Lovers, to bed' (V.i.350), constituting itself as a micro-narrative that proposes the fulfilment of desire as the logical outcome of the linearity of narrative. It is as if the enjoyment of a story, no matter what its subject matter, is in itself aphrodisiac and logically leads to sex. Shakespeare's play explores and celebrates the arbitrariness and the inexorability of desire, and explicitly links that inexorability with our passion for fictional stories, fusing the two types of desire in the consolidation of a new genre: romantic comedy. The cinema, and particularly Hollywood cinema, in its relentless construction of scenarios of desire, soon adopted the old genre as one of its most durable staples, and at the outset of the new millennium continues to offer representations of intimate matters through the comic perspective and conventions of this genre.

   V.O.S. ostensibly places itself within this tradition. *Bringing Up Baby* (1938) and the films of Meg Ryan are evoked at key moments and, more importantly, Ander is writing the script of a romantic comedy. He links his wish to write a romantic comedy with his freedom to manipulate chronology and multiply the flashbacks within flashbacks. Clara disagrees, demands linearity and warns that romantic comedy spells disaster. She obviously wants her boyfriend to write an important film and, given the cultural bias against romantic comedy, his choice of genre is not a promising start. In any case, the text associates rom-com with jumbled narrativity and realism with linearity. To students of Hollywood cinema these are unexpected connections, since romantic comedy has generally been described as being far from narratively or thematically complex. The most superficial of popular genres, rom-com is felt to be as far as one can get from sophisticated cinema, whether we call it art cinema, independent cinema or auteur cinema. The majority of film critics and the kind of spectator parodied through Clara dismiss the genre and decry its unswerving ideology, as encoded, especially, in an all-powerful ending that is predictable, unrealistic and wholly conservative. For Ander, however, romantic comedy is complex, rejects linearity and welcomes a certain degree of experimentation.

The ideology of the genre, however, is more flexible in its exploration of issues of desire and intimate matters than critics have allowed. In recent decades, for example, rom-com has chronicled the important changes that have taken place in contemporary societies in terms of gender relationships and sexual discourses, protocols and practices while actively contributing to those changes. In a recent interview along with his habitual scriptwriter Tomàs Aragay, Gay has described the current sexual and intimate climate as one of deep disarray and uncertainty for men and women (Deleyto 2008: 357). *V.O.S.* reflects this state of affairs through a comic lens. The arrangement that Manu and Clara, two friends who may or may not be attracted to one another, make to have a baby together is at the centre of the film's perspective on the fluidity, ineffability and also excitement of contemporary relationships. Gay and Aragay had already included a similar bargain in their previous film, *Ficció/Fiction* (2006), as part of their exploration of contemporary sexual protocols and friendship patterns. In an analysis of this film and their previous *En la ciudad/In the City* (2003), María del Mar Azcona has demonstrated the importance of the conventions of romantic comedy in the articulation of a specifically Spanish tension between tradition and modernity in sexual matters (2009: 245). *V.O.S.* is more openly convinced of its status as a romantic comedy than the two previous films, but narrates a similar attitude towards intimacy and sexuality, acknowledging both the unstoppable force of desire and its power to generate ever-changing interpersonal permutations. The visibility of the narrative carpentry reinforces this feeling: deprived of its realistic trappings, desire sails along as strong as ever and, like the Shakespearean specta-tor, we have no option but to accept its supremacy.

Ander, the diegetic puppet-master, believes in the commensurability between romantic comedy and narrative complexity. The resulting 'comic fragmenta-tion' speaks to the multiplicity of intimate options that have become possible in contemporary societies. Relationships may be short-lived or long-lasting, based on sexual desire or friendship; men and women may be in love or intimate in other respects; there is suffering and frustration in *V.O.S.*, but ultimately all these options are blessed with the comic mantle of the genre: Vicky loses her boyfriend to her rival but finishes the story asking Manu to have a baby with her, overawed as she is by the wonders of incipient motherhood. Clara may be one of the most unsympathetic lovers in recent examples of the genre, yet Roca's nuanced per-formance and the film's powerful comic atmosphere allow the spectator to accept and enjoy the micro-narrative of her falling in love with Ander. Manu may not have had the courage to confess his love for Clara and has missed his chance,

28. Romantic comedy and rear projection: the four characters discuss having babies and being in love in the fake reality of *V.O.S.*

but his experience of living with her for a few months leaves him immune to her charms and stronger in his independence. Conventional heterosexual monogamous relationships seem impossible to achieve and not particularly desirable, yet traditional forms of intimacy continue to pop up in the protocols used by the characters to relate to one another, underlining the reappearance of the mixture of past and present conventions identified by Azcona in the two previous films. In sum, Gay subtly employs the conventions of the genre in order to suggest the multifariousness, confusion and exhilaration of the current intimate climate.

Since Shakespeare, the best romantic comedies have conveyed the excitement of sexual attraction and the pleasures of coupledom through a form of textual energy that links sex and identity (Greenblatt 1988: 88–90), but in a postcolonial and, according to some authors, postnational world (Appadurai 1996), contemporary films may be using a similar textual energy to represent other forms of desire and other articulations of identity. In films like *Babel* (Alejandro González Iñárritu, 2006), *It's a Free World …* (Ken Loach, 2007), *Auf der Anderen Seite/ The Edge of Heaven* (Fatih Akin, 2007), *Frozen River* (Courtney Hunt, 2008), *Etz Limon/Lemon Tree* (Eran Riklis, 2008), *The Visitor* (Thomas McCarthy, 2007) or *Amreeka* (Cherien Dabis, 2009), the desire for a place, the desire to belong or not belong, and the desire for movement and settling down have taken centre stage, combining in various ways with more traditional forms of desire. Many of these films are particularly interesting because of their juxtaposition of sexual desire and these other forms of desire. At first sight, *V.O.S.* may be felt to be very distant in its interests from narratives of immigration, transnationalism and globalisation like those mentioned above. In fact, however, the complexity of its use of the conventions of romantic comedy and of its approach to contemporary intimate mores does not exhaust the particular form of textual energy it deploys. The attentive spectator may discern a more powerful undercurrent beneath the romantic comedy narrative, one that never materialises as a visible discourse but whose presence can be felt throughout. In my view, this excess of textual energy is closely related to the issue of Catalan identity, and it becomes almost visible in the way the characters address one another.

Catalan identity, film and language

Historically, Catalan identity has been strongly linked with language. The law of 'linguistic normalisation', approved by the Catalan Parliament after the advent of democracy in Spain and the 1978 Constitution which consecrated the *Estado de las Autonomías* [State of Autonomies], has had a considerable impact in Catalan society. This curious euphemism, which means resolute institutional support for the consolidation of Catalan as the main language in Catalonia, has reached all areas of social intercourse and everyday life, from education to entertainment. Based on the belief in the existence of two separate 'ethno-linguistic' communities, one Catalan-speaking and one Castilian-speaking (Boix 1993: 203–9), it seeks to promote Catalan as a minority language under constant threat from the sociolinguistic context. This has produced incessant political friction as well as social discrimination. As this chapter was being researched in the summer of 2010, new legislation about the exhibition of commercial films dubbed into Catalan and political wrangles over the obligation to have proficiency in Catalan in public higher-education institutions continued to locate language at the centre of the struggle over Catalan identity (see, for example, Bilbeny 2010 and Tobarra 2010). Around the same time, the heated debates over the reform of the Catalan Statute of Autonomy, which brought about a surge of nationalist feeling in the region and renewed political squabbles among Spanish and Catalan political parties (see Sala i Martin 2010 and Chacón y González 2010), predictably featured various aspects of linguistic normalisation. For Manuel Castells, the Catalan language is what made Catalans distinctive from the beginning, and it has been seen by Catalan nationalists as the core of national identity (2004: 51–2). On the other hand, Joan-Lluís Marfany has argued that the language soon transcended the policies of the nationalists and became the property of the vast majority of Catalans. For him, Catalan as a marker of national identity is problematic because it is the language of all Catalans, and not only of those defending a national Catalan identity (1995: 352). This dichotomy of Catalan as the constant bone of political contention and as the common linguistic practice of millions of people is crucial for an understanding of contemporary Spanish and Catalan history. The normalisation of something that already appears to be normal reveals some of the anxieties and contradictions of political appropriation of everyday practices, as well as the nagging refusal on the part of many Spanish speakers and politicians outside Catalonia to recognise and accept the linguistic reality of their own country. The lived bilingualism of Catalan people, and their ability to survive and thrive while remaining bilingual, seems to be difficult to accept within the political discourses of both Catalan and Spanish nationalists.

Cultural policies, as part of the larger political activity, have reproduced these tensions and anxieties. According to Josep Lluis Fecé, for the Catalan government cultural policy has been practically synonymous with linguistic policy (2003: 291). Understanding that cultural texts are a potent channel for the construction of national identity, those in power have sought to control and promote certain cultural manifestations in order to construct a monolingual fantasy whose success has in turn influenced people's perception of themselves. However, the cinema, because of its industrial profile, has been excluded from a space shared by the theatre and television. In the view of Matilde Obradors, the failure of Catalan cinema to reflect a national identity and to convey a collective soul contrasts with the theatre, which has managed to show Catalan artists as visual storytellers far more successfully (2003: 73). TV3, the prime Catalan channel, was created, according to Fecé, mainly as an instrument to consolidate the Catalan language in the public sphere (2003: 289), that is, as a tool of linguistic normalisation. Precisely because of the absence of an indigenous film industry, what he calls the Catalan star system has been built around actors' transitions between theatre and television (299). In this way, both media have collaborated in creating a collective imaginary around monolingual fictional stories addressed, according to Obradors, to a variety of social and intellectual classes (73). Enric Castelló has explored the ideological and institutional context of these constructions in an analysis of soap operas on TV3. He explains that monolingualism in this channel is a very consistent practice based on criteria of cultural policy. The producers and scriptwriters that he interviews support this policy enthusiastically and argue that the presence of Spanish in fictional stories would be a serious impediment to linguistic normalisation. They argue that fiction never reproduces reality as it is (in this case bilingual), but plays with conventions that audiences interpret easily, that is, characters always speaking Catalan are perfectly understood by the spectators as not a reality but a convention. Yet, this convention also has a pedagogical dimension, aimed at immigrant spectators: when an immigrant spectator sees that the immigrant character who speaks Catalan is perfectly integrated and accepted, s/he will feel the urge to learn Catalan, too (2006: 203). In other words, when an immigrant speaks Catalan in one of these programmes, it means simultaneously that s/he is and is not speaking Catalan. Castelló also explains that this television channel has a department of linguistic correction that carefully monitors scripts and shoots and implements a strict oral standard that reduces variety, even among Catalan speakers, and erases linguistic inconsistencies, strictly implementing a previously decided-upon linguistic norm (203–4).

Both theatre and television, for different reasons, have acquired a cultural identity that, according to most observers, is lacking in the cinema. Because of this lack, Catalan cinema has become, according to Obradors and others, a marginal phenomenon (2003: 68). This does not mean that films are not made in Catalonia or by Catalan filmmakers; rather, with some exceptions such as Ventura Pons or Albert Serra, they are not perceived as 'Catalan'. The financial complications involved in making commercial films in Catalan have been at the root of the marginality of the cinema with respect to the theatre and television, both of which based their cultural specificity largely on their commitment to monolingual production. Given the financial and/or institutional feasibility of two forms of entertainment addressed exclusively to Catalan audiences, the theatre and television have managed to be successful with texts only in Catalan and have in fact turned their monolingualism into a commercial strength. This is not the case for most films, which cannot survive without the box-office receipts of Spanish-speaking audiences, both in and outside Spain. Films with Catalan dialogues practically condemn themselves to the margins of the industry (Obradors 2003: 70). Wanting to reach wider Spanish audiences, Catalan filmmakers have often made their films in Spanish even when the action of their films has taken place in Catalonia, a situation that remains unchanged in the first decade of the twenty-first century.[1] For example, the characters in *Yo soy la Juani/My Name is Juani* (2006), by Bigas Luna, one of the most important contemporary Catalan directors, speak only Spanish both when they live in a small Catalan town and when Juani (Verónica Echegui) decides to emigrate to Madrid, whereas Gay's *In the City*, a film about a very recognisable and culturally specific Barcelona intellectual middle class, is spoken exclusively in Spanish, with the DVD offering the option of a Catalan-dubbed version. Even a film like José Luis Guerín's prestigious Barcelona documentary *En construcción/Work in Progress* (2001) keeps Catalan to a minimum, as if afraid that too much of that language will harm the film's prospects outside Catalonia, however modest those prospects may be for an art documentary. Conversely, attempts have been made to reproduce the all-Catalan convention in the cinema, as in the case of Ventura Pons's *Barcelona (un mapa)/Barcelona (A Map)* (2007) and *Forasters/Strangers* (2008), both adaptations of plays with most of the dialogues in Catalan, with comparable aesthetic results and very poor performances at the box office.

Hollywood cinema has accustomed us to similar conventions: film characters speak English even when their original language is French, Swedish or Hungarian. Such examples also abound in French and other national cinemas. Spanish spectators, like those of other European countries, are well used to seeing films dubbed into their own language, and the fact that this is not the characters' original language does not make the illusion of reality for them different than for spectators who watch the film in the original version. These industrial practices, however, have cultural and ideological consequences and find particular difficulties when representing a global age in which multilingual experiences are becoming more and more common. Catalan society has had a long history of bilingual communication and a present reality in which Catalan and Spanish, as well as other languages, habitually coexist in various degrees depending on the specific area. This is an important part of the experience of living in Catalonia and of the identity of the many people for whom bilingual communication is part of their everyday practice. The erasure of this experience from narrative texts, whether for political, institutional, cultural or industrial reasons, constitutes a remarkable loss. A Moroccan character (played by a Catalan actor) speaking Catalan in *Strangers*, a film from the twenty-first century, makes it old-fashioned and even culturally irrelevant, even if we accept the convention. The presence of an Argentine character in one of the stories of *Barcelona [A Map]* forces the other character in the scene to speak Spanish to her, but the very presence of Spanish in only one of the stories makes the text strangely contrived and inconsistent. When all the characters speak to one another only in Spanish in *In the City* (or only in Catalan in the dubbed version), we feel that the representation is seriously impaired. In general, the use of language in Catalan films, as in plays or TV programmes, follows ideological or industrial requirements rather than realistic conventions. The linguistic reality is felt to be threatening for dominant institutions and is hidden under a monolingual rule. This curious situation affects both the industrial feasibility and the cultural credibility of Catalan cinema in a world in which linguistic hybridity and heterogeneity are fast becoming the norm rather than the exception.

To return to *V.O.S.*, it is now tempting to interpret the nurse's words at the beginning of the film differently. With the two men mixing Catalan and Spanish (with a smattering of Basque for good measure), she would not be puzzled if she were a real nurse working in a real hospital in Barcelona. But, being a fictional character in a Catalan film, she needs to ask those who, within the film's conceit, have created the story, what is going on. She never gets a reply from the people off screen, but the linguistic pattern of this short dialogue is reproduced in the rest of the narrative: two Catalan women and two Basque men, one of whom has only recently arrived in Barcelona and is not yet proficient in Catalan, speak primarily Catalan to one another but constantly shift to Spanish when the situation requires it, often starting their sentences in one language and finishing it in the other. The characters' rather strong accents (Basque and Catalan) when they speak Spanish, and the occasional lines in Basque, suggest a linguistic complexity which Spanish cinema in general has never been able – or indeed inclined – to capture. Being exposed to Spanish, their Catalan is very different from that spoken by characters in TV3 soap operas, and being Catalan speakers their

Spanish often incorporates linguistic turns from the other language. Linguistic correction and purity of the type enforced in TV3 are clearly not the name of the game here, and yet a powerful sense of identity is being articulated through their mixed dialogues.

V.O.S. is not exactly an isolated case within contemporary Catalan cinema. More and more films are being made in which both languages coexist in various degrees. After writing a monolingual script for *In the City*, Gay and Aragay created a bilingual scenario for *Fiction*, a story that takes place in a small village in the Pyrenees, in which the presence of a Spanish speaker allows the characters to mix, even though Catalan is realistically the predominant language. *V.O.S.* is an adaptation of a play by Carol López, who also collaborated with Gay on the script (three of the actors in the film had also played the same parts in the play). As the film was being made, López's next theatrical piece, the comedy *Germanes/ Sisters* (2008), was being produced in Barcelona to critical acclaim. The play, which like Gay's films elicited comparisons with Woody Allen, Eric Rohmer and Agnès Jaoui, also mixed Spanish and Catalan in the dialogues (Ordóñez 2008). A film from the same year as *V.O.S.*, *Tres dies amb la família/Three Days with the Family*, by first-time director Mar Coll, tells an intimate story of a middle-class Catalan family who get together for the funeral of the patriarch, Josep Maria Vich i Cardó. Léa (Nausicaa Bonnín), the protagonist, speaks Spanish to her French mother, Joëlle (Philippine Leroy-Beaulieu), who sometimes speaks French to her daughter but Spanish to everybody else, but she can read and understand Catalan and sometimes speaks Catalan. Joëlle and her husband Josep Maria (Eduard Fernández) speak Spanish to one another but he and his daughter communicate in Catalan. In spite of their very strong Catalan identity, their Catalan, like that in *V.O.S.*, is noticeably contaminated by Spanish, as is their Spanish by Catalan. As in *V.O.S.*, the apparent effortlessness of the script creates the illusion that most of the time the characters are not even aware of the language they speak or of changing from one language to the other. This makes for a very different type of experience than that promoted by other Catalan films and visual texts. The impact of *Pa Negre/Black Bread* (Agustí Villaronga, 2010) may or may not be an indication that things are beginning to change in the industry. The film tells a story of the immediate post-Civil War years which takes place in a village in the Catalan mountains in which all the characters realistically speak Catalan, except for the occasional school-classroom scenes. Like most foreign films it was dubbed into Spanish for exhibition in Spain outside Catalonia, but its Catalan original version did not stop it from collecting nine awards at the 2011 edition of the 'Premios Goya' [Goya awards], including best film and best director, or from being nominated as Spain's entry for the 2011 Oscars.

As already noted, in *V.O.S.* the two female characters are Catalan, the two male ones Basque. Given their heterosexual orientation, the difference between the way the male and the female characters speak is part of their attraction to one

29. Sex and the city: the many faces of desire in *V.O.S.*

another. Linguistic otherness energises desire, while their linguistic promiscuity facilitates the multi-directionality and ever-shifting nature of their sexual drives. Given the relative scarcity in filmic representations of the type of fictional scenario that they inhabit, it is as if the characters felt liberated from the burden of the monolingual rule and that freedom allowed their desire to flow more freely. While in the society which this and other Catalan films represent this linguistic proliferation is far from special or extraordinary, cinematic representations, as the nurse's surprise suggests, are not used to it. Its desirability is turned by the text into narrative and sexual desirability, as if the characters of *A Midsummer Night's Dream* had been converted into words and sentences from different languages longing to merge with one another in the Athenian forest, a Utopian Tower of Babel whose variety produced fulfilment rather than frustration and lack of communication. It could be argued, then, that sexual desire in *V.O.S.* functions as a metaphor of the desire for a different type of identity, one that would take as its starting point everyday experience rather than carefully monitored cultural policy. The striving for monolingual purity openly reproduces a struggle for a national identity that, in the heavily politicised scenario of contemporary Catalonia and Spain, can only be envisaged in terms of either/or. Texts like *V.O.S.* may be seen as fantasies that strive to locate themselves outside that binary system and to reproduce reality in a cultural context in which linguistic reality has been strictly repressed. The characters' desires are not only propelled by their linguistic impurity but they have that impurity as their hidden object of desire. Or maybe not so hidden: after all, the film is called *V.O.S.*, which is not only a statement of its intention to separate itself from the majority of dubbed films in its country, but also an accurate description of what the film is (a *versión original*), as opposed to the majority of narrative texts coming from Catalonia, which are already dubbed, even in their original versions. Ander may insist that he is *only* writing a romantic comedy, but what makes his romantic comedy different is not so much the complexity of its narrative structure as the simplicity of its original version. *V.O.S.* uses the generic framework as a useful tool to articulate a transnational form of identity which in Catalan society has had a very long history, and to represent the desire for something that amidst the din of the political and cultural struggle for purity is in danger of being lost.

Conclusion

Barcelona, the capital city that has historically been a crucible of many different civilisations, the space in which purity and homogeneity have never made much sense and in which, no matter the number of laws and policies, the coexistence of Catalan and Spanish remains unstoppable, encapsulates this mongrel identity and is the text's ultimate object of desire. From the beginning of the narrative, even within its constant frame-breaking and apparent assault on reality, the 'real' Barcelona is ever-present and recognisable, but what we get is not necessarily a tourist-guide city or a Gaudí-laden symbol of Catalan national identity. From a ring road north of the city to a pedestrian street inside the Barceloneta, from a little square in Gràcia to a corner in Via Laietana, these are spaces of the bilingual practice and multifaceted identity that for many inhabitants of the city constitute an unremarkable fact of everyday life but that Catalan cinema has found it so difficult to reproduce. In *V.O.S.* these relatively ordinary places are lifted from the everyday and become the magic space of romantic comedy, a space in which, on this occasion, something more than the characters' sexual longings and intimate feelings is being protected. It is ultimately this idea of Barcelona, simultaneously real and Utopian, that becomes the final target of the textual multilayered desire: a new cinematic Barcelona, finally in the original version.[2]

Notes

1 The case of Isabel Coixet, one of the central figures of contemporary Catalan and Spanish cinema, is significant: her films tell transnational stories with dialogues mostly in English.
2 Research for this chapter was funded by the Ministerio de Ciencia y Tecnología (Ref. HUM2007-61183/FILO) and the DGA (Ref. H12). I would like to thank María del Mar Azcona and Gemma López for their valuable suggestions on the manuscript, and Josep Lluis Fecé for his help with the research.

Bibliography

Appadurai, Arjun (1996) *Modernity at Large: Cultural Dimensions of Globalization*, Minneapolis: University of Minnesota Press.

Azcona, María del Mar (2009) 'Spaces of Sincerity and Deception: The Representation of Desire in Cesc Gay's *En la ciudad* and *Ficción*', *Hispanic Research Journal*, 10:3, 233–46.

Bilbeny, Norbert (2010) 'Hay otros problemas', *El País* (6 September), www.elpais.com/articulo/sociedad/Hay/otros/problemas/elpepisoc/20100906elpepisoc_2/Tes [accessed 6 September 2010].

Boix, Emili (1993) *Triar no és trair: Identitat i llengua en els joves de Barcelona*, Barcelona: Llibres al'abast.

Castelló, Enric (2006) 'La construcció nacional a les sèries de ficció: visió sobre una dècada de producció de Televisió de Catalunya', *Quaderns del CAC*, 23–4, 199–209.

Castells, Manuel (2004) *The Power of Identity*, 2nd edn, Malden, Oxford and Victoria: Blackwell.

Chacón, Carme and González, Felipe (2010) 'Apuntes sobre Cataluña y España', *El País* (26 July), 21.

Deleyto, Celestino (2008) 'Aquellas pequeñas cosas: una entrevista con Cesc Gay y Tomás Aragay', *Hispanic Research Journal*, 9:4, 354–68.

Fecé, Josep Lluís (2003) 'Teleseries de producción propia e identidad nacional', in Víctor Fco. Sampietro Blanco (ed.), *La pantalla de las identidades: medios de comunicación, políticas y mercados de identidad*, Barcelona: Icaria.

Greenblatt, Stephen (1988) *Shakespearean Negotiations*, Oxford: Clarendon Press.

Marfany, Joan-Lluís (1995) *La cultura del catalanisme*, Barcelona: Empúries.

Ministerio de Cultura, Base de datos de películas actualizadas, www.mcu.es/bbdd peliculas/cargarFiltro.do?layout=bbddpeliculas&cache=init&language=es [accessed 23 September 2010].

Obradors, Matilde (2003) 'Una aproximació al cinema català des de l'estudi del seu procés creatiu', *Quaderns del CAC*, 17, 67–75.

Sala i Martín, Xavier (2010) 'Españosaurios', *La Vanguardia* (17 July), 19.

Tobarra, Sebastián (2010) '¿El idioma antes que el talento?', *El País* (6 September), www.elpais.com/articulo/sociedad/idioma/talento/elpepisoc/20100906elpepisoc_1/Tes [accessed 6 September 2010].

17

También la lluvia/Even the Rain
(Iciar Bollaín, 2010): social realism,
transnationalism and (neo)colonialism[1]

Duncan Wheeler

In 2000, a predominantly Spanish cast and crew arrive in Cochabamba, Bolivia, to make a socially conscious film denouncing Columbus's exploitation of the New World. The turnout for a public audition to cast the film's Indian characters far outweighs expectation. Daniel (Juan Carlos Aduviri), who is accompanying his young daughter, leads a protest demanding that they all be seen as they were promised; his presence and belief in justice and dignity mark him out as a leader whom the director, Sebastián (Gael García Bernal), thinks will be perfect as the film's protagonist. Costa (Luis Tosar), the producer, agrees, albeit reluctantly, as he fears that the non-professional actor's combative nature will make him difficult to control.

As filming commences, tensions escalate concerning attempts by the government to prevent the local inhabitants from collecting rain so as to allow a North American multinational to privatise water supplies. Daniel is a ringleader in the protest movement, leading to his arrest. Costa uses bribes to have him released temporarily so that filming can continue. When the police arrive on set to take Daniel back, the Bolivian actors, still in costume, overpower his assailants. The city descends further into chaos and many of the Spanish cast ask to return home. When Costa contracts a private security firm, they reluctantly agree to continue shooting outside Cochabamba.

As they prepare to leave, Daniel's wife begs the producer to help her find her young daughter who has been injured in the demonstrations. He tries to brush her aside but she insists that her only chance of getting through armed blockades is if she is accompanied by a foreigner. Costa agrees, much to the director's frustration. The cast and crew witness military brutality, and Sebastián is distraught when everyone else decides to return home. Costa finds the severely injured girl and secures their safe passage to a hospital with cash bribes. He subsequently finds Daniel's hideout, and the men embrace warmly. The producer shows him a newspaper story featuring a photo of the Bolivian actor alongside details of the multinational pulling out. The two friends bid farewell as Costa prepares to leave Bolivia and help Sebastián complete his film.

The striking visual image of the 15-year old Iciar Bollaín, red-haired and wide-eyed, in *El sur/The South* (Víctor Erice, 1983), ranks amongst the most iconic in the history of Spanish cinema. This debut screen performance in a period piece set in the 1950s also provided a template for subsequent roles that, as Isabel Santaolalla notes, tend to 'draw on her appearance, persona and ability to portray modern, active, intelligent women, often with a political or social conscience, relatively untouched by the ephemera of taste and fashion' (2012: 6). In what is but one of several instances of her work in front of and behind the camera impacting on each other, these are also the very same qualities that have defined her career as an activist, director and producer.

Bollaín may be indelibly linked with the national cinema and yet she resembles Isabel Coixet – currently, Spain's only other readily exportable female director – in the sense that success at home is also the result of her foreign influences, and in the esteem in which she is held in global markets. This is manifest, for example, in Bollaín becoming the first female director to have a film entered as the official Spanish entry to the Oscars, or in the fact that the parallels with Ken Loach's directorial style and political agenda are often identified and praised. In this chapter, I am particularly interested in examining how *También la lluvia/Even the Rain* (2010) functions at the interface between the local and the global whilst simultaneously negotiating different realist traditions at the level of content and form. I will begin by briefly locating Bollaín within wider patterns in (inter)national cinema(s), before introducing some key concepts which will be fundamental to my subsequent reading of the film.

Iciar Bollaín and social realism

It was almost by chance that the Madrid-born filmmaker entered the cinematic profession. The makers of *El sur* came to her secondary school in search of an adolescent with the right attributes to embody a precocious teenager curious about her enigmatic father's personal and political past.[2] This critically acclaimed debut marked the beginning of a professional career that flourished in the remainder of the 1980s and the early 1990s when the young actress appeared in a variety of films directed by some of Spain's most respected auteurs, including Felipe Vega, Gerardo Herrero and Manuel Gutiérrez Aragón. These early performances were instrumental to her subsequently forging a multifaceted cinematic career.

From the outset, Bollaín established friendships with the crews, and was keen to learn about the technical elements of filmmaking (Rodríguez Merchán 2005: 67). Somewhat less positively, she was frustrated by the fact that she felt unable to identify with the majority of male-authored female roles she played, in spite of the fact that their backgrounds and characters were ostensibly similar to her own (Bollaín 2001: 13). In 1991, she became one of the founding partners of the production company La Iguana, which allowed for a degree of freedom in developing projects, including her own first short films, whilst also continuing her acting career. A crucial turning point occurred when she was cast as Maite, a member of the Republican militia, in Loach's film about the Spanish Civil War: *Land and Freedom* (1995).

The Spanish actress and nascent filmmaker studied the British director's working methods closely. She publicly acknowledged the formative influence he had on her first feature film as a director, *Hola, ¿estás sola?/ Hi, Are You Alone?* (1995), speaking of how she reworked the script after the experience of working on *Land and Freedom*, paying more attention, for example, to the kind of flat that the two female protagonists would be able to afford (cited in Heredero 1997: 232). Her presence on the set of his next film, *Carla's Song* (1996), resulted in the publication of a book based on her observations where she spoke admiringly, for example, of the fact that the British director recorded sound directly rather than adding it in post-production, thereby, in her view, making his cinema more realistic and imbuing it with an integrity lacking in much commercial filmmaking (Bollaín 1996: 70).

Over the course of her following three films – *Flores de otro mundo/ Flowers From Another World* (1999), *Te doy mis ojos/ Take My Eyes* (2003) and *Mataharis* (2007) – Bollaín's directorial signature would come to be associated with two major trends in Spanish cinematic production. First, she formed part of a new wave of female directors who, for the first time in the mid-1990s, established a collective foothold and identity in the traditionally male-dominated national cinema.[3] Their films widened the parameters of what Spanish cinema was willing or able to show, centring as they often did on the personal and political circumstances of psychologically and sociologically plausible women who, as Bollaín was fully aware, had often been (in)conspicuous in their absence.

In addition to settling a gendered cultural deficit, many of these women's works also participated in a broader trend by a new generation of male and female Spanish filmmakers to deploy social realism as a form of political protest. Hence, for example, *Take My Eyes* engaged with the furore in the Spanish media surrounding the perceived escalation of domestic violence, and the seeming inability and/or unwillingness of the government to address the problem (see Wheeler 2008: 187–92). The realist trend emerged largely as a response to the aggressively market-driven policies of the centre-right Partido Popular [People's Party] (PP) who, under the leadership of José María Aznar, came to power in 1996 and ruled with an absolute majority from 2000 to 2004.

Given the relationship between social realism and reactionary political rule in the Spanish context, it is not perhaps surprising that the trend became less visible in the wake of the 2004 general elections won by the Partido Socialista Obrero Español [Spanish Socialist Workers' Party] (PSOE) (see Thibaudeau 2007). What is, however, more perplexing is the fact that the potential for increased gender parity suggested by the influx of female directors has not been realised, with male dominance arguably reasserting itself in Spanish cinema.[4] There are, of course, exceptions, and amongst the most striking features of the select group of women such as Bollaín, Chus Gutiérrez, Coixet and Gracia Querejeta who have been able to forge successful careers as directors is that they have continued to reflect the quotidian aspects of female experience and champion the kind of social realist filmmaking which is, in general, now far less prominent on Spanish screens than it was at the turn of the century.

Bollaín may not have gone as far as some of Loach's more extreme methods – shooting in sequence and withholding the script from the actors – but she has incorporated many of the techniques seen to be pivotal to his social-realist style and approach: extensive preliminary research and interviews; attention to detail; location shooting; the conscious attempt to eschew glamour in favour of everyday settings and characters. Nevertheless, the intuitive belief that we know what cinematic social realism is – or, at least, recognise it when we see it – belies the fact that it is a relative rather than absolute term. According to John Hill:

> While it is in the nature of 'realism' to profess a privileged relationship to the exter-
> nal world, its 'reality' is always conventional, a discursive construction rather than
> an unmediated reflection. What then identifies a 'realist' innovation in the arts is
> less the quality of its relationship to an external referent than its place in the history
> of artistic conventions, its 'intertextual' relationship to what has preceded. (1986:
> 127)

Within the Spanish context, oppositional directors under Franco tended to employ an elliptical and metaphorical style to evade censorship, and there is a widespread perception, be that real or imagined, that filmmakers in the democratic period have not always exploited the new-found freedoms available to them in order to eschew fantasy and reflect real life, however that may be construed. This helps explain why Loach is lionised in Spain where, unlike in the UK, all of his films are given extensive theatrical runs; especially following *Land and Freedom*, he has come to epitomise ethical and cinematic integrity. A wide-spread faith in what we might term 'naïve realism' – the ability of the camera to present an unmediated image of the world as it is – has been instrumental in the critical validation of filmmakers such as Bollaín who are seen to address difficult subjects and not relinquish social commitment for commercial gain.

Transnationalism and neocolonialism

As Susan Martín-Márquez notes, the yearning for a mythical homeland is central to *The South* yet, in Bollaín's directorial films, the 'treatment of notions of home, of displacement, and of cultural difference emerges from the contemporary contexts of globalization rather than from the traumas of the post-Civil War period' (2002: 257). *Flowers From Another World,* for example, is based on the true story of how rural depopulation led the male inhabitants of one small Castilian village to invite busloads of women from Central and South America in order that they become prospective partners. An increasingly pronounced transnational tendency is also indicated by Bollaín's most recent screen appearance in *Rabia/ Rage* (2009), directed by the Ecuadorian Sebastián Cordero and produced by Mexican filmmaker Guillermo del Toro, in which she is cast against type as Marimar Torres, a well-dressed and somewhat solipsistic woman from high society.

The narrative centres on Rosa, a young Ecuadorian maid, who works in a rural Basque mansion for a dysfunctional Spanish couple whose son rapes her. In spite of its international origins, *Rage* can clearly be grouped with a number of recent Spanish films such as *Princesas/Princesses* (Fernando León de Aranoa, 2005), *Retorno a Hansala/Return to Hansala* (Chus Gutiérrez, 2008) and *El dios de madera/Wooden God* (Vicente Molina Foix, 2010), which focus on the plight of immigrants in twenty-first-century Spain. These films, which all adopt a broadly progressive stance towards their subject, reflect the huge demographic changes caused by immigration in a very short period of time: between 1998 and 2008, the proportion of the population who were not born in Spain had risen from 3 to 13 per cent (Reher and Requena 2009: 11).

Whilst the Bollaín character might not provide a close match for her on- and off-screen persona, *Rage*'s well-crafted script, strong lead performances and liberal credentials do. The irony of a film of this kind which clearly intends to critique some effects of globalisation is, however, that its production and distribution are often conditioned and enabled by some of the very same processes that it sets out to denounce. The real boom in Spanish co-productions with Latin America occurred as business concerns increased in Latin America under the PP government – see Maria M. Delgado's Chapter 14 in this volume. Crucially for the audiovisual sector, Ibermedia, a collaboration between Spain and 13 Latin American countries, was established in 1997. On the one hand, this flow of capital has provided a lifeline to ailing national cinema industries; nevertheless, as Anne Jäckel has recently noted:

Co-production arrangements present opportunities but also risks. Unequal power relationships between partners have created problems for the producers and/or film-makers from the economically subordinate vis-à-vis the dominant country, with the latter being able to establish firmer control over the production. (2010: 84–5)

What this can effectively mean is that decisions about what kind of films should be made in Latin America and/or by Latin American practitioners are often made in Spain. Furthermore, it is generally easier to see films from a wider cross-section of Spanish-speaking countries in Madrid than it is on the other side of the Atlantic. In the specific case of *Rage*, 80 per cent of the money came from Spain, and 20 per cent from Colombia.[5] There is no reference to immigration in the source novel by the Argentine Sergio Bizzio, which focuses instead on class divisions. The superimposition of a national concern in Spain can be interpreted in two ways: an opportunity for an Ecuadorian director to give voice to his compatriots, or of cultural appropriation designed to cater to foreign tastes which may, in fact, reinforce existing hierarchies and prejudices.[6] Although the immigrant characters are in many respects more sympathetic than their Spanish counterparts, their depiction is nevertheless problematic. Rosa's boyfriend, the muscular José María is, for example, the embodiment of the noble savage: verbally inarticulate and predisposed to physical aggression, he is never violent without provocation.

In other words, co-productions of this kind may be seen as a critique of and/or the perpetuation of imperialist mentalities at the level of content, production and reception. If we opt for the latter, then even socially conscious transnational filmmaking comes to constitute the kind of surreptitious subjugation which, as Robert Young explains, has been seen as characteristic of modern-day capitalism:

Neocolonialism denotes a continuing economic hegemony that means that the postcolonial state remains in a situation of dependence on its former masters, and that the former masters continue to act in a colonialist manner towards formerly colonized states. (2001: 45)

The complicity with neocolonial practices and the ideological contradictions that beset co-production with ostensibly progressive credentials are central to the narrative and thematic logic of *Even the Rain*. In the main part of this chapter, I would like to discuss how Bollaín's fifth film as a director deconstructs not only imperial mythologies but, more surprisingly, its own means of production and circulation, alongside the kind of socially committed filmmaking for which her name has become a byword.

Even the Rain

Paul Laverty, Loach's habitual screenwriter since *Carla's Song*, and Bollaín's long-term partner – they met on the set of *Land and Freedom* – originally wrote the script for what would become *Even the Rain* to form part of a cycle of English-language films. The project stalled, as did his subsequent attempts to collaborate with Mexican director, Alejandro González Iñárritu. Bollaín then came on board in what constitutes the couple's debut professional collaboration; in terms of budget, location, ambitious set-pieces and potential global distribution, this is clearly the most ambitious project in which either of them has been involved. Indicative of this is that the modest La Iguana has not financed the film; Spain's Morena Films and France's Mandarin each contributed 40 per cent to the $6.8 million budget, with Mexico's Alebrije supplying the remaining 20 per cent.

My analysis, split into three sections, is designed to reflect the film's principal themes. I begin with a discussion of its depiction of imperialism in relation to Christopher Columbus and his 'discovery' of the New World, which makes reference both to the historical record and previous screen representations. This is followed by an examination of the political significance of the water war in Cochabamba, and how the subject matter relates to the traditional preoccupations of social-realist cinema. Then, in the final section, I examine how these two historical moments collide on screen, and question to what extent the film interrogates ostensibly realist modes of representation. This should then facilitate some closing remarks on how and why *Even the Rain* challenges traditional notions of ontologically pure national cinema(s).

The film is a long overdue reappraisal of Spain's imperial past which, at least in cinematic terms, has been systematically evaded. During the early Franco period, it was hoped that, in the absence of a physical empire, Spain could at least be at the helm of a spiritual community comprising its ex-colonies. In a clear antecedent to the current vogue for co-productions, cinema was to play an important role in this mission, as is reflected in attempts to create transatlantic collaborations, and the content of a number of films set in the past and present. *Alba de América/Dawn of America* (Juan de Orduña, 1951), for example, was designed as an antidote to the lies told about the discovery of the New World in the British *Christopher Columbus* (David Macdonald, 1949). In the Spanish film, the Admiral is depicted as a morally virtuous widower whose religious vocation is constantly stressed.

Dawn of America was a commercial failure, and did little to encourage filmmakers in the dictatorship to deal with a historical subject likely to require a hefty budget. Puncturing the heroic rhetoric of Francoism became an increasingly widespread practice in the transition period, as is reflected, for example, in *Cristobal Colón, ... de oficio descubridor/Christopher Columbus ... on a Mission of Discovery* (Mariano Ozores, 1982). In general, however, Rafael de España is right to conclude that 'el afán revisionista del cine de la Democracia no llega a la Historia de América' [the revisionist drive of the cinema of the democracy has not extended to the History of America] (2002: 27). In other words, Francoist visions of the past may be ridiculed, but they have not always been subject to serious reappraisal. Imperial celebration is now out of fashion and politically incorrect but – as Agustín Sánchez Vidal demonstrates in Chapter 4 in this volume on Carlos Saura's *El Dorado* (1988) – any film which is seen to reinforce the black legend too strongly may also be subject to censure.

Even the Rain constitutes a milestone in that it is the first major Spanish film to depict a flesh-and-blood Columbus who is neither caricatured nor idealised. As is also the case elsewhere, casting is paramount in this regard. Karra Elejalde is a versatile actor whose screen persona and weatherbeaten face suggest a combination of bravura, fragility and jaded cynicism. This equips him well to portray Antón, an alcoholic Spanish star struggling with his divorce and the breakdown of his relationship with his children, whilst still having the gravitas to embody an intimidating figure in the film-within-a film. In this depiction, the coloniser's sin is shown not so much to be cruelty as a rush to certainty instigated by intellectual and moral blindness.

There is a pedagogical and ethical dimension to this reappraisal of Columbus and his formative role in Spain's imperial past. Bollaín has noted how '[c]uando yo lo estudié nos quedábamos en sus cuatro viajes y en la gesta de encontrar América' [when I studied the subject, we looked only at his four trips and the feat of discovering America] (cited in Belategui 2010). *Even the Rain* examines Columbus's activities as a Governor in the Caribbean, and its pedagogical remit is designed to extend beyond the cinematic auditorium: it was screened in Spanish secondary schools prior to its official release, and a handbook for teachers can be downloaded from the official website.[7] An unfortunate correlative to this laudable endeavour is the film's principal aesthetic shortcoming: a formal neatness and schematic exposition that sometimes verges on earnest didacticism.

The action frequently cuts between various levels of fiction: we are privy to rehearsals; backstage conversations; footage shot by María, a young woman making a behind-the-scenes documentary; and social occasions. This gives the fictional filmmakers ample scope for self-reflection, but much of their dialogue is laboured in its exposition and gives the impression of having been shoehorned into the narrative. Hence, for example, there is a rather verbose exchange at dinner over the real historical debate as to whether Bartolomé de Las Casas's acceptance and even endorsement of black slavery undermine his liberal credentials (see Todorov 1992: 170–1).

The water war in Cochabamba clearly lends itself to the romanticisation of subaltern solidarity and the 'feel-good' anti-corporate social realism in which Laverty and Bollaín often trade. As in many of his scripts, the principal narrative is set in the recent past; this brief time lapse reflects the intention to balance the desire for political intervention with the need to carry out extensive research prior to writing. In 1999, the government of former dictator Hugo

Banzer sought to privatise Bolivia's water supplies by selling them to the North American corporation, Bechtel, and to prevent local citizens from collecting the rain through their own irrigation systems. A popular movement in Cochabamba, the country's fourth largest city, rose up and forced the reversal of the decision in what Tom Lewis has characterised as 'the first great victory against corporate globalization in Latin America' (Olivera and Lewis 2004: xiii). This popular uprising 'weakened the legitimacy of political parties and traditional unions, and strengthened the power and confidence of horizontally organised coalitions of workers and citizens such as the *Co-ordinadora*' (Dangl 2007: 69).

Even the Rain is the first film Bollaín has directed based on a script which she has not at least co-written, and it appears to be a genuine collaboration with Laverty, as is reflected in their equal billing on publicity materials. In spite of its broad and expensive canvas, the film resembles both of their previous efforts in that it uses a charged political backdrop to frame a compelling human drama, and vice versa. Where Laverty's influence can, perhaps, be felt most strongly is that it is the first of Bollaín's films to focus on male protagonists and their interpersonal relationships; there is, in fact, a complete absence of major female characters. The complex narrative is structured around two male friendships: first between Sebastián and Costa, and then between Daniel and Costa in the final third.

Although Sebastián's film is set in the Caribbean, Costa has decided to shoot in a country full of, in his words, starving Indians; it will allow them to shoot the film's epic scenes on a reasonable budget without recourse to computer-generated images. Bolivia's weak economy has, in real life, made it attractive to Ibermedia productions (Falicov 2007: 28).[8] Early on, the Spanish producer risks the personal safety of the local force by erecting crosses, on which the natives in the film will be burnt, cheaply; he shows none of his colleagues' interest in learning individual words in Quechua; and, unlike Sebastián, he initially seems to have no qualms about agreeing to return Daniel to the police chief once the film's key sequence has been shot. In other words, the hypocrisy of making an ostensibly ethical film under such conditions is manifest and there is little to suggest that Costa, an agent of multinational capitalism, will show compassion. If the structuring principle of the political battle can be traced back to David and Goliath, the personal narrative provides a modern-day equivalent to the parable of the Good Samaritan.

Costa may be the boss in the Bolivian context but he had wanted to film in English, and he is accountable to financiers elsewhere. The Spanish producer first comes into conflict with Daniel when he foolishly speaks in a derogatory fashion about the Indians on the phone, in front of him; the actor has worked for two years in Los Angeles and understands him perfectly. As is the case in real life, the on-screen characters from Spain and Latin America are, to borrow a phrase from Teresa Hoefert de Turégano, 'framed in an imperial triangle with the United

States' (2004: 15). Although Bollaín also opted to make the film in Spanish, the continued dependence on the USA was manifest in the excitement raised at home by its prospects at the Academy Awards (see Wheeler 2011).

From the open casting shown at the beginning of *Even the Rain*, the camera's gaze is associated with – to quote the title of Mary Louise Pratt's book – 'imperial eyes' (1992). When Daniel is badly assaulted in a street demonstration, the crew's only concern is whether the make-up department can conceal his wounds so that he can continue shooting. Bollaín often frames the cast and crew inside cars and vans. This enables us to learn more about their respective relationships whilst also giving them – and, by implication, us – a kaleidoscopic view of their new surroundings and its inhabitants. As we are encouraged to adopt their point of view from inside a moving vehicle, the windows become both a barrier and a screen through which the natives can be viewed.

This dichotomy of separation and omniscience is indicative of how, according to Homi K. Bhabha, 'colonial discourse produces the colonized as a social reality which is at once an "other" and yet entirely knowable and visible' (2004: 101). Both facets of this claim are evident throughout. Hence, for example, Costa believes that he will be able to control the extras as if they were computer-generated pixels. He boasts on the phone to the money men in English about how the indigenous actors are well behaved because they feel like kings on their meagre salaries, and subsequently offers to raise Daniel's salary if he keeps out of trouble. The local inhabitants, nevertheless, exceed the visual plane afforded by the totalising gaze of the imperial eye. Daniel reneges on his deal with Costa and returns to organise the street protests, whilst Sebastián is unable to complete one key sequence due to his failure to recognise the existence of a different system of values. The director wants some of the female actresses to pretend to drown their babies in order to save them from the jaws of the colonisers' hunting dogs; they refuse, claiming that they cannot conceive of such a horrific scenario. He becomes infuriated, as he claims it is very important for the film, to which Daniel responds that there are more important things in life.

This is not the first time that issues of this kind have been addressed in the cinema. *Para recibir el canto de los pájaros/ To Hear the Birds Singing* (Jorge Sanjinés, 1995) is a Bolivian film made by the country's most prominent director. The narrative is centred on a European crew who arrive to shoot a film criticising the Spanish occupation in the sixteenth century. A French woman who has lived amongst the local indigenous Aymara community since 1968 acts as an intermediary. The recently arrived foreigners are perplexed, as Columbus had been before them, by the natives' seeming indifference to financial gain. Relations gradually deteriorate and the filmmakers reproduce precisely the abuse, authoritarianism and racist attitudes which they had set out to denounce, whilst bemoaning the Indians' perceived stupidity in not realising that they are making the film for them.[9]

In both *To Hear the Birds Singing* and *Even the Rain*, the juxtaposition of two historically distinct imperial occurrences is facilitated not only by the common colonial impulse but also by the visual means through which it is achieved. As Andrea Noble remarks:

> If the contemporary global moment has become associated with a new turn to the visual, it is tied to an earlier cultural event, namely Western expansion, the legacy of which we are living with today. It should perhaps not surprise us then that Columbus's 'discovery' of America and its aftermath similarly gave rise to strikingly image-centred colonial cultures. In other words, by taking the long view, it is possible to bring into focus the powerful historical role that visual culture played in the formation of cultural identities in Latin America. (2003: 157)

The visual can, however, also be used as a weapon against invading forces. In the sixteenth century, published accounts of imperial adventures began, for the first time, to be used against the colonising power: 'It needed only the horrific illustrations of Theodore de Brye's new editions of Las Casas at the end of the century to stamp an indelible image of Spanish atrocities in the European consciousness' (Elliott 1970: 96). A similar ambivalence persists in the twenty-first century-context: 'Just as the media can exoticize and otherize cultures, they can also reflect and help catalyze multicultural affiliations and transnational identifications' (Shohat and Stam 2003: 1). As regards the case in hand, James Dunkerley has observed how the 'Bolivian experience shares with other recent radical episodes a *combination* of mass mobilisation and mass' (2007: 25; original emphasis). In *Even the Rain*, this is reflected in Costa seeing Daniel being arrested on television, whilst some of the Spanish actors voice their desire to return home on viewing images of violent street demonstrations in their hotel.

Bollaín and Laverty have both long shown an interest in the possibilities and constraints inscribed in new visual technologies. What distinguishes *Even the Rain* is the hitherto unprecedented degree of self-reflexivity. Hence, in one scene, the camera cuts between a cinema screen on which the daily rushes are projected and Daniel's daughter, Belén, who is in awe at seeing herself projected onto such a vast canvas. Antón is impressed by her performance, and says that he hopes they are paying her a dignified wage; she replies affirmatively, and is visibly happy about the fact that she received much more than the $2 a day paid to the extras. This is, however, soon put into context when the Spanish actor reveals his salary. The centrepiece of both Sebastián and Bollaín's respective films is when Daniel's character becomes a martyr of local resistance as he remains defiant as he is burnt on a cross. Sebastián and Costa are positioned on top of a hill so as to have a panoramic view of what proves to be a resounding success. Just after the director shouts 'cut' through his megaphone, and there is a collective round of applause, the police arrive to take Daniel back to jail. Costa bows his head in his first intimation of guilt, and angrily places his hand over María's diegetic camera; this material is not suitable for inclusion in the kind of 'making of' features which are now de rigueur in many DVD releases.

In addition to the playfulness of these meta-cinematic scenes, there is an ethical correlative that finds its equivalent in Bertolt Brecht's distancing effects which have often been construed as antithetical to the faith in the indexicality of the photographic image and sound championed by André Bazin. This distinction is, however, often predicated on a misreading of the French theorist whereby his complex theories are inaccurately subsumed within naïve realism. As Richard Rushton notes, 'Bazin's conceptions of realism and reality were far more complex than a reductive correspondence theory of realism can indicate' (2011: 59), whilst in the words of Dudley Andrew, 'true realism gets to the essence of its subject through the self-alienating operations of allusion and ellipsis' (2010: 140). The reductive opposition with Brecht might therefore prove to be a red herring. Furthermore, Lúcia Nágib has highlighted the political parallels that can also be drawn between their respective critical endeavours:

> A basic faithfulness to the profilmic phenomenon, combined with the inherent honesty of the film medium, was indeed the main requirement of Bazin's realism, one which emerged from the experience of the disastrous consequences of Nazi-Fascist lies. This was also Brecht's main concern, when he championed the unmasking of representative artifice as the only possible realist method. (2011: 11)

Within the Spanish cinematic context, not only has the former concern consistently been privileged over the latter but, lacking Bazin's theoretical complexity, the result has often been a blind and even evangelical faith that false representations from both home and abroad ought to be combated with more rather than less realism. Whilst there have been numerous examples of the conceit of the film-within-the-film,[10] they have emerged more frequently from popular rather than so-called auteur traditions, and the aim has not generally been to radically deconstruct the realist conventions of classical cinema. Beyond the occasional director and movement – e.g. the Barcelona school – there has never been a sustained attempt to create a counter-cinema based on the rupture of classical conventions on a par with what took place during the 1960s and 1970s in many Latin American countries. Social realism is thereby construed as an ideal to which to aspire rather than as a form to be interrogated. It is in this regard that *Even the Rain* marks new ground within the context of Spanish national cinema.

Bollaín's film does not, however, carry out its formal interrogation by deserting social realist conventions altogether. It resembles *Moloch Tropical* (Raoul Peck, 2009) in that it constitutes a high-profile example of what Nágib and Cecília Mello term 'world cinema's "realist revival"' (2009: xiv),[11] which also proffers a cinematic response to their rhetorical question: 'would it not make sense to question the opposition between Bazin and Brecht, as representatives respectively of realism and anti-realism?' (2009: xix). In both films, the development of psychologically plausible characters and interpersonal relationships, grounded in specific socioeconomic circumstances considered characteristic of social realist cinema, coalesce with alienation effects designed to question various modes and forms of representation, including their own. *Even the Rain*'s most Brechtian device is, in fact, provided in the guise of an idealistic filmmaker whose artistic narcissism is shown at the end, when he rants against the popular uprising for interfering with the completion of his masterpiece; he claims that the former will soon be forgotten about, but the latter will last forever.

The high-profile presence of Gael García Bernal not only optimised possibilities for the film's funding and distribution, but also provided a perfect match for the role. As Jethro Soutar notes: '[h]is brooding image has seen him labelled the Latin James Dean, although Bernal is more a rebel with than without a cause' (2008: 173). He spoke out against the Iraq War at the 2003 Academy Awards Ceremony and co-founded Canana, a production company largely inspired by Loach's example, to encourage the kind of socially committed productions which are often ignored by the world of commercial filmmaking. In other words, he might be nicknamed 'Sex-Mex' by the French press, but consumers can rest assured that he has solid fair-trade credentials.

Both he and Bollaín are thereby reflecting and undercutting their star personas on screen, whilst questioning the ethics of their relationship to the subjects they set out to represent. The problem, however, is that there are inevitable blind spots. Sebastián is irritated by the affectations of the Peruvian television actor Costa has lined up for the role. Daniel's ability to look directly at the camera in his screen test marks him out as, to use a popular colloquialism, the 'real deal'. Bollaín arguably encourages us to view the Bolivian agitator in a similar fashion. Indicative of this is the fact that Alberto Iglesias's recurrent elegiac score is employed as diegetic music when Sebastián reads his own script and imagines it in his head and, subsequently, as an extra-diegetic aural presence when Daniel is leading street protests. In one sense, Daniel is an idealised hero but, as we have seen, the flipside of this kind of romanticisation can be blindness to flesh-and-blood human beings.

As Alberto Moreiras has asked in relation to postcolonial studies, 'what good is it to engage in a metacritics of intellectual activity if that very metacritics is ultimately destined to be absorbed in the systemic apparatus whose functioning it was once thought designed to disrupt?' (2001: 41). In a similar vein, it is not always clear what *Even the Rain*'s self-reflexivity is intended to achieve. Although it is beyond the remit of this chapter, any genuinely ethical appraisal of the film would have to look at concrete information about the treatment and payment of the indigenous cast and crew, examining how the Bolivian extras were treated.[12] In terms of reception, Bollaín is consciously trying to make Spanish audiences more aware of their trespasses in the past and present in order to inculcate an

30. The filmmaker and his subject: Daniel and Sebastián have an on-set discussion in
Even the Rain.

ethics of humility. To what extent she will succeed in her goal, and whether this
will have tangible effects, is again open to speculation.

Conclusion

A social-realist aesthetic may be frequently construed as the antithesis of
Hollywood filmmaking, but both *Even the Rain* and Sebastián's film-within-a-
film are the kind of prestige co-productions which paradoxically seek to counter
North American hegemony whilst simultaneously courting its approval. Having
previously forged her reputation largely through the importation of a social
realist aesthetic from Britain, Bollaín here refashions that discourse through the
kind of realist self-reflection which is increasingly prominent in world cinema
generally in order to interrogate her country's imperial past and complicity with
neocolonial practices in the present.

   Even the Rain is a product and dissection of post-national filmmaking that
raises important questions about a classificatory system based around state
borders. It also, however, provides a concrete illustration of Will Higbee and
Song Hwee Lim's claim that 'the national continues to exert the force of its presence even within transnational film-making practices' (2010: 10). As I hope to
have demonstrated, the ethical and aesthetic achievements of this international
co-production only begin to come to the fore when contextualised within the

framework of discourse surrounding Spanish cinema and history. In the simplest of terms, *Even the Rain* is as much a transnational film about Spain as it is a Spanish film about transnationalism.

Notes

1 The research for this chapter was enabled by a Leverhulme Research Fellowship. My intellectual horizons were also broadened by bibliographical advice and comments made by Laura Rodríguez Isaza on film funding and co-productions in the Latin American context. I am very grateful to Stephanie Dennison and Lúcia Nágib for their feedback on an earlier draft.

2 This process is recounted in a documentary about Elías Querejeta: *El productor/ The producer* (Fernando Méndez Leite, 2006).

3 For a guide to female directors, see Camí-Vela (2001) and Heredero (1998).

4 Between 2000 and 2006, only 7.4 per cent of Spanish films were directed by women; and in the 1990s 17.08 per cent of new directors were female but, between 2000 and 2007, this figure fell to 10.4 per cent (Arranz 2010: 20, 60).

5 Information on the funding of individual films alongside box-office figures supplied in this chapter is taken from the Filmoteca Española database of films available via the Ministry of Culture website: http://www/mcu.es.

6 These were precisely the qualities that led the film to being well received at film festivals such as Tokyo, Málaga – where it won the Best Film prize – and Guadalajara, alongside a release in metropolitan centres in the USA such as New York.

7 See http://www.tambienlalluvia.com/en/.

8 Following the end of a military dictatorship in 1982, the landlocked country became a 'showpiece of neoliberal reformism in the 1980s and 1990s' (Grindle 2003: 318). This did not, however, always equate to an improvement in living conditions in a country that is 'not just averagely poor – 35 per cent of its population (2,966,000 people) are completely indigent, subsisting on an income of less than $1 per day' (Dunkerley 2007: 1). In 2000, 49 per cent of Bolivia's population was described as being of Indian extraction (Klein 2003: 250), and they generally constitute the most marginalised sections of society.

9 For a detailed study of this film, see Hart (2002).

10 See, for example, *Esa pareja feliz/ That Happy Couple* (Juan Antonio Bardem and Luis García Berlanga, 1953), *Al ponerse el sol/At Sunset* (Mario Camus, 1967), *Las 4 bodas de Marisol/Marisol's Four Weddings* (Luis Lucia, 1967), *Yo soy esa/I'm the One* (Luis Sanz, 1990), *La niña de tus ojos/ The Girl of Your Dreams* (Fernando Trueba, 1998) or *Los abrazos rotos/Broken Embraces* (Pedro Almodóvar, 2009).

11 Future studies might want to examine the parallels between *Even the Rain* and this co-production between France and Haiti.

12 According to the information given to Spanish newspapers by Bollaín and the film's producers, the extras were paid 20 dollars a day (Santaolalla, 2012: 211).

Bibliography

Andrew, Dudley (2010) *What Cinema Is! Bazin's Quest and its Charge*, Chichester: Wiley-Blackwell.

Arranz, Fátima (2010) 'La igualdad de género en la práctica cinematográfica española', in Fátima Arranz, Javier Callejo, Pilar Pardo, Inés París and Esperanza Roquero, *Cine y género en España: una investigación empírica*, Valencia: Cátedra, 17–68.

Belategui, Oskar L. (2010) 'Si llegamos a los Oscar es que algo hemos hecho mal', interview with Iciar Bollaín, *La Verdad*, 13 December.

Bhabha, Homi K. (2004) *The Location of Culture*, London: Routledge.

Bollaín, Iciar (1996) *Ken Loach: un observador solidario*, Madrid: El País Aguilar.

—(2001) 'El cine no es inocente', in *II Encuentro de Nuevos Autores, 2000*, Valladolid: Semana Internacional de Cine de Valladolid and Sociedad General de Autores y Editores, 13–19.

Camí-Vela, María (2001) *Mujeres detrás de la cámara: entrevistas con cineastas españolas de la década de los 90*, Madrid: Ocho y Medio.

Dangl, Benjamin (2007) *The Price of Fire: Resource Wars and Social Movements in Bolivia*, Edinburgh: AK Press.

Dunkerley, James (2007) *Bolivia: Revolution and the Power of History in the Present (Essays)*, London: Institute for the Study of the Americas, 1–56.

Elliott, J.H. (1970) *The Old World and the New: 1492–1650*, Cambridge: Cambridge University Press.

España, Rafael de (2002) *Las sombras del encuentro (España y América: cuatro siglos de historia a través del cine)*, Badajoz: Diputación de Badajoz.

Falicov, Tamara L. (2007) 'Programa Ibermedia: Co-production and the Cultural Politics of Constructing an Ibero-American Audiovisual Space', *Spectator: The University of California Journal of Film and Television*, 27:2, 21–30.

Grindle, Merilee S. (2003) 'Shadowing the past? Policy reform in Bolivia, 1985–2002', in Merilee Grindle and Pilar Domingo (eds), *Proclaiming Revolution: Bolivia in Comparative Perspective*, Cambridge, MA: Harvard University Press, 318–44.

Hart, Stephen (2002) 'The Art of Invasion in Jorge Sanjinés's *Para recibir el canto de los pájaros* (1995)', *Hispanic Research Journal*, 3:1, 71–81.

Heredero, Carlos F. (1997) 'Icíar Bollaín', in Carlos F. Heredero (ed.), *Espejo de miradas: entrevistas con nuevos directores del cine español en los años noventa*, Madrid: Festival de Cine de Alcalá de Henares, 203–42.

—(ed.) (1998) *La mitad del cielo: directoras españolas de los años 90*, Málaga: Ayuntamiento de Málaga and Ministerio de Educación y Cultura.

Higbee, Will and Song Hwee Lim (2010) 'Concepts of Transnational Cinema: Towards a Critical Transnationalism in Film Studies', *Transnational Cinemas*, 1:1, 7–21.

Hill, John (1986) *Sex, Class and Realism: British Cinema 1956–1963*, London: BFI.

Hoefert de Turégano, Teresa (2004) 'The International Politics of Cinematic Coproduction: Spanish Policy in Latin America', *Film and History: An Interdisciplinary Journal of Film and Television*, 34:2, 15–24.

Jäckel, Anne (2010) 'State and Other Funding for Migrant, Diasporic and World Cinemas in Europe', in Daniela Berghahn and Claudia Sternberg (eds), *European*

Cinema in Motion: Migrant and Diasporic Film in Contemporary Europe, Basingstoke: Palgrave Macmillan, 76–95.

Klein, Herbert S. (2003) 'Social Change in Bolivia Since 1952', in Merilee Grindle and Pilar Domingo (eds), *Proclaiming Revolution: Bolivia in Comparative Perspective*, Cambridge, MA: Harvard University Press, 232–58.

Martín-Márquez, Susan (2002) 'A World of Difference in Home-Making: The Films of Icíar Bollaín', in Ofelia Ferrán and Kathleen M. Glenn (eds), *Women's Narrative and Film in Twentieth-Century Spain: A World of Difference(s)*, New York: Routledge, 256–72.

Moreiras, Alberto (2001) *The Exhaustion of Difference: The Politics of Latin American Cultural Studies*, Durham, NC: Duke University Press.

Nágib, Lucía (2011) *World Cinema and the Ethics of Realism*, New York: Continuum.

—and Cecília Mello (2009) 'Introduction', in Lúcia Nágib and Cecília Mello (eds), *Realism and the Audiovisual Media*, Basingstoke: Palgrave Macmillan, xiv–xxvi.

Noble, Andrea (2003) 'Latin American Visual Cultures', in Philip Swanson (ed.), *The Companion to Latin American Studies*, London: Hodder Arnold, 154–71.

Olivera, Oscar and Tom Lewis (2004) *¡Cochabamba! Water War in Bolivia*, Cambridge, MA: South End Press.

Pratt, Mary Louise (1992) *Imperial Eyes: Travel Writing and Transculturation*, London: Routledge.

Reher, David-Sven and Miguel Requena (2009) 'Introducción: el impacto de la inmigración en la sociedad española', in David Sven Reher and Miguel Requena (eds), *Las múltiples caras de la inmigración en España*, Madrid: Alianza, 7–19.

Rodríguez Merchán, Eduardo (2005) 'Icíar Bollaín: una limpia mirada, delante y detrás de la cámara', in Pedro Medinas and Luis M. González (eds), *Cortos pero intensos: las películas breves de los cineastas españoles*, Alcalá: Festival de Cine de Alcalá de Henares, 66–72.

Rushton, Richard (2011) *The Reality of Film: Theories of Filmic Reality*, Manchester: Manchester University Press.

Santaolalla, Isabel (2012) *The Cinema of Icíar Bollaín*, Manchester: Manchester University Press.

Shohat, Ella and Robert Stam (2003) 'Introduction', in Ella Shohat and Robert Stam (eds), *Multiculturalism, Postcoloniality, and Transnational Media*, New Brunswick, NJ: Rutgers University Press, 1–17.

Soutar, Jethro (2008) *Gael García Bernal and the Latin American New Wave: The Story of a Cinematic Movement and its Leading Man*, London: Portico.

Thibaudeau, Pascale (2007) '¿Hacia un nuevo realismo social en el cine español?', in Nancy Berthier and Jean-Claude Seguin (eds), *Cine, nación y nacionalidades en España*, Madrid: Casa de Velázquez, 233–46.

Todorov, Tzvetan (1992). *The Conquest of America*, trans. Richard Howard, New York: Harper Perennial.

Wheeler, Duncan (2008) 'Intimate Partner Abuse in Spain (1975–2006)', *Cuestiones de Género*, 3, 173–204.

—(2011) 'La imagen y la repercusión del cine español en el Reino Unido', *Academia: Revista de la Academia de Cine*, 177, 25–7.

Young, Robert J.C. (2001) *Postcolonialism: An Historical Introduction*, Malden and Oxford: Blackwell.

Index